CORNWALLIS

CORNWALLIS

Soldier and Statesman in a Revolutionary World

RICHARD MIDDLETON

YALE UNIVERSITY PRESS
NEW HAVEN AND LONDON

Published with assistance from the Annie Burr Lewis Fund.

For information about this and other Yale University Press publications, please contact:
U.S. Office: sales.press@yale.edu   yalebooks.com
Europe Office: sales@yaleup.co.uk   yalebooks.co.uk

Set in Adobe Garamond Pro by IDSUK (DataConnection) Ltd
Printed in Great Britain by TJ Books, Padstow, Cornwall

Library of Congress Control Number: 2021944144

ISBN 978-0-300-19680-1

A catalogue record for this book is available from the British Library.

10 9 8 7 6 5 4 3 2 1

The noble Marquess . . . stands justly so high in the affections and good opinion of his country, that every man is satisfied that in whatever situation he may be placed, his best endeavours will be used, not only for their honour but for their advantage.

George Tierney, speech to the House of Commons, 7 November 1796

I have to a degree made it a rule to resist the requests of those, who, because they were men of rank and fortune, thought they had a right to a favour of this kind.

Cornwallis to Alexander Ross, 26 December 1800

Contents

CONTENTS

Illustrations

12. Portrait miniature of Cornwallis on his return to Calcutta, by John Smart, 1792. © National Portrait Gallery, London.

13. Tipu, Sultan of Mysore ('Tippoo Sultaun'), by William Ridley, published by John Sewell, 1 July 1800. © National Portrait Gallery, London.

14. 'The coming-on of the monsoons; - or - the retreat from Seringapatam', by James Gillray, published by Hannah Humphrey, 6 December 1791. © National Portrait Gallery, London.

15. 'The Bengal levee' by and published by James Gillray, published by Hannah Humphrey, 9 November 1792. © National Portrait Gallery, London.

16. View of Fort William, Calcutta, by Jan van Ryne, 1754.

17. East India House, by Thomas Malton, 1800. Yale Center for British Art, Paul Mellon Collection.

18. *Great Court Yard, Dublin Castle*, by James Malton, 1792. The Stapleton Collection / Bridgeman Images.

19. *The House of Commons 1793-94*, by Karl Anton Hickel, 1793. © National Portrait Gallery, London.

20. Arial view of Fort Tilbury. Mervyn Rands / CC-BY-SA-4.0.

21. Henry Dundas, Lord Melville, *c.* 1810. © National Portrait Gallery, London.

22. Frederick, Duke of York, by unknown artist, 1800–20. Royal Collection Trust / All Rights Reserved.

23. Charles Cornwallis (1738–1805), 2nd Earl and 1st Marquis Cornwallis, Military Commander and Colonial Governor, by John Singleton Copley, 1795. Guildhall Art Gallery/ CC-BY-NC.

24. St Paul's monument to Cornwallis. Angelo Hornak / Alamy Stock Photo.

MAPS

Preface

As the light began to fade on 2 January 1777, a group of red-coated figures gathered in discussion on a small hill overlooking the village of Trenton, New Jersey. The urgency of their deliberations was emphasised by the rumbling sound of nearby musketry and cannon fire. Closer inspection revealed their uniforms to be those of senior British offices, richly enhanced with gold facings and epaulettes. At their centre was the thirty-eight-year-old Charles, Earl Cornwallis, a major-general in the army that King George III had sent to quell Britain's rebellious thirteen colonies. Listening to him, hunched for protection against the icy cold, were three other senior officers: Major-General James Grant, Colonel Sir William Erskine, and Colonel Alexander Leslie. Trenton was not where any of them had expected to be so early in the New Year. Only ten days before, the rebellion had seemingly collapsed, allowing Cornwallis to board ship for an eagerly anticipated reunion with his beloved wife and children in England. Then, news arrived that the rebel commander, George Washington, had for a second time crossed the Delaware River into New Jersey, threatening the recent resurgence of Loyalist support. The response of Sir William Howe, the British commander-in-chief, was immediate. Cornwallis was to gather the cream of his army and administer a final crushing blow. After marching from Princeton, the British commander arrived at Trenton to find the rebel army cowering behind Assunpink Creek and seemingly trapped. However, three initial attempts to force the rebel position had failed. The question now posed by Cornwallis to his companions was whether to press home the attack or to wait until morning. Erskine proposed an immediate assault, fearing the enemy might otherwise escape during the night. Grant and Leslie advised caution, preferring to wait until daylight, when the troops were refreshed and the task facing them clearer. To Cornwallis such advice seemed eminently sensible. Night attacks were always problematic. Why rush ahead when a few hours would bring success? Looking at his aristocratic companions, he summed up the position with a metaphor that he knew they would appreciate. 'We've got the Old Fox safe now. Let's go over and bag him in the morning.'[1]

Within hours Cornwallis knew that Erskine had been right: the fox had escaped. But he could never have imagined that four and a half years later the roles would be reversed, with Washington the hunter and he, Cornwallis, the fox, cornered this time without escape. The surrender at Yorktown inevitably spelt disaster for the British prosecutors of the war, whether generals, admirals, ministers, or even George III, who momentarily considered abdication. Remarkably, Cornwallis was not among them. Instead, he emerged to play a leading role in British public life, first as a reforming governor-general of Bengal; then as master-general of the Ordnance responsible for war production during the French revolutionary conflict; next as lord lieutenant of Ireland entrusted with ending the 1798 rebellion and passing the Act of Union; and lastly as minister plenipotentiary for concluding peace with Napoleonic France.

Despite these important roles there has been only one biography of Cornwallis, and that was more than forty years ago. The diversity of his life perhaps explains the relative lack of biographical attention, except for his involvement in the War of American Independence. The biographer of Cornwallis, therefore, must master the details of a career spent in widely differing roles on three separate continents.

Seventy years ago, the title of this book might have been *Cornwallis: Pro-Consul of the British Empire*, since this best describes the role he was called to fulfil, first in America, then in India, and later in Ireland. In America he attempted to save the first British Empire; in India he endeavoured to reform Britain's burgeoning second empire; and in Ireland he sought to preserve the centre of that empire from the scourge of Jacobin France. Until the 1960s it was seemingly a story of national pride. Since then, the word 'empire' has become a pejorative term, suggestive of racism, colonialism, and the denial of human rights. Nevertheless, even dead white men have a claim to be understood, not least because the heroes and noble causes of today will surely become the misguided zealots or disregarded ideologies of tomorrow. Cornwallis's career, in any case, was not one of unalloyed imperialism. Although he began life as the dutiful soldier, he developed into a leader who was habitually progressive in his views. Above all, he was imbued with a deep sense of humanity for those less favoured than himself, no matter what their race, religion, or circumstance.

Constraints of space have necessarily imposed limitations in the scope of this book. I have, accordingly, restricted details about the wider Cornwallis family and matters regarding his lands and estates. The focus is essentially on Cornwallis's public career, though even here certain topics have had to be curtailed or omitted. This is especially true of his time in India.

Although Cornwallis has lacked biographers, much of his public life was recorded in the three densely filled volumes of published papers, edited by Charles Ross, the son of Cornwallis's former aide and long-time friend, General Alexander Ross. Ross not only scoured the Cornwallis family correspondence, but also numerous public and private archives to give a fuller picture of his father's friend and mentor. Since Ross transcribed his documents with meticulous accuracy, I have cited these rather than the archival source. But all citations include the type of document used, the name of the writer, recipient, and date of composition. As the original manuscript sources often have conflicting page and folio references, I have only cited these where a source is not arranged chronologically. I have also modernised the spelling and punctuation of quoted material where necessary for readability.

Inevitably, I have incurred many obligations to scholars, both personally and through their books. I should especially like to thank Peter Marshall for supporting my original proposal to Yale University Press; also Andrew O'Shaughnessy for inviting me to apply for a Jefferson Foundation Fellowship at Monticello. This gave me access to the foundation's considerable data resources at a critical point in my research. Working as an independent scholar, after retirement from the fray of academic life, can be an isolating experience. The fellowship gave me a chance to meet other scholars working in contiguous fields to my own.

Grateful acknowledgement is also due to the peer reviewers of this book in manuscript form, both for recommending publication and for their pertinent comments. The text has additionally benefited from the assistance of several non-specialist readers of the manuscript, notably Henderson Downing, Bill Cook, and Basile Poulopoulos, who gave me valuable advice regarding readability and presentation. I am additionally indebted to Dr Hilary Flett for advice about Cornwallis's medical condition.

Regarding illustrative materials, I must thank Chris Bryant for locating various portraits of Cornwallis. These included a previously unidentified miniature by the American artist Matthew Pratt. He was additionally helpful in explaining the details of eighteenth-century British military uniforms. My thanks too go to Ian Cranston for alerting me to some little-known Cornwallis family portraits at Audley End, and Bob Swayne for advice on maps.

This project additionally benefited from the helpful endeavours of numerous librarians and archivists, who obtained documents for me and suggested other sources where I might find relevant materials. Chief among these were the staff of the William L. Clements Library, the Bodleian Library, the British Library, the Kent Record Office, the National Archives at Kew, the National Army Museum, the National Library of Scotland, the Scottish Record Office, and the National Library of Ireland.

Finally, I should like to thank Yale University Press, especially Heather McCallum for accepting the project, and Marika Lysandrou for acting as principal editor. I also wish to acknowledge the important contribution of the copyeditor Jacob Blandy in preparing the text. All other errors of omission or commission are mine alone.

Richard Middleton, October 2020

Part I
AMERICA

ONE

An Irresistible Impulse

Charles Cornwallis, son and heir of the first Earl Cornwallis, was born on 31 December 1738 in Grosvenor Square, London, not far from St James's Palace in the heart of fashionable Mayfair. It was a world away from the family's obscure origins, which may have been Cornish, given the custom in a pre-literate age of using place names to identify people.[1] However the name also appears in Ireland, where it was spelt Cornwallys or Cornwaleys, and this connection is supported by evidence that the family had once owned lands there. The first identifiable mention of the name in a British context occurred in the reign of Edward III when a man called Thomas Cornwallis gained prominence as sheriff of London. It was this Cornwallis who first purchased property in Suffolk, and it was his son, John, who in 1384 acquired the lands and manor in the hamlet of Brome.[2]

The next Cornwallis to achieve notice was also named Thomas. He rose progressively in the service of Edward VI and then Queen Mary, receiving a knighthood in 1548 from the crown. In 1554 he was made treasurer of Calais, England's last territory in France. Popular rumour suggests that he was responsible for its loss the following year, after betraying the town for money to meet the cost of rebuilding his home. The accusations appear unfounded, but whatever his part in that event, he proved less adept during Elizabeth I's reign, perhaps because he remained a Catholic recusant.[3]

Nevertheless, these associations did not prevent his son Charles from holding positions at court, while his heir, William, advanced the family fortunes by acquiring a second Suffolk estate at Culford, near Bury St Edmunds. But it was William's son

3

Map 1. England.

Frederick who was first ennobled in 1661 as Baron Cornwallis, in recognition of his support for the crown during the Civil War. The family hereafter made Culford Park their principal residence, though Frederick retained the manor of Brome, since it gave its owner electoral influence in the neighbouring parliamentary constituency of Eye. The new baron adopted as his heraldic motto *Virtus vincit invidiam* ('Virtue conquers envy'), featuring in his coat of arms three Cornish choughs, to emphasise the family's English origins.[4]

The tortuous rise of the Cornwallis family continued with Charles, the third Baron Cornwallis. He too proved politically shrewd, joining the Whig cause at the start of the 1689 'Glorious Revolution' following the flight of James II. For the next hundred years the family remained firm supporters of parliamentary supremacy, limited monarchy and membership of the Church of England as the fundamental principles of the constitution. His reward was to become the first member of the family to be a privy counsellor, and briefly first lord of the Admiralty. His successor Charles, the fourth baron, also held office, first as postmaster-general and then paymaster of the forces. Had he lived to enjoy the perquisites of the latter post, he might have greatly increased the wealth of the Cornwallis dynasty. In the event death removed him from office after twelve months.[5]

The fifth baron, Charles, Cornwallis's father, like his two predecessors, remained a loyal Whig and a supporter of the Hanoverian monarchy. This resulted in his appointment as a groom of the royal bedchamber, constable of the Tower, and member of the Privy Council. He also advanced his fortunes by marrying Elizabeth, a daughter of Lord Townshend, head of one of the most prominent Whig families and noted agricultural innovator who had demonstrated the benefits of rotating crops like turnips. She was also a niece of Thomas Pelham-Holles, duke of Newcastle, George II's long-standing secretary of state and later first lord of the Treasury. It was these connections that secured the fifth baron's elevation in 1753 to an earldom, with the subsidiary title of Viscount Brome, which was held hereafter as a courtesy title by the earl's eldest son.[6]

Cornwallis thus arrived in the world with the proverbial silver spoon in his mouth, though much would be expected of him in view of his lineage. Present at his christening in St George's Church, Hanover Square, were Newcastle and the

Honourable Thomas Townshend; the bishop of Norwich officiated.[7] Little is known of his early life, which was most likely spent at Culford Park under the watchful eye of a private tutor until he was ready for Eton. Undoubtedly, he spent much time outdoors, learning how to ride and shoot, all proper recreational activities for a young nobleman. For company he was joined in 1741 by brother Henry, then James in 1742, and finally William in February 1744. The birth of several male heirs was fortunate for the Cornwallis dynasty, since the four boys had been preceded by five daughters, two of whom died in infancy. This left three sisters, Charlotte, Elizabeth, and Mary, to look after their baby brothers.[8]

It is not known when Cornwallis entered Eton, though by 1753 he was enrolled in the sixth form as an 'oppidan', a student who lodged outside the school, a privilege preserved for the offspring of noble families. Judging from the subsequent arrangements for his own son, Cornwallis was probably accompanied by a personal tutor, as was customary at the time. A principal part of the curriculum was Latin, which had been an essential qualification for entering the church or practising the law since pre-Reformation times. Although less useful now, the achievements of ancient Greece and Rome remained models for the understanding of architecture, art, literature, and history, with which all educated members of society should be familiar. But life at Eton was not confined to the classroom. Various sports, official and unofficial, were readily available. It was during a game of hockey that Shute Barrington, a future bishop of Durham, accidentally struck Cornwallis in the eye, leading to strabismus, commonly called a squint or wall-eye.[9] It was to be a feature of his subsequent portraits.

Two years later Cornwallis enrolled as a scholar at Clare College, Cambridge, though he did not graduate from the university.[10] He may have attended classes to further his education until deciding on a profession. Most likely he had already made his choice, for he later told his son that he had been 'actuated by an irresistible impulse' to be a soldier.[11] One influence may have been his uncle Edward, now a major-general and colonel of the 24th Foot Regiment. Certainly, by early December 1756 the decision had been made, with his commissioning as an ensign in the prestigious 1st Foot or Grenadier Guards.[12] Not that his choice was in any way unusual, being a well-trodden path for many aristocratic heirs, who took an officer's commission while waiting to inherit their titles and estates.

The average cavalry or infantry officer in the eighteenth-century British army normally joined a regiment to learn the craft of soldiering from more senior officers and experienced non-commissioned personnel. Dedicated entrants might also supplement their training by reading such works as Humphrey Bland's *Treatise of Military Discipline* (1727). But Earl Cornwallis seemingly decided that this was not sufficient for his son and heir. Exposure to continental ideas and methods of warfare were thought desirable for anyone wanting to advance in their profession. However, no institution existed in Britain to teach such matters, since the Woolwich Royal Military Academy was limited to training the army's technical services of the artillery and engineers. The decision was therefore taken to send Cornwallis to a military school at Turin in Italy, which had a reputation for producing officers of a high calibre. Accompanying him would be an experienced Prussian officer, Captain de Roguin, who was to act as tutor and companion until he reached Turin. For Cornwallis it would be the military equivalent of the Grand Tour.[13]

Early 1757 was not a good time for such an undertaking, given the start of the Seven Years' War between Britain and France in May 1756. Although the rest of Europe was still at peace, war clouds were gathering along the Rhine following the diplomatic revolution that year, which committed Frederick II of Prussia to act as the guarantor of George II's Hanoverian territories, an unfriendly act in French eyes. In these turbulent circumstances, royal consent was necessary. Fortunately, George II's younger son, the duke of Cumberland, then captain-general of the army, was agreeable to the proposed course of study, telling the first earl that the mission 'if properly attended to' would be 'very useful'. Cumberland was seemingly already acquainted with Cornwallis's sober disposition, for he continued: 'I must do Lord Brome the justice to say he has less of our home education than most young men', a reference to the drinking, gambling, and womanising that were all too prevalent in the ranks of the British officer corps.[14] However, Cumberland was wrong in supposing that Cornwallis was above the 'common levities of youth'. When discussing his own son's future many years later, he confessed that he himself had been 'guilty of thousands of follies', having committed 'perhaps what strict people might call vices'.[15]

Tutor and pupil accordingly set off in the spring of 1757 for Lake Constance on the Swiss border, where Roguin suggested they spend a few months. Cornwallis later recounted it as one of the dullest places imaginable, though it also prompted memories of 'parties to Lausanne and Geneva'.[16] They finally arrived in Turin in early January 1758, where Cornwallis was formally introduced to the king of Sardinia and his family before receiving a private audience as a peer of the realm. Then, on 20 January 1758, his studies began in earnest, as Roguin reported to Cornwallis's father. The routine five days a week started at 7 a.m. with an hour's dancing lesson, a necessary skill for those in society. Next followed an hour's instruction in German, as befitted an institution dedicated to the Prussian method of warfare. After breakfast the cadets received drill instruction from the master of arms until one o'clock, when they took their main meal of the day in the company of the governor and deputy governor. Classes resumed at three with the professor of mathematics and fortifications, who instructed the cadets in the mechanics of siege warfare for two hours, after which there was a further hour of dancing. Evenings were devoted to attending the opera, visiting friends, and eating supper. Thursdays and Sundays were spent at the Sardinian court.[17]

Cornwallis proved a quick learner, not least with the dance master. However, now that the Seven Years' War had spread to most of Europe, the decision was taken to limit his stay at Turin to six months. He and Roguin consequently left for Geneva in June 1758, visiting several minor Swiss courts on their way. Here, Cornwallis heard that his regiment had been ordered on an expedition to the French coast. This determined him to return to England to join the troops then assembling on the Isle of Wight. However, at Cologne he found to his frustration that the expedition had long since sailed, as he told his cousin Thomas Townshend: 'Imagine having set out without leave, come two hundred leagues, and my regiment gone without me.'[18] Then he learnt that other British troops had been earmarked for service in Germany under Duke Ferdinand of Brunswick, one of the Frederick II's leading generals. Excited by the prospect of action, Cornwallis decided to seek employment there, even though George II had ordered that no volunteers would be allowed to join: officers must remain with their regiments to preserve discipline. But Cornwallis was not deterred, sending an impassioned letter to his father, asking him to intercede with the king through Newcastle, who was now first lord of the Treasury and partner in a coalition government with William Pitt.[19] In the meantime, he resolved to try his luck by joining Ferdinand's army, fully expecting to be sent home. To his surprise he was 'received in the kindest manner', being appointed shortly afterwards aide-de-camp to Lord Granby, the British second in command. Cornwallis's defiance of the royal wishes had been conveniently overlooked, as Newcastle had forecast might be the case.[20]

For the next twelve months Cornwallis served in Germany and was present at a number of important battles, including Minden, following which he was promoted captain in the newly formed 85th Foot Regiment. This necessitated his return to Britain at the end of the campaign to help complete his new corps. During the next eighteen months he appears to have impressed his seniors, for in June 1761 he returned to Germany as lieutenant-colonel of the 12th Foot Regiment.[21] This was a rapid promotion, though not exceptional when family influence counted for so much. His father certainly had no doubts about the reasons for Cornwallis's rapid advancement, as he emphasised to William Cornwallis, now serving in the navy. The key to promotion was to be respected by senior colleagues. 'Your Brother . . . is known to every General in the army he serves in, and has their universal good word and approbation.' This had 'helped him with ease to be a lieutenant-colonel very young', and would carry him even further to general 'applause'.[22] To raise his heir's profile even higher, the earl had also arranged for Cornwallis to be returned to Parliament for the Eye constituency.[23]

But the uncertain fortunes of life were ever present, even for the most privileged families. In May 1761 Cornwallis's closest brother, Henry, succumbed to a fever while returning home on military leave. Cornwallis admitted to his brother William that 'the loss of a brother and friend that I loved so sincerely as I did my dear Harry, is a most shocking and irreparable stroke'. It was equally hard for his parents. Their only consolation was that Cornwallis appeared 'to be in perfect health', and 'a great comfort to us all as he seems to be a very promising young man'.[24] Nevertheless, his promotion to the 12th Foot Regiment meant that he would have to return to Germany. The old earl comforted himself that recent talk of peace indicated that the war was about to end and that there would be no further bereavements in the family. Before returning Cornwallis sat for a three-quarter-length portrait by Sir Joshua Reynolds depicting him in his colonel's uniform. The impression is of a thoughtful young man who was ready to assume the Cornwallis name. His wall-eye is clearly visible.

During the following eighteen months, Cornwallis commanded his regiment in a number of engagements, including the Battle of Vellinghausen in July 1761, when the 12th Foot Regiment suffered over 100 casualties, a testimony to the severity of the fighting. Happily, the rest of the campaign was spent in minor skirmishing around Hesse and Paderborn until the onset of winter sent the regiment into quarters at Osnabrück.[25] It was during this period that Cornwallis came into contact with a number of officers with whom he was later to serve in America, notably Sir Henry Clinton of the 1st Foot Grenadier Guards, and William Philips of the Royal Artillery Regiment. Another important acquaintance was William Petty, earl of Shelburne, then serving as aide-de-camp to Granby.

The next campaign duly began in the spring of 1762 with several sharp actions in which Cornwallis's regiment more than fulfilled the tasks set by Granby. But his military career was to be temporarily halted by the news that his father had died while drinking the waters at Bristol Springs, a popular alternative to Bath Spa. From 23 June 1762, Cornwallis was now Earl Cornwallis and head of the family. Heavy fighting, however, prevented him from attending the funeral at Culford Park, where his father was interred in the family vault. Nevertheless, Cornwallis appears to have received compassionate leave during a subsequent lull in the fighting to attend to his late father's estate. This was undoubtedly a comfort to his mother, the Countess Elizabeth, who admitted to William Cornwallis that she was looking to her children to lighten her grief, above all by doing well in their 'several stations'.[26] Another consequence of succeeding to the earldom was the need to vacate the Eye constituency, since he was no longer eligible to sit in the Commons. His place was now in the upper legislative chamber.[27] With the war finally ending that autumn, Cornwallis was able to take his seat in the Lords on the next opening of Parliament.[28]

The main business facing Parliament in November 1762 was to debate the peace terms negotiated by the ministry of Lord Bute and George Grenville, which had replaced the wartime coalition of Pitt and Newcastle. Considerable opposition was being expressed, especially by the former ministers, because the terms did not adequately reflect Britain's gains on the battlefield. Though present, it is doubtful that Cornwallis spoke in these debates.[29] He was not a ready speaker, being diffident about expressing himself in public, a reserve which was to beset him for the rest of his life.[30] This did not prevent him from participating in committee work, though as a new and youthful member, he was assigned relatively mundane tasks, preparing private bills to pave the streets of Coventry and enclose lands in Bedfordshire.[31]

Nevertheless, the family tradition of supporting the Whig cause made Cornwallis a natural invitee to a series of dinners which his godfather, Newcastle, began holding in March 1763 to organise a more effective opposition in Parliament.[32] The first issue to arise was a proposed tax on cider, which Bute's chancellor of the Exchequer, Sir Francis Dashwood, wanted to include as part of a programme to balance the budget. Such excise duties were always unpopular, being associated with the heavy hand of government because of the use of inspectors. Cornwallis's allies accordingly decided to oppose Dashwood's bill, posing as the champions of liberty and the rights of the West Country apple growers.[33] Their action was unusual because it breached the convention that the Lords did not meddle in matters of taxation. Newcastle's group countered this by arguing that the measure was not purely financial, since the extension of excise duties had dangerous implications for liberty.[34] They were strongly applauded by the radical *London Evening Post*.[35]

Cornwallis was equally supportive of the Whigs during the next session of Parliament in November 1763, when the party opposed the decision of the ministry, now headed by Grenville and the duke of Bedford, to expel the firebrand John Wilkes from the Commons for lampooning the recently delivered king's speech on the opening of Parliament. The ministers argued that parliamentary privilege did not extend to the writing of seditious libels. To the Newcastle Whigs, the ministry's action appeared yet another dangerous extension of executive power and contrary to the principles of the 1688 Glorious Revolution. Cornwallis became one of seventeen peers, led by Shelburne, who condemned the Commons' action when it was debated in the upper house. They argued that Wilkes's expulsion fatally undermined the privileges of both houses of Parliament and was incompatible with the freedom of its members.[36] Cornwallis's radical stance did not go unobserved by Grenville, especially after he was seen walking with the firebrand Wilkes in Hyde Park.[37] The young earl was keeping dangerous company.

Aside from his political interests and regimental duties, Cornwallis, as head of the family, was responsible for the well-being of his widowed mother and younger siblings. The dowager countess was comfortably settled in London with a house near Berkeley Square in Mayfair, though she complained about spending summers there when society migrated to the country.[38] Two of Cornwallis's three surviving sisters were already married with their own households, and therefore no longer his responsibility. This left Molly, the sister closest in age to Cornwallis, who probably alternated stays with her mother with visits to Culford Park and the residencies of relatives like the Townshends. In 1769 she married Samuel Whitbread, the brewer, though her life was cut short in childbirth within a year.[39] As for Cornwallis's two male siblings, James, his middle brother, had completed his theological studies at Oxford in preparation for the church. He could expect help in his career from his uncle Frederick Cornwallis, currently the bishop of Lichfield and Coventry, who became archbishop of Canterbury in 1769. Finally, William, Cornwallis's younger sibling, was progressing in his naval career, though any assistance from his brother could not but be helpful. Even before his elevation to the peerage, Cornwallis had promised his filial support, affirming that 'half the contents of my purse will be always at your service'.[40] Nor was this all, as his mother reported in the summer of 1763. Although Cornwallis was then in Scotland with his regiment, he was using his contacts to get William appointed a post-captain, despite his youth.[41]

Despite the offer to his brother, Cornwallis was not a wealthy man compared to most of his peers. He had rents from the farms on the family estates at Culford Park and Brome, though the latter comprised just 750 acres. There were also several other small manors, including one in Huntingdonshire. However, he had to maintain not only Culford Park and Brome Hall, but also a town house in London. And wherever he resided, he required a proper establishment of butlers and other domestic servants, plus horses, grooms, and carriages. The problem was that the Cornwallis family had not progressed financially since the time of Charles II's restoration. One indication of this was the dilapidated state of Culford Park, which had received little refurbishment since its purchase a century before.[42] He was naturally prudent with money, anxious to avoid the embarrassment of being indebted to tradesmen. Nevertheless, he necessarily entertained 'a great deal of company' at Culford Park, when his regimental duties allowed, as the dowager countess informed William in October 1764.[43] It was an essential part of advancing himself and the family.

Peacetime service in the army was naturally different from that of wartime. Cornwallis was fortunate that his regiment, being a long-established corps, was not disbanded at the end of the conflict, but reduced to a smaller peacetime establishment. As lieutenant-colonel, it was his task to manage the corps's discipline, appearance, and general welfare, subject to occasional inspections by its titular colonel, Lieutenant-General Robert Napier, or directives from the War Office. This necessarily required Cornwallis to be frequently domiciled with his regiment, either in barracks at one of the forts around the kingdom or in temporary quarters with local innkeepers.

Nonetheless, life was not all seriousness and attention to duty. Cornwallis enjoyed foxhunting and the other outdoor pleasures that were open to the landowning classes, such as shooting pheasant and partridge. He also participated in the aristocratic social scene in Suffolk and London. Not least was the need to reciprocate the hospitality of the many prominent figures who invited him to their various receptions, balls, and entertainments. Especially pressing was his godfather Newcastle, who hosted lavish entertainments at Claremont, his country estate in Surrey.[44] Many others too wanted to be on good terms with the young earl. Though naturally modest and thoughtful, Cornwallis had a wry sense of humour and was good company at such events. But whatever his previous behaviour, he had firmly laid aside the 'levities of youth'.

Meanwhile, Cornwallis's support for the Whig party was about to pay a dividend. By the middle of 1765 the Grenville ministry had become politically embroiled over the issues of American taxation and its use of general warrants to silence opposition journalists and printers employed by Wilkes. The result in August 1765 was the formation of a Whig ministry under the marquess of Rockingham. Cornwallis followed these events closely in the House of Lords, since his connections with the Whigs naturally placed him in line for political advancement. He was not disappointed, being appointed a lord of the royal bedchamber. This was a merely an honorary post and may have been the reason why he exchanged it shortly afterwards to become an aide-de-camp to the king.[45] Nevertheless, Cornwallis's greater political standing was reflected by his membership of the committee to draft the reply to the king's speech, whose other members included such political heavyweights as Rockingham, the duke of Grafton, and Shelburne.[46]

Cornwallis was naturally expected to support the government's key measures, notably the repeal of the Stamp Act and passage of a Declaratory or Dependency Bill. However, he initially broke ranks during the second reading of the Dependency Bill to support Lord Camden, Shelburne, and two other lords, who contested the view that Parliament had the right to legislate for the American colonies 'in all cases whatsoever', meaning taxation. Cornwallis's opposition on 3 February 1766 is surprising because such conduct was likely to anger the king as well has his Whig allies. Most historians have assumed that he acted thus because he sympathised with the American cause, but a more likely explanation is that he was momentarily swayed by his friend Shelburne, as he did not show such sympathies again. He appears in any case to have explained his position beforehand to the Whig leadership, since Rockingham assured George III the following day that 'no consequence' was to be drawn from the votes of Camden's allies.[47] In the event the repeal of the Stamp Act proved the more controversial measure, being vigorously opposed by Grenville and Bedford, who sought to defend their record on America.[48] The Declaratory Act in contrast passed its final reading without a division.

Nevertheless, for a while Cornwallis's name acquired some notoriety, being toasted at a celebratory ball hosted by an eminent timber merchant with links to the American Patriots. He was also hailed as a friend of liberty during a rally in King's Lynn.[49] However, when Rockingham and his supporters were replaced by a government headed by Pitt, now earl of Chatham, Cornwallis retained his post as aide-de-camp. He may have become embarrassed by his newfound popularity and felt it unbecoming for a royal aide to be linked with opposition. Whatever the reason, he was rewarded for his abandonment of the Rockingham Whigs in December 1766 with the sinecure post of chief justice for the royal forests south of the River Trent. Apart from a useful supplement to his income, the position had sentimental value since it had previously been held by his father.[50]

Cornwallis's military career was similarly progressing, with his promotion to full colonel coming in August 1765, though without the command of a regiment. However, in March 1766 he received the colonelcy of the 33rd Foot Regiment.[51] He had no previous affiliation with this corps, which recruited principally in the West Riding of Yorkshire and was currently doing garrison duty on the island of Minorca.[52] His promotion meant that much routine administration could be left to his deputy, Lieutenant-Colonel Hildebrand Oakes, or the regimental agent, James Meyrick. However, like most ambitious colonels, Cornwallis wanted his corps to be the best in the army. Judging by the comments of one of the 33rd Foot Regiment's lieutenants, its relaxed life on the island meant that Cornwallis had much work to do to make it an effective fighting unit.[53]

Cornwallis left Britain to join his corps in late July 1766.[54] However, he appears to have spent only a few months in Minorca, for by mid-February 1767 the newspapers reported that he had returned to England.[55] Indeed, from early March to the end of the parliamentary session in June he was once more attending the House of Lords. But the only significant mention of him in the House journals was his selection with the duke of Ancaster to carry the Lords' congratulatory message to Queen Charlotte on the birth of her fourth son, Edward, duke of Kent.[56]

As he entered the twenty-ninth year of his life, Cornwallis's thoughts turned to marriage. The young lady in question was Jemima Jones, the daughter of James Jones, a former lieutenant-colonel of the 3rd Foot Guards Regiment. Cornwallis may have known Jemima's father when he was himself an ensign in the Guards. However, an introduction more likely occurred through the agency of a fellow officer. Her portrait by Reynolds in 1771 shows her to have been a slender young woman of poise and elegance. The union seems to have been entirely romantic on Cornwallis's side. Jemima's family were not socially prominent, nor was she desirable as an heiress. Her father left only a modest estate on his death in 1758. His total effects comprised a house in Henrietta Street near Covent Garden, valued at £1,430, and a similar sum for his furniture, books, and paintings. Among the latter were works by Rubens, Van Dyck, Tintoretto, and Rembrandt. The most valuable, a David Teniers landscape, sold for £5 2s 6d.[57]

Despite her relatively modest circumstances, Jemima was the young lady to whom he proposed just before her twenty-first birthday. The marriage itself took place on 14 July 1768 at Jemima's home in Stratton Street off Piccadilly, with James Cornwallis officiating as minister.[58] It was to prove a remarkably strong and loving union. During the next few years Cornwallis sought her company as much as possible, subject to his regimental duties. Within a year of their marriage, they were blessed with a daughter, Mary, followed in October 1774 by a son, Charles, known as Viscount Brome, providing at least one male heir to preserve the family name and title.[59]

Shortly after his marriage in February 1769 Cornwallis was appointed vice-treasurer of Ireland, another sinecure, in place of his chief justiceship in eyre.[60] There was no obvious reason for the appointment, other than Cornwallis's continued support for the ministry, now headed by the duke of Grafton. Political opposition no longer had much appeal for him, since he associated it with people who wanted power for personal gain or aggrandisement. Though he remained attached to the principles of the 1688 revolution, integrity, honour, and reverence for the country's institutions were more important than narrow tribal allegiances. This made him a natural supporter of George III and his ministers.

It was this association with the ministry that produced a scathing attack in the *Public Advertiser* by the anonymous letter writer Junius, using on this occasion the alternative pseudonym of 'Domitian', the Roman emperor.[61] The essence of the attack of 5 March 1770 was Cornwallis's abandonment of his former allies. 'Where is now . . . his zeal for the Whig interest of England, and his detestation of Lord Bute, the Bedfords and the Tories', which at one time 'were the only topics of his conversation?' Seemingly he had changed both 'his company as well as his opinions'. He was to be commended, therefore, for having taken the 'wise resolution at last' of 'retiring into a voluntary banishment in hopes of recovering the ruin of his reputation'.[62]

The attack had little impact and was misinformed, since Cornwallis had not retired from the political arena. For another twelve months he continued to support the ministry in the Lords on both its American and domestic issues. One sign of this was his elevation to the Privy Council in November 1770.[63] Then in January 1771 he was appointed constable of the Tower of London in place of his vice-treasurership of Ireland.[64] This post was usually given to a military man and his appointment probably reflected his growing reputation as a soldier rather than as a politician. It was now that Cornwallis stepped back from the political sphere: he made only three appearances in the Lords in 1771 and was also absent for most of 1773. The one time when Cornwallis invariably appeared was at the opening of Parliament, as was customary for loyal supporters of the government.

His reduced political activity reflected his increased duties elsewhere. As constable of the Tower, he had to ensure its security as an arsenal for small arms and as a prison. The post also included the office of *custos rotulorum* ('keeper of the Rolls'), which gave Cornwallis the powers of a magistrate for the borough of Tower Hamlets. This included responsibility for ensuring that its militia could assist the fort should it be attacked. But he had few prisoners to deal with, and only one of note, when in the autumn of 1775 the sheriff of London, Stephen Sayre, was incarcerated on a charge of treason. A supporter of the American cause, Sayre was accused of plotting to kidnap George III with the aid of the London mob in order to send him back to his ancestral electorate of Hanover.[65] Sayre's incarceration proved short-lived, since he was released within days for lack of evidence.

Otherwise, Cornwallis appears to have concentrated on making his regiment the best in the British army following its return from Minorca in June 1769. The annual inspection for that year suggested that all was not well with the corps. The reviewing officers noted the slow pace of the regiment in some exercises and that it 'deviated from the practice of the army' in forming its ranks. They also observed the comparative youth of the officers in contrast to the superannuated age of the rank and file, fifty-seven of whom had to be discharged.[66] However, by June 1771 Cornwallis appears to have achieved his objective. According to the *General Evening Post*, the 33rd Foot Regiment under his command had been twice reviewed 'at the particular request' of the king, first on Blackheath and then in Hyde Park, where 'they again exhibited all their new manoeuvres as light infantry'. The paper continued: 'Their quickness of motion and marching, and various order of firing, is really astonishing.' Once back before the king 'they formed in an instant the Indian file, and fired in ambuscade'. The whole performance rightly merited 'the just applause of His majesty' and numerous senior officers.[67] Two days later the same newspaper noted that the Guards were to try 'the new exercises introduced by Lord Cornwallis with the 33rd Foot Regiment, now deemed the best regiment in the army'.[68]

It is unclear why Cornwallis adopted such tactics for the whole of his regiment. The light infantry normally comprised only one company per regiment. As an elite group, their role was to provide flanking parties, undertake reconnaissance, and execute other dangerous assignments. Such training would clearly be advantageous in the woods of eastern North America, though there is no evidence that Cornwallis was anticipating conflict there. Nevertheless, it was to prove fortuitously far-sighted and was the start of his lifelong belief in the value of such corps.

The early 1770s seemingly passed in quiet contentment, as Cornwallis enjoyed the pleasures of domestic life, while fulfilling his responsibilities as constable of the Tower and colonel of his regiment. He was generally in good health, though in 1770 he began to be troubled by 'eruptions' on his legs, indicative of varicose veins, the consequence perhaps of being overweight. This suggests that he suffered from a congenital condition like diabetes, given Cornwallis's aversion to any sort of overindulgence. Swollen legs and ankles were to afflict him periodically for the rest of his life.

All this while Cornwallis continued his efforts to ensure that his regiment remained one of the best in the British army, as was again shown in April 1774, when the 33rd Foot Regiment received its annual inspection from Sir William Howe at Plymouth. The *Morning Chronicle* reported that 'the spectators seemed astonished at the quickness and regularity' of the 33rd Foot Regiment's 'motions and manoeuvres'. It also praised the corps's behaviour while quartered among the population.[69] Howe seconded these verdicts in his official report. The officers were 'exceedingly expert in their duty', while the rank and file comprised 'a very fine corps', despite their youth – a big change from the unfavourable comments in 1769. Howe was especially impressed by the light infantry company and concluded: 'The discipline of this regiment is established upon the truest principles, far superior to any other corps within my observation.'[70] The inspection seems to have inspired Howe to organise a wider demonstration of light infantry tactics on Salisbury Plain, which one participant noted were clearly intended for the 'woody and intricate districts' of North America, where 'an army cannot act in line'.[71]

Cornwallis, however, was not present, since the 33rd Foot Regiment had been ordered to Ireland as part of the garrison there.[72] The regiment now had a new lieutenant-colonel, James Webster, the son of a Scottish Presbyterian minister. According to Sergeant Roger Lamb, who was to serve in America with Cornwallis, it was here that his own regiment, the 9th Foot Regiment, was instructed by the 33rd Foot Regiment in the use of the new light infantry tactics. The 33rd, he noted, 'was in a high state of appointment . . . I never witnessed any regiment that excelled it in discipline and military appearance.'[73] Thirty years later, Wellington, then lieutenant-colonel of the 33rd Foot Regiment, acknowledged that his 'uniform object' was 'to maintain the system of discipline, subordination, and interior economy' established by Cornwallis.[74]

Immersed in his regimental duties, Cornwallis seems to have paid little attention to the increasing tensions between Britain and her colonists, though he made a point of returning to London for the opening of Parliament. When his old political allies, Rockingham, the duke of Richmond, Shelburne, and Camden attempted on 30 November 1774 to amend the address to the king, deploring the government's repressive measures against the colonists, Cornwallis voted as usual with the ministry.[75] Like most of his colleagues, he believed that the American colonists had been subverted from their natural fidelity by a few malcontents. Thus, when the Rockingham Whigs attempted on 21 March 1775 to amend the bill restraining the trade of New England, Cornwallis again voted with the ministry.[76] To his mind the measure was the least that could be done to secure the colonists' obedience.

With hostilities in prospect, it was incumbent on Cornwallis and Webster to ensure that the regiment was up to strength and in good order. Accordingly, Cornwallis returned at the end of the parliamentary session to Dublin, where the 33rd Foot Regiment now comprised part of the city's garrison. Here the corps was reviewed on 17 July 1775 by Lieutenant-General John Irwin and other senior officers. With Cornwallis at the head, the 33rd performed the various evolutions, firings, and manoeuvres 'exceedingly well'. The only adverse comment was that the corps still required forty-two men to complete its ten companies. Nevertheless, Irwin concluded that the regiment was 'in perfect good order and in every respect fit for service'.[77] The incomplete ranks may have reflected Cornwallis's exacting standards. A recruiting poster in Herefordshire required those enlisting in the 33rd Foot Regiment to be no younger than seventeen and no older than twenty-two. They must also have an honest character since only those who promised 'to be a credit to their officers and honour to their country' would be accepted. He was not going to fill his regiment with inmates from the local gaols.[78]

Cornwallis left no record of his stay in Dublin. As a peer of the realm he would have had ready access to the society of the ruling Anglo-Irish elite. He does not appear to have been impressed, judging by his reaction to Ireland's governing class when he returned twenty-three years later as lord lieutenant.

TWO

The Call of Duty

Cornwallis had few doubts about suppressing the American rebellion that had broken out on 19 April 1775 following the armed clashes at Lexington and Concord. Like most of his contemporaries, he believed the British constitution offered the best possible system of governance, incorporating a judicious Aristotelian blend of monarchy, aristocracy, and democracy. The only explanation for the current unrest was that the colonists had fallen victim to the wiles of a malevolent minority. As he told his mother after the Battle of Brooklyn: 'The unhappy people have been kept in utter darkness by the tyranny of their wicked leaders' and were 'astonished to hear how little is required of them' to renew their loyalty.[1] It was a view that the British establishment would retain for the rest of the war.[2]

Neither Cornwallis nor his regiment were among the officers and corps selected in July 1775 to relieve General Thomas Gage, who was then being besieged in Boston by the New England militia. He was certainly disappointed at not being chosen for the task of restoring British authority, being naturally envious of contemporaries like Howe, Clinton, and Guy Carleton, who had been summoned. All three were close to Cornwallis in age and only one rank higher in seniority. Martial prowess was the essence of being a soldier. It was what one did when the nation was in peril.

For the moment he had to bide his time and be content with promotion in October 1775 to the rank of major-general.[3] However, when he learnt a few weeks later that the ministry was planning to send an expedition to help the Loyalists in the southern colonies, Cornwallis promptly petitioned the new secretary of state for America,

Map 2. America: The Northern Theatre.

Lord George Germain, for permission to take charge of the troops until they reached their destination. He was supported by Lord North, now prime minister, who suggested to George III that Cornwallis's offer 'to serve as second on the expedition' should be accepted, as his 'example will give credit and spirit to our proceedings against America'.[4] The king readily consented and also agreed that Cornwallis's regiment should be included in the embarkation.[5] However, not everyone applauded Cornwallis's offer. The *London Evening Post* reminded its readers that Cornwallis had been 'one of the memorable minority of five in the House of Lords' who had championed the principle 'that the British Parliament had no right to tax the American colonies'.[6] But that was ten years ago and overlooked Cornwallis's subsequent record, which demonstrated that any sympathy he might have had for the American cause had long since disappeared.

Cornwallis undoubtedly consulted his wife Jemima about his wish to serve in America. It is equally likely that she objected, since their son, Viscount Brome, was barely a year old. Family tradition suggests that she asked Cornwallis's uncle, Archbishop Frederick, to intercede with the king in an attempt to prevent his departure. However, she was unlikely to have been so disloyal.[7] Paradoxically, the *Morning Post* claimed that the archbishop's help had been sought, not to prevent Cornwallis from serving in America, but to secure permission to go![8] That was a more likely scenario.

The force leaving Ireland was to consist of seven infantry regiments and two companies of artillery. On reaching America, Cornwallis was to place himself 'under the command of such superior officer as you shall find to have been sent there by Major-General Howe', the commander-in-chief.[9] The most likely candidate was Henry Clinton. A mutual friend, William Philips, conscious of Clinton's sensitive temperament, attempted to smooth the way by telling him that Cornwallis 'has a most confirmed good opinion of you and is happy beyond measure at being to serve under your orders'. Clinton should thus 'throw off all reserve', treating Cornwallis 'at once in confidence and friendship'. Since both men had been trained in the Prussian methods of warfare, they would hopefully be able to 'stand by each other' in the trials to come.[10] Philips's concern about Clinton's ability to work with others was to prove well founded.

After a final audience with the king, Cornwallis set off in mid-December for Portsmouth to take ship for Ireland.[11] But assembling the necessary shipping took longer than expected, and the expedition, comprising several warships and twenty-one transports under the supervision of Rear Admiral Sir Peter Parker, only left Cork on 12 February 1776.[12] The voyage proved a remarkably slow one: three weeks later the convoy was still only 200 miles from its point of departure. Although Cornwallis was accommodated on one of the larger warships, the fifty-gun *Bristol*, the constant buffeting of the waves made even writing a letter difficult.[13] The flotilla finally reached Cape Fear, its rendezvous, in early May 1776. Here, they were met by Clinton, who informed them that they were too late to help the North Carolina Loyalists. They had risen in the New Year only to be crushed at Moore's Creek Bridge on 27 February 1776.[14]

Since further operations at Cape Fear appeared inadvisable, the commanders decided to look elsewhere for a target. Loyalist strength had been reported in both Virginia and South Carolina by their former governors, Lord Dunmore and William Campbell.[15] However, Parker and Clinton were constrained by the need to join Howe in time for the campaign in New York. This effectively ruled out any attempt to restore the king's government in either colony, though the remaining time might allow them to establish a post, 'where the King's persecuted subjects and his officers might find an asylum'.[16] Clinton favoured the Chesapeake, but Parker preferred the area around Charleston. Two of his officers had discovered that Sullivan's Island on the eastern approaches to the city was weakly defended by just one principal fortification, Fort Moultrie. The city itself appeared relatively defenceless.

Clinton and Parker, accordingly, decided to make the capture of Sullivan's Island their primary objective. Cornwallis himself necessarily agreed, having no personal knowledge of the area. The initial plan was to land directly on the island until it was found that the shore there was subject to heavy surf. It was agreed instead to land on nearby Long Island and wade across the intervening channel, which was said to be no more than 2 or 3 feet deep at low tide. Prior to the operation, Clinton and Cornwallis spent several nights reconnoitring possible landing sites, only for the engineers to discover that the water between the two islands was never less than 7 feet deep even at low tide. This meant that the troops would be unable to get across, given the lack of landing craft. With time running out, Parker offered to manoeuvre his ships close to the fort to subdue it with their heavy guns. This too proved inopportune, for after a nine-hour bombardment on 28 June the British had nothing to show for their endeavours other than three badly damaged warships, one of which had to be destroyed. The decision was consequently taken to sail for New York. The rescue of the southern Loyalists would have to wait.[17]

The flotilla reached New York on 1 August where they found that Howe had yet to open the campaign. He had been assembling his army on Staten Island since late June, but was still awaiting two Guards battalions and both divisions of Hessian troops, which the ministry had hired from the Landgrave of Hesse Kassel for service in America. Howe's plan, as he informed Germain on 10 August, was to land on Long Island, engage Washington's forces entrenched on Guana Heights, after which he expected to capture the city and complete the destruction of the rebel army. Rhode Island might then be occupied and a junction made with Carleton's army advancing from Canada via Lake George. The encirclement of New England would then be complete.[18]

The campaign finally started on 22 August, when the troops landed on Long Island, close to the settlement of Flatbush. Cornwallis had been placed in command of the reserve, with two battalions of light infantry and a Hessian corps under Colonel Carl von Donop. Nevertheless, Howe quickly ordered him to inspect the main pass through Guana Heights, though without attempting to engage. As expected, Cornwallis found Washington's army firmly entrenched on the heights to the north.[19] Howe responded by adjusting his plan. While Major-General James Grant and the Hessian general Leopold Philip de Heister confronted the rebels on Guana Heights, the main army would march under cover of darkness to the unguarded Jamaica Pass on the left of Washington's position. The rebel flank could then be turned, allowing their centre and right wing to be surrounded. On this occasion Clinton was to lead the advance with Cornwallis in close support. In the event the plan worked perfectly. While Grant and Heister distracted the rebels, Clinton, Howe, and Cornwallis gained the heights a few miles to their left. Despite gallant resistance, the disciplined firepower and use of the bayonet at close quarters proved too much for the inexperienced colonials, who fled back towards their fortified encampment on Brooklyn Heights overlooking the East River. In the mêlée the 33rd Foot, Cornwallis's own regiment, reached the rebel camp and was about to storm a key redoubt when they were called back by Howe, fearful that events were spiralling out of control.[20] Cornwallis himself spent most of the battle directing the 71st Highland Regiment in a move to trap the American right wing. Among those captured was General William Alexander, Lord Stirling, one of Washington's most experienced corps commanders.[21]

Howe's failure to let the 33rd Foot Regiment storm the American lines proved an expensive error, since it gave Washington time to evacuate his shattered forces over the East River to Manhattan. It was to be one of many examples of Howe's caution when a bolder approach might have completed the destruction of Washington's army. However, his reluctance to press home the attack on 27 August seems to have been deliberate. As Cornwallis informed his mother, everyone believed that 'in a short time their army [would] disperse and the war ... be over'. Unnecessary bloodshed would merely render reconciliation more difficult, though Cornwallis was pleased with his part in the battle, despite the casualties. 'Judge of my happiness, having had a share in the late glorious action.' His joy was doubly great, given 'the prospect of being soon restored to my family'.[22]

During the next two months Cornwallis played a relatively minor role with the reserve, which befitted his volunteer status. Clinton took the lead on 15 September during the landing at Kip's Bay on Manhattan Island, though Cornwallis was close behind with his corps. Clinton again commanded in the engagement at White Plains on 28 October, while the Hessian general Wilhelm von Knyphausen and Lieutenant-General Hugh Percy led the subsequent attack on Fort Washington. In mid-November, however, Howe decided to give Cornwallis a chance to prove himself, ordering him to cross the Hudson River with a substantial force to capture Fort Lee, thus opening the river for British shipping. Among the corps allotted to the operation were several elite units, including the British and Hessian light infantry, two Guards battalions and some Hessian jaegers or riflemen. It was Cornwallis's first time commanding a full brigade of infantry, cavalry, and artillery.[23]

Once the necessary shipping had been assembled, Cornwallis crossed the Hudson unmolested on the night of 19 November with 4,000 men for the assault on Fort Lee.[24] In the event, the recent setbacks on Manhattan had so demoralised the rebel forces that Washington ordered the fort's hasty evacuation, leaving behind thirty cannon, numerous stores, and several thousand cattle in the nearby meadows.[25] Cornwallis welcomed the lack of bloodshed. When the Hessian captain Johann Ewald suggested a vigorous pursuit, he replied: 'Let them go my dear Ewald and stay here. We do not want to lose any men. One Jaeger is worth more than ten rebels.' Ewald suddenly understood the reason for the slow pace of Howe's operations. He 'wanted to spare the King's subjects and hoped to terminate the war amicably'. Ewald was strengthened in this assumption 'the next day by several English officers'.[26]

Further operations, therefore, were not Howe's immediate priority, other than the dispatch of Clinton to secure Rhode Island as a base for future operations in New England. Cornwallis's subsequent orders of 22 November were limited to following the remnants of Washington's army to Brunswick on the Raritan River. Here his troops could go into winter quarters, since supplies were likely to be plentiful in that part of New Jersey.[27] Accordingly, Cornwallis set off the next day with his corps, reaching Newark on 28 November, Elizabethtown on the 29th, Perth Amboy on the 30th, and finally the Raritan River opposite Brunswick on 1 December, arriving just as Washington's rearguard reached the other side.[28]

The next few days were spent preparing winter billets and repairing the bridge into Brunswick. But Howe had not reckoned with the Loyalist outcry that there was nothing to stop him reaching Philadelphia. The capture of the rebel capital would be a handsome Christmas bonus. This prompted Howe not only to reinforce Cornwallis, but take charge himself, arriving at Brunswick on 6 December with an additional corps of 3,000 men under Grant. The advance was resumed that afternoon, with Cornwallis leading the vanguard, heading first for Princeton and then Trenton beside the Delaware River.[29]

The march was still a leisurely one, reinforcing Ewald's conclusions about Howe's pacific intentions.[30] The same dilatory progress was noted by another Hessian officer, Captain Friedrich von Muenchhausen. The army in consequence arrived at Trenton just as Washington's last detachments reached the Pennsylvanian side of the river, taking all the boats with them. While Howe and Cornwallis pondered on how to proceed, the rebel artillery opened fire from across the river. Howe insisted on standing his ground until a cannonball removed the hind leg of Muenchhausen's horse. Only then did he allow his companions to take cover.[31]

Since no crossing was immediately possible at Trenton, Howe ordered Cornwallis to ascend the river to Coryell's Ferry in hopes of finding sufficient craft. In this he was disappointed, as Washington had secured every boat for more than 60 miles.[32] With cold weather setting in, Howe determined to revert to his plan of going into winter quarters. The Loyalist historian Charles Stedman believed in retrospect that another golden opportunity for destroying Washington's army had been lost by Howe, an opinion that is difficult to contradict, despite Cornwallis's subsequent defence of him during a parliamentary enquiry.[33]

With the rebellion on the verge of collapse, Cornwallis decided to ask permission to return to England. Howe readily consented, telling Germain: 'I cannot too much commend Lord Cornwallis's good services during this campaign.' His pursuit of the enemy from Fort Lee to Trenton, a distance of more than 80 miles, was especially noteworthy. This had only been possible through the 'ardour of his corps who cheerfully quitted their tents and heavy baggage' to expedite their march.[34] It was an early example of the respect in which Cornwallis was held by his men, explaining the hardships they readily endured during his subsequent campaigns.

His departure from America, however, was to be unexpectedly delayed and for longer than he could have imagined. On Christmas night, Washington re-crossed the Delaware and surprised the Hessian garrison at Trenton, capturing two-thirds of the men quartered there before retreating back into Pennsylvania. Howe had earlier admitted to Germain that his chain of posts was 'rather too extensive, but I was induced to occupy Burlington to cover the county of Monmouth', since there were 'many loyal inhabitants' there. The danger of such dispersion appeared small, given the 'almost general submission of the country' and 'the strength of the corps placed on the advanced posts'.[35] Cornwallis later testified that he had encouraged Howe to extend his posts in this fashion, believing that the protection of a loyal population was paramount if the policy of conciliation was to work.[36] Unfortunately, the commander at Trenton, Colonel Rall, had failed to fortify his position against a surprise attack, partly because of contempt for the Americans, and partly because the frozen ground made it impossible to construct earthworks.[37] The result, nonetheless, was a damaging blow to the British cause.

The seriousness of the situation was further emphasised on 30 December when Washington recrossed the Delaware River for a second time to take post once more at Trenton. In this crisis Howe turned to Cornwallis as the commander most likely to remedy the situation. Cornwallis was about to sail for England aboard the warship *Bristol*.[38] Leaving aside all thoughts of home, he immediately set off through New Jersey with an escort of just three dragoons, before picking up various detachments along the way to Princeton, where he arrived late on 1 January 1777. Here he found

Grant with the advanced guard, bringing his total force to nearly 7,000 men, seemingly more than enough for the task in hand. The only discussion was whether to proceed in one column down the post road to Trenton, which he and Howe had taken four weeks earlier, or send part of the army on an alternative route, which would enable it to approach the town from the east.[39] Cornwallis preferred the route with which he was familiar.

He set out early on the morning of 2 January for the 10-mile march to Trenton, leaving Lieutenant-Colonel Charles Mawhood with three regiments at Princeton in reserve. Progress proved difficult, with the road muddy following an overnight thaw. Precautions also had to be taken against the rebel sharpshooters who infested the surrounding countryside, though the dangers of rifle fire had been greatly exaggerated. As Captain Dansey of the 33rd Foot Regiment had earlier commented, the colonists believed their familiarity with firearms and possession of rifles would make them invincible. The reality was 'that being a good marksman is only a trifling requisite for a soldier'. After the landing on Manhattan, Dansey had stood 'for upwards of seven hours at their favourite distance about 200 yards', inflicting several casualties without suffering one in return. This showed 'that a good soldier with a good firelock was beyond a Rifleman with all his skill'. It was a view that Cornwallis shared for the rest of his life.[40]

A more serious obstacle to progress proved to be Washington's rearguard, which occupied a series of intersecting creeks, compelling the British to deploy each time as though for battle. The main column only reached the outskirts of Trenton around 4 p.m., where it was discovered that Washington had taken post to the south-east of the town along Assunpink Creek. Three attempts by the Hessian and British infantry to storm the only available bridge all failed, as did tentative probes to cross at two fords.[41] With dusk fast approaching, Cornwallis decided to consult his senior officers; it was now that he made his alleged remark about bagging the 'Old Fox' in the morning. Apart from the arguments of Erskine, Grant, and Leslie, Cornwallis wanted to await the arrival of Mawhood, whom he had summoned with reinforcements from Princeton. Everything pointed to the advantage of waiting until daylight.

The army, accordingly, settled down for the customary evening meal, while the light infantry patrolled the banks of the creek to check on the rebel positions. All seemed in order as campfires illuminated the night sky and rebel sentries were heard issuing their challenges. But unknown to Cornwallis, the fires and challenges were all part of an elaborate ruse. Once night had fallen, Washington and his army departed on a back road around the eastern flank of the British position before heading northwards.[42] The first that Cornwallis knew all was not well was the sound of distant gunfire from the direction of Princeton. The vanguard of the rebel army had fallen on Mawhood, who was marching southwards with two regiments in response to Cornwallis's call for reinforcements. The weight of numbers soon scattered the British corps, resulting in heavy casualties.[43] Washington had clearly outfoxed his adversary, as patrols confirmed that his camp was empty.

In this crisis Cornwallis quickly assembled his men for a rapid march back to Princeton in hopes of catching his foe. He feared that Washington would advance to Brunswick, where the army had its stores, baggage, and a large amount of specie. Washington momentarily considered the idea. However, the hard frosts and snow persuaded him that it was time for his men to go into winter quarters. After destroying a key bridge to slow his pursuers, he set off for a previously planned encampment at Morristown, deep inside New Jersey's hilly interior. Cornwallis reached Princeton two hours later, but decided against further pursuit in such wintry conditions. The morale of his troops had been undeniably shaken. Their enemy, of whom they had been so contemptuous, had suddenly acquired wings, seemingly able to strike at will.[44]

Writing briefly to Germain four days later, Cornwallis attempted to put a brave face on the affair. Rall's surprise at Trenton had revealed that 'our quarters were too much exposed'. It had therefore become 'necessary to assemble our troops' in more compact formations. This was 'now done and all is safe'. Washington, in contrast, would not be able to feed his men for long at Morristown; should he attempt to return to Pennsylvania, 'the march alone will destroy his army'. Cornwallis made no mention of Mawhood's loss of approximately 250 men, or his own substantial casualties the previous day.[45] He was perhaps fortunate to be supported in these sentiments by Howe.[46]

Clearly, Cornwallis had been thoroughly out-manoeuvred by the rebel commander. He was probably wise not to press home his attack on first arriving at Trenton. But he should have ensured that Washington was securely trapped before settling down for the night, which he could have done by blocking the eastern exit from Assunpink Creek. As a result, Cornwallis squandered one of the best chances that the British were to have of capturing the wily American.

The affair does not seem to have damaged Cornwallis's reputation with the army or the public in Britain. Nevertheless, the setback at Trenton ultimately proved fatal to British hopes of regaining the middle colonies, since the withdrawal of their forces to Brunswick and Perth Amboy meant surrendering the rest of New Jersey to rebel control. The Loyalists, who had so recently cheered the arrival of Howe's army, now had the cruel dilemma of making peace with their former persecutors or of fleeing to New York without their possessions. They would be doubly cautious of welcoming the British again, as Cornwallis was to find (see below, p. 80).

The setback had one other consequence for Cornwallis. He would not now be able to return home to Jemima and the children. Instead, Howe placed him in charge of the 7,000 British forces cantoned at Brunswick and Perth Amboy. Such locations offered few comforts, especially in winter, in contrast to New York, where the officers had balls and concerts to entertain them.[47] Cornwallis was not envious, as such frivolity seemed inappropriate in the current circumstances of his king and country.

In London it was assumed that Washington's successes at Trenton and Princeton were merely the spasms of a dying cause. The ministers believed that Howe still had the means to complete the subjugation of New England and the middle colonies, after which the southern colonies should be easily recovered, given the alleged depth of Loyalist support there. Unfortunately for Germain and his colleagues, their assumption that the war was almost over was far from Howe's view of the situation, especially regarding the means for achieving such outcome. His initial intentions in December 1776 were to take the bulk of his army to Philadelphia, the rebel capital, which he assumed Washington was bound to defend, resulting in a final decisive battle. Elsewhere, he proposed to post strong detachments in New York and Rhode Island to facilitate co-operation with the army of Major-General John Burgoyne, which was to advance on the Hudson River from Canada.[48] However, the events at

Trenton and Princeton persuaded Howe in early January 1777 that he must have another 15,000–20,000 men to carry out these plans, otherwise he would be limited to an advance on Philadelphia by way of New Jersey. Elsewhere a strict defensive would be necessary.[49]

It is not clear how far Howe communicated his ideas with Cornwallis and the other corps commanders. In his testimony to the House of Commons in 1779, he asserted that he only took the decision to go to Philadelphia 'after the most mature deliberation and frequent consultation with the Admiral, Lord Cornwallis and other officers'.[50] However, when Cornwallis was asked during the same enquiry whether Howe had consulted him about going to Philadelphia, he declined to say.[51] The indications are that Howe kept his views to himself, other than talking to his brother Richard, Admiral Lord Howe. The fateful decision to go to Philadelphia, rather than to co-operate with Burgoyne, as the ministers expected, appears to have been Howe's alone.

Cornwallis's main task during the next few months was to maintain the discipline of the troops in New Jersey, while keeping a watchful eye on the enemy. Much of the time was spent searching for forage. Six such sorties were made in January, a further six in February, and another ten in March 1777. The forces deployed had to be sufficiently strong to deter Washington from intervening from his retreat at Morristown. As one British officer ruefully noted, these exercises 'kept the army the whole winter in perpetual harassment', costing 'more men than the last campaign'.[52] Nevertheless, Johann Ewald believed that these forays had helped revive morale, following the setbacks at Trenton and Princeton.[53] Occasionally they provided an opportunity to inflict more substantial damage on the enemy. One such clash occurred in mid-April, when Washington sent a brigade out on reconnaissance. As Howe noted to Germain: 'Lord Cornwallis, ever watchful to take advantage of the enemy's situation', surprised and defeated a corps of rebels at Bound Brook, north-west of Brunswick, killing thirty and capturing another eighty with three brass field guns. Benjamin Lincoln, one of Washington's senior officers, narrowly escaped capture. The British losses were trifling.[54]

The arrival of more clement weather meant that preparations for the forthcoming campaign could begin in earnest. Howe now knew that any reinforcement would be less than half what he had requested. He therefore informed Germain on 2 April that he had abandoned his scheme of marching through New Jersey and crossing the Delaware near Trenton. Instead, he would reach Pennsylvania by sea, arguing that it offered a safer and easier route. Cornwallis's forces in East Jersey, in consequence, would be withdrawn to conserve manpower.[55] Burgoyne, he informed Carleton in Quebec, would have to look after himself.[56]

Nonetheless, before embarking for Philadelphia, Howe determined to try an alternative method of defeating the rebels. After Princeton and Trenton, he had concluded that the war could only be terminated 'by a general action' with Washington's army.[57] In pursuit of this objective he now proposed to attempt this in New Jersey before setting out for Philadelphia. At the end of May 1777, he accordingly dispatched two brigades to Brunswick, ostensibly to cover the evacuation of Cornwallis's forces, but covertly hoping to lure Washington out of his Morristown retreat and into a trap of Howe's making.[58]

The first attempt at implementing this scheme came early on 14 June when Cornwallis set off from Brunswick with the first division of Howe's army, while General Heister marched with a second division on a parallel route. The ploy proved to no purpose, other than the burning of some buildings and exchange of shots with rebel parties.[59] Nevertheless, Howe determined to persist in his design. He knew that several of Washington's brigades had moved from their hilltop positions in readiness to harass the British when they attempted to embark their forces. Two columns were again formed on 26 June, with Cornwallis commanding the right division. This time he successfully engaged one of Washington's brigades under Alexander, near the hamlet of Woodbridge, capturing three brass cannon and inflicting some 300 enemy casualties. But despite a hot pursuit to Westfield, the rebel corps successfully regained the heights at Middlebrook. Their escape persuaded Howe that it was time to resume his plan of going to Philadelphia by sea. With Cornwallis commanding the rear, the army successfully evacuated Perth Amboy on 1 July without further incident.[60]

A few days later, Clinton returned from England after a short visit, expecting to be Howe's deputy. In this he was to be disappointed, since Howe had decided that Cornwallis should accompany him to Philadelphia, having found Clinton a tiresome colleague. Clinton in consequence would remain at New York to await Burgoyne from Canada. When he queried these arrangements, Howe replied jocularly that he understood Clinton would prefer the command of 'three companies at a distance from him to serving in any capacity immediately under him'. Clinton remembered using some such words privately to Cornwallis during the New York campaign, after Howe had insulted him in the presence of a junior officer. Now it appeared that Cornwallis had not only taken his rightful position as second-in-command, but had spread gossip to Clinton's disadvantage.[61]

Had Cornwallis betrayed his colleague? It seems generally out of character. However, once back at headquarters after a hard day's campaigning, in the warm glow of a campfire and with a glass of claret in hand, he may have related the story. Although Cornwallis was a moderate drinker, indiscreet talk can easily occur in such circumstances, especially as Clinton was absent in London pursuing his own interests. But whether true or false, the result in Clinton's mind was that Cornwallis, 'my junior in rank, was placed on the high road to glory', with 'all the agreeable advantages of an active and separate command'.[62] Clinton was a sensitive man, as Philips had noted, and Cornwallis's alleged betrayal was not something he would forget.

With the command structure settled, it was time for the embarkation to proceed, though it was not until 23 July that the flotilla finally left New York. On board the 200 transports were 14,000 troops, escorted by twenty-two warships. Howe travelled with the admiral on his flagship, the *Eagle*.[63] Cornwallis too had a brother to accommodate him, since William Cornwallis had joined the squadron as captain of the fifty-gun *Isis*.[64] After clearing Sandy Hook, the flotilla headed for the Delaware River, expecting to disembark near Philadelphia. However, on arriving in Delaware Bay, Howe changed his mind, fearing that Washington's fortifications along the river might be too strong to effect a landing.[65] After a private conference with his brother, he announced that the flotilla would instead approach Philadelphia via Chesapeake Bay and Head of Elk. Neither Cornwallis nor the other senior officers were consulted.[66]

For another three weeks the expedition tacked southwards at the hottest time of the year before finally entering Chesapeake Bay. A further week was then spent sailing back towards Head of Elk. Not until 23 August was the army able to disembark, with Cornwallis leading an elite corps of Hessian Jaegers, light infantry, and Guards.[67] By now most of the cavalry's horses had been lost for want of forage, while many of the troops were also in poor health and in need of recuperation.[68]

While the men refreshed themselves and looked for horses, Cornwallis, Major-General Sir Charles Grey, and Erskine reconnoitred the road to the north. The countryside appeared deserted, contrary to expectation, since Howe had been assured that the area was full of Loyalists.[69] Nevertheless, he had no option but to proceed, sending three brigades to occupy Head of Elk. Several days were then spent foraging for supplies, while Howe issued a proclamation assuring the inhabitants that they had nothing to fear from the army's presence. Despite this, numerous complaints were received of plundering by the British and Hessian troops.[70]

Cornwallis left no record of his thoughts at this point, though he was undoubtedly glad to leave Head of Elk on 3 September, since reports suggested that Washington was preparing to dispute the army's progress at Brandywine Creek. The campaign might finally result in a decisive action. The army marched in two columns, one commanded by Cornwallis and the other under Knyphausen. Since Washington's forces occupied an advantageous position on the northern bank of the river at Chad's Ford, Howe decided on a flanking movement, similar to the one he had executed at Guana Heights. While Knyphausen threatened Washington's front, Howe and Cornwallis set off early on 11 September for a 15-mile detour, to take advantage of an unguarded ford further upstream. According to Ewald, who was reconnoitring with his Jaegers, Cornwallis came forward himself to inspect both the river crossing and the passage of a deep embankment which would be necessary before the army could reach open country.[71] There a sympathetic young Quaker admiringly noted that Cornwallis 'was on horseback, appeared tall and sat very erect. His rich scarlet clothing, loaded with gold lace' made 'a very brilliant and martial appearance'.[72]

The detour meant that Howe and Cornwallis were not ready to launch their attack until after 4 p.m. The sound of the ensuing gunfire was the signal for Knyphausen to force the passage of the Brandywine. Although Washington redeployed Sullivan's division to counter Howe and Cornwallis, his army was unable to escape the jaws of this pincer movement. The result was another British victory, though the rebel rearguard under Nathanael Greene stemmed the rout sufficiently to permit a relatively orderly withdrawal. Nevertheless, Howe was correct in asserting that his victory would have been complete but for the arrival of nightfall.[73]

Two days later Cornwallis led the light infantry and grenadiers towards Chester, where the rebel army had reformed.[74] Several days of cat-and-mouse manoeuvring then followed along the Schuylkill River, as Washington sought to preserve his army while protecting Philadelphia, where the rebel Congress was still in session. Eventually, the challenge proved too much for his exhausted army, when Howe succeeded on 22 September in crossing the Schuylkill River near Valley Forge. Three days later, the main army occupied Germantown, allowing Cornwallis with three battalions of British and Hessian grenadiers to enter Philadelphia next morning.[75] Here, they received an apparently warm welcome, though many of those applauding had been 'publicly on the other side' the day before.[76]

Despite the applause, there was no respite for Cornwallis and his men from the gruelling task of winning the war. Batteries were immediately required along the waterfront to prevent rebel vessels escaping upstream. Washington's army also remained a danger, as was demonstrated two weeks later when he attacked the British camp at Germantown, which Howe had neglected properly to entrench. The battle of 4 October was sufficiently serious for Cornwallis to race with his grenadiers towards the action, though the enemy had retreated by the time he arrived. Even so, he continued the pursuit for a further 8 miles but without result.[77]

Cornwallis's principal task hereafter was to help open the Delaware River so that British shipping could reach Philadelphia's vital port. The rebels, as Howe had earlier feared, had done everything possible to strengthen the river's defences. Among the obstacles downstream were several booms or *chevaux de frise*, consisting of large timbers bolted together with outward pointing iron spikes.[78] Washington had also reinforced two key fortifications, namely Fort Mifflin on Mud Island in the river's mid-channel, and Fort Mercer on the eastern side in New Jersey, commonly referred to as the 'Red Bank'.[79] In preparation for an assault on the latter, Cornwallis crossed the Delaware on the night of Monday, 17 October with the light infantry and grenadiers, plus the 27th and 33rd Foot Regiments.[80] The attack itself on 23 October was given to Colonel Donop and a Hessian brigade. Howe's plan was for the Hessians to storm Fort Mercer while the fleet subdued Fort Mifflin. It was now that Washington's recent dispatch of reinforcements proved opportune, for despite several attempts, the Hessians were beaten back, suffering 400 dead and wounded.[81] The British also lost a sixty-four-gun ship of the line and a frigate, though happily not William Cornwallis's *Isis*. Not until mid-November were the Howe brothers ready to make another attempt. The navy was again to force the rebels to evacuate Fort Mifflin, while Cornwallis renewed the attack on Fort Mercer. Both operations were this time successful. The channel to Philadelphia was finally cleared. On 23 November the first vessels reached the city.[82]

However, there was little celebration in the British camp, since the opening of the river was overshadowed by the news that Burgoyne's army had been forced to surrender at Saratoga. For all its efforts, Howe's army had merely exchanged Brunswick and Perth Amboy for the city of Philadelphia. Cornwallis left no thoughts on who was responsible for the disaster, but he correctly surmised that Burgoyne's defeat had 'greatly changed the face of affairs in this country'. 'God only knows how this business will end', he told his mother, indicating that he had become deeply pessimistic about the war. At least William Cornwallis had 'gained the greatest credit' during the attack on Fort Mifflin. Another consolation for the family was news of Cornwallis's own promotion to the rank of lieutenant-general.[83]

One immediate consequence of Saratoga was a request from Howe to resign his command, though he had to await permission to do so. In the meantime, he instructed Cornwallis to secure Fort Mifflin before returning to Philadelphia for winter quarters.[84] But his men were not long in residence before being ordered once more into the field. At the beginning of December Howe learnt that Washington had taken post at Whitemarsh, 14 miles north of the city, which was seemingly vulnerable to attack. Cornwallis was to command the vanguard, while Knyphausen followed with the main army. Howe's plan was to tempt Washington into more open country, which he must do to attack Cornwallis's seemingly outnumbered corps. To increase the odds, Cornwallis's force was deliberately dispersed as though on a foraging expedition. On 5 December the bait succeeded to the extent that one of Washington's corps attacked a light infantry battalion under Lieutenant-Colonel Robert Abercromby, before being driven off by Cornwallis. To Howe's disappointment, the rest of Washington's army remained sensibly out of harm's way.[85]

With the army secure inside its defensive perimeter, Howe was ready to grant Cornwallis his long-delayed leave 'to attend to his private business in Europe'.[86] Apart from being reunited with Jemima and the children, he was probably glad to escape the hedonistic atmosphere in Philadelphia, where the Howe brothers' love of luxury and licentiousness set the tone. According to Stedman the whole winter was 'spent in dissipation', even though Washington's army at Valley Forge was on the verge of starvation and might have been destroyed.[87] Nevertheless, Cornwallis remained supportive of Howe, who entrusted him with his dispatches for England. In a covering letter, Howe commented that he was sending Cornwallis so that Germain might 'have the earliest communication' from an officer 'whose knowledge of the war, in which he has had so great a share of service, will, I am confident, enable him to give Your Lordship the most ample information'.[88]

Cornwallis had hoped to travel home with his brother, but the navy had other duties for the *Isis*.[89] Before sailing he wrote to Ewald thanking him for his 'services during the two campaigns in which I have had the honour to command the Hessian Chasseurs [Jaegers]'. If their paths did not cross again, he would 'ever remember' Ewald's 'distinguished merit and ability'.[90] Cornwallis appreciated ability in a subordinate and was happy to say so. The next day, 16 December 1777, he boarded the armed ship *Brilliant* for home.

The *Brilliant* enjoyed favourable headwinds and reached Plymouth on 18 January 1778. From here Cornwallis headed for London, pausing for only a few minutes at Salisbury for a change of horses.[91] According to the *General Evening Post* he 'went straight to the Queen's Palace for an audience with the king'. This lasted three hours, after which he called 'on Lord North with whom he stayed a considerable time'.[92] A key task for Cornwallis was to explain Howe's reasons for not conducting winter operations in the southern colonies, which their governors continued to urge. In reality Howe lacked sufficient troops and believed it foolish to make fleeting appearances, which left the Loyalists at the mercy of their opponents once the army departed. In any case he doubted the governors' estimates of Loyalist support, which was likely to amount to nothing more than an 'equivocal neutrality', as had proved so far 'the case in every province'.[93] The propriety of continuing the war was seemingly not discussed.

These duties completed, Cornwallis was free to reunite with his wife and children, before travelling to Culford Park to inspect his estate and attend to other private matters. Yet his stay in Suffolk cannot have been long, since he had various engagements to fulfil in London and elsewhere. One was his responsibilities as constable of the Tower. Another was a promise to visit the families of Clinton and Grey, who were both still in America.[94] He had also been invited to Norwich to receive the freedom of the city in recognition of 'his private virtue, military character and constitutional zeal'. Cornwallis modestly replied that he was pleased if 'any part of his conduct [had] met with their approbation'.[95] A few weeks later Great Yarmouth made a similar grant.[96] Clearly any damage to his reputation on account of Trenton had been forgotten.

In London his main preoccupation was attendance in the House of Lords, where the Rockingham Whigs were calling for an enquiry into the 'state of the nation', as part of their campaign to end the American war and discredit the ministry. The measure, with Cornwallis's help, was defeated by ninety-four votes to thirty-one.[97] However, he did not attend the debates on Lord North's proposed appointment of commissioners to negotiate peace with the American rebels. He was absent too when the repeal of the Declaratory Act was discussed, abandoning Parliament's right to tax the colonies, which North considered a necessary concession for the talks to be successful. Cornwallis may have doubted the wisdom of these measures and preferred to abstain, knowing they were likely to be adopted. But he attended the Lords on 17 March 1778 when the opposition attempted to blame George III's 'evil ministers' for the difficulties facing the country, and again on 23 March when the duke of Richmond presented a motion condemning 'the present system of reducing America by force of arms'. Both were comfortably defeated, with Cornwallis supporting the majority.[98] His final appearance was on 7 April, when the Elder Pitt collapsed while making an impassioned speech about preserving the Empire. These were sentiments with which Cornwallis agreed and for which he was still ready to fight.[99]

It is unclear when Cornwallis knew that Howe's request to resign had been granted and that Clinton was to succeed him, making Cornwallis his deputy in America. But he was certainly aware of the situation by 10 March 1778, when George III signed a dormant commission making him a full general in America and commander-in-chief should Clinton be incapacitated.[100] The ministers were anxious to prevent one of the king's Hanoverian officers claiming the post through seniority.[101]

However, Germain confirmed in a letter to Clinton that Cornwallis could return to England, if a ceasefire occurred, suggesting that he wished to avoid any negotiations that might undo what he and his men had been fighting for. It was a concession that undoubtedly pleased Jemima.[102]

In an attempt to dispel any latent tension, Cornwallis wrote to Clinton before he returned, promising to do everything possible 'to contribute to your ease in a situation which I fear you will not find a bed of roses'. He could only assure him 'that health, happiness and success . . . is the sincere wish of your very faithful servant and friend'.[103] Whatever Clinton's reaction, Ewald noted that the 'entire army' was pleased at Cornwallis's impending return.[104]

One consequence of the British defeat at Saratoga was the signing of an alliance between France and the American rebels. This suggested that war with France was now inevitable, making Cornwallis's prompt return to America desirable, though not before he had received a final briefing from the ministers, at which the peace commissioners and the king himself were present.[105] This time he was accompanied to Portsmouth by Jemima, his son Brome, and his daughter Mary. One of his fellow passengers commented on the misery caused by such partings. 'Poor Lord Cornwallis is going to experience' the agonies of all contented couples: 'my heart bleeds for them'.[106] Of course Jemima, as the daughter of a professional soldier, had been taught to place duty to king and country above personal considerations. Such values, nonetheless, did not make the parting any easier for either husband, wife, or children.

Cornwallis eventually left England on 21 April 1778, after a stay of just three months, having found accommodation on the sixty-four-gun line of battleship *Trident*. Travelling with him were North's three peace commissioners, the earl of Carlisle, William Eden, and George Johnson. They were initially upset at having to share their accommodation with Cornwallis and his aides.[107] However, relations improved as the passengers walked the quarterdeck, took meals in the captain's cabin, and played whist of an evening. The passage was remarkably quick: on 3 June the *Trident* entered Delaware Bay, docking three days later at one of Philadelphia's busy wharfs.[108]

Here the passengers received the unexpected news that Clinton was about to evacuate Philadelphia and retreat to New York. Cornwallis knew that the conduct of the war would have to change if France entered the conflict. However, he was seemingly unaware of Germain's secret orders to Clinton of 21 March 1778 to make the dispatch of reinforcements to the West Indies his priority, thereby facilitating operations against the French sugar islands. If his remaining forces were insufficient to hold Philadelphia, he could withdraw to New York or even Halifax.[109] But whatever Clinton decided, the ministry's instructions meant that the war in America would necessarily become a defensive one, far different from what Cornwallis expected. Within a week he was writing to Germain that as 'no offensive measures can be undertaken against the enemy in this part of the world, I must beg' that the king be 'graciously pleased to permit me to return to England'.[110] He was not alone in his dismay. The peace commissioners were even angrier, recognising that the rebels were unlikely to negotiate with an enemy intent on running away to New York.[111]

The next day, 18 June, the army began leaving Philadelphia, encumbered by an enormous baggage train that contained everything from mobile bread ovens and forges to the officers' furniture. It would have been even larger but for Clinton's decision to send 3,000 Loyalists to New York by sea. His plan was to have one division of the army under Knyphausen at the front of the convoy while he and Cornwallis with some 6,000 British troops commanded the rear, it being the point of greatest danger. Progress was unsurprisingly slow with a baggage train 12 miles long, as men, horses, and wagons trudged along two parallel roads towards Allentown, where they arrived on 24 June. Much of Cornwallis's time was spent trying to stop the troops from plundering from the hapless inhabitants.[112]

At Allentown the road divided, one route going northwards to Perth Amboy, the other a more easterly road to Sandy Hook. Clinton opted for the latter.[113] By now Washington was approaching the British rear, having left Valley Forge on 19 June, intending to strike at the first opportune moment. On 28 June near Monmouth Court House he decided that the terrain was right for such an attempt, instructing his vanguard under Major-General Charles Lee to engage the flanks and rear of the British. Clinton, however, was prepared for such eventuality and quickly ordered the rear division to about-face the enemy. According to one officer, Clinton and Cornwallis galloped up to the front, urging the grenadiers to charge rather than waste time forming their ranks.[114] The sight of the advancing redcoats prompted Lee into a hasty retreat, resulting in several of his units becoming entangled with one another. Fortunately for the rebels, Washington was on hand to reform his army along a steep ridge. When Cornwallis attempted to break through, his men met with stubborn resistance. Especially galling was the fire from the rebel artillery.[115] It was the first time that the British had confronted the remodelled Continental Army, which Washington and Friedrich Wilhelm, baron von Steuben had been training at Valley Forge. Now it was the British who broke off the engagement, using nightfall to cover their departure. Although Clinton had taken personal direction of the battle, he acknowledged to Germain that he was 'much indebted to Lord Cornwallis for his zealous services on every occasion'.[116]

Once safely in New York, Cornwallis faced the unappetising choice of doing garrison duty, searching for forage, or raiding the coastal towns of southern New England (as Germain wanted).[117] It was to avoid such 'desultory raids' that he had requested permission to return home, so far without success. He was also frustrated by Clinton's refusal to allow his newly appointed aide-de-camp, Captain Alexander Ross, to purchase the commission of major in the 45th Foot Regiment. Ross had held his captaincy for eighteen years and was clearly a meritorious officer. He assured Clinton: 'I do not by any means wish to press you on this subject or to cause you one moment's trouble or uneasiness'.[118] It was all to no avail. Ross had to wait another two years before he secured his promotion.

With the summer almost ended, attention focused once more on the need to ensure that the army had sufficient forage for the winter. On 22 September Clinton ordered Cornwallis to cross the Hudson and forage along the Hackensack River, while Knyphausen took a similar corps to the Bronx.[119] During the operation, Cornwallis received intelligence that a rebel regiment of light dragoons under Colonel George Baylor was quartered at Old Tappan and that a body of militia was similarly lodged in nearby New Tappan. Cornwallis quickly devised a plan for an attack on the night of 27 September. One column under Grey was to attack Baylor's dragoons while Cornwallis marched against the militia. Simultaneously, part of Knyphausen's division was to be ferried across the Hudson from Manhattan to complete the encirclement of the rebels. Frustratingly for Cornwallis, deserters alerted the militia to their danger, allowing them to flee. Grey in contrast was more successful, totally surprising the dragoons, few of whom escaped.[120] The only downside was the accusation that Grey had refused quarter until most of Baylor's men were dead.[121] Nevertheless, Clinton was well pleased with the outcome, commenting to Germain about Cornwallis's 'well-projected plan'.[122]

Not long afterwards Cornwallis received news that Jemima was unwell. In a letter to William Cornwallis that September she described herself as being 'as yellow as an orange' and felt 'very ill': clearly she was suffering from jaundice or another liver complaint.[123] The uninspiring nature of the American conflict was a further inducement to request compassionate leave. Clinton, now that the army was ready to go into winter quarters, saw no objection. He too wanted to be recalled, angry at the lack of reinforcements and dispatch of so many men to the West Indies.[124] Relations were sufficiently harmonious for him to entrust Cornwallis with the delicate task of briefing the ministers on the progress of the war. In a covering letter, he commented that Germain should find Cornwallis's 'knowledge of this country and of our circumstances . . . as serviceable as I have found his experience and activity during the campaign'.[125] For Clinton, this was indeed a ringing endorsement.

Cornwallis accordingly sailed on 27 November 1778, again in the company of the peace commissioners, whose mission had ended in abject failure. Also on board was Grey, who was similarly disenchanted with the war.[126] Driven by strong westerly winds, the ship made a remarkable crossing of just sixteen days, reaching the Channel on 13 December. This time Cornwallis went straight to his house in Mansfield Street where the dowager countess was tending to Jemima. Perhaps buoyed by her husband's return, Jemima thought herself recovered, but Cornwallis did not conceal from William Cornwallis that his wife was 'in a very weak state indeed'.[127] Her condition immediately confirmed what he must do. The next day, 23 December 1778, he requested an audience with the king to resign his command.[128] George III reluctantly agreed, though not before complaining that Cornwallis should have stayed in America in case Clinton persisted in his request to resign.[129]

After this he was free to devote his time to Jemima and his two children in what was the bleakest period of his life. Writing to Clinton on 22 January, he affirmed that he was not 'indifferent' to American affairs. The reason for his delay in corresponding was simple: 'The very ill state of health in which I found Lady Cornwallis has rendered me incapable of any attention but to her.' As a result, he had 'had no conference with any minister, nor with the King except to resign' his command. Had he been asked for his sentiments, he would have advised the ministers that if they were 'tolerably certain of a superiority at sea and of feeding your army', it would 'be right to keep New York and Rhode Island'. However, Clinton's interests had not been neglected: his aide-de-camp, Major Duncan Drummond, and his cousin, Henry Fiennes Pelham-Clinton, now duke of Newcastle, had successfully lobbied Germain for reinforcements, though not sufficient in number to 'tempt you to stay'. He concluded: 'in the present agitation of my mind, I am sure you will excuse a longer letter'.[130] In spite of his every effort, Jemima died on 14 February 1779.

Until this crisis, Cornwallis had appeared to be a man in command of himself, whether directing soldiers in battle or entertaining guests at Culford Park. Now, according to Drummond, everyone noticed his 'greatest distress' and refusal to see anyone.[131] Even eight months later he confessed to William Cornwallis that Jemima's death had 'effectually destroyed all my hopes of happiness in this world'. The slightest memory of her was enough to 'harrow up' his soul.[132] Nevertheless, a sense of *noblesse oblige* compelled him to appear in public once more, in control of his emotions. This was not easy: everything in England reminded him of Jemima. Hence, like many others suffering bereavement, he looked to travel to alleviate his distress. One option was to request a new military posting. Six weeks after Jemima's death his thoughts turned to America, as he informed Clinton on 4 April 1779. Although operations there might have stalled, if Clinton had any offensive in mind against the southern colonies or French West Indies, Cornwallis would 'with great pleasure' offer his services. The main thing was to escape his current torment; 'This country has no charms for me, and I am perfectly indifferent as to what part of the world I may go.'[133] But he was not seeking personal fame and glory. As he confided to his brother William a few weeks later, 'I am now returning to America, not with views of conquest and ambition', since 'nothing brilliant can be expected in that quarter'. It was simply that 'I find this country quite insupportable'; he must have a change of scenery. He had 'many friends in the American army. I love that army and flatter myself that I am not quite indifferent to them.' Should Clinton still insist on retiring, then 'of course I cannot decline taking the command'.[134]

Rather than approaching Germain, Cornwallis decided to make his request to General Jeffery Lord Amherst, the recently appointed commander of the army in Britain and effectively the Cabinet's key military adviser. There was just one obstacle: Major-General John Vaughan had been promised the position of second-in-command to Clinton. However, Amherst believed that Vaughan, who was junior in rank to Cornwallis, would not take offense, provided he was found a suitable alternative. The king favoured the request, since the military establishment thought Cornwallis's return would be 'for the good of the service and should give great pleasure to every officer serving in America'.[135] In the event Vaughan was happy to accept a command in the West Indies. The appointment, therefore, was quickly authorised. As Germain informed Clinton on 11 April: 'You are well acquainted with His Lordship's military merit'. His return consequently must be highly pleasing, 'having so able an officer to second you in your operations and share with you the cares and fatigues of so extensive a command'. Hopefully, this would persuade Clinton to withdraw his own request to resign.[136]

One concession to Cornwallis was the king's readiness to allow him to return with his aides, Alexander Ross and Henry Brodrick.[137] Ross was only five years' Cornwallis's junior and was to become his closest friend and confidant in the years ahead. Brodrick was a distant relative, the son of an Irish peer. The arrangements made for Cornwallis's children are less clear. He appears to have appointed the rector of Culford parish, Dr Nicholas Wakeham, to act as tutor for Brome. Aristocratic families customarily left the upbringing of their male offspring to others, sending them to boarding school until they approached adulthood. Nevertheless, Cornwallis must have experienced pangs of guilt about absenting himself at such a sensitive time. It was undoubtedly with great relief that he informed William Cornwallis before his departure: 'My children are, thank God, vastly well.'[138]

Despite his anxiety to leave, one matter still required his attention: the need to testify in the House of Commons regarding Howe's conduct in America. The demand for an enquiry came from Howe himself, who saw it as a means of exculpating himself for the lack of success there. North was not keen, fearful that the proceedings might embarrass the government. No one had made any formal accusation against Howe, and no indictment had been issued. Nevertheless, North's attempt to prevent the enquiry proved unsuccessful.[139] Cornwallis might still have avoided the ordeal had the Lords refused him permission to attend, but the peers left it to his discretion. With Howe anxious to call him as a witness, Cornwallis felt obliged to appear, though, as he told Clinton, 'in my present state of spirits' it was something 'truly distressing'.[140]

As a courtesy to a member of the upper house, Cornwallis was permitted to sit inside the bar of the house while giving his testimony on 6 May 1779. One can only imagine his inner turmoil, divided by loyalty to Howe, while conscious that the war had not been well conducted. He also had to resolve the contradiction of volunteering to serve once more in a war with which he had become disenchanted. He attempted to avoid these dilemmas by adopting the line that he had not come 'to answer questions of opinion', limiting his replies 'to questions . . . of fact'. Overall, he believed Howe 'deserved greatly of his country', having served it 'with fidelity, assiduity, and with great ability'. Cornwallis's one awkward moment came when he was asked about the halt at Brunswick in early December 1776. He began by asserting that he 'could not have pursued the enemy from Brunswick without greatly distressing the troops', only to qualify his response by admitting: 'Had I seen that I could have struck a material stroke by moving forward I should certainly . . . have done it'.[141] But that was with the advantage of hindsight.

Captain John Peebles of the 42nd Black Watch Highland Regiment, on reading a printed version of the enquiry in New York, thought that the Howe brothers had much to thank Cornwallis for. He had supported them while leaving the Commons 'not much the wiser' about what had happened during four hours of testimony.[142] Grey, in contrast, had fewer inhibitions when giving his evidence, having retired from the service. He told his audience that Howe had done everything possible to carry 'on a war in the strongest country in the world', with limited resources against an almost 'unanimous people to defend it'. The implication was clear: the war was unwinnable.[143] Cornwallis's desire to leave England had perhaps overridden his duty to speak more openly.

Before departing, Cornwallis sought medical advice from Dr Robert Knox, a former army surgeon. He had for some time been suffering 'eruptions' on his skin, similar to what he had experienced in 1770 (see above, pp. 17–18). The doctor's diagnosis was eminently practical (Knox not being an advocate of medicines). The best remedy was 'as much regularity in diet and exercise as the service can admit'. Cornwallis should avoid highly seasoned and fried meat, taking instead his food 'plain dressed with a due portion of vegetables'. As for beverages, he should drink spruce beer at meals, with a moderate quantity of wine afterwards. Spruce beer, Knox believed, was a most effective remedy, since it would 'supply the defect of vegetables for the cure of scurvy', which afflicted many serving personnel. However, if his eruptions were especially troublesome, he could take an additional powder to 'keep your body open'. But everything should be taken in moderation, even if serving in the tropical West Indies.[144] Unknowingly, Knox was offering sound advice for the treatment of a congenital condition like diabetes, from which Cornwallis may have suffered.

Cornwallis took his leave of George III on Wednesday 26 May, setting off the same day for Portsmouth with Ross and Brodrick, no doubt reminded of his journey the previous year with Jemima and the children. At Portsmouth he found the twenty-gun frigate *Greyhound* awaiting him; several other army officers would be fellow passengers. The vessel cleared harbour on 4 June and tacked down the Solent before entering the Channel.[145] Hopefully the sea air and prospect of seeing old comrades would revive his spirits. Surely life in America would be kinder to him than his recent stay in England?

THREE

Implementing Britain's Southern Strategy

The passage across the Atlantic was relatively smooth, allowing Cornwallis to reach New York by 21 July 1779. Once ashore he immediately reported to Clinton for a briefing and delivery of Germain's dispatches. The meeting was seemingly cordial, since Clinton informed Germain shortly afterwards 'how happy' he was at 'the return of Lord Cornwallis to this country'. Cornwallis's 'indefatigable zeal, his knowledge of the country, his professional ability, and the high estimation in which he is held by this army must naturally give me the warmest confidence'. But another reason for Clinton's pleasure was that Cornwallis, being so eminently qualified, could relieve him from his own disagreeable situation, caused by the lack of adequate reinforcements.[1] Nevertheless, his readiness to welcome a successor was not without a hint of jealously: he confided to a correspondent that 'I am by no means the fashion here with civil or military' people, whereas 'my successor, if I am permitted to resign the command, will start fair with both'.[2]

For the moment, however, Clinton would have to remain, until the king changed his mind. The army was currently confined to Manhattan and Staten Island, which allowed Cornwallis to visit the different corps and renew old friendships. Outwardly he was his former sociable self, as Captain Peebles noted after a dinner, which his host conducted 'with ease, elegance and temperance'. Such sensibility was in contrast to headquarters, where knowledge of Clinton's desire to resign made for a febrile atmosphere.[3] Even so, the lack of military activity was distasteful and Cornwallis was ready to seize any chance of escaping such tedium. An opportunity to do so appeared to have arrived with news of a Franco-Spanish threat to Jamaica, Britain's

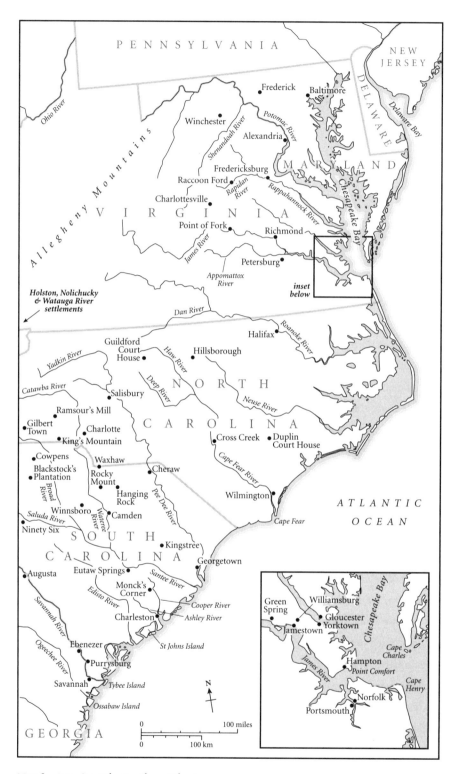

Map 3. America: The Southern Theatre.

most valuable sugar island. Although Clinton was contemplating a winter expedition to South Carolina, he felt obliged to help the Jamaican governor, and offered 4,000 of his best troops. Cornwallis quickly volunteered to take command, which Clinton seemed genuinely to appreciate. Cornwallis's orders were to secure Jamaica and then to reinforce Pensacola in west Florida. After this he could seize New Orleans, if feasible, before returning in time for Clinton's southern expedition.[4]

The flotilla left New York Harbour on 24 September with an escort of three ships of the line commanded by Commodore Drake, with whom Cornwallis travelled on the seventy-four-gun *Russell*.[5] However, Cornwallis's desire for an independent command was quickly dashed: news arrived a few days after leaving port that the rumoured attack on Jamaica was false. The danger, in reality, was closer to New York, the objective of the French fleet under Admiral Charles Hector, comte d'Estaing being the capture of Savannah. D'Estaing had twenty-four ships of the line with several thousand troops on board. Drake, of necessity, had to abort the mission.[6]

Nevertheless, Cornwallis's return to New York allowed Clinton to resume his plans for a southern offensive, which Germain had long been urging.[7] Clinton had responded in October 1778 by dispatching a force of 3,000 men to Georgia under the command of Lieutenant-Colonel Archibald Campbell.[8] To everyone's surprise, Campbell not only secured Savannah but quickly overran the inhabited parts of the province as far as Augusta. Equally encouraging was the number of Loyalists who welcomed the restoration of royal government. Nor was this the end of British success, since Campbell's successor, Major-General Augustine Prévost, then advanced on Charleston, until compelled to retreat before the superior numbers of Major-General Benjamin Lincoln.[9] These events were sufficiently positive for Clinton to consider a further attempt there, once the outcome of d'Estaing's visit to Savannah was known. Prévost eventually succeeded in holding the town, despite several attempts to storm his defences. After one final bloody repulse, d'Estaing returned to France.[10]

The way was now open for Clinton to launch his southern offensive, which he acknowledged was risky, since the attack on Savannah showed how vulnerable the British were without naval superiority. Nevertheless, he believed his plan for 'separating the southern colonies from the northern' colonies had much to recommend it, as it would allow the re-establishment of 'civil government', which could then be maintained by arming the friends to the crown. The downside was that spreading resources so thinly opened 'the risk of being beat in detail', especially if command of the sea was lost.[11] On balance it seemed a risk worth taking.

Before making a final decision, Clinton sought the advice of Admiral Marriot Arbuthnot, the senior naval officer, and Cornwallis, his most senior colleague. Both were favourably disposed, despite the risks. The main difference from his previous visit in 1776 was that Clinton proposed to land to the south of Charleston rather than force the channel past Fort Moultrie. Privately his only doubt was that he might receive permission 'to resign the command' before the operation was finished. Perhaps he ought to let Cornwallis and Arbuthnot undertake the business, but then reflected that 'should success attend us in Carolina', the same process could 'be tried in the provinces bordering on Chesapeake'. The result might be the recovery of all the colonies outside New England, making him a national hero.[12] Nevertheless, in anticipation of his possible recall, Clinton arranged for William Smith, the chief justice of New York, to hand over his office correspondence and commission as commander-in-chief to Cornwallis once his recall became official.[13] He informed Cornwallis of these arrangements and implied that he would let him take the lead in conducting the campaign.[14] The inadvisability of this arrangement was soon revealed.

Cornwallis undoubtedly welcomed the prospect of a campaign, since life in New York had not eased the pain of 'his fatal loss', as he told his brother William in October 1779. However, he would 'not dwell on this wretched subject'. He could only pray that 'success, honour and riches' attended his brother, adding quickly: 'I put honour first', which 'you will approve of'. He was comforted by reports that both Brome and Mary were in good health, adding with obvious pride: 'I must say, although I am their father, they are charming children'.[15] He confided similarly to his mother: 'the accounts of my children give me the greatest satisfaction'. As for himself, he was resigned to his fate, having 'in this world neither hopes nor fears . . . I will endeavour to do my duty to my country, and be honest, and then, with perfect resignation to his will, put my trust in God's mercy.'[16]

The flotilla eventually left New York on 26 December 1779, comprising ninety transports with 8,700 troops on board, escorted by fourteen warships. Cornwallis travelled on the forty-gun *Roebuck*, while Clinton chose the thirty-six-gun *Romulus*.[17] A series of storms unfortunately dispersed the fleet, resulting in the loss of the cavalry's horses. Nevertheless, both men reached the designated assembly point at the mouth of the Savannah River by early February 1780. Since many of the transports were still missing, Clinton decided to visit Savannah with Cornwallis, to assess progress in returning Georgia to royal government. Their inspection indicated the need for more troops. A corps of 1,500 men under Brigadier James Patterson was accordingly dispatched 'to Augusta to try the temper of the back settlements', and to divert enemy resources from the defence of Charleston.[18]

The transports were finally assembled on 11 February, allowing the flotilla to enter the North Edisto River Inlet. The troops then disembarked on Simmons Island before crossing to the larger Johns Island, 16 miles south of Charleston, leaving the fleet to blockade the approaches to Fort Moultrie and the harbour beyond. For the next fortnight the army consolidated its base, before Cornwallis, with a select corps, crossed to the adjacent James Island, giving them the first, albeit distant, view of Charleston.[19] Progress was slow because the area was intersected by rivers and waterways, and it was not until 10 March that the troops completed a bridge over the Wappoo Cut (canal), bringing them to the Ashley River directly opposite Charleston. This was an important milestone, since the navy could now use the canal to bring its flat-bottomed landing craft and armed galleys into the Ashley River, without waiting for Arbuthnot to force the entrance to Charleston Harbour.[20]

So far relations between Clinton and Cornwallis had been courteous. As Clinton informed Germain in his letter of 9 March, his operations had been advanced by 'the great assistance I have from Earl Cornwallis'.[21] True to his word he had treated Cornwallis as the de facto commander-in-chief, though he was exasperated by the widespread assumption 'that my resignation is accepted and that I am to give up the command immediately when this expedition is finished'.[22] Then on 19 March he learnt from Germain that the king was 'too well satisfied with your conduct to wish to see the command of his forces in any other hands'.[23] Clinton of necessity would have to remain for this campaign at least.[24] Inexplicably, he kept the information to himself.

Unsurprisingly, relations between the two men began to sour, as Clinton increasingly reasserted control. One early disagreement concerned the occupation of James Island which Cornwallis asserted had not been 'done as he advised'. Another discordant exchange occurred over some artillery that had been sent to Lighthouse Island 'contrary to [Cornwallis's] opinion'. More serious was the two men's disagreement about crossing the Ashley River onto Charleston Neck, the thin strip of land on which the city stood. Cornwallis wanted to delay this until Arbuthnot had manoeuvred some warships past Fort Moultrie into Charleston Harbour. Cornwallis, who was to direct this operation, feared that he would otherwise not have sufficient support for securing a bridgehead, given that the enemy had 5,000 men in the city.[25]

In the event, Cornwallis's concern proved unfounded, since the light infantry and grenadiers successfully established themselves 2 miles above the city on 29 March without interference, though Clinton privately criticised Cornwallis for delaying to deploy some cannon, which he described as very 'un-soldierly behaviour'. The main army was then successfully ferried over in the next two days, allowing the British their first view of Charleston from the landward side. Clinton noticed some rising ground on the left, known locally as Hampstead Hill, which he thought would assist the siege, even if its capture proved costly. He asked Cornwallis for his opinion and it was with seeming agreement that the trenches for the first parallel were successfully begun on the night of 1 April, 800 yards from the enemy lines.[26]

Nevertheless, the simmering question as to who was in command finally came to a head on 2 April, when Cornwallis directly confronted Clinton about the issue, forcing him to acknowledge that his request to resign had been refused.[27] At a stroke the position of the two men was reversed, to Cornwallis's embarrassment. The likelihood of his succeeding Clinton had made him the target of officers seeking to ingratiate themselves. Now everyone would know of his de facto demotion and flock to Clinton instead. More seriously, Clinton's lack of candour had destroyed Cornwallis's trust in him. According to Clinton's account of the conversation, he must now be 'responsible' for all decisions, as Cornwallis 'no longer would take the lead' and 'wished to be less consulted'. Clinton 'might consult him as a Lieutenant-General under his orders', but that was as far as he could go, though Cornwallis would continue to 'serve with zeal and responsibility in any distinct service I should employ him on'.[28]

Clinton noted that the exchange was entirely civil, though, as he admitted in a memorandum to himself, 'what all this means I do not guess'. He inferred from Cornwallis's response that 'he sees things more desperate than they were', and 'from this day's discovery he wishes not to be answerable on any opinion'.[29] Uncertain how to react, Clinton asked his aide, Major John André, for advice. To André it was clear that Cornwallis wished to avoid responsibility for the campaign, though not because he thought the siege would fail. He was not refusing to help Clinton; he merely wanted a separate role away from the main army. André concluded that Cornwallis 'may be very useful to Your Excellency upon his own terms (I mean with a kind of distinct concern)', until he could be moved to another theatre.[30]

Unfortunately, another issue now clouded the relationship between the two men. In 1777 a number of regular officers had been encouraged to form provincial units, with the inducement of enjoying a higher rank while keeping their commissions as regulars. The authorities in Britain disliked the practice, as it disadvantaged those officers who, denied such privilege, might then have to take orders from colleagues who had previously been their juniors. Germain had made more than one attempt to end the practice, and in November 1779 renewed the instruction that those holding dual commissions must choose which service they wished to retain by resigning the other.[31] This letter arrived simultaneously to the one informing Clinton that the king wanted him to remain in post.[32] When Clinton still took no steps to rectify the anomaly of dual commissions, Cornwallis, perhaps undiplomatically, reminded him of the matter. He was probably right to do so on the grounds of fairness, but it increased Clinton's belief that his subordinate had been fanning the flames of discontent in anticipation of becoming commander-in-chief himself. After Clinton demanded a public apology, Cornwallis visited his quarters on 5 April in an attempt to defuse the situation, though it did him no favours.[33] In the privacy of his journal, Clinton pondered: 'Was it friendly, was it military for a lieutenant-general next in command to me to hear, encourage, and approve discontent in the army without being sure of the fact?' He continued: ''Tis not time for altercation, but I can never be cordial with such a man.'[34] He was reminded again of the incident in 1776, when Cornwallis had betrayed a confidence about serving under Howe (see above, pp. 32–3).[35]

Neither man emerged with much credit from these exchanges. Cornwallis should have accepted the situation and bided his time, however temporarily embarrassing for him. But Clinton was also at fault in undertaking an operation when he was expecting to be recalled, giving Cornwallis the status of heir apparent only to resume full command without clarifying the situation. He would have done well to have remembered Philips's advice in December 1775 to 'throw off all reserve', and to meet Cornwallis 'in confidence and in friendship'.[36] Open and friendly Clinton had not been. Indeed, his only response was to request Arbuthnot to exclude Cornwallis from divulging his operational plans.[37]

For the next two weeks Cornwallis supervised the troops as they dug the trenches and built the redoubts necessary for a siege, telling Clinton that the more often he 'employed him the better'.[38] Completing the first parallel between the Ashley and Cooper rivers was a formidable task, since the works stretched for over a mile and were under constant fire. Nevertheless, by 8 April the batteries were ready to test Charleston's defences, providing covering fire for those digging the next parallel 450 yards from the city's perimeter. Arbuthnot too had finally manoeuvred some warships into Charleston Harbour, despite heavy fire from Fort Moultrie.[39] But the rebels still had access to the interior across the Cooper River, since Clinton did not have enough troops to occupy its eastern bank.[40] He originally anticipated that Arbuthnot would get some frigates into the Cooper River to complete the city's isolation. However, this option disappeared when the enemy sank several of their own vessels across the river's entrance.[41]

Fortunately, Clinton had recognised the need for more troops on first landing, and had recalled Patterson's corps from Georgia in response. He had also asked Knyphausen in New York for reinforcements. The arrival of the latter on 18 April now gave Clinton the resources to complete the encirclement of Charleston by occupying the east bank of the Cooper River. Initially he assigned this task to Webster with the 33rd Foot Regiment. However, several days later he remembered André's advice about giving Cornwallis a separate command, away from the main army, and accordingly placed him in charge of an enhanced force of 2,300 men.[42] Among the corps allotted to him was Lieutenant-Colonel Banastre Tarleton's British Legion, which had just routed the enemy's cavalry in a surprise attack at Monck's Corner. The Legion had been formed at New York in the summer of 1778 by Clinton to harness Loyalist support in the middle colonies, and was unusual in that it comprised both cavalry and mounted infantry, giving it exceptional mobility and flexibility. Tarleton was to prove an enterprising commander, as Cornwallis quickly came to appreciate in the course of the next eighteen months.[43]

Cornwallis's plan was for Tarleton to keep guard between the Cooper and Wando rivers, while he advanced on two enemy batteries at Lempriere's Point and Mount Pleasant, which Clinton hoped would expedite the navy's entry into the Cooper.[44] Cornwallis began his mission on the night of 23 April, promising to pay 'the greatest attention' to Clinton's orders. After crossing the Cooper, he proceeded to the battery near Mount Pleasant, which he reached on 26 April, only to find it abandoned. Here he consulted Arbuthnot about a joint attack on Lempriere's Point. However, it appeared too strong to storm, and Cornwallis did not have time for a formal siege, since his main task was to prevent the enemy escaping higher up the river. He fell back in consequence to the fork of the Wando and Cooper rivers as the best position for intercepting Lincoln's garrison.[45] No assault on Lempriere's Point proved necessary, since the rebels evacuated the post the next day.[46] Despite the successful outcome, Clinton still brooded in his journal: 'I repent that I sent him; he will play me false, I fear; at least Ross will.'[47] In Clinton's fevered imagination, Ross had metamorphosed into Cornwallis's evil counsellor.

By now, the troops before Charleston were completing the third parallel, just 200 yards from the city's main defences, allowing the batteries to open a final bombardment on 6 May. Since Lincoln still refused terms, the gunners continued breaching the rebel defences as the prelude to a general assault. As the siege was clearly coming to its climax, Cornwallis asked Clinton 'as a favour if you will let me be of the party' storming the city. He would be especially 'happy to attend my old friends the grenadiers and light infantry'.[48] Alas, he was not to be gratified in his wish. On 11 May Lincoln requested a renewal of peace talks.[49] Under the terms granted, the Continental soldiers were to become prisoners of war until exchanged for British equivalents, while the militia were given parole and allowed to return home. All other inhabitants were similarly to be considered as prisoners on parole until they had taken an oath of loyalty.[50]

Despite the previous acrimony, Clinton affected an air of unity in his official report to Germain, paying tribute alike to the officers of both services. These included Arbuthnot, whom he by now detested even more than Cornwallis because of his perceived idiosyncratic behaviour.[51] Cornwallis himself merely headed a list of general officers who had given 'animated assistance'. The star performer for Clinton was the chief engineer, Major James Moncrieff; others to receive a fulsome acknowledgement were Webster and Tarleton.[52] In a further slight to his subordinate, Clinton ensured that Cornwallis was not present at the surrender ceremonies when the Stars and Stripes were lowered as the British and Hessian grenadiers entered the city's main gate.[53] With such distrust prevailing between the two senior army officers it is surprising that the siege had progressed as well as it did. In reality, neither man had allowed their disagreements to interfere with the operational conduct of the war.

Even so, the events of the preceding weeks had proved a 'painful and distressing' experience for Cornwallis, leaving him in a position he was anxious to escape. Two days after the surrender, he wrote to Amherst suggesting that, as Clinton was to remain in America, there was less need for Cornwallis's services there. Consequently, if 'any offensive operations should be carried on in another part of the world, I request the favour of Your Lordship to lay my situation humbly before His Majesty'. The king could be assured 'of my most zealous exertions wherever he may think proper to employ me, and of my having no objection to any climate or distance'.[54]

His letter proved premature, for within days Clinton announced that he was returning to New York, having heard that a powerful French armament was about to sail for North America from Brest. Fears for that city were never far from Clinton's thoughts.[55] This raised the question of who should succeed him in the Carolinas, which were too distant to be controlled from New York. One option was to choose Cornwallis, despite Clinton's fear that he would double-cross him. The other was to take Cornwallis back to New York and to appoint instead the next most senior officer, Major-General Alexander Leslie. In the event, Cornwallis pre-empted the situation by asking directly for the position, which Clinton had difficulty refusing. As Cornwallis later explained to Leslie, he had told Clinton he was 'ready to serve wherever he thought fit to employ me, and had no objection to remain in South Carolina'. Clinton responded by saying 'something civil about the climate' but 'on my assuring him that it was not objection, he then wished me to take this command'.[56] Leslie must surely understand that Cornwallis, 'as a military man', preferred commanding in the south to playing second fiddle to Clinton in New York. Clinton in any case was anxious to put the disputes behind him. Writing to William Eden, Germain's principal secretary, he affirmed that whatever the previous difficulties between the two men, they were now 'upon good terms' and 'must be so while serving together'. The reality was that 'a certain Mr Ross, his aide-de-camp, and not His Lordship' was to blame for the dissensions.[57]

Before departing, Clinton made various arrangements for the administration of South Carolina. Most important was the establishment of a Loyalist militia. Two kinds of corps were envisaged. One, composed of male heads of households, would 'remain at home', assembling occasionally 'in their own district, under officers of their own choosing, for the maintenance of peace and good order'. The second was to consist of 'young men' without family responsibilities, who were to be 'ready to assemble when required', for service 'with the King's troops for any six months of the ensuing twelve'. Each recruit was to receive a certificate stating that they would never be enrolled involuntarily into the regulars, or have to serve outside the Carolinas and Georgia.[58] To implement these proposals Clinton appointed Major Patrick Ferguson, who currently commanded a small corps of riflemen, as inspector of militia and commandant of its first battalion.[59]

Before any such militia could be established, however, further pacification was necessary. So far only Charleston and its immediate environs had been secured. Now it was time to extend royal authority throughout the province, which Clinton proposed to effect by organising three discrete corps. The largest, under Cornwallis, was to proceed to Camden in the northern part of South Carolina, while Lieutenant-Colonel Nisbet Balfour advanced to the north-west frontier settlement of Ninety Six, and Colonel Thomas Brown retook Augusta.[60] Camden was an important crossroads and commercial centre, advantageously placed for an advance into North Carolina. Cornwallis himself acknowledged to Clinton the importance of his mission: 'without some success in the backcountry, our success at Charleston would but little promote the real interests of Great Britain'.[61]

Accordingly, on 18 May Cornwallis set off from his camp at Manigault Plantation for Camden with some 2,540 rank and file. Shortly afterwards he learnt that a detachment of Virginian Continentals under Colonel Abraham Buford was retreating towards North Carolina. Cornwallis immediately ordered Tarleton, 'that excellent officer', to overtake the enemy with his British Legion and destroy them as a fighting unit. Tarleton found his quarry at Waxhaws, 20 miles north of Camden, having covered 105 miles in just fifty-four hours.[62] He immediately offered Buford terms, similar to those granted at Charleston, only for these to be rejected. Tarleton then launched a furious attack and successfully routed the Virginians. But in the heat of the moment he failed to restrain his men from continuing the slaughter, even when their opponents were trying to surrender.[63] Tarleton believed he had conformed to the European convention that a refusal to surrender meant an enemy had forfeited the right to mercy.[64] The ill consequences of this action for Cornwallis and the British cause were to be shortly revealed.

Cornwallis himself reached Camden on 1 June. Everywhere the attitude of the inhabitants appeared favourable.[65] On 4 June he published the details of Clinton's proposed militias, adding the requirement that disaffected persons, who were excluded from the militia, were to furnish 'provisions, horses, [and] wagons in lieu of their personal services'. He also attempted to address the problem of the ringleaders, by announcing that all those who had held public office during the rebellion were to be sent on parole to one of the coastal islands until their culpability could be established. Finally, known persecutors of the king's loyal subjects were to be imprisoned, while lesser offenders were to be disarmed and sent home on parole.[66] He was unaware that Clinton was making different arrangements at Charleston.

To consolidate the restoration of the king's peace, Cornwallis then distributed his troops at a number of strategic posts. At Camden, the lynchpin of the British position, he placed Lord Rawdon with the 23rd and 33rd Foot Regiments, and several provincial corps, including Tarleton's Legion. Further east he stationed Major Archibald McArthur with the 71st Highland Regiment at Cheraw Hill to cover the frontier between Camden and the Pee Dee River. Finally, to the north-west he established a strong post at Rocky Mount on the Wateree River, leaving Ferguson's militia to maintain the communication with Ninety Six.[67]

By now Clinton was ready to return to New York. It was time to give Cornwallis his instructions about future operations and the governance of South Carolina. First, he was to command 8,500 British, Hessian, and provincial regulars, close to the number that Clinton had first brought to South Carolina, thereby allowing Clinton to take some 5,000 men back with him to reinforce New York. Cornwallis could deploy his men as he saw fit for the defence of Charleston and its dependencies. He was also responsible for the safety of East Florida and Georgia, though not for their civil administration. 'At the same time', Clinton informed him, 'it is by no means my intention to prevent your acting offensively', should an opportunity arise. But any such action had to be 'consistent with the security' of Charleston, 'which is always to be regarded as a primary object'. Finally, he was to send Clinton regular accounts and 'such intelligence as you think interesting to His Majesty's service'.[68]

In a separate letter, Clinton then outlined his views on future operations, to be carried out once the pacification of South Carolina was complete. Intelligence suggested that North Carolina was ready to fall. If that were to prove the case, Cornwallis could assist Clinton in his plans for the Chesapeake Bay. Clinton had recently received a letter from Colonel William Rankin about Loyalist strength in the bay's upper reaches.[69] However, such a project could only be contemplated once the French threat to New York had receded.[70] The exploitation of Loyalist support in the upper Chesapeake was a project that Clinton was to return to more than once, as Cornwallis discovered. Nevertheless, for the first time in his life, Cornwallis had an independent field command, something which every ambitious officer dreamt about.

Before leaving Charleston, Clinton published two proclamations, the first on 1 June as joint peace commissioner with Arbuthnot. All inhabitants now had to declare whether they supported the crown or intended to continue in their misguided defiance. Those who chose the former path would 'be received with mercy and forgiveness', though royal clemency would not be extended to persons 'who were polluted with the blood of their fellow citizens'. When a sufficient number had taken the necessary oaths, they could expect the restoration of civil government, with an assembly possessing the sole right of levying taxes.[71] However, to speed the return to normality, Clinton decided to issue a second proclamation of his own on 3 June, abolishing the inhabitants' paroles. He believed these were allowing 'a great number of inveterate rebels' to remain in the country, 'and by their underhand and secret counsel . . . prevent the return of many well-disposed persons to their allegiance'.[72] Now, those who refused to take the oaths of allegiance and support the government were to be treated as rebels, liable to the seizure of their persons and property.[73] In his eagerness to end the emergency, Clinton overlooked the danger that many former rebels would take the oaths without intending to keep them, enjoying in the meantime the same privileges and status as the genuinely loyal. It was to prove an unfortunate oversight.

Clinton sailed with Arbuthnot on 5 June without discussing the matter of paroles with Cornwallis. The consequences were soon revealed when two leading rebels attempted to surrender under the terms of the joint proclamation of 1 June, which seemingly allowed them to resume normal life without penalty. Cornwallis admitted to being ignorant of the matter, but was certain that the rebel interpretation was inadmissible. A general pardon irrespective of the crimes committed was contrary to reason and justice.[74] The situation was further complicated because Clinton had issued a large number of protections, many to the very people against whom his proclamation of 3 June was supposedly aimed. Cornwallis's first action, hence, was to annul the protections of all those 'who cannot be safely received into the militia'. Instead, such people were to be put back on parole, confining them either to their homes or to incarceration on one of the coastal islands.[75] As he shortly confided to Arbuthnot: 'nothing can in my opinion be so prejudicial to the affairs of Great Britain as a want of discrimination' in the treatment of friends and foes. There was only 'one way of inducing the violent rebels to become our friends and that is by convincing them it is their interest to be so'.[76]

Yet whatever the differences between Cornwallis and Clinton, they both failed to appreciate that many former rebels saw these changes as a breach of the surrender terms. They erroneously believed that their paroles had given them the right to remain neutral for the duration of the war.[77] The consequence of 'the unfortunate proclamation of 3 June', Rawdon reported from Camden, was that many inhabitants assumed they were free to resume hostilities.[78] The process of restoring royal authority, Charles Stedman later argued in his *History*, had been implemented far too quickly and in a manner that was not calculated to win either rebel or Loyalist hearts and minds. A 'proper discrimination' ought to have been made at the time of surrender between 'the inhabitants who were really loyal, and those who were nominally so'.[79]

Nevertheless, affairs appeared sufficiently promising for Cornwallis to leave the backcountry for Charleston, where he had various matters to settle for the governance of South Carolina. He accordingly left Camden on 20 June, giving Rawdon the task of patrolling the interior. Four days later he arrived in the capital. Here he was greeted by the principal officers to the accompaniment of church bells and the 'great glee and joy' of the inhabitants.[80] His arrival proved well timed, for everything appeared to be in confusion. Patterson, Clinton's nominee as garrison commander, was in poor health and anxious to return to New York. Cornwallis was not sorry to see him go, as he had his own candidate for this important position. Lieutenant-Colonel Nisbet Balfour was a former aide-de-camp of Howe who had impressed Cornwallis with his quiet efficiency, though like most officers he wanted an active assignment with his regiment. But as Cornwallis now explained: 'Men of merit must go where they are most wanted.' He continued: 'it is absolutely necessary for the good of the service that you should take the management of the town, which will in fact be the management of the province'.[81] Balfour was to prove a loyal, able, and dedicated appointee.

Cornwallis's first report to Clinton on 30 June was relatively optimistic. The organisation of the militias was proceeding under Ferguson and the watchful eye of the regulars. In addition, the last embers of rebellion had seemingly died with the surrender of Colonel Andrew Williamson, a key rebel leader. As to North Carolina, Cornwallis had opened discussions with 'several people of credit and undoubted fidelity'. They all confirmed 'the good disposition of a considerable body of the inhabitants', and he had in consequence 'sent emissaries to the leading persons amongst our friends, recommending in the strongest terms that they should attend to their harvest, prepare provisions, and remain quiet until the King's troops were ready to enter the province'. This would not be long, since Cornwallis was anxious to start his campaign there, believing that the possession of 'so valuable a province . . . would prove an effectual barrier for South Carolina and Georgia'.[82] His optimism about the war was reflected in a letter to William Cornwallis of 4 July, informing him that 'the province of South Carolina has totally submitted, and American affairs wear a better aspect than they have done for some time'. Most promisingly, 'the people of the backcountry . . . seem most sincerely happy at returning to their union with Great Britain and execrate the tyranny of their late rulers'.[83]

In reality, the situation was far from stable, as Cornwallis discovered within days of writing to his brother. In mid-July South Carolina experienced a renewed upsurge of violence along its northern borders, seemingly set off by the arrival in neighbouring North Carolina of 2,000 Continentals under General Johann de Kalb, and the prospect of an even larger number of Virginian militia to come. Equally destabilising were the 1,500 South Carolinians who had enlisted under the partisan leader Thomas Sumter. They, like many, believed that Clinton's annulment of their paroles had left them free to re-join the Patriot cause. Clearly the enemy intended an offensive once their preparations were finished. This made the completion of Cornwallis's own arrangements even more necessary, as he informed Clinton on 14 July: 'I am using every possible dispatch in transmitting to Camden rum, salt, regimental stores, arms and ammunition, which on account of the distance and excessive heat of the season is a work of infinite labour.' However, he was hopeful that, once in North Carolina, he would able to 'get supplies up some of the principal rivers', thus reducing his lines of communication.[84]

Meanwhile, the violence continued to spread in South Carolina, following the defeat of a provincial corps on 12 July by Sumter at Williamson's Plantation near Rocky Mount.[85] The situation was no better further east at Cheraw Hill, despite the arrival of 800 Loyalists from North Carolina with Colonel Samuel Bryan, who had attempted an abortive uprising. Rawdon decided to reinforce McArthur with the Royal Welch Fusiliers and part of the Legion, only for Cornwallis to advise against such a move.[86] 'I think your force at Camden ought to be very respectable and I have seen in this war so many bad consequences from a distant separation that I would not risk it without an absolute necessity.'[87] Cheraw Hill was accordingly abandoned and a new post established at Hanging Rock, closer to Camden. Nevertheless, Cornwallis conceded that this left the vacated area open to rebel incursions and was likely to shake the confidence of the Loyalists.[88]

This quickly proved the case, not least when it came to the new militias that Ferguson was attempting to organise, which refused to enlist 'under any kind of regularity'.[89] Simultaneously, Balfour observed that 'the enemy were exerting themselves wonderfully and successfully in stirring up the people' in more settled areas. Many of those with protections had already joined the rebels, and 'a very great number' more were ready to join them 'at the smallest reverse of our fortune'.[90] Nonetheless, one thing that Cornwallis ruled out was the employment of Indians as some were urging. Colonel Thomas Brown at Augusta was about to negotiate a treaty with the Creek and Cherokee nations. Cornwallis agreed that they should 'be kept in good humour by civil treatment and a proper distribution of such presents as are sent from England for that purpose. But I would on no account employ them in any operations of war.' Apart from committing outrages contrary to the conventions of European warfare, they were notoriously unreliable. At Pensacola the Creeks recently stayed 'only as long as they could extort presents', leaving promptly when a Spanish attack became imminent.[91]

Fortunately, Cornwallis's labours in Charleston were bearing fruit with the publication of several proclamations for the better governance of the province. The first on 18 July threatened severe punishment to anyone stealing cattle under the pretence of supplying the army. In future, only militia field officers were to exercise such powers.[92] A second proclamation on 22 July permitted the export of surplus rice to Britain to assist the merchants and planters in settling their debts, a necessary precondition for the opening of trade. A third on 25 July prohibited suspected persons from selling their property to escape 'the limits of His Majesty's government'. Those wishing to sell lands, houses, or slaves must first obtain a license to do so.[93] Finally a board of police was to be established in Charleston for the administration of justice until civil government was restored.[94] James Simpson, a former attorney-general of the province, was appointed its first superintendent.[95]

Important as these measures were, Cornwallis's attention was necessarily focused on the frontier with North Carolina where Sumter, 'an active and daring man', had recently attacked the British posts at Rocky Mount and Hanging Rock. The assaults were only repulsed with difficulty, necessitating the abandonment of both posts. As a result, 'the whole country between [the] Pee Dee and Santee has ever since been in an absolute state of rebellion'. The discontent was further increased by the news that General Horatio Gates, the victor of Saratoga, had arrived to take command of the rebel forces and was preparing to attack Rawdon. It all reinforced the need for an offensive into North Carolina, as Cornwallis informed Clinton on 6 August 1780. He conceded that some might think it an imprudent measure, but 'I am convinced it is a necessary one'. 'If we do not attack that province, we must give up both South Carolina and Georgia and retire within the walls of Charleston.' Assurances of support in North Carolina were as strong as ever, where the Highland immigrants of Cross Creek had offered to form a regiment, once the army arrived. Finally, Clinton's plan for a military presence in Virginia merited attention, given the level of rebel support from that province. 'An early diversion in my favour in Chesapeake Bay will be of the greatest and most important advantage to my operations.'[96]

Cornwallis finally left Charleston on the evening of 10 August, reaching Camden early on the morning of 14 August, 'to the great joy of Lord Rawdon and the whole army', according to the former governor, Josiah Martin.[97] Throughout his journey, he had 'suffered the most anxious suspense', conscious that 'if our affairs did not speedily take a more favourable turn, the greatest part of the inhabitants between Camden and Charleston would appear in arms against us'.[98] His fears were not assuaged on reaching his destination, where he found widespread sickness among Rawdon's troops. Only 2,043 men out of 3,026 were fit for duty.[99] In contrast, Gates had reportedly between 5,000 and 6,000 men, of whom 1,500 were Continentals, and was about to advance.[100]

Despite the odds, Cornwallis immediately resolved on a pre-emptive attack. He explained his reasons subsequently to Germain. Camden itself was defensively a weak position, while a retreat would necessitate abandoning 800 sick and numerous stores. Even more importantly it would entail the loss of the whole province except Charleston. A similar collapse was likely in Georgia, which would mean 'forfeiting all pretensions to future confidence from our friends in this part of America'.[101]

After assessing the latest intelligence, Cornwallis set off on the night of 15 August to attack Gates at dawn in his encampment at Rugeley's Mill, 12 miles to the north. With Cornwallis were the 23rd Welch Fusiliers, the 33rd Foot Regiment, the 71st Highland Regiment, and several provincial units, notably Rawdon's Volunteers of Ireland and Tarleton's British Legion. After proceeding a few miles in column formation, the vanguard suddenly clashed with the enemy marching in the opposite direction. Cornwallis immediately formed his line, though he declined to engage until daylight, when he could be sure of the situation. He placed Webster on the right with 23rd and 33rd Foot Regiments and Rawdon to the left with the provincial infantry, leaving the 71st Highland Regiment and Legion cavalry as a central reserve. His position, rather fortuitously, was protected on either flank by swamps, denying Gates an opportunity to outflank him with his superior numbers.[102]

Like Cornwallis, Gates had decided on a night march to surprise his opponent. However, contaminated provisions left many of his troops suffering from diarrhoea. His intelligence was also faulty, making him think that Rawdon's forces were still dispersed. Confident that his 4,000 men were sufficient for victory, Gates placed the Virginian militia on his left opposite Webster's brigade, while the Continentals under Kalb opposed Rawdon's division. This meant that the strongest units on both sides were opposed by their opponent's weakest corps.[103]

As dawn broke, Cornwallis observed that the Virginian militia were still forming a line. He needed no further invitation before ordering Webster to attack. The serried ranks of the regulars with their gleaming bayonets were too much for Gates's disorganised militia, who fell back in panic, exposing the flank of Kalb's

Continentals.[104] Up to this point the provincial corps under Rawdon had been struggling to contain Kalb's men: Cornwallis, seeing that Webster's corps was in control of his sector, accordingly switched his attention to the left wing of the army. As one of the Volunteers of Ireland noted: 'For half an hour the event was doubtful', until Cornwallis 'came up to them with great coolness', in the midst of especially heavy fire, calling out, 'Volunteers of Ireland, you are fine fellows! Charge the rascals – by heaven you behave nobly.' The regiment was instantaneously energised.[105] After a bitter resistance of forty-five minutes, Kalb's men also gave way, whereupon Cornwallis unleashed Tarleton's cavalry in pursuit, which continued for 20 miles to Hanging Rock. Gates lost all his artillery and stores, while 1,500 men were killed, wounded, or taken prisoner. He himself did not stop his flight until reaching Charlotte, 60 miles away.[106]

Soon there was another British success. Cornwallis knew before the battle that Sumter, acting independently of Gates, was intending to attack the communication with Charleston. Accordingly, on the day after the battle he ordered Tarleton with his Legion and some light infantry to seek out Sumter, who was then in the vicinity of Waxhaws. The surprise was total when Tarleton burst into Sumter's encampment at Fishing Creek on 18 August, killing, wounding, and capturing almost half of the 700 rebels there. As a bonus, a number of regulars and Loyalist militia were also freed.[107] However, the British success was not universal, since a corps of provincial troops under Lieutenant-Colonel Alexander Innes was defeated that same day at Musgrove's Mill by a large force of irregulars from the Georgia and the Carolina backcountry. Only news of the British successes elsewhere persuaded the rebels to retreat.[108] It was a reminder to Cornwallis that the situation was still fluid and that he would need every resource to restore the authority of the crown.

Given the distance from New York, Cornwallis decided to communicate the news of his victory directly to Germain, rather than wait for Clinton to forward his letters to London. Historians have consistently asserted that he did this secretly, undermining his superior officer. However, Cornwallis was quite open about the correspondence, since Clinton had given him permission before he returned to New York. 'As Your Excellency told me in a conversation . . . that if I fought a battle and took cannon I should write directly to England, I have on this occasion dispatched my aide-de-camp, Captain Ross, with the letters to Lord George Germain, of which

I have the honour to enclose to you the copies.'[109] Clinton subsequently acknowledged to Germain his consent to this arrangement, which continued until Cornwallis entered Virginia in April 1781.[110] Even Clinton refrained from accusing Cornwallis of this particular offense.

In writing his dispatches, Cornwallis was as usual generous in acknowledging the part played by others. 'The behaviour of His Majesty's troops was beyond all praise: it did honour to themselves and to their country.' Among the officers, Rawdon and Webster had distinguished themselves by their 'courage and ability'. Also deserving special mention were Tarleton and Lieutenant John McCleod, commanding the artillery, as well as Cornwallis's two aides, Haldane and Ross. He recommended Tarleton and Ross for promotion, describing the former to Amherst as 'one of the most promising officers I ever knew', though he quickly added that he had 'no private connection with him nor any motive for recommending him but the desire of seeing extraordinary merit rewarded'.[111] Ross finally secured his promotion to major after delivering Cornwallis's dispatches to London. Tarleton had to wait, since Amherst judged that his advancement to lieutenant-colonel was premature, he having only just become a major in the regulars.[112]

Victory on the battlefield was to prove the easier part of the campaign. Cornwallis still had to turn military success into political advantage, though he was hopeful that the 'internal commotions and insurrections in the province will now subside', as he told Germain. But he was determined not to repeat the mistake of being too lenient, as had happened on the surrender of Charleston. 'I shall give directions to inflict exemplary punishment on some of the most guilty', to deter others from breaking their oaths and treating with contempt the 'generosity of the British government'.[113] Accordingly, Colonel John Cruger at Ninety Six was to punish 'with the greatest rigour' any inhabitant who had previously 'submitted' and then participated in the latest violence. Their fate should be imprisonment and the confiscation of their property, so that compensation could be paid to those who had 'been plundered and oppressed' on account of their loyalty. In addition, 'every militiaman who had borne arms with us and had afterwards joined the enemy should be immediately hanged'.[114] Lastly, Balfour was to send 'a number of the principal and most violent inhabitants', who had conspired 'to keep up the flame of rebellion', to St Augustine in Florida to serve out their paroles.[115]

Cornwallis originally anticipated that a victory in South Carolina would be followed by an immediate advance into North Carolina. For the moment this appeared unwise, because of continued sickness among the troops. Among those affected was Tarleton, which caused Cornwallis considerable concern, since it was his abilities which met 'every deficiency'.[116] But another reason for not proceeding was the continued unrest between the Santee and Pee Dee rivers, orchestrated by a second partisan leader, Francis Marion. To nip this menace in the bud, on 28 August Cornwallis ordered Major James Wemyss to scour the countryside from King's Tree Bridge on the Black River to Cheraw Hill. Wemyss was to 'disarm in the most rigid manner all persons who cannot be depended upon', punishing 'the concealment of arms and ammunition with the demolition' of the offenders' plantations. Cornwallis also reiterated that those who had voluntarily enrolled in the Loyalist militia and then defected to the enemy were to be hanged, 'unless you should seize a very great number'. In that case Wemyss could select 'the properest objects' for mercy.[117] Lastly, Wemyss was to address the problem of rebel propaganda: 'The infamous falsehoods so industriously circulated by our enemies have done us infinite mischief.' He was consequently to 'seize the busy retailers of those pernicious lies' and have them whipped in 'some public place of their district'.[118]

One final reason for delaying entry into North Carolina was the need to assemble stores and prepare a wagon train. Responsibility for the latter lay with the quartermaster-general, Major Richard England. The department's effectiveness had long been impaired by the practice of allowing officers to supply the wagons themselves, usually at exorbitant rates. The abuse was especially widespread in New York. Cornwallis now resolved to dismiss 'everybody belonging to the quartermaster-general's department'. His plan was simple: 'By paying conductors, drivers etc. their wages instead of putting them into our own pockets', he hoped to 'procure a sufficient provision train to enable us to subsist'. The army could then return the wagons and horses which it had impressed from the loyal inhabitants of Orangeburg and Ninety Six.[119] Cornwallis later informed Balfour that the quartermaster's department was in ''wonderfully good order'. Now Major England's 'thoughts are taken up with supplying the army, and not making money'.[120] Preventing such waste and profiteering was to become a consistent feature of Cornwallis's career.

Before marching northwards into North Carolina, Cornwallis instructed Balfour about the forwarding of supplies via the Cape Fear River. He then thanked him for his support during the recent campaign: 'I cannot express how much I am obliged to you. Without your assistance I could not have carried on the King's Service.'[121] As a sign of his confidence, he gave Balfour wide powers to act in his absence, since communication with Charleston might be difficult once the army crossed the border. To prevent any questioning of his authority, Balfour could preface all orders with the phrase: 'I am particularly directed by Lord Cornwallis.'[122] Lastly, Balfour was to forward Cornwallis's dispatches to London. Since these would be in cipher, Balfour should supplement them with a covering letter of his own.[123] The settling of these preliminaries suggested that everything was ready for the next phase of the campaign.

FOUR

Taking the War to the Enemy

Cornwallis left Camden on 7 September 1780 to begin the recovery of North Carolina. However, he got no further than Waxhaws, still inside South Carolina, as he informed Clinton on 22 September. The halt had been necessary because many of the troops were still too ill with the 'fever'. He had therefore quartered himself on Waxhaws's rebellious inhabitants, where provisions and forage were plentiful. Hopefully the return of cooler weather would restore the men to health. His plan was to march on Charlotte with such troops as were fit, where he hoped to establish a base for policing the South Carolina frontier. After this he proposed marching deeper into the countryside to Salisbury, 'to see what assistance we may really expect from our friends in North Carolina'. If nothing else it would open a communication with the Highlanders of Cross Creek 'on whom my greatest dependence is placed'.[1]

To add to Cornwallis's problems, news now arrived that a rebel force from the backcountry had laid siege to Augusta, just as Brown was conferring with the Creek Indians. This was both unexpected and serious. Everything depended on Cruger at Ninety Six to organise a rescue.[2] Cornwallis was consequently relieved to learn a few days later that Cruger had raised the siege. The incident led Cornwallis to reconsider 'making use of the Indians', as he admitted to Balfour. However, they should only be engaged under tightest 'restrictions'.[3]

Cornwallis thus set off for Charlotte on 24 September in a slightly more positive mood. The march itself was uneventful until the Legion were fired upon as they entered the town on 27 September by enemy riflemen under Colonel William Davie. In the absence of Tarleton, the Legion faltered until Cornwallis reminded them that they had 'everything to lose and nothing to gain' by their timidity. The attack was promptly resumed, resulting in the killing and capture of fourteen of Davie's men for the loss of one wounded legionnaire and a dead horse.[4] Cornwallis then issued a proclamation promising that all those who surrendered their arms and took an oath to remain peaceably at home would 'be protected in their persons and properties'. They would also 'be paid a just and fair price in gold or silver' for supplies furnished to the army, since the king preferred 'to reclaim his deluded subjects . . . by justice and mercy' rather than through the 'force and terror of his arms'.[5]

Cornwallis's intention at this point was to leave Wemyss with a garrison at Charlotte while he marched to Cross Creek. But, unknown to him, events elsewhere were about to disrupt his plans. At the end of August he had allowed Ferguson to enter Tryon County with a battalion of his militia, despite concern that he would play 'some cussed trick'.[6] Cornwallis appreciated Ferguson's organisational abilities, though not his talents as a field commander, given his tendency to disregard orders. His hope now was that Ferguson could protect the army from attack by the backcountry inhabitants from the Holston, Watauga, and Nolichucky river settlements. He might also be able to demonstrate that the militia had some value.[7]

Ferguson accordingly set off in September with some 700 militia and a few New York provincials, reaching Gilbert Town on 28 September 1780. Here he issued a rambling proclamation, denouncing the rebels while promising all peaceable individuals protection for their lives and property. He particularly singled out the inhabitants of backcountry Georgia and the Nolichucky River as deserving punishment.[8] The inevitable consequence was that the backwoodsmen began assembling for an attack under the leadership of Colonel Isaac Shelby. But far from feeling threatened, Ferguson saw their gathering as a chance to strike a decisive blow, provided he was reinforced. Instead of retreating, he suggested to Cornwallis that if Tarleton's Legion was diverted towards the Little Broad River, the entire area could be cleared of rebels.[9]

Until early October Cornwallis was not concerned about Ferguson's situation. However, on hearing about Shelby, he instructed Ferguson on 5 October to fall back towards the forks of the Catawba River, where McArthur would support him with the 71st Highland Regiment.[10] Ferguson began to do so, though he was still confident of a successful outcome if supported by '400 good soldiers'. The next day his route led him past King's Mountain where he decided to 'take post', believing he would be safe even if confronted by a 'stronger enemy than that against us'. He then repeated his view that 'two or three hundred good soldiers as reserves behind our riflemen . . . would enable us to act decisively and vigorously'.[11]

In reality Ferguson was grossly exaggerating the capacity of his half-trained militia to deal with an enemy, who now composed several corps of backcountry militia and mountain volunteers. Using the trees as cover, the westerners inflicted a deadly rifle fire on Ferguson's men, despite several charges to drive them back down the hill. After an hour's bitter fighting it was all over, following one last charge by Ferguson, who died in the attempt.[12] It was now that the rebels remembered the fate of Buford's men (see above, pp. 57–8), shouting 'Tarleton's quarter!' as they killed those offering to surrender. The fate of the survivors was not much better. After being marched to Gilbert Town without food or water, several of their officers received a mock trial before being hanged.[13]

In his account to Clinton, Cornwallis exonerated Ferguson, describing the outcome at King's Mountain as an accident rather than the fault of its commander. Ferguson had entered Tryon County 'whilst the sickness of my army prevented my moving'. Because Ferguson promised to be careful, 'I thought he could do no harm and might help to keep alive the spirit of our friends in North Carolina'. Then a 'numerous and unexpected enemy came from the mountains . . . As they had good horses their movements were rapid.'[14] Therein lay the cause of the defeat. In reality Cornwallis should have kept a tighter rein on Ferguson, knowing his cavalier attitude to orders.

Although the loss of men was not serious, the political consequences meant that hopes of establishing royal authority with local support were all but extinguished. Even before Ferguson's defeat, appeals for support at Charlotte had fallen on deaf ears, perhaps unsurprisingly, since Mecklenburg County had been one of the first areas to call for independence. The army's isolation was evidenced by the repeated murder of its messengers, which helped explain the lack of intelligence about Ferguson's situation. In this disheartening setting Cornwallis decided temporarily to abandon North Carolina, not least because of the need to deal with renewed violence in South Carolina. At Winnsboro he would be closer to Ninety Six and Camden and able to deploy his forces more effectively. Not that the decision came easily, since fighting 'a defensive war' ran counter to Cornwallis's nature.[15]

It was at this point that Cornwallis developed a 'severe fever'. As his condition deteriorated, he decided to place Rawdon in command.[16] The cause of his illness was probably malaria, though Balfour ascribed it to 'the little care' that Cornwallis habitually took of his health.[17] Heavy rains made progress excruciatingly slow, especially crossing rivers. According to the Loyalist Charles Stedman, who was in charge of the commissariat and responsible for feeding the army, 'the soldiers had no tents', even though 'it rained for several days without intermission', and 'the roads were over their shoes in water and mud'. 'Sometimes the army had beef and no bread; at other times bread and no beef.' Nevertheless 'the soldiers bore' their hardships 'with great patience and without murmur . . . supported by their attachment to their commander', knowing that their officers' 'fare was not better than their own'.[18]

Although confined to bed, Cornwallis continued to monitor the situation closely. One reassuring piece of news was that Clinton had answered Cornwallis's appeal for a diversion in the Chesapeake. Two and a half thousand men had been placed under the command of Major-General Leslie with orders to prevent rebel supplies reaching the Carolinas. After destroying enemy magazines on the James River, Leslie was to establish a base at Portsmouth on the Elizabeth River, and await further orders from Cornwallis.[19] However Ferguson's defeat made Cornwallis aware of his own need for more troops. Accordingly, on 24 October he told Rawdon to suggest that Leslie embark for Cape Fear, since 'a descent there would be the surest means of joining and arming the friends of government as well as of co-operating with this army'.[20] But Leslie was only to do this if it was compatible with Clinton's orders. Cornwallis was anxious to avoid any further misunderstanding with his superior.[21]

The army's arrival at Winnsboro on 31 October coincided with Cornwallis's ability to hold a pen for the first time in three weeks.[22] This was fortunate, as he had much to do. The region between the Santee and Pee Dee rivers remained in rebellion, fanned by the activities of Marion, who constantly threatened the communication between Camden and Charleston. A post on the Black River would help counter such threats, but Cornwallis did not have sufficient troops for this.[23] He decided instead to unleash Tarleton in the hope of hunting down Marion and other partisan activists. This was no easy task without reliable intelligence, as Tarleton quickly discovered, reaffirming his belief that only a policy of widespread 'fire and sword' could remedy the situation.[24] Cornwallis for once disagreed with his subordinate, not seeing 'any advantage' in the use of such tactics, even 'from a partial destruction of the country'.[25] Undeterred, Tarleton burnt a number of rebel plantations, which he claimed on 11 November was having a good effect. Yet he also admitted that 'if there had been one individual . . . attached to our cause and exempt from fear, the total destruction of Mr Marion' would have been accomplished.[26] Before returning to Winnsboro he issued a proclamation promising to pardon rebels who returned peaceably to their homes by 25 November. Those who did not could be assured that their 'treachery, perfidy and perjury' would 'be punished with instant fire and sword'.[27]

Tarleton had no time to assess the success of his policy, since Cornwallis had to recall him in the second week of November to quell another insurrection to the north-west, where Wemyss had been defeated by Sumter at Fishdam Ford.[28] Tarleton consequently set off with his Legion together with some mounted infantry and two field guns. He found his quarry on 20 November at Blackstock's Plantation near the Tyger River. However, in his haste to engage, he failed to await his infantry or 3-pounder guns. Though he remained in possession of the battlefield, he lost fifty of his precious cavalry, and was still powerless to restore royal authority.[29] The ephemeral impact of Tarleton's operations did not go unnoticed by Balfour in Charleston. Within days of the foray against Marion, the rebel leader had not only 'appeared with 500 men before Georgetown', a supposedly safe Loyalist area, but remained in the vicinity undisturbed.[30] So much for the policy of 'fire and sword'.

It was at this point that Cornwallis was accused by Washington of having broken the Charleston surrender terms, by imprisoning 'respectable citizens' on British warships.[31] Clinton replied that those confined had been plotting to destroy the town, making their detention unavoidable. The humanity of Cornwallis was in any case well known.[32] Washington then broadened his complaint by sending copies of alleged correspondence showing additional misdeeds by the British commanders in the south.[33] One from Cornwallis seemingly authorised Balfour to seize the property of those who refused to support the crown, even though they had not committed any violence. Cornwallis quickly replied that his letter had originally been sent to Cruger at Ninety Six, not Balfour, and subsequently amended by rebel propagandists. It therefore bore no relation to the alleged complaint. As to an additional charge about indiscriminate hangings, Cornwallis could affirm that the only persons so punished were those who had first volunteered for royal service and then deserted with their weapons. British treatment of their opponents in any case was infinitely better than that given to Ferguson's 'unhappy men'. It was difficult to 'describe the shocking tortures and inhuman murders which are every day committed by the enemy, not only on those who have taken part with us, but on many who refuse to join them'.[34]

Amid these recriminations, Cornwallis continued to ponder his next move. Winnsboro was proving a healthy place for the army and was also well situated for protecting the frontier between Camden and Ninety Six. The problem was that he did not have enough troops to renew the offensive into North Carolina while sustaining the royal cause further south. This led him to make an important change to his previous plan, as he informed Clinton on 3 December 1780. The defeat at King's Mountain meant that any co-operation with Leslie via 'the Cape Fear River would be attended with many difficulties'. He had accordingly directed Leslie to sail to Charleston instead. A union of their two corps would then ensure that Cornwallis had sufficient strength to march into North Carolina, while still protecting the Loyalists of Georgia and South Carolina. But after everything that had happened, he would not make Clinton 'any sanguine promises', though he acknowledged that Leslie's force was far stronger than expected.[35]

Cornwallis's resolve to renew the offensive against North Carolina was strengthened by the news that Clinton was sending another force to the Chesapeake under the rebel commander Benedict Arnold, who had recently defected to the British cause. Arnold's mission, like Leslie's, was to stop supplies from Virginia reaching the Carolina rebels.[36] He too would be under Cornwallis's control. Cornwallis was further encouraged by the readiness of the Cherokee to respond to his appeal to attack the Watauga, Holston, and Nolichucky river settlements, which were all 'new encroachments on the Indian territories'. The backwoodsmen along the frontier had retreated in consequence and would no longer threaten the army's flank as it marched northwards.[37] The only shadow over his proposed campaign was a rumour that the French were planning to seize Wilmington on the Cape Fear River. If that happened it would be 'madness to think of penetrating to North Carolina', given the need for supplies via that route.[38] Fortunately, the report proved erroneous. Balfour should therefore occupy Wilmington without delay.[39]

Finally, Cornwallis was buoyed by his return to good health. 'I am now perfectly stout', he informed Dr John Hayes in Charleston, indicating that he had regained his normal weight after his recent debilitating illness. But his main concern was for the soldiers under Hayes's care, for whose treatment 'no reasonable expense should be spared'. He accordingly much approved of Hayes proposal to send a surgeon to Camden. Its central location made it eminently suitable for treating the sick and wounded from the frontier posts.[40]

Towards the end of December Cornwallis received news that Major-General Nathanael Greene, Gates's replacement, had split his command into two divisions, sending Brigadier Daniel Morgan with Colonel William Washington's cavalry to threaten Ninety Six, while he occupied the former British position at Cheraw Hill. Ninety Six was already threatened by backcountry rebels, which made immediate reinforcement necessary.[41] As usual Cornwallis turned to Tarleton to execute this task. Taking with him the Legion and the first battalion of the 71st Highland Regiment, Tarleton's assignment on 2 January was 'to push' Morgan 'to the utmost' back across the Broad River.[42] Tarleton responded by suggesting a modification to Cornwallis's plan. The danger was that Morgan might threaten Ninety Six a second time, once the army began its northwards march. What Tarleton proposed was a more decisive strike, forcing Morgan either to fight where he was, or once over the Broad River, having to confront Cornwallis with the rest of the army. Either way the rebel corps would be caught in a pincer movement and destroyed.[43]

Cornwallis readily approved Tarleton's scheme, affirming in his reply of 5 January: 'You have exactly done what I wished you to do, and understood my intentions perfectly.'[44] However, bad weather prevented Tarleton from crossing the Pacolet River for several days, though the delay suited Cornwallis, since it gave Leslie time to join him, thus greatly increasing his force.[45] He currently had fewer men than Tarleton, and had a large baggage train to protect. But he would correspond daily and recommended that Tarleton did the same.[46]

Rain delayed the execution of Tarleton's plan for several more days, and he was only able to cross the Pacolet on 16 January, where he received news that Morgan was retreating a few miles to the north-west.[47] A swift night march brought him up to his quarry on the morning of 17 January, drawn up on open ground at Cowpens,

6 miles from the Broad River. Although Morgan's force was slightly superior in numbers, the majority comprised militia, whereas Tarleton's corps were either British or provincial regulars. Tarleton also had two pieces of field artillery and a great superiority in cavalry. However, he failed to assess the terrain properly or to realise that Morgan had arranged his forces in three distinct lines, the first two composed of militia who were only to deliver a couple of volleys before withdrawing to the rear of the Continentals. By the time that Tarleton's infantry reached the third line, believing victory was already theirs, they were hit by a devastating fire from Morgan's regulars. The result was a loss of cohesion, which was made all the worse by the reappearance of the rebel militia on the flanks and rear of the British line. After one final charge with some cavalry, Tarleton fled the field, leaving over 600 of his men either dead, wounded, or prisoners of war.[48] But mere numbers did not tell the whole story, since the British losses included most of the light infantry, who were indispensable 'in a wooded and thinly settled country'. The new campaign could not have had a worse start.[49]

In the immediate aftermath, Tarleton blamed the defeat on an unexpected panic on the part of the British soldiers and Legion cavalry, who failed to respond to the orders of their officers. Other participants disagreed, attributing the disaster to Tarleton's haste to engage. Nevertheless, Cornwallis accepted Tarleton's version in his reports to Clinton and Germain.[50] He also refused Tarleton's request for a court-martial, telling him: 'You have forfeited no part of my esteem as an officer by the unfortunate event' of 17 January. Tarleton's efforts 'to bring the enemy to action were able and masterly, and must ever do you honour'. It was 'the total misbehaviour of the troops' that had deprived him 'of the glory which was so justly your due'.[51]

Had Cornwallis probed a little deeper, he might have questioned why this had happened to troops who 'had upon all former occasions behaved with the most distinguished gallantry'.[52] In his later *History of the Campaigns of 1780 and 1781*, Tarleton made the further excuse that Cornwallis had wasted time waiting for Leslie, which had not been part of the plan. Tarleton's corps in consequence, like Ferguson's, had been defeated by a lack of support from the main army.[53] But support from Cornwallis had been the last thing on Tarleton's mind before the battle, since he wrote only one brief note before the engagement, and at no point requested help. Moreover, no other British participants accepted his arguments. Lieutenant Roderick

Mackenzie castigated Tarleton's failure to halt before engaging the enemy, so that he could properly assess the situation with experienced officers like McArthur. A pause would also have given Cornwallis more time to arrive, while allowing Tarleton's infantry to refresh themselves after a long march. Above all there was anger that the troops had been blamed for the debacle when the real cause was Tarleton's faulty positioning, indecent haste, and lack of precaution.[54]

Although Cornwallis attempted to minimise the damage to the British cause at Cowpens, it was nevertheless a severe blow to his hopes for the campaign. 'The late affair has almost broke my heart', he confided to Rawdon in the aftermath.[55] However, he was determined to persevere with the advance into North Carolina, as he informed Clinton on first news of the disaster. Whatever consequences 'this unexpected and extraordinary event may produce', Clinton could 'be assured that nothing but the most absolute necessity shall induce me to give up the important objects of the winter's campaign'.[56] Events since Camden had demonstrated that little could be accomplished while the enemy still drew their supplies from North Carolina and Virginia. He also wanted to establish irrevocably the extent of Loyalist support in North Carolina. Maintaining the initiative was another consideration, as he subsequently told Germain. 'Defensive measures' would bring 'certain ruin to the affairs of Britain in the southern colonies', and he was resolved that Tarleton's setback would not deter him 'from prosecuting the original plan'.[57] In this he had the support of senior officers like Charles O'Hara, the commander of the Guards brigade with Leslie, who agreed that the only way to 'retrieve our affairs in this quarter, was the beating or driving Greene's army out of the Carolinas'.[58] Cornwallis, like Howe before him, had fallen into the error of thinking that the war could be won with victory in one big battle.

But first Cornwallis must deal with the immediate consequences of Cowpens. Six hundred prisoners were still in rebel hands, and he quickly recognised the need to intercept Morgan before he crossed the Catawba River. Leslie joined the army the day after Cowpens, allowing it to move towards King's Creek. However, the intelligence about Morgan was sketchy, and Cornwallis had to dispatch Tarleton to reconnoitre. First indications suggested that he was then at Gilbert Town, north-west of the British position.[59] In reality Morgan was marching eastwards to join Greene, which Cornwallis only learnt about on 21 January.[60] He immediately altered his route for Ramsour's Mill only to arrive three days too late.[61] The best that he could do for the prisoners was to propose an exchange for the rebels captured at Charleston.[62]

Hard decisions now had to be made, as Cornwallis acknowledged to Rawdon at Camden. 'My situation is most critical. I see infinite danger in proceeding but certain ruin in retreating. I am therefore determined to go on, unless some misfortune should happen to you, which God forbid.' He remained convinced that Greene's army and the resources of Virginia were the principal supports for the rebellion in the Carolinas and Georgia. Eliminate these and the flames of discontent would die down. Despite everything, morale was high and the men 'healthy and full of zeal'.[63] Nevertheless, destroying Greene's army would be no easy task, as O'Hara commented. North Carolina was 'a very mountainous country', covered by 'thick forest' and 'cut with numberless broad, deep and rapid waters'. Few fords existed over these swirling torrents, while the roads were equally challenging.[64] To help overcome these challenges, Cornwallis decided to burn his supply train, except for the wagons carrying rum, salt, spare ammunition, and hospital stores. This meant that everyone had to dispose of their personal possessions. Cornwallis quickly set an example, which was 'cheerfully followed by all the officers'.[65] Then, as O'Hara later commented, 'Without baggage, necessaries, or provisions of any sort for officer or soldier, in the most barren inhospitable unhealthy part of North America', and equipped 'with zeal and with bayonets only, it was resolved to follow Greene's army to the end of the world'.[66]

The army accordingly resumed its march on 26 January, but at a more leisurely pace, while searching for a suitable place to ford the Catawba River. To ensure success, Webster was sent as a decoy to Beattie's Ford, 4 miles upstream, leaving Cornwallis to make the real attempt downriver early on the morning of 1 February. Even so the militia on the opposite bank proved more tenacious than expected. Nevertheless, Cornwallis ordered the Guards to brave the waters, holding their fire until across the river, which was chest-deep and 500 yards wide. According to Sergeant Lamb, Cornwallis 'in his usual manner, dashed first into the river, mounted on a very fine spirited horse'. The animal was wounded but did not collapse until its rider reached the other side unscathed. Here the militia were quickly dispersed by a brisk use of the bayonet.[67]

The army then set off after Morgan, only to find that he had crossed the next obstacle, the Yadkin River, with the aid of boats, though his rearguard suffered some casualties. Everything now indicated that Greene and Morgan had been able to unite their forces. This at least simplified Cornwallis's task of bringing the rebels to a single decisive battle. He accordingly marched upstream to cross the Yadkin and several other rivers where they forked into smaller tributaries, since heavy rain made the fording of the main channels again impossible. He momentarily believed that he had trapped Greene on the south side of the Dan River where the waters were deep and currents fast, thus barring any sanctuary in Virginia. To Cornwallis's disappointment, however, Greene had been able to assemble a number of flat-bottomed boats with which to ferry his men to safety.[68] But it had been a close-run thing, as Greene acknowledged to Washington: 'The enemy's movements have been so rapid and the country under such terror that few or no militia have joined us.'[69] He commented similarly to Steuben: the British commander 'marches from twenty to thirty miles a day, and is organised to move with the same facility as a light infantry corps'. Without reinforcements 'we must be finally ruined'.[70]

In reality, Cornwallis did not have the strength to follow Greene into Virginia. He decided instead to return to the town of Hillsborough, this being a central point for raising the king's standard and appealing for volunteers. Although he had not destroyed Greene, he had driven him from North Carolina itself. He was also encouraged by Balfour's dispatch of 300 men under Major John Craig to Wilmington, raising the possibility of an alternative supply route via the Cape Fear River.[71] This was vital since the troops were 'in the greatest want of shoes and other necessaries'.[72] Unsurprisingly, many of them had taken to plundering, compelling Cornwallis to warn yet again that if 'duty to their King and country and their feelings for humanity' were not sufficient to ensure discipline, he would 'reluctantly' have to use the full severity of 'the military laws' to ensure compliance.[73]

In his proclamation of 20 February 1781 Cornwallis reaffirmed the king's wish 'to rescue his faithful and loyal subjects from the cruel tyranny under which they have groaned for several years'. All well-disposed subjects should 'repair without loss of time, with their arms and ten days provisions, to the royal standard now erected at Hillsborough'. Here, they would not only receive a 'friendly reception', but find Cornwallis ready to concur in 'effectual measures for suppressing the remains of the rebellion'. Once that had been achieved, they could work together for 'the reestablishment of good order and constitutional government'.[74]

The response was modest, producing enough recruits for one additional company in the new Royal North Carolina Regiment. More pronounced was the effect on Greene, after he heard erroneously that the people around Hillsborough were swarming to 'take the oath of allegiance to the King of Great Britain'.[75] To prevent further Loyalist recruiting, Greene re-crossed the Dan River, even though the Virginian militia had yet to join him.[76] His move proved highly effective, especially after he sent Colonel Henry Lee, with his legion of Virginian cavalry and mounted infantry, to the area between the Haw and Deep rivers, where Loyalist support was strong. On 25 February Lee encountered 200 Loyalists under Colonel John Pyle, who were travelling to Hillsborough in answer to Cornwallis's proclamation. Lee's men wore a similar green uniform to that of Tarleton's corps, causing the unsuspecting Loyalists to parade in front of his cavalry while the rebel infantry crept up behind. Few escaped the subsequent carnage.[77]

After this, few Loyalists openly supported the crown. As Stedman observed: 'if the Loyalists were before cautious and slow, they now became timid to an excess'. The ties of loyalty were further stretched by the need to requisition their cattle and other provisions to feed the troops. This was not the way to consolidate support, especially when the lack of provisions forced Cornwallis to leave Hillsborough before the expiry of his proclamation inviting Loyalists to enlist.[78] Nevertheless, Greene's reappearance at least gave Cornwallis the chance of fighting a decisive battle, which was clearly essential, as 'no material rising of our friends can be expected whilst his army is in the neighbourhood'.[79]

At length on 14 March Cornwallis received news that Greene had posted his army at Guilford Court House, 12 miles from the British camp, seemingly ready for battle. Although Cornwallis would be fighting on ground of Greene's choosing, he determined to seek out his foe immediately, setting off at dawn the following day. A five-hour march finally brought him face to face with Greene, who had placed himself on rising, partly wooded ground, with a force estimated to be between 6,000 and 10,000 men.[80] Like Morgan, he had arranged his troops in three distinct lines, the first two comprising the North Carolinian and Virginian militia and the third composed of Continentals.

It was now mid-morning. Having questioned local inhabitants about the terrain, Cornwallis made his dispositions for an attack, dividing his army of 1,600 men into three brigades with Webster on the left, O'Hara in the centre, and Leslie on the right.[81] After a short bombardment, all three brigades advanced, though in doing so their lines became increasingly extended to avoid being outflanked. This compelled Cornwallis to commit his remaining infantry, the 2nd Guards regiment, leaving Tarleton's cavalry as the only reserve. The first rebel line, consisting of North Carolinian militia, was quickly routed, allowing the army to continue its advance against the enemy's second line, composed of the Virginian militia. They similarly gave way after discharging a couple of volleys, though pursuit was obstructed by thick brushwood which allowed them to maintain sporadic fire. When Cornwallis went forward to clarify the situation, he was nearly captured according to Lamb, until the sergeant guided his horse back to the safety of the 23rd Royal Welch Fusiliers.[82]

Eventually the British emerged from the woods close to Guilford Court House. Here they found Greene's third line of defence, the Continentals, drawn up on open ground, supported by Washington's cavalry. Initially the 2nd Guards captured some rebel artillery but the effort proved too much, especially when they were charged by Washington, threatening a collapse of the whole line. It was at this point that Cornwallis allegedly ordered his artillery to fire grapeshot at the seething mass in an effort to separate the two sides.[83] Whatever the truth, the superior discipline of the British allowed them to reform for one final effort, supported by Tarleton's cavalry.[84] Greene, realising that he was about to be outflanked, ordered a retreat to a previously prepared rallying point at Troublesome Creek.[85] There was no pursuit. The British were too exhausted after a long march and two hours of bitter fighting. Common humanity also required Cornwallis to attend to the wounded of both sides, who were scattered over a wide area. The battle had cost him ninety-three dead, 413 wounded, and 26 missing, almost a third of his army.[86]

O'Hara later commented: 'I never did, and hope I never shall, experience two such days and nights, as these immediately after the battle. We remained on the very ground on which it had been fought, covered with dead and dying', expecting 'every moment to be attacked'.[87] Heavy rain added to the discomfort, lasting for almost two days; the troops had no tents. In reality, Greene lacked the resources for a counterattack. He had lost his artillery and, equally importantly, most of his militia, who had gone home with their dead and wounded. Of his Continentals, Greene had lost 57 killed, 111 wounded, and another 161 missing.[88] He too could only lick his wounds and await events.

Cornwallis left no record of his feelings, though he probably reflected that Cowpens had robbed him of the resources for a truly decisive victory at Guilford Court House. In any case, he was not given to introspection: his ingrained stoicism directed his thoughts to the needs of the moment. That included acknowledging 'the extraordinary valour displayed by the officers and soldiers'. They could be assured of his determination to do them justice in his 'representations to their sovereign'. Personally, it had been 'the greatest honour of his life to have been placed at the head of so gallant an army'.[89] Among the officers he paid special tribute to the gallantry of Leslie, O'Hara, Webster, and Tarleton. Also deserving of mention was Lieutenant McLeod of the artillery and the men of the Hessian Regiment von Bose.[90]

But whatever his public utterances, Cornwallis acknowledged privately that the battle had been a desperately close contest, telling Philips: 'we had not a regiment or corps that did not at some time give way'.[91] Indeed, the Pyrrhic nature of this victory could not be disguised, as Stedman later recalled: 'When the extent of the British loss was fully ascertained, it became too apparent that Lord Cornwallis was not in a condition either to give immediate pursuit, or to follow the blow the day after the action.'[92] The army had almost no forage for the horses, while the troops had been without bread for two days. When they did have their first meal, twenty-four hours after the conclusion of the battle, it consisted of a quarter of a pound of flour and a little lean beef.[93] The prospects for a successful military outcome appeared as distant as ever.

Unable to seek out Greene, and stranded in a hostile country with a dangerously weakened army, Cornwallis had no option but to reconsider his campaign. Above all he needed supplies. The most promising location appeared to be Cross Creek, where Loyalist support was strong. The settlement was also close to the Cape Fear River, offering the possibility of supplies from Wilmington. He was additionally encouraged by the report that a reinforcement of three regiments was coming from Ireland.[94] With such assistance he might yet be able to revive his flagging campaign.

Because the army had no wagon train, Cornwallis decided to leave his most seriously wounded at Guilford, taking only Webster and two other critically injured officers with him. Accordingly, he arranged hospital accommodation at the nearby Quaker meeting-house, together with medicines, a surgeon, and surgeon's mate. To facilitate this work of humanity, Cornwallis requested Greene to allow the two medics to stay under a flag of truce on the understanding that the wounded men would become prisoners of war on their recovery.[95] His appeal was duly acknowledged by Greene, who was 'much obliged' for the attention paid to the American wounded left on the field of battle.[96]

The army finally prepared to march to Cross Creek on 21 March. Since the troops would 'be marching through a country chiefly inhabited by friends', Cornwallis requested the officers to do everything possible 'to preserve order and save the country from ruin'.[97] The journey itself was without incident, allowing the army to reach Cross Creek by the end of March. Here Cornwallis experienced further disappointment. The Highland immigrants, on whom so much had been staked, declined like others earlier to enlist until they were certain that they and their families 'were out of reach of their nearest enemies and unmerciful tyrants'.[98] Equally disconcerting was that little forage or provision was available. Worst of all was the discovery that 'the navigation of the Cape Fear River . . . was totally impracticable'. The distance to Wilmington was 150 miles, the river scarcely 100 feet wide, with high banks, and the 'inhabitants on each side almost universally hostile'.[99] Clearly a retreat to Wilmington itself was necessary, meaning the abandonment of yet another district where Loyalist support had been strong. All that Cornwallis could do was to invite volunteers to join him on his march. At Wilmington they could be equipped for the task of restoring the country to its allegiance.[100]

The troops consequently set off once more, this time following the course of the Cape Fear River. In appearance they were far from the victorious army being portrayed by the ministers in London. As O'Hara informed his relative, the duke of Grafton, 'the excessive fatigues of the campaign' had 'totally destroyed this army . . . No zeal or courage is equal to the constant exertions we are making.'[101] The truth of his observations was reflected in the muster returns. At the start of the year Cornwallis had 3,224 rank and file fit for duty. Now he had just 1,723 men.[102] Nevertheless, O'Hara still praised him for his attempt to expel Greene from the

Carolinas, which 'must ever do the greatest honour to Lord Cornwallis's military reputation'.[103]

During the march, Cornwallis wrote to Balfour about his army's urgent need for shoes and other items of equipment. Above all, clothing was required for Tarleton's Legion, who were 'quite naked' since 'the fatal 17th of January'. The army was also 'in the utmost distress for money'. Speed in dispatching these items was essential, 'for should the enemy threaten South Carolina I must not stay here'.[104] So far Greene had followed him at a discrete distance, and was currently at the forks of the Deep River. He doubted that his opponent would march southwards, but added: 'this war has taught me to think nothing impossible'.[105]

It was at this point that Cornwallis had to report the death of 'poor Webster' on 2 April, after suffering much pain from his battlefield wounds. Webster had been a meticulous disciplinarian of the 33rd Foot Regiment and an able field officer, 'whose loss is severely felt by me and the whole army'.[106] Writing his condolences to Webster's parents, Cornwallis admitted that the task brought 'a bitter renewal of my own grief'. Of one thing the Webster family could be assured: their 'son fell nobly in the cause of his country, honoured and lamented by all his fellow soldiers'. His life had also been one of honour and virtue, 'which must secure him everlasting happiness'.[107] Yet while lamenting the dead, Cornwallis had to consider the future by requesting the appointment of Lieutenant-Colonel John Yorke in Webster's place.[108]

The army finally reached Wilmington on 7 April. Here Cornwallis found dispatches from Rawdon that his forces had twice rebuffed Sumter and also kept Marion in check. The only disappointment was Rawdon's poor health, though he hoped to leave the Camden district 'in a state of tolerable quiet', should he have to resign his command.[109] Two days later, two further promising pieces of news arrived. The first was that Arbuthnot had fought a successful naval battle off the Capes of Virginia and relieved Arnold, who had been trapped in Portsmouth by rebel forces under the command of the French volunteer, Major-General Gilbert du Motier, marquis de Lafayette. The second was that Cornwallis's old friend William Philips was on his way with a force of 2,500 men to reinforce the British presence in the Chesapeake. This suggested the possibility of conducting the war in a different way, as he informed Philips on 10 April: if an 'offensive war' was to be pursued in America, 'we must abandon New York and bring our whole force into Virginia'. A successful battle might then consolidate British control of some, if not of all the colonies. On the other hand, 'if our plan is defensive, mixed with desultory expeditions, let us quit the Carolinas (which cannot be held defensively whilst Virginia can be so easily armed against us) and stick to our salt pork in New York, sending now and then a detachment to steal tobacco etc.'.[110]

Cornwallis's contempt for coastal expeditions or 'desultory' warfare was clear, though he was naturally more circumspect in his letter to Clinton. 'I am very anxious to receive Your Excellency's commands, being as yet totally in the dark as to the intended operations of the summer.' However, it was incumbent on him to express his 'wishes that the Chesapeake may become the seat of the war', even to the extent of abandoning New York, for 'until Virginia is in a manner subdued, our hold of the Carolinas must be difficult if not precarious'. The rivers of Virginia offered great advantages to an invading army, unlike those of North Carolina, where 'a total want of interior navigation' was the norm.[111] Cornwallis may have been influenced in his views by a paper from Hector McAlester, a Loyalist, who argued that even operations in North Carolina should be launched from Petersburg on the Appomattox River or other places along the James and Roanoke rivers.[112]

Meanwhile, Cornwallis continued to assume that Greene was in the vicinity of the Deep River, waiting to intercept him if he marched back into North Carolina. Initially, this proved the case, since Greene, like Cornwallis, had found it necessary after Guilford Court House to reorganise his troops in preparation for his opponent's next move. However, like Cornwallis, he had no interest in a defensive war. Two weeks after the battle he resolved to change his strategy by marching southwards into South Carolina, as he informed Washington on 29 March. Should Cornwallis follow him, as was likely, such a move would liberate North Carolina, allowing that state to contribute more effectively to the war effort. If Cornwallis did not follow him, Greene might still wrest South Carolina from British hands, thus upsetting their southern strategy.[113] He commenced his new mission on 6 April, heading for Camden by way of Salisbury.

Cornwallis as usual lacked reliable intelligence about Greene's movements. Although he received a vague report on 15 April that the American had 'marched or detached in force' towards the south, he only learnt this for certain on 21 April.[114] He immediately recognised the danger to Rawdon. Indeed his first thought was to return at once to South Carolina via Georgetown on the Pee Dee River. But whatever route he chose would 'be attended with great difficulty', as he told Balfour on 22 April.[115] It was now that the consequences of his Pyrrhic victory at Guilford became obvious. His army was too weak to follow Greene without reinforcement, and would be too late to save South Carolina should Rawdon be defeated.

However, the danger to Rawdon was not the only thing on Cornwallis's mind. He was also preoccupied by the knowledge that Clinton had placed Philips, like Arnold, under his command.[116] This prompted him to change his plans, like Greene, except that he proposed to march northwards to Virginia, rather than follow his opponent back to South Carolina. The temptation to do so was increased because there was no sign of the three regiments from Europe. Writing to Germain the following day, 23 April, he listed his reasons for not marching southwards to help Rawdon: 'The distance from hence to Camden, the want of forage and subsistence on the greatest part of the road, and the difficulty of passing the Pee Dee when opposed by an enemy, render it utterly impossible for me to give immediate assistance.' The reality was that such a course would be attended with 'the utmost hazard to this little corps', without offering any benefit to Rawdon, since the growing spirit of rebellion would 'enable Greene to hem me in among the great rivers and by cutting off our subsistence render our arms useless'. The only other way of joining Rawdon was to remain at Wilmington and await transports to facilitate a return via Charleston, but that would 'be a work of time' and result in the loss of the cavalry's horses. Since Charleston appeared to be safe from an immediate attack, he had 'resolved to take advantage of General Greene's having left the back part of Virginia open', by marching 'immediately into that province to attempt a junction with General Philips'. If nothing else, such a move might compel Greene to abort his southern advance.[117]

In forwarding copies of his correspondence to Clinton, Cornwallis acknowledged the critical nature of what he was about to do. 'It is very disagreeable to me to decide upon measures so very important and of such consequence to the general conduct of the war without an opportunity of procuring Your Excellency's directions or approbation.' However, 'the delay and difficulty of conveying letters and the impossibility of waiting for answers' rendered it 'indispensably necessary' to do so, since no time was to be lost. He was naturally anxious about South Carolina and was not taking his decision lightly. Indeed, 'my present undertaking sits heavy on my mind'. But although he was adopting 'this hazardous enterprise hastily and with the appearance of precipitation', it was essential to do so, given the lack of reinforcement from Europe and the danger that Greene might return to prevent a junction with Philips. For without that union no offensive operations would be possible in the south.[118]

The following day Cornwallis wrote a final letter to Balfour advising him of his intentions. His plan was to march towards either Hillsborough or Halifax on the Roanoke River, in the hope of forcing Greene to quit South Carolina. If that failed, he would then proceed to a union with Philips in Virginia. The worst that could happen in South Carolina was that Rawdon might have to evacuate some interior posts. But nothing was yet fixed, and Balfour should dispatch as many transports as possible in case a junction with Philips proved impracticable, making a return to Charleston necessary. He finished by acknowledging Balfour's own difficulties, his zeal for the service, and friendship for Cornwallis: 'God bless you my dear Balfour.'[119]

The army left Wilmington on 25 April, heading for Duplin County Court House, its numbers swelled to perhaps 1,800 by the recovery of the sick and wounded.[120] Here on 30 April Cornwallis informed Balfour 'the die is cast'. Nevertheless, the situation at Camden still preoccupied him, though he could do nothing 'unless my present move should recall Greene'. If required, Balfour should evacuate Ninety Six to provide support for Rawdon. But he was still to send transports to Wilmington in case the route to Virginia proved impractical or because Philips had left the province.[121]

In an effort to obtain intelligence, Cornwallis dispatched Tarleton ahead of the army towards Halifax on the Roanoke River. For once he criticised his protégé, suggesting that Tarleton's reports paid too much attention to 'the sanguine opinions of friends and your own prejudices'. Above all he must 'attend to dates and distinguish between *is* and *has been*'.[122] Precise information was essential, since he was determined not to cross the Roanoke River 'without some certain information of Philips or of the state of things in Virginia'.[123] News then arrived on 12 May 1781 that Rawdon had defeated Greene at Hobkirk's Hill near Camden. South Carolina was seemingly safe, thus precluding the need to embark for Charleston. To mark the occasion Cornwallis ordered guns to be fired and a double allowance of rum issued to the troops.[124] The conundrum of whether to march into Virginia was finally solved on 14 May, when he heard that Philips and Arnold were at Petersburg, and that Colonel John Simcoe of the Queen's Rangers was waiting at the Roanoke River to greet him.[125] A new phase in the war was about to open that might yet bring success to British arms.

FIVE

Reckoning at Yorktown

Cornwallis reached Petersburg on the morning of 20 May 1781. It was not a happy event. He had just learnt that Philips had died from a fever. 'You will conceive my distress at the loss of my poor friend', he told Rawdon.[1] Death was never far from a soldier's lot, for either officer or private.

After a briefing from Arnold, Cornwallis perused Philips's correspondence to assess Clinton's intentions regarding the forces in Virginia. One, variously dated between 30 April and 2 May, undoubtedly caught his eye, containing the news that Clinton was sending another 1,500 men to the Chesapeake. The letter also detailed Clinton's continued difficulties with Arbuthnot, whose recall he had requested. 'If the next packet does not satisfy me in this particular, I shall probably retire and leave him to Lord Cornwallis's management.'[2] Cornwallis of course had heard such declarations before, and probably discounted this one too.

Cornwallis recognised that his first duty was to inform Clinton of his arrival in Virginia. He accordingly sat down that same day to communicate his whereabouts and request further orders. Two points needed clarification: one concerned future operations in Virginia; the other the situation in South Carolina. Regarding Virginia, Cornwallis promised to refrain from any 'precipitate movement' in case the French resumed their designs on Portsmouth, as was rumoured they were about to do. Regarding South Carolina, Cornwallis believed that Rawdon's success at Hobkirk's Hill had stabilised the position. However, if Greene persevered in his attempts to overrun the province, Rawdon could evacuate Camden and Ninety Six, 'two very bad posts', which would be no sacrifice, since the crown had lost control of the backcountry for 'some months past'. Rawdon could then occupy a more secure frontier along the Congaree and Santee rivers.[3]

Within days the intelligence about French designs on the lower Chesapeake proved erroneous, leaving Cornwallis free to execute the orders that Clinton had originally given to Philips. One was to maintain Portsmouth as a base for future military operations in Virginia. The other was the destruction of the stores and magazines along the James River destined for Greene's forces in the Carolinas.[4] However, he also knew from the correspondence now in his possession that Clinton had more recently proposed to Philips and Arnold an expedition to the upper Chesapeake or Philadelphia via the Delaware River, which Rankin continued to assert would attract widespread Loyalist support. It was for this reason that Clinton was sending another 1,500 men to Virginia.[5]

The new reinforcement opportunely reached the James River on 22 May, thus relieving Cornwallis of any further worries about garrisoning Portsmouth.[6] He could now think about future operations. However, he was not enamoured of the Rankin plan. The promises of local support bore 'too strong a resemblance to those of the emissaries from North Carolina to give me much confidence'. The reality was that 'when a storm threatens, our friends disappear'. He continued: 'one maxim appears to me to be absolutely necessary for the safe and honourable conduct of this war, which is that we should have as few posts as possible and that, wherever the king's troops are, they should be in respectable force'. For this reason, he ruled out any temporary occupation of Philadelphia. He then returned to the question of an offensive in Virginia, which he believed was the only place where such operations could prove effective. But he was not seeking to pre-empt the command, since 'few things could give me greater pleasure than being relieved' by Clinton 'from a situation of so much anxiety and responsibility'.[7]

He accordingly informed Clinton that until he heard to the contrary, he would dislodge Lafayette from Richmond, before destroying 'any magazines or stores in the neighbourhood' which had been collected for Greene's army. Cutting off Greene's source of supplies still seemed the best way of helping Rawdon and Balfour. After this Cornwallis would move to the Williamsburg peninsula, which 'is represented as healthy, and keep myself unengaged from operations . . . until I have the satisfaction of hearing from you'. He would also be better placed to find a site for 'a proper harbour and place of arms'. Portsmouth appeared unsuitable because of the number of men required to defend it. Its location was also unhealthy, and it offered no protection for ships of the line. Perhaps Yorktown would prove a more promising site.[8] Finally, Cornwallis confirmed that Arnold would return to New York on the first safe conveyance in conformity with Clinton's wishes.[9] Cornwallis probably regretted Arnold's departure, recognising him as a soldier of ability and resource.

The army began its operations on 26 May, moving northwards to Westover on the James River as the prelude to driving Lafayette from Richmond. Cornwallis's intention was to make a wide sweep around Hanover Court House to get between Lafayette and General Anthony Wayne, who was reported to be marching southwards with 700 Pennsylvanian Continentals to reinforce him. However, Lafayette immediately retreated towards Fredericksburg to keep contact with Wayne. Instead of pursuing his foe, Cornwallis decided to advance on Point of Fork, where Steuben was reputably training some newly raised recruits while guarding stores for Greene's army.[10] A brief halt was made on 3 June to celebrate George III's birthday with an extra measure of rum, though the day was marred by the rape of a young local girl by two men of the Queen's Rangers. Cornwallis immediately ordered an inquiry and, when the offense was proven, hanged the two perpetrators before the assembled troops.[11]

That evening the army pitched camp on the Elk Hill plantation of Thomas Jefferson, currently the rebel governor of Virginia. Here Cornwallis unleashed Simcoe to attack Steuben with his mounted rangers, while Tarleton visited Charlottesville, where the Virginia legislature was in session. Both detachments set off early on 4 June. Simcoe had only limited success, as Steuben succeeded in retreating over the Rivanna River, though he left behind a considerable quantity of stores which were duly destroyed.[12] Tarleton also reached his target, capturing several members of the legislature. He then sent a detachment to seize Jefferson himself at his home of Monticello, but the dragoons arrived ten minutes too late: the governor had fled. Remarkably no damage was done to the house. The same could not be said for Jefferson's Elk Hill plantation. Here the crops were destroyed, barns burnt, and the livestock eaten, leaving a trail of devastation which Jefferson believed was beyond the rules of war. Ironically for him, Cornwallis, not Tarleton, was the unacceptable face of British warfare.[13]

Having done as much damage as possible to the rebels in the interior of Virginia, Cornwallis began retreating on 13 June back towards Richmond. Here he stayed only a few days, mindful of his promise to Clinton to inspect Yorktown with a view to establishing a base there. Ewald, who was again under Cornwallis's command, was struck by the army's changed appearance. It was now accompanied by several hundred runaway slaves, who, after plundering the wardrobes of their masters and mistresses, gave the flanks and rear of the army the appearance of a wandering Tartar horde. Cornwallis had exacerbated the situation by permitting his officers and subalterns to employ the runaways as baggage handlers, cooks, and maids. The relationship was entirely symbiotic. The slaves did menial tasks in return for protection from vengeful masters and the hope of eventual freedom. But much as Cornwallis may have disliked slavery, their liberation was not a priority.[14]

Cornwallis reached Williamsburg on 25 June. Here he received his first letter from Clinton since leaving Wilmington. The commander-in-chief was not pleased, as he informed his subordinate on 29 May. Had he known that Cornwallis was considering a junction with Philips, he would 'certainly have endeavoured to have stopped' him, believing such a move was 'likely to be dangerous to our interests in the southern colonies'. However, what had been done could not now be altered. Accordingly, Cornwallis was to conduct such operations 'as you shall judge best in Virginia', until the climate made it advisable to send the troops northwards. Then, if Cornwallis had no immediate use for the 7,500 men presently in Virginia, he should send some of them back to New York. But whatever Cornwallis decided, he should remember that operations in the Chesapeake were only secure 'whilst we are superior at sea', though he had no reason to suppose that Britain's naval superiority would be challenged.[15]

Two weeks later, Clinton made a more pressing call for Cornwallis to return some troops to New York. Since the dispatch of Leslie in October 1780, Clinton had sent 7,724 men to Virginia. Even if the number of men fit for service had been reduced to 5,304, Clinton still believed they were more than sufficient for Cornwallis's current operations, given the weakness of the enemy in Virginia: Lafayette had barely 1,200 Continentals and Wayne a maximum of 1,000. In contrast, Clinton's forces at New York numbered barely 10,931, and were about to be threatened by a Franco-American force of at least 20,000 men. Clinton based his assessment on intelligence from a recent conference at Wethersfield between Washington and Jean-Baptiste Donatien de Vimeur, comte de Rochambeau, the commander of the French land forces at Rhode Island. Hence, if Cornwallis did not intend to attack Baltimore or Philadelphia, he should 'take a defensive station in any healthy situation you choose (be it at Williamsburg or Yorktown)'. Then, after 'reserving to yourself such troops as you may judge necessary for an ample defensive and desultory movements by water', he should send the rest of his command back to New York.[16] He ended by rejecting Cornwallis's call to make Virginia the centre of the British operations. Such redeployment would be pointless 'without the hearty assistance of numerous friends', who were clearly not to be found in the lower Chesapeake.

Despite the shrill tone of Clinton's letter, Cornwallis persisted in arguing his case on how the war should be conducted. 'Until Virginia was to a degree subjected', he wrote in reply on 30 June, 'we could not reduce North Carolina or have any certain hold of the backcountry of South Carolina'. As to an attack on Philadelphia, he knew from personal experience the many difficulties posed by navigating the Delaware River. It would be impossible to achieve any form of surprise while 'our appearance there, without an intention to stay, might give false hopes to many friends and occasion their ruin'. However, he acknowledged this was a matter for Clinton to decide as commander-in-chief.[17]

Cornwallis then reported the results of his recent inspection of Williamsburg and Yorktown. Williamsburg had no port, while Yorktown 'far exceeds our power consistent with your plans to make safe defensive posts there and at Gloucester, both of which would be necessary for the protection of shipping'. Perhaps Portsmouth was the best option after all. He would give a more considered view once he had been able to inspect it. But if desultory raids were to be the limit of British operations in Virginia, 'I submit it to Your Excellency's consideration whether it is worthwhile to hold a sickly defensive post in this bay, which will always be exposed to a sudden French attack' and 'makes no diversion in favour of the southern army'. He concluded by expressing his concern about Rawdon's poor health, offering to go to South Carolina himself in replacement: 'As I came to America with no other view than to endeavour to be useful to my country and, as I do not think it possible to render any service in a defensive situation here, I am willing to repair to Charleston if you approve of it.' In the meantime, he would do as Clinton desired, by assembling the necessary shipping for sending a portion of his army back to New York.[18]

The army accordingly prepared itself for a crossing of the James River before marching along its southern bank to Portsmouth. Cornwallis planned to complete the exercise on 7 July, only for word to reach him on the 6th that Wayne was approaching with his Continentals. He immediately ordered his pickets to appear as though in hasty retreat, making the enemy think that only a vulnerable British rearguard remained to oppose them. The ruse at Green Spring plantation almost succeeded when Wayne advanced to attack before confronting the massed ranks of Cornwallis's army. After a sharp exchange the enemy gave way, though nightfall prevented any pursuit. Nevertheless, the rebels had clearly lost between 200 and 300 men, a tenth of their corps, together with two cannon.[19]

After crossing to the south side of the James, the army continued its march towards Portsmouth. On reaching Suffolk, he received another letter from Clinton, dated 19 June, confirming his view that the French and Americans were still likely to attack New York, after being reinforced by the fleet of Admiral François Joseph Paul, comte de Grasse, then in the Caribbean. It was possible that Grasse might visit the Chesapeake on his way, making it incumbent on Cornwallis to have a respectable defensive post ready on the Yorktown peninsula to meet such eventuality. Providing Cornwallis had secured the 'York River before him, I think it most likely he will come to Rhode Island' to release the French squadron of Commodore Barras, which Arbuthnot was currently blockading. Their combined forces would then attack New York. Nevertheless, Clinton was more relaxed about this prospect, 'as Sir George Rodney' – who currently commanded the Royal Navy's powerful Leeward Islands fleet – 'seems to have the same suspicions of de Grasse's intentions . . . and will of course follow him thither'.[20]

Cornwallis had barely time to digest this letter before receiving another one, dated 8 July, taking issue with Cornwallis's assertion that he had insufficient troops to garrison Yorktown and Gloucester, which Arnold believed could be done with 2,000 men. Clinton also criticised Cornwallis's decision to leave the Jamestown peninsula, being 'strongly impressed with the necessity of our holding a naval station for large ships of war as well as small'. Yorktown appeared a strong contender for such purpose. He could not, therefore, 'but be concerned that Your Lordship should so suddenly lose sight of it, pass the James River, and retire with your army to the sickly post of Portsmouth', which was only ever intended as a 'station to cover our cruising frigates and other small vessels'. He continued: 'It has ever been my opinion that if a better [facility] could be found, especially for covering line-of-battle ships, it ought to have the preference.' One alternative might be Old Point Comfort overlooking Hampton Road. However, Clinton would consult Arbuthnot's successor, Rear Admiral Thomas Graves, as to what was best. But he was adamant about not relying on New York for desultory operations, as Cornwallis advised, since he was planning further operations in Virginia, whenever the season permitted. Regarding the command in South Carolina, Clinton affirmed, 'I can by no means consent to Your Lordship's going thither'. He was needed where he was.[21]

Clinton had previously mentioned the idea of a base for the navy's ships of the line, yet never as a priority.[22] One reason for his insistence now was the recall of Arbuthnot, which offered Clinton an opportunity to mend his fences with the navy. Its senior officers had long disliked New York as their principal base in North America, because sand bars at the entrance to its harbour frequently damaged the keels of the larger warships. The harbour was also prone to freeze in winter, immobilising the vessels and making them vulnerable to land attack. The latter danger was demonstrated at the end of 1779 when exceptionally cold weather froze the harbour waters to such a degree as to support 'the heaviest cannon'.[23] The possession of an ice-free anchorage had obvious appeal.

Four days later Clinton relayed the results of his conference with Graves. 'We are both clearly of the opinion that it is absolutely necessary we should hold a station in Chesapeake for ships of the line as well as frigates.' As to location, Graves thought that Hampton Road would be best. To speed construction of the new facility, Cornwallis could retain his present troop establishment. However, once the fortifications were complete, he was 'not to detain a greater proportion of the troops . . . than what may be absolutely necessary for defensive operations'. The rest were to be sent back to New York.[24]

These constant changes of direction were naturally frustrating for Cornwallis. Nevertheless, Clinton's orders were now clear: Cornwallis was to evacuate Portsmouth and find another post which could provide an anchorage for the navy's ships of the line. Cornwallis accordingly dispatched one of his engineers to 'examine and survey Point Comfort and the channels adjoining it', before visiting the site himself. But as he reported to Clinton on 26 July, both the engineer and the senior naval officer present, Captain Charles Hudson, were clear 'that a work on Point Comfort would neither command the entrance, nor secure His Majesty's ships at anchor in Hampton Road'. Cornwallis would, therefore, 'in obedience to Your Excellencies' orders, take measures with as much dispatch as possible to seize and fortify Yorktown and Gloucester', which between them provided the only harbour capable of giving 'effectual protection to line of battle ships'. The river there was sufficiently deep for the largest vessels, while the 100-foot-high banks should partially shield the ships anchored beneath. He would simultaneously evacuate Portsmouth, though he would be unable to send any troops to New York until the new works were finished. A substantial corps was needed to secure forage and prevent Lafayette and Wayne from disrupting the construction.[25]

Fortifying Yorktown and Gloucester was the antithesis of the war that Cornwallis wanted to wage. He was also dispirited by Clinton's constant carping, which indicated that he was 'determined to throw all the blame' on Cornwallis should any mishap occur. Only a determination not to 'hurt our affairs in this country', he confided to Rawdon, prevented him from asking to be relieved of his command.[26] Serving his king and country still came before personal inclination.

Early on the morning of 29 July Cornwallis boarded the frigate *Richmond* with Hudson for Yorktown. Staying behind was O'Hara with several corps to salvage stores and complete the evacuation of Portsmouth. Contrary winds prevented Cornwallis from reaching Gloucester until 1 August and Yorktown the following day. Both landings were unopposed. But Cornwallis was no more enamoured of Yorktown than on his previous visit, describing it to O'Hara as 'bad', since it provided no command of the surrounding countryside. Progress was not helped by a lack of entrenching tools and 'labouring Negroes'.[27] Fortunately Hudson was co-operative, answering with alacrity Cornwallis's request for 12-pounder cannon to defend Gloucester.[28] By 12 August, he was able to report that 'the works on the Gloucester side are in some forwardness' and hopefully 'in a situation to resist a sudden attack'.[29] Even so there was still much to do, as he informed Clinton on 16 August 1781. So far 'we have bestowed our whole labour on the Gloucester side, but I do not think the works there . . . are at present, or will be for some time to come, safe against a *coup de main*'. The works at Yorktown were even less advanced, since the plans for its defence still had to be settled with the engineer. Hence Clinton's continued hopes of receiving reinforcements from Cornwallis were unrealistic.[30]

One reason for the slow progress was the lack of African-American labourers, the heat being 'too great to admit of the soldiers doing it'.[31] However, Cornwallis's plea to O'Hara for more working runaways met with a negative. O'Hara had barely fifty himself, despite the hundreds who had taken refuge with the British. The reason was smallpox, which had infected more than 1,000 camp followers, who were 'dying by scores every day'. O'Hara was perplexed as to how to act, given his pending departure.[32] Cornwallis acknowledged the dilemma: 'It is shocking to think of the state of the Negroes, but we cannot bring a number of sick and useless ones to this place.' All he could suggest was that O'Hara left some flour for their nourishment and a local superintendent 'to prevent their perishing'.[33]

O'Hara finally evacuated Portsmouth on 18 August, bringing with him hundreds of Loyalist refugees from the surrounding area. By the time of his arrival on 22 August the engineer had completed the survey of Yorktown and drawn up plans for its fortification, which Cornwallis had 'directed to be executed'. However, a minimum of six weeks would be necessary for putting the place 'into a tolerable state of defence', without ruining the health of the troops. Since Clinton was proposing to resume operations in Virginia in early October, Cornwallis suggested that he keep his whole command in the Chesapeake to expedite the works at Yorktown. Lafayette was currently posted between the Pamunkey and Mattaponi rivers and had a considerable body of militia, but posed no immediate threat. The main problems for Cornwallis were a lack of cannon to defend the river approaches and a shortage of other artillery and engineer's stores. But he was also concerned about the heavy consumption of provisions by the refugees and African-Americans employed on the works.[34] The difficulties prompted him to suggest once more that Clinton take command. If that was not possible, Cornwallis must have 'explicit instructions . . . on all points that will admit of them'.[35] His lack of belief in the Yorktown project and distrust of his superior were deeply troubling for Cornwallis.

Before leaving Portsmouth, O'Hara jocularly asked Cornwallis whether he was 'ready to receive the French if they make you a visit?'[36] Unknown to both men this scenario was about to be realised. Clinton in New York knew from intercepted intelligence that Grasse had orders to send part of his fleet to North America before the onset of the hurricane season, his objective being the release of Barras's squadron at Rhode Island. Only then was Grasse to join Rochambeau and Washington in a combined operation, the most obvious target being New York.[37] Until early August this information was correct. However, despite the agreement at Wethersfield, Rochambeau had privately suggested to Grasse that Cornwallis's army in Virginia might make a more attractive target. Grasse's original orders also required him to join the Spanish in an attack on Jamaica, before aiding Barras. However, the timetable for that operation had become unrealistic with the approach of the hurricane season. The Spanish commanders in Havana suggested instead that Grasse take his entire fleet of twenty-nine ships of the line plus troops to North America, so that he could strike a decisive blow against the British. Jamaica could then be captured once the hurricane season ended.[38] The result was the dispatch of a much larger force than the British commanders anticipated. Rodney at Antigua remained convinced that the fourteen ships of the line allotted to his deputy, Rear Admiral Samuel Hood, would more than suffice against Grasse in North American waters, especially when added to the seven ships of the line with Graves.[39] Hood himself had no doubts about his mission, writing to Clinton on 25 August that his fleet was 'fully equal to defeat any designs of the enemy, let de Grasse bring or send what ships he may in aid of those under Barras'.[40]

The first sign for Cornwallis that all was not well came late on 31 August, when he was informed that an enemy ship of the line and two frigates had anchored at the mouth of the York River. Cornwallis immediately sent a naval officer with a suitable escort to investigate. He reported ominously that there were 'between thirty and forty sail within the Capes, mostly ships of war and some of them very large'.[41] For the moment, however, Cornwallis was not unduly perturbed, since the enemy's aim might be simply to obtain water and provisions before heading northwards, as Clinton had implied. Two days later he could take no such comfort, after learning that forty boats with troops had gone up the James River and that four ships of the line were now guarding the mouth of the York River.[42] Reports then confirmed on

4 September that the French troops had landed at nearby James Island.[43] Clearly Cornwallis's army was the objective of these manoeuvres.

Nevertheless, nothing was certain, since the following morning the French fleet had disappeared, leaving just two ships of the line and five frigates in the bay. That afternoon distant gunfire was heard, suggesting some kind of naval engagement, though without any indication of the outcome.[44] The firing on 5 September had indeed been an action between the main French and British navies. The British fleet, consisting of twenty ships of the line, had departed from New York on 31 August, still confident of defeating the French. It was only when Graves and Hood reached the Capes of Virginia and met Grasse emerging from Chesapeake Bay that the French superiority became clear. Nevertheless, the decision was taken to engage. Grasse, mindful that his task was to protect the French and American land forces, tacked with the wind while firing at his opponents' rigging. His aim was to prevent the British from engaging at close quarters, where the sturdier construction and heavier armament of their ships were most effective. By early evening much of the British fleet had been damaged, drastically reducing its manoeuvrability. After drifting several days in a vain attempt at repairs, Graves and Hood decided to return to New York for a more complete refurbishment. They were encouraged to do so by the knowledge that reinforcements were coming from England under Admiral Robert Digby. A second attempt could then be made to rescue Cornwallis.[45]

All this remained unknown to Cornwallis, still labouring on his works at Yorktown. However, by 8 September he knew that the French had landed 3,800 troops under General Henri de Saint-Simon, and that Lafayette was at nearby Williamsburg with his Continentals and a considerable militia. Most ominous was the news that 'Washington is said to be shortly expected' with Rochambeau, giving the enemy a numerical advantage of more than two to one. Cornwallis accordingly informed Clinton that as 'my works [are] not in a state of defence, I have taken a strong position out of town': this would facilitate the construction of several redoubts along the outer perimeter.[46] He made no recommendation about what Clinton should do, though the implications were clear: he must either reinforce Cornwallis or allow him to evacuate his position.

Although the completion of his works remained Cornwallis's priority, more offensive measures were also considered. According to Tarleton, two schemes were discussed for attacking Lafayette and Saint-Simon. The first was a surprise pre-dawn assault, using several small ravines to approach the enemy lines undetected. The second was the dispatch of 2,000 men upstream to attack the enemy rear while Cornwallis engaged their front. However, letters then arrived from Clinton promising relief, which led to the plans being laid aside.[47]

The first inkling for Clinton that something unusual was happening came on 27 August, when he heard that Washington and Rochambeau had crossed the Hudson River. However, he remained confident that New York remained their objective.[48] It was only when the allies reached the Delaware River that he recognised this might not be the case. Writing to Cornwallis on 2 September, he assured him that, if the enemy really were concentrating their resources in the Chesapeake, 'I shall either endeavour to reinforce the army under your command', or alternatively 'make every possible diversion in your favour'. At this point Clinton still shared the general conviction that Graves and Hood would prevail in any naval engagement.[49] Four days later, on 6 September, he wrote more precisely about his response, now that the allied intentions were certain. 'I think the best way to relieve you is to join you as soon as possible with all the force that can be spared from hence, which is about 4,000 men.' The troops were 'already embarked' and would 'proceed the instant' it was safe to do so. Finally, he informed Cornwallis about Digby's reinforcement, though he did not give the number of ships. Cornwallis in the meantime should advise Clinton how the troops from New York could 'be best employed' for his relief.[50]

Clinton's two letters reached Cornwallis on 15 September. By now the French fleet had returned to Chesapeake Bay after forcing Graves and Hood to retire. Cornwallis's next dispatch to Clinton was accordingly a sombre one. 'If I had no hopes of relief, I would rather risk an action than defend my half-finished works, but as you say Digby is hourly expected and [as you] promise every exertion to assist me, I do not think myself justified in putting the fate of the war on so desperate attempt.' Meanwhile, 'by turning out useless mouths, my provisions will last at least six weeks'. However, one thing was clear: diversionary tactics would not suffice, Cornwallis being 'of [the] opinion that you can do me no effectual service but by coming directly to this place'. The seriousness of his plight was even greater now that Barras had joined Grasse, raising their strength to thirty-six ships of the line. Clearly Digby's reinforcement would have to be substantial. As to Yorktown, Cornwallis confirmed that it was 'in no state of defence'. Hence, if Clinton could not relieve him, 'very soon, you must be prepared to hear the worst'.[51]

Tarleton later asserted that Cornwallis should at this point have implemented one of his schemes for attacking Lafayette and Saint-Simon before Washington and Rochambeau arrived. He now knew the strength of the forces ranged against him and the likelihood that the navy would have difficulty relieving him. In particular he should have realised that Clinton had promised relief in his two letters of 2 and 6 September before he knew about the disparity between the two fleets.[52] Alternatively, Cornwallis could have abandoned Yorktown by ordering a forced march to South Carolina.[53]

However, Cornwallis had good reasons for not adopting such risky ventures, as he later explained. He no longer enjoyed a superiority of numbers after the arrival of Saint-Simon, while the ground at Williamsburg by no means favoured attack. Moreover, Clinton had recently castigated him for marching into Virginia without permission and it was clearly Clinton's responsibility to decide on so dramatic a change as an evacuation of Yorktown, for which he had not given Cornwallis 'the smallest particle of discretionary power'. Cornwallis would also have had to abandon a considerable number of sick and wounded, as well as the transports and frigates. Duty for the moment required him to await events, relying on Clinton's promise of relief.[54]

Work consequently continued on the defences, though as October approached it was clear that the enemy were about to start their siege operations in earnest. To raise the troops' spirits, Cornwallis assembled his men one last time outside the lines 'to look General Washington's whole force in the face'. As he informed Clinton on 29 September: 'There was but one wish throughout the whole army, which was that the enemy would advance.'[55] This bravado was prompted by another letter from Clinton, dated 24 September, informing him that the navy and army in New York had agreed unanimously to the dispatch of 5,000 troops on board the British fleet, now reinforced by three ships of the line with Digby. The flotilla was expected to sail by 5 October.[56] Although Digby's reinforcement was much smaller than hoped, Cornwallis responded that Clinton's latest communication had given him 'the greatest satisfaction'. He would accordingly retire from his incomplete outer works, confident that 'if relief arrives in any reasonable time, Yorktown and Gloucester will be both in possession of His Majesty's troops'.[57] However, he retained two of the outer redoubts on the left of his position, to prevent the enemy from enfilading his inner defence lines.

Within twenty-four hours of writing his last letter, Clinton had to acknowledge that the relief flotilla would be further delayed, because repairs on the warships were taking longer than expected. Until then Cornwallis should inform Clinton how best to effect a junction, stationing messengers at the entrance of Chesapeake Bay to guide the ships to a suitable rendezvous.[58] The news of the fleet's problems reached Cornwallis on 2 October, by which time the allies had begun the siege.[59] On 28 September they had advanced to a new camp nearer the British lines, with the Americans on the right and the French to the left, as Cornwallis informed Clinton on 3 October. Nevertheless, the 'uncommon exertions of the troops' meant that the British earthworks were in 'a better state of defence than we had reason to hope'. But he reiterated that only a junction with Clinton on the York River could save the situation, and that would require a successful engagement with the French fleet, which was currently anchored near the York River and had increased in size to between thirty-five and thirty-six ships of the line following the arrival of Barras.[60] To conserve provisions, he was expelling any African-American who had the smallpox, though Washington quickly castigated the measure as the 'act of an ungenerous enemy'. Unlike the British army, few of Washington's troops had been inoculated against the disease.[61]

Nevertheless, the allies continued digging their first parallel, which they completed on the night of 6 October, 600 yards from the British lines. Cornwallis noted that they had done this 'with great regularity', making sorties by the garrison difficult. He had refrained from using his own artillery, because of the distance of the enemy works and the need to conserve his gunpowder. However, by 9 October the allied batteries were ready to fire with some forty cannon, mostly heavy 18- and 24-pounders, supported by sixteen mortars. In the next few hours Cornwallis's army lost seventy men, while his soft earthworks soon showed signs of serious damage. Writing to Clinton on 11 October he affirmed that with 'such works on disadvantageous ground against so powerful an attack, we cannot hope to make a very long resistance'. To escape the cascade of cannonballs and mortar shells, Cornwallis sought shelter under some overhanging rocks along the river as another thirty men were killed in just five hours. The conclusion was inescapable: 'Nothing but a direct move to York River, which includes a successful naval action, can save me.'[62] He emphasised this because Clinton's latest letter of 30 September stated that if the relief force was further delayed, 'I will immediately make an attempt upon Philadelphia by land' to draw off 'part of Washington's force', thereby giving 'you an opportunity of doing something to save your army'. Otherwise, Clinton would persist in attempting 'a direct move even to the middle of November'.[63] He still made no specific mention of abandoning Yorktown.

The siege, meanwhile, continued on its remorseless way, affecting not only the army but the navy too, as red-hot shot ignited fires aboard the frigate *Charon* and several transports. Then, on the morning of 12 October, it was discovered that the enemy had completed their second parallel just 300 yards distant, except for the area around the two British redoubts.[64] It was now that the consequences of withdrawing from the outer defence line became apparent. Cornwallis had done this to concentrate his manpower in case of a sudden attempt to force his lines. The downside was that the perimeter was scarcely 400 yards from the river, exposing the entire army and its shipping to enemy bombardment. Rochambeau certainly believed the withdrawal had helped the allies.[65]

Any hope that the remaining two redoubts might slow the enemy advance were soon extinguished. Both were quickly stormed by the allies on the night of 14 October and were promptly incorporated into their second parallel. As Cornwallis commented to Clinton the next day, 'my situation now becomes very critical'. Currently, 'we dare not show a gun to their old batteries and I expect the new ones will open tomorrow'. He continued: 'Our fresh earthworks do not resist their powerful artillery, so that we shall soon be exposed to an assault in ruined works, in a bad position, and with weakened numbers.' The safety of Yorktown was 'so precarious that I cannot recommend that the fleet and army should run great risk in endeavouring to save us'.[66] The writing was truly on the wall.

Up to this point, Cornwallis's defence had been one of restraint, as Washington had observed in puzzlement.[67] However, the capture of redoubts nine and ten not only dispirited the troops but added to the murderous fire thinning their ranks. Some counterattack became essential to slow the enemy's progress. Accordingly, in the early hours of 16 October, Cornwallis ordered Colonel Robert Abercromby with a detachment of 350 men to make a spoiling attack on two enemy batteries in the second parallel. Both attacks achieved their objective, resulting in the spiking of eleven cannon. Unfortunately, the work was necessarily done in haste and the guns were soon ready to fire as planned.[68]

This left Cornwallis the chance to make one last throw of the dice, as he subsequently informed Clinton. 'There was no part of the whole front . . . on which we could show a single gun and our shells were nearly expended.' Cornwallis in consequence 'had to choose between preparing to surrender next day or endeavouring to get off with the greatest part of the troops'. He decided to try the latter. Arrangements were quickly made to ferry the men across the river to Gloucester in a final bid to save the army.[69] The first detachments crossed without incident, but shortly afterwards 'a most violent storm of wind and rain' arose, driving the boats in different directions. After consulting his engineer and senior officers, Cornwallis concluded that further resistance was inadvisable, as he informed Clinton in his official account three days later. 'I thought it would have been wanton and inhuman to the last degree to sacrifice the lives of this small body of gallant soldiers, who had ever behaved with so much fidelity and courage.' He currently had barely 3,200 men fit for duty, with another 600 at Gloucester. The enemy in contrast had 7,500 French regular infantry and a further 8,000 Continentals and Virginian militia. They had in addition 'an immense train of heavy artillery, most amply furnished with ammunition and perfectly well manned'.[70] Only one outcome was possible.

Accordingly at 10 a.m. on 17 October the British drummers beat a parley, so that Cornwallis could deliver a brief note to Washington, proposing a cessation of hostilities for twenty-four hours and the appointment of officers to discuss terms for the surrender of Yorktown and Gloucester.[71] Washington immediately granted a cessation of hostilities, but insisted on a quick outcome, fearing that the Royal Navy might yet arrive to relieve his beleaguered foe. He therefore suggested that prior to the appointment of negotiators, Cornwallis should indicate in writing what terms he thought appropriate. Two hours would be allowed for this purpose.[72]

At half past four Cornwallis sent his reply, observing that the allotted time did not permit him to provide much detail. His main points were that the garrisons of Yorktown and Gloucester should be granted the customary honours of war and allowed to return home to Britain or Germany under an engagement not to serve against America, France, or their allies until released or exchanged. All arms and stores were to be surrendered, though the officers should keep their sidearms and all prisoners their personal effects. Finally, Cornwallis requested that the interests of those serving the British in a civil capacity should be respected.[73]

Washington quickly ruled out several of these preliminary suggestions. The British and Germans were not only to be prisoners of war but were to serve their terms in such places as the allies deemed suitable, though their treatment would be 'benevolent'. As to the honours of war, these would be the same as the British had granted Lincoln's army at Charleston (see above, p. 55). Regarding civilian employees, Washington could give no opinion until more was known about them. He allowed two hours for the acceptance or rejection of these conditions. In the case of the former, commissioners could then be appointed to finalise the details.[74]

Cornwallis had little option but to accept, since there was no sign of Clinton's relief force. Nevertheless, he was determined to secure some compensation for the surrender of Gloucester, which had not been tested by the French and American forces. His first demand was that the sloop *Bonetta* should be allowed to sail unmolested with his dispatches for New York. A second was that the property of Loyalist traders and inhabitants should be respected. Finally, he requested that 'no person may be punished or molested for having joined the British troops'. Cornwallis wanted to protect both prominent Loyalists, as well as more humble supporters of the crown, who had enlisted in his army.[75]

Washington indicated a partial readiness to accept these caveats. Talks accordingly began in the house of local plantation owner Augustine Moore, about a mile from the British lines. To execute this task, Cornwallis appointed Ross and Lieutenant-Colonel Thomas Dundas; the American and French representatives were John Laurens, son of the former president of Congress, and Louis-Marie, viscount de Noailles. After eighteen hours, terms were finally agreed. Cornwallis could send the *Bonetta* to New York without it being searched. However, Washington refused to grant the Loyalist soldiers and civilians the right to amnesty. Their fate would have to be determined by the American civil courts. As to the surrender ceremonies, the British, Loyalist, and German forces were to march out of Yorktown at two o'clock 'with shouldered arms, colours cased, and drums beating a British or German march'. Then, after grounding their weapons, they would be sent to Virginia, Maryland, or Pennsylvania to serve their term of captivity, accompanied by a proportionate number of officers. The remaining officers, including Cornwallis, were granted parole with permission to go to New York or Europe, though they were liable at any time to be recalled.[76]

The document was finally signed on the morning of 19 October amid the ruined earthworks of Yorktown, first by Cornwallis and Captain Thomas Symonds, currently the senior naval officer present, and then by Washington, Rochambeau, and Barras. Although the total number of military personnel was 5,950, only 4,017 were fit to attend the surrender ceremonies, together with 1,100 seamen.[77] When the time arrived, Cornwallis was not at the head of his men, as they marched slowly past the allied armies, with the Americans on the left and the French on the right, along the road to the field of surrender. The most likely reason for his absence was a renewed attack of malaria, triggered by the unhealthy conditions at Yorktown. Unaware of this, many local Virginians flocked to view the spectacle, not least to witness the British commander in his hour of humiliation. Instead they had to be content with seeing O'Hara at the head of their defeated foe, marching to the tune of 'The World Turned Upside Down'. Consequently, it was O'Hara who performed the task of handing over Cornwallis's sword as a token of the British defeat. He initially offered it to Rochambeau, who promptly directed him towards Washington, only to be again rebuffed and sent to the American second in command, Lincoln, as the appropriate recipient.[78] That evening, in accordance with European convention, the victors hosted a dinner for the defeated commanders. Once again Cornwallis excused 'himself on account of health', leaving O'Hara to deputise for him. This he did with remarkable sociability, as one of Washington's aides noted.[79]

Yet however ill, Cornwallis still had matters to attend to, not least that of informing Clinton of the debacle. He began his letter on 20 October by expressing his mortification at having to surrender to 'the combined forces of America and France', the first time he had formally acknowledged the United States. He then mentioned what for him was the heart of the matter: 'I never saw this post in a very favourable light, but when I found I was to be attacked in it in so unprepared a state by so powerful an army and artillery, nothing but the hopes of relief would have induced me to attempt its defence.' Had no such relief been promised, he would 'either have endeavoured to escape to New York by rapid marches from the Gloucester side . . . or I would, notwithstanding the disparity of numbers, have attacked them in the open field', where fortune might have 'favoured the gallantry of the handful of troops under my command'. However, 'being assured by Your Excellency's letters that every possible means would be tried by the navy and army to relieve us, I could not think myself at liberty to venture upon either of those desperate attempts'. He had therefore retired inside his half-finished defensive earthworks, relying on Clinton's promise of 24 September to attempt a rescue.[80]

Cornwallis then sketched the main details of the siege, before giving his customary tribute to the officers and men who had served beyond the call of duty to their king and country. During the capitulation he had done everything possible 'to alleviate the misfortune and distress of both officers and soldiers'. Fortunately, the treatment from the enemy since the surrender had been 'perfectly good and proper'. The French officers had been especially sensible of 'our situation' in generously lending money. Cornwallis himself had received such help from Rochambeau. He concluded by restating his view that a successful defence had been impossible at Yorktown, 'for the place could only be reckoned an entrenched camp'. The ground in general was 'so disadvantageous, that nothing but the necessity of fortifying it as a post to protect the navy could have induced any person to erect works upon it'.[81] The dispatch was to be delivered to Clinton by Abercromby, travelling on the *Bonetta*.

Other urgent tasks requiring his attention concerned the choice of the officers who were to accompany the soldiers into captivity. Provision also had to be made for the sick and wounded. A further perplexing issue was the treatment of Loyalist refugees. To ease his burden, Cornwallis delegated this task to James Hubbard, a Williamsburg Loyalist, whom he appointed inspector of refugees. To him fell the delicate job of deciding who should travel on the *Bonetta*.[82] But Cornwallis also wanted clarification about the parole terms, especially the clause that they could be recalled, 'whenever required by the commander-in-chief of the American army or the commissary of prisoners'. No reason had to be given for this.[83] In Cornwallis's view this left him and his officers in an arbitrary and uncertain status. Washington, however, proved unbending.[84] The only alternative was for Cornwallis to be exchanged with an officer of equal rank. This would be difficult: the British had no captive equivalent to a lieutenant-general, though Washington was prepared to accept three brigadiers in lieu.[85]

Meanwhile, Cornwallis's health had improved sufficiently by 22 October for him to accept an invitation to dine at Washington's headquarters in company with O'Hara and the other senior officers. During an exchange of toasts, Cornwallis allegedly replied by predicting that Washington would be remembered, not for Yorktown, but for saving the American cause at Trenton.[86] After this, it was the turn of Rochambeau to host a dinner at which were present 'a large company'.[87] Undoubtedly, Cornwallis found these entertainments trying, though his natural sociability and knowledge of French allowed him to sustain the necessary pleasantries. What was talked about is unknown, though one regimental doctor claimed to have overheard Washington advise his convalescing prisoner to protect his head from the cold, to which Cornwallis replied, 'it matters not Sir what becomes of this head now'.[88]

Having done all he could for the captives, Cornwallis's thoughts turned to his own departure from a place that had brought such misery for himself and his men, and such loss to his king and country. But he still hoped to do so as a free man through an exchange, rather than as a prisoner on parole. One possibility remained. Henry Laurens, the former president of Congress, had been captured in August 1780 by a Royal Navy frigate en route to Europe, where he was to represent the United States in any subsequent peace negotiations. Laurens was duly confined in the Tower of London, creating the paradoxical situation whereby Cornwallis, the constable of the Tower, was himself a prisoner of Laurens's son John, then acting as Washington's commissary of prisoners.[89] Cornwallis had raised the idea of an exchange through Ross during the capitulation talks at Moore's house. Laurens believed that Congress would 'consent to the exchange', and agreed to expedite matters. But nothing had been decided by 4 November, when Cornwallis finally departed on the armed ship *Cochrane* for New York.[90]

Cornwallis eventually reached New York on 19 November 1781 after a tiresome passage, as he informed Rochambeau, when thanking him for his 'acts of kindness'.[91] However, his first obligation was to visit Clinton at his headquarters for a debriefing about the siege. The interview, which lasted about an hour, was naturally difficult for both men.[92] In the immediate aftermath, Clinton firmly attributed the disaster to the navy's lack of ships and the ministry's false promises about reinforcements. He told Germain: 'Your Lordship's former letters . . . encouraged me to expect that our fleet here would not only have been augmented at least in proportion to that of the enemy, but that our naval reinforcement would have arrived on this coast even before theirs'. Hence, 'my surprise was great when I heard de Grasse had brought with him 28 sail of the line and that Sir Samuel Hood had only 14 . . . To this inferiority, then, I may with confidence assert, and to this alone, is our present misfortune to be imputed.'[93]

Face to face, the two men skated round the issue of responsibility, preferring once more to blame the navy, though Cornwallis admitted he should have made more sorties during the siege.[94] Clinton then consented, surprisingly, to the publication of Cornwallis's letter, which he had received with the arrival of the *Bonetta* on 31 October.[95] But the truce did not last, since his staff belatedly pointed out that Cornwallis's account contained passages which implied that Clinton was partly to blame for the disaster. Most damaging were three assertions made by Cornwallis: first, that he 'had been compelled' by Clinton to take post at Yorktown against his 'own preference'; second, that he had warned Clinton about 'the defects of the ground'; and third, that he had been 'detained there contrary' to his own judgement. Clinton now demanded a correction of these assertions, otherwise he would be compelled to take 'measures to obviate your letter being viewed in the same light in England'.[96]

In response, Cornwallis explained that Clinton's orders were specific about finding 'a harbour in the Chesapeake for line-of-battle ships', and that following the inspection of Point Comfort and Hampton Road, Yorktown appeared the only feasible alternative, despite Cornwallis's frequent expressions of concern. As to promises of support, he could only remind Clinton that all his letters 'held out uniformly hopes of relief'. He had in consequence not felt justified in either abandoning 'these posts with our numerous sick, artillery, stores and shipping', or of risking 'an action which in all probability would . . . have precipitated the loss of them'. However, he acknowledged that his letter had been 'written under great agitation of mind and in great hurry, being constantly interrupted by numbers of people coming upon business or ceremony'. His only intention had been 'to explain the motives that influenced' his conduct, and 'to narrate the incidents that preceded the extremity that forced us to surrender'.[97] He was not blaming Clinton.

Another disagreement to embroil Cornwallis while in New York concerned the Loyalists. They had taken exception to his wording of Article 10 of the capitulation, which stated that native inhabitants at Yorktown who had joined the British army should not be 'punished'. This implied that even the British thought that the Loyalists had broken their allegiance to the country of their birth.[98] They accordingly wanted Cornwallis to clarify publicly that he only meant that no one should suffer for having supported the crown. Most importantly, the Loyalists wanted the British to ensure that in future they were given prisoner-of-war status as the prelude to any peace settlement. Even Burgoyne had secured this for them. Instead, they were currently 'in no better light than runaway slaves'. However, Cornwallis could do little for them as a prisoner on parole other than issue a declaration clarifying his meaning.[99] The reality was that Washington would never have given the Loyalists what they wanted.

On 8 December Cornwallis boarded the seventy-four-gun *Robust* for his journey home.[100] Travelling with him was Arnold, who recognised his life would be in peril if he remained in America. No record survives of what the passengers said or how they occupied themselves. Doubtless Cornwallis spent time pondering his own responsibility for what had happened and how he might be received in England. A parliamentary enquiry was likely, while countless debates were inevitable in the taverns and dining rooms of Britain. Would he be cast as villain, victim or hero in these discussions?

But first he and his companions had to reach their destination. The *Robust* sprang a leak shortly after leaving New York, compelling its passengers to transfer to the transport *Greyhound*. The convoy was then scattered in the Western Approaches, leaving Cornwallis's ship an easy prey to a French privateer, the *Boulogne*.[101] The privateer's captain wanted to take his prize into Saint-Malo or Morlaix in Brittany, but was thwarted by a second storm which drove him instead towards the rocks at Rame Head in Cornwall. After attempting to keep the vessel afloat for three days, Cornwallis and his exhausted companions beseeched the captain to take refuge in nearby Plymouth Sound, promising that they would ensure his safe return to France with his prize. Their pleas succeeded, allowing the grateful passengers to disembark as prisoners on parole.[102] But one passenger who did not wait for such outcome was Arnold. Fearing that he would be executed if taken to France, he leapt into a small boat and rowed to safety near Falmouth.[103]

The journey from Plymouth to London must have both surprised and reassured Cornwallis. Instead of hostility, his appearance elicited the ringing of church bells and applause from bystanders, as he passed through the towns and villages along the way.[104] On reaching the capital, the welcome became even louder, especially when Archbishop Frederick Cornwallis ordered the bells of Lambeth Palace to be rung in grateful thanks for his nephew's safe return.[105] It was something that everyone could celebrate.

Cornwallis left no thoughts about his time in America, preferring to look to the future rather than dwell on the past. His conscience was clear: he had done his best for king and country. Yet even a sympathetic biographer must draw some conclusions, however briefly, about his subject's achievements. Certainly, Cornwallis's period of service in America was not beyond criticism, even before Yorktown. His performance at Trenton had been seriously flawed by his failure to trap Washington at Assunpink Creek. In the Carolinas he had conducted a vigorous campaign, more so than any other commander. He had also attempted to wage the war humanely, though, like all the British generals, he failed to understand the nature of the business he was engaged in. As the Loyalist Joseph Galloway commented, his progress through the Carolinas was like that of a bird which 'passes through the country but conquers no part of it'.[106] Furthermore, his advance into Virginia in April 1781 was culpable, given its likely impact on the war in the south and disregard for Clinton's orders to make the pacification of South Carolina his primary objective. His strategy for winning the war in Virginia was also questionable. However, Clinton's subsequent charge that Cornwallis's march to Petersburg resulted in Yorktown was not well founded. Clinton had twice reinforced the army in Virginia and was planning further operations there himself. Moreover, it was Clinton who agreed to establish a base for ships of the line in the Chesapeake, making the possession of Yorktown a hostage to fortune, should command of the sea be lost. Finally, it was Clinton's promise of relief, and his refusal to give Cornwallis any discretion about remaining at Yorktown, that made his entrapment certain.

Nevertheless, it is wrong to blame Clinton alone for the Yorktown debacle or for the failure to prosecute a successful war between 1778 and 1781, since it was a collective failure of the British establishment to understand the ideological underpinning of the Revolution. They believed that once the Patriot leadership was defeated, the natural loyalty of the colonists would reassert itself. This was despite increasing evidence to the contrary. Few had the courage to follow the example of Grey in telling Parliament that the war was unwinnable. Cornwallis should perhaps have done the same, given his doubts after 1777 about the war. The problem was that serving officers were necessarily trained to obey orders. They had to believe that what they did was right and would produce success, even while harbouring doubts, as Cornwallis undoubtedly did. To do otherwise was to betray the sacrifice of fallen comrades and the expectations of the nation. It was the politicians and the monarch who were responsible for deciding the issues of war or peace.

The other principal reason for the British defeat was a lack of resources. Britain simply did not have the population and materials to fight a war over such distances, while simultaneously fighting much of Europe. This was the reason why the Royal Navy lost control of American waters in 1781, having nearly done so on several previous occasions. Yorktown in reality was a disaster waiting to happen.[107] The limits of British power was to be one of the lessons that Cornwallis remembered when the nation had to face the challenges of Revolutionary France. Another was his realisation that no government could maintain its authority without the passive consent of the population. It was something he would not forget subsequently in India and Ireland.

Part II
INDIA

SIX

The Search for a New Role

Although Cornwallis was naturally anxious to see his family, duty required that he first report to the ministry; etiquette, however, prevented him from appearing at court as a prisoner of war. Nevertheless, the king promised him a private audience, and any fear that he might be blamed for the disaster was quickly dispelled. George III did 'not lay anything at the charge of Lord Cornwallis' and could not 'see why he shall not be presented at my levee tomorrow' (referring to his weekly reception of dignitaries at the palace).[1] Others quickly followed in exonerating him, as Captain Sir John Jervis, a rising star in the navy, informed Clinton: 'No officer was ever so popular under misfortune as he.' Those who had served with him in America 'sound his praises beyond example, the Court flatters him, and John Bull is delighted with the blood spilt under His Lordship's auspices'. Grey alone had 'not sacrificed to Lord Cornwallis's shrine'.[2]

Cornwallis's movements after completing his official duties are unclear. Undoubtedly his first concern was a reunion with his children Brome and Mary, followed by meetings with old friends at his club. Another consideration was the need to find somewhere to live while in London. Being uncertain about the future, he decided to rent a property on the less fashionable side of Oxford Street to keep his expenses down. But Brome and Mary were the immediate focus of his attention, as his mother, the dowager countess, testily informed William Cornwallis. Charles 'talks of writing, but he has got his children with him'. She could only hope that they would 'give him time' to attend to the rest of his family, since 'they are always with him' when at home.[3] He was clearly making up for lost opportunity.

Nevertheless, there was no escape from public affairs, even if popular sentiment exonerated Cornwallis for what had happened. Although George III wanted to continue the war in America, opposition to it was growing, both in Parliament and the country, which made an enquiry into Yorktown inevitable. This duly came on 4 February 1782, when the dukes of Richmond and Chandos called for the Lords to investigate 'the causes of the great loss which the nation has sustained'.[4] However, his cousin, Charles Townshend, quickly assured Cornwallis that he was not the target of the motion, but rather the ministry of Lord North.[5] Nevertheless the request 'for copies or extracts of all correspondence between Sir Henry Clinton and Earl Cornwallis' relating to Yorktown was naturally of concern, given his recent differences with Clinton.[6] He could only hope that the requested documents at least exonerated him from being held the main architect of the disaster.

He had one advantage: Clinton was still in America and was thus unable to challenge Cornwallis's version of events, as contained in his letter of 20 October 1781, which Germain had published without amendment. But he had no wish to inflame the dispute, as one of Clinton's friends confirmed.[7] Nevertheless, Jervis warned: 'Cornwallis will have the first opportunity to avow the facts.'[8] The consensus had already formed that either Clinton, Graves, or Rodney were to blame for the disaster: Rodney for not sending enough ships; Graves for mismanaging the naval battle; and Clinton for not intercepting Washington and Rochambeau as they marched through New Jersey.[9] In contrast, the only critics of Cornwallis were the Loyalists, still embittered about Article 10 of the surrender document.[10]

Cornwallis could not attend the proceedings himself as a prisoner on parole. He was, in any case, involved in a separate inquiry by the Commission for Examining the Public Accounts. This body was looking into the financial conduct of the war as part of a wider inquiry into the failings of government.[11] Key targets for investigation were the military supply departments of the quartermaster-general and the commissary-general. Cornwallis was accordingly summoned to testify on oath before the Commission on 27 February and again on 1 March 1782. Among the issues discussed was the practice whereby regimental quartermasters gave receipts for the full value of the rations received, whether they had been brought from Europe or obtained more cheaply from local sources, which produced a considerable profit in the latter case for the officials in charge. Cornwallis, in reply, explained that he had not been responsible for the commissariat until taking command in the Carolinas, though he was aware of such malfeasance. 'To remedy this evil' he had appointed commissaries of captures who issued no receipts for locally sourced supplies unless the provisions had been provided by Loyalists, to whom payment was legitimate. He had also endeavoured to prevent profiteering in the quartermaster's department whereby officers owned and hired the wagons and horses at exorbitant rates to the army.[12] Unsurprisingly, the Commission found no fault with Cornwallis's management, reserving its criticism instead for Clinton's officials in New York. Their findings were published just as Clinton arrived from America. It was to be another cause of contention between the two men.[13]

Any concern Cornwallis might have felt about the House of Lords inquiry proved unnecessary. At the end of March 1782, North's wartime ministry succumbed to opposition pressure, paving the way for a new government headed by Rockingham and Shelburne.[14] Once in office, the new ministers had no further interest in parliamentary enquiries. Nevertheless, Cornwallis felt obliged to resign as constable of the Tower, given his role in executing the former ministry's American policies. But before doing so, he decided to explain himself to George III, affirming that he would gladly resign as constable if it would 'contribute to the convenience of your arrangements'. Hopefully his 'unwearied endeavours to serve Your Majesty and my country' would lead the king 'to consider favourably my pretensions' to military preferment, 'when a proper opportunity offers'.[15] George III was touched by Cornwallis's offer, assailed as he was by office-seekers. 'The whole tenor of your conduct has so manifestly shown that attachment to my person, to your Country, and to the military profession', that he should not 'from a false delicacy think of resigning' his office.[16] Cornwallis should stay on as constable.

His audience with the king was prompted in part by the need to supplement his moderate income. The prospects for employment were not entirely bleak. The dowager countess noted in early April 1782 that Cornwallis was again on friendly terms with Shelburne, the new secretary of state for home affairs and the colonies.[17] Their renewed friendship was not accidental, since Shelburne wanted Cornwallis to replace Warren Hastings as governor-general of Bengal, who was about to be recalled because of difficulties with his council. The offer was certainly welcomed by Cornwallis. Though 'the military part of the prospect is not brilliant', he mused to

William Cornwallis, what other opportunities were there? His remuneration would 'be great and without deviating from the strictest honour, I must have it in my power to put my children in a better situation'.[18] Moreover, competition for the post was unlikely to be high: 'few of our generals' would 'wish to quit their easy chairs, unless it is to command an English camp'.[19] Only one obstacle blocked his appointment: he was still on parole. However, Henry Laurens remained in the Tower, renewing the possibility of an exchange. A plan was accordingly devised for Ross to travel to France on a diplomatic passport to contact Benjamin Franklin, the American ambassador in Paris.[20] The strictest anonymity was to be preserved.

Franklin duly agreed to forward the proposed plan to Congress, while the British in turn released Laurens as evidence of their good faith. The king, believing that everything was settled, quickly lifted the ban on Cornwallis's attendance at court, telling Shelburne that he would receive Cornwallis with 'pleasure' at his next levee.[21] The audience on 19 June 1782 coincided with Clinton's own presentation, following his return from America. Clinton initially believed he had been exceptionally well received by George III until he witnessed Cornwallis's turn.[22] Equally galling was that Cornwallis was still receiving the freedom of towns like Leicester in recognition of his 'very gallant and distinguished behaviour and meritorious service in America'.[23] No such honours were flowing Clinton's way.

Nevertheless, the prospect of becoming governor-general of Bengal remained tantalisingly out of reach. Cornwallis's release from parole was proving more tortuous than expected, especially when Congress demanded his recall to America, if Laurens was not promptly released.[24] This was frustrating given that Laurens had already been freed. To expedite matters, Cornwallis wrote in early August 1782 to Guy Carleton, Clinton's replacement in North America, asking him to intercede with Washington.[25] Still nothing happened. With Christmas approaching, Cornwallis contemplated writing to Lafayette, and asked Ross to correct any mistakes in his French. Nevertheless, it seemed his 'wretched state of uncertainty must continue', since he was anxious to avoid the humiliation of being 'publicly named for the command in India' and then being unable to accept.[26] Eventually the muddle between London, Paris, and Philadelphia was settled with the signing of the peace preliminaries in January 1783, which automatically freed all prisoners. But by this time Shelburne's administration was in a state of collapse and about to be replaced by a ministry headed by North and Charles James Fox, who had their own plans for India. Seemingly this route to employment had been closed.

One thing that had not changed was Clinton's determination to lay the blame for Yorktown onto Cornwallis. After his disappointing reception at court, Clinton resorted to writing anonymous letters, masquerading as 'an old officer', who wished to refute the slur that his former commander-in-chief should have intercepted Washington and Rochambeau before they reached Virginia.[27] When such endeavours failed, he published on 14 January 1783 a more lengthy *Narrative* under his own name, repeating for the most part what he had told Cornwallis in New York.[28] Cornwallis was not impressed, telling Ross: 'It is a bad performance, and I think not likely to do the cause much good with people of judgement.'[29] He was right to think so. The *Gentleman's Magazine* suggested that 'the impartial reader' was 'unlikely to accept Sir Henry Clinton's argument that he had no responsibility for choosing Yorktown', while the *Monthly Review* similarly noted that Clinton absolved himself of all blame and was disingenuous in asserting that Cornwallis had misconceived his orders.[30] Nevertheless, Cornwallis still felt he should respond, especially as Clinton 'so often arraigns my march into Virginia, as a measure undertaken without waiting for his command'.[31] The result was the publication on 15 February 1783 of his *Answer*.[32] Like Clinton, Cornwallis included a selection of documents, but unlike his adversary, he printed them in full, providing 260 pages of original materials, compared to just fifty-four in Clinton's *Narrative*.[33] The response was generally favourable.[34]

The dust had barely settled before Clinton published a second pamphlet in response to Cornwallis's *Answer*.[35] To give his work extra incisiveness, he employed the historian Edward Gibbon to polish the text.[36] The reception was no more favourable. Cornwallis in any case did not reply. He knew that others were ready to take up the challenge. He himself was anxious to put the episode behind him. Whatever his failings, he had done his best to serve his king and country in what had proved a forlorn cause.

Although Cornwallis had yet to find a new role, he was kept busy with his responsibilities for the 33rd Foot Regiment and the Tower of London. He also had his estates to manage and friends and family to entertain, all the while keeping watch on the political situation in London. One thing he now had time for was the painting of his portrait by the fashionable artist Thomas Gainsborough. The result was a half-length figure of him, dressed in the uniform of a lieutenant-general, though without background battle scenes, as befitted a commander who had recently lost his army. Though its subject was by now middle-aged, the portrait is suggestive of someone who has experienced life's travails, yet still possessing a quiet authority and confidence in himself.

A major cause for concern during 1783 was the poor health of Brome. He was now enrolled at Eton, where Cornwallis spent several days in August, tending to his son, who had scarlet fever, only to suffer a swollen foot himself, similar to what he had experienced four years earlier. 'God knows whether it is gout or not', he told Ross.[37] Then in October 1783 he was back at Eton: Brome had succumbed to another fever. He admitted to Ross that 'these repeated attacks are very discouraging and distressing'. However, he would 'make one more trial of Eton', before entrusting the education of his son to private tutors.[38]

Politically Cornwallis remained unattached, though his preference was for the opposition led by Shelburne and William Pitt the Younger. However, he was cautious about supporting them, fearing that their radical wing, led by Richmond, would 'overturn the constitution of this country' by implementing parliamentary reform. Cornwallis was adamant about that issue and its advocates: he could 'have nothing to do with them'. The legislature was sufficiently representative as it was.[39] Nevertheless, his lack of affiliation raised once more the dilemma of his position as constable of the Tower. Perhaps he should resign from what was still a quasi-political appointment, to avoid the humiliation of being turned out of office in the next ministerial reshuffle. But he would make no hasty decision until the next opening of Parliament.[40]

Cornwallis's good standing with George III resulted in his being briefly consulted about the household of the king's second son, Frederick, duke of York. The prince was currently in Germany under the tutelage of Major-General Richard Grenville, an old colleague of Cornwallis during the Seven Years' War. George III had originally sent York to Hanover to separate him from his brother, the prince of Wales, and other undesirable companions.[41] But he also wanted him to become head of the British army like his great uncle, the duke of Cumberland. The time of York's majority was approaching, when Grenville's supervisory role would cease. The king remained anxious to surround York with persons who might be a steadying influence on him and turned to Cornwallis for suitable nominees. Cornwallis responded by proffering his former aide, Colonel Henry Brodrick, to whom York seemed favourably inclined.[42] To prepare Brodrick for his new role, Cornwallis recommended 'a little reading' to make him a more knowledgeable companion. He himself was currently perusing a French translation of the Greek historian Polybius, detailing the advantages of forming a column, phalanx, or square when engaging an enemy.[43] 'I am every day more convinced on the necessity of military reading', he told Ross a few weeks later, 'and I assure you that it is very agreeable to me'.[44] Yet despite his efforts to find a suitable companion for York, Cornwallis noted in the New Year that York had appointed 'three or four boys of the Guards for aides-de-camp, which will be of great disservice to him'.[45] Cornwallis knew too well that corps's supercilious culture of aristocratic entitlement.

The approach of the new parliamentary session in October 1783 coincided with a rumour that North was considering Cornwallis for the position of governor-general of Bengal, once the ministry had passed its bill regulating the East India Company, which had become responsible for the administration of that province and other territories in India following the Seven Years' War.[46] But a month later Cornwallis had still heard nothing and concluded that the story was unfounded.[47] This seemed a blessing, given the controversy that immediately ensued on the publication of the new bill. Most contentious was the patronage the government would acquire for its supporters through the creation of a board of commissioners to supervise the Company's future management. The political temperature became so heated that Cornwallis decided to leave London before the Lords voted to avoid any political embarrassment. Word then arrived that George III vehemently opposed the measure, and that 'whoever voted for the India Bill were not only not his friends, but that he should consider them his enemies'.[48] Cornwallis felt bound to support his beleaguered monarch, even though voting against the Fox–North ministry would end his chances of employment.[49]

In reality, Cornwallis had become sceptical about going to India, whatever government was formed. As he told Ross, 'I am handsomely off and, in the present fluctuating state of affairs and violent animosities about India, I can see no prospect of any good.'[50] But ease and quiet were not his only considerations. After its defeat in the Lords, the Fox–North ministry had been promptly replaced by an administration headed by William Pitt the Younger. This time Cornwallis felt he must resign as constable of the Tower, to avoid the imputation of 'having kept my place' while voting 'against the ministry', of which he was notionally a member. At least he would maintain his honour, whatever the loss of income.[51]

Cornwallis was aware that his resignation would raise doubts about his political attitude to the new ministry. However, he doubted that Pitt's 'mince pie' administration would survive the Christmas recess.[52] He was accordingly surprised on 8 January when he received an invitation to dine with his cousin, Thomas Townshend, now Lord Sydney, who had become home secretary. In the event Sydney's main concern was to canvass parliamentary support for the new ministry, though he hinted that an offer of employment might follow. Cornwallis jocularly responded by offering Sydney some 'hares, partridges and pheasants', but refused to speak for the two members for Eye regarding support for the ministry.[53] He had previously told William Cornwallis that he should act according to his own judgement in all parliamentary matters, and had given the same freedom to his friend, Richard Burton Phillipson, the other member for Eye.[54] As to holding office, Cornwallis must reluctantly decline, given the current political uncertainty. The conversation was nevertheless friendly.

Over the New Year Cornwallis entertained Rawdon – now fully restored to health since leaving South Carolina – at Culford Park. Another old colleague from the American war, Charles O'Hara, might have been present but for 'his merciless creditors'.[55] That conflict had also left many other ruined beggars on the streets of London, as Cornwallis noted to Ross. 'I am still plagued to death and impoverished by starving Loyalists.' Though he wished to be generous, the loss of income from the Tower made it essential 'to shut the purse, except in the most moving instances of misery'.[56] In any case he was determined to pursue 'the most rigid economy' and live within his income: he was 'not afraid of being called shabby' while looking for employment.[57]

The political temperature, meanwhile, remained high, with many of Cornwallis's relatives adopting 'violent opposition language' to show their support for the recently dismissed Fox–North ministry.[58] Cornwallis, in contrast, felt growing admiration for Pitt, as he battled to save his minority administration, though he still doubted that he could survive, despite his dazzling performances in the Commons.[59] But, like most observers, he underestimated Pitt's dexterity and the king's resolve not to reappoint Fox and North. Just when it seemed that the ministry was doomed, Pitt asked George III at the end of March 1784 to dissolve Parliament, even though it still had three of its seven years to run. The election threatened both expense and management for Cornwallis, because William Cornwallis had agreed to contest Portsmouth instead, at the request of the ministry. Cornwallis in consequence had to find an alternative candidate for Eye. The election itself was eventually uncontested for Cornwallis's two nominees, Phillipson and Peter Bathurst, another old army acquaintance.[60] Fortune also smiled on the ministry, which secured a handsome majority. Among the casualties, to Cornwallis's amusement, was Clinton, who had quarrelled with his patron, Newcastle. 'The worthy knight', in consequence, had no seat to contest.[61]

The election was barely over before Sydney contacted Cornwallis, this time with the specific offer of becoming commander-in-chief of the army in India. Cornwallis quickly declined, telling Ross: 'I see no field for extraordinary military reputation', only a situation in 'every light dangerous to the greatest degree'. It would be intolerable 'to abandon my children and every comfort on this side [of] the grave' for a quarrelsome relationship 'with the supreme government in India, whatever it may be'. How frustrating it would be 'to find that I have neither power to model the army or correct abuses', while running the 'risk of being beat by some nabob' (Indian prince) and 'disgraced to all eternity'.[62] He had been disturbed by the news that an East India Company force under General Richard Matthews had been forced to capitulate in May 1783 to Tipu Sultan, the ruler of Mysore.[63] One consequence of Sydney's approach was a review by Cornwallis of his finances. These showed that he could live decently in the country for six months and still afford the rest of the year in London. Moreover, on resigning the constableship of the Tower he had been led to expect some military position, which might produce an additional income of between £700 and £1,000. 'All this is hardly affluence', he conceded, yet 'to a man of my turn it is not distress'.[64]

Nevertheless, the ministry persisted in its approaches, resulting in a second meeting with Sydney on 25 May 1784. This time Cornwallis stressed that it was not only 'the circumscribed power of the military command', but the lack of any civil authority that made it impossible for him to accept. Sydney responded that he was sure that Pitt would give him both posts.[65] After the meeting, Cornwallis indulged in an agonised soliloquy about his situation, as he told Ross that evening. The ministry and Company were seemingly 'desirous of my going, but I feel how precarious their favour must be'. The problem was this: 'I can come to no resolution till I know the plan; yet inclination cries out every moment, do not think of it; reject all offers; why should you volunteer [to endure] plague and misery? Duty then whispers, you are not sent here merely to please yourself; the wisdom of Providence has thought fit to put an insuperable bar to any great degree of happiness.' If he stayed at home contentment might still elude him, should Brome die or some other calamity occur. Instead he ought to 'try to be of some use; serve your country and your friends'. Currently he could do neither. He should therefore embrace the means 'which God is willing to put into your hands'.[66]

For the moment no decision was necessary, since the ministry still had to complete the drafting of its new India bill. Sydney eventually forwarded the ministry's proposed bill to Cornwallis on 3 August, adding that if there was 'any situation that would be agreeable to you, I am persuaded that you might command it'. The directors of the East India Company were 'desirous to trust their affairs to you', the ministry even more so.[67] The bill's aim was to rectify the perceived weaknesses in North's previous India Act of 1773, especially the lack of authority vested in both the government and Bengal's governor-general. It proposed to rectify this by creating a new Board of Control, giving the ministry power to vet all Company appointments and policies affecting the governance of its territories.[68] Nevertheless the bill had a number of objectionable features for Cornwallis. Most importantly, it still seemingly precluded the holding of both offices of commander-in-chief and governor-general, which Cornwallis considered essential if he was to implement the government's proposed reforms.[69]

Cornwallis accordingly once again declined Sydney's offer, though he added that whatever his 'vexations and disappointments' in America, 'no consideration of personal inconvenience or safety' would prevent his accepting an appointment if it appeared that 'my poor abilities would be useful to my country'. However, he remained convinced that he must have both offices to be effective. If he settled for 'the place of Governor-General, I should not only abandon a profession to which I have from my youth wholly turned my thoughts', but would most likely be 'in competition with some person whose habits of business' differed from his own. The army was still his 'favourite passion', which 'I cannot give up'. Equally, he could not accept the military command alone. The 'present circumscribed situation of the Commander-in-Chief, without power or patronage', meant that the holder 'would neither get credit to himself, nor essentially serve the public'.[70] The recent setbacks clearly showed that the military establishment in India needed reforming and that required someone with the necessary authority to effect it.

There, for the moment, the matter rested. Indeed, by early September 1784 Cornwallis believed the 'business as absolutely and finally concluded'.[71] He was about to make his annual visit to Brome Manor to keep open house for a month to maintain his influence with the electors and corporation of Eye. This was not a task that Cornwallis enjoyed. To make his stay bearable he invited Phillipson to accompany him, though this proved a mixed blessing, as his companion was increasingly deaf and had 'most provokingly left all his [ear] trumpets in London'. More pleasurable was the arrival of Brome and Mary.[72] Mary had recently assisted him with his correspondence, and at fifteen years old was developing into a companionable young lady.[73] Brome also promised much, providing he remained in good health. Their presence reminded him of his earlier conclusion that he could 'live comfortably in England', attended by his children, who were approaching an 'age when an anxious and affectionate father would wish to be constantly watching them'.[74]

Despite his refusal to go to India, Cornwallis assumed that his relations with the ministry were harmonious and that he could still expect some military appointment in place of the constableship of the Tower. One possibility was the governorship of Plymouth, which had become vacant with the death of General Waldegrave. He was surprised therefore to learn in early November 1784 that the ministry had appointed to the post Lord George Lennox, who had replaced Cornwallis at the Tower only eight months before. Cornwallis was genuinely hurt on this occasion, though he attempted to hide his feelings with the jocular observation that, like Falstaff, he was always waiting for the summons that never came.[75]

Despite this, Cornwallis realised that he had been too passive in seeking preferment. He determined accordingly to ask Sydney why he had not been named either governor of Plymouth or a colonel of the Guards. Sydney replied that strengthening the ministry was the main reason for the recent appointments. This cut little ice with Cornwallis, since both posts were of a military, and not a political, nature. He had clearly been treated with 'contempt and neglect', prompting him to tell Ross that he was 'done for ever with kings and ministers'.[76] His temper was not improved when, in a second interview on 6 November, Sydney said that Cornwallis had been excluded because it was assumed that he would go to India. But the more Sydney attempted to explain, the more exasperated Cornwallis became: he answered that he 'could talk no longer on the subject, and wished him good morning'. Sydney interjected: 'we must not part on these terms'. Cornwallis responded: 'we can part on no other'. It was seemingly the end of the bid to make him governor-general.[77]

Nevertheless, Cornwallis believed that his honour required a fuller explanation as to what had happened. In so hierarchical a society, tongues would wag if he was perceived as lacking influence in the political and military world. Fearing that Sydney was an unreliable channel of communication, he resolved to write to Pitt himself. He began by saying that after his previous dealings with the ministry, he had foolishly imagined that his sacrifices 'to the King's service in America' and his 'disinterested attachment' over 'the last twenty years' would have procured him 'a place in His Majesty's affections'. Instead Cornwallis had been exposed to ridicule, while Sydney's apologies had 'only added insult to the injury'. Had the king or Pitt told Cornwallis 'that it was necessary for the support of their government that I should not only waive my pretensions, but give up half of the income of my estate, I would cheerfully have complied'. It was the ministerial insincerity that so disgusted him. Nevertheless, Cornwallis was careful to express his admiration for Pitt's political leadership, assuring him: 'I will not be base enough, from a sense of personal injury, to join faction' in order to 'obstruct the measures of government'. 'Private confidence', however, might not be 'so easily restored'.[78]

The result was a meeting two days later with Pitt, at which the prime minister made copious apologies before offering Cornwallis his old position of constable of the Tower of London. The whole meeting was conducted with much civil language and 'a proper dignity' on both sides. Nevertheless, Cornwallis still considered declining Pitt's offer, fearing it would be construed as a political bargain rather than a spontaneous recognition of merit. But after a few hours' consideration he accepted the proposition, assuring Pitt that all previous difficulties would be forgotten.[79] Three weeks later he took the oath of office in the Privy Council 'to truly serve the King' as constable of the Tower.[80]

Pitt's conciliatory stance was because the ministers still wanted Cornwallis to go to India, and were prepared to introduce a bill allowing him to become both governor-general and commander-in-chief. Accordingly, in early February 1785 Pitt again contacted Cornwallis, informing him of the absolute necessity 'that the appointment of a Governor-General of India should take place in a short time'. He continued: 'The security of India and all the utility to be derived from that place' depended 'upon its administration being speedily put on a good footing'. This could only be done by reforming both 'the civil and military establishments', thereby eliminating the present 'abuses in both'. He continued: 'I do not ask this as a personal favour, because I wish to rest it upon the great public grounds which are really involved.' Nevertheless, it would be 'one of the most flattering circumstances' in 'Pitt's public life', should Cornwallis accept.[81]

Pitt left the details of the appointment to Henry Dundas, his political ally in Scotland, who was now effectively in charge of the Board of Control. Dundas assured Cornwallis that if he agreed to go to India, the obnoxious parts of the recently passed act would be amended. Despite this, Cornwallis still declined with a 'very civil negative', although 'violently attacked' to accept what was proposed. The reality was that he would not initially go to India both as commander-in-chief and governor-general. He feared that the ministerial pledges to amend the appointment might subsequently fall foul of divisions in the Cabinet. He also disliked several recent military appointments, notably that of General Robert Sloper as commander-in-chief in Bengal.[82] As was now his custom he discussed the matter with Ross, who supported his resolution to decline. This was a considerable comfort to Cornwallis: 'you know how much I value your approbation'.[83] Ross now filled the role of confidant, which Jemima had previously performed.

With no further commitments other than periodic inspections of the Tower and the 33rd Foot Regiment, Cornwallis decided to join York and Grenville in Germany for the annual review of the Prussian army. Frederick II's military establishment was still considered the best in Europe, and Cornwallis remained anxious to improve his professional knowledge. Invitations were sparingly granted, though this one was warmly endorsed by the Prussian king.[84] News of Cornwallis's trip reached the ministers, who decided to entrust him with an informal diplomatic mission. They were anxious to end Britain's political isolation in Europe, and saw an alliance with Prussia as the best means of doing so. Such an agreement might not only improve the security of Hanover, but also counteract French influence in Holland, which was threatening the ruling House of Orange. Pitt's foreign secretary Francis Osborne, the marquess of Carmarthen, explained the ministry's reasoning in approaching Cornwallis: 'The high opinion which the King of Prussia, in common with the rest of the world, entertains of Your Lordship's character' would hopefully 'induce him to be more communicative to you upon these subjects, than to any other person'. Cornwallis's role would be that of a listener rather than the initiator of any proposals. Throughout, 'great caution' was to be observed 'with so artful as well as so experienced a character in every branch of political intrigue' as the king of Prussia. The mission was to remain secret.[85]

Cornwallis accordingly set out in mid-August 1785, travelling first to The Hague, where he was joined by York and Grenville, before continuing to Berlin. Here Frederick II honoured Cornwallis and Grenville with an invitation to dine with him each day. Cornwallis also met his old commander-in-chief in Germany, Duke Ferdinand of Brunswick, who 'received [him] very graciously'.[86] However, no opportunity arose for a private talk with Frederick II. The court then travelled to Breslau to inspect the forces in Silesia. Cornwallis's reception here was less flattering, since Frederick II showed a marked preference for Lafayette, who was also attending the manoeuvres. Cornwallis was unsure whether this reflected Frederick II's greater knowledge of France or was an indication of Prussia's diplomatic priorities. As to the review itself, Cornwallis admired the Prussian cavalry but was less impressed with the infantry, whose movements were slow and slightly ridiculous.[87] He confessed to Ross 'that on the whole, from the first person I met, I have been throughout rather disappointed'.[88]

The party then returned to Berlin to attend the Potsdam manoeuvres. Awaiting Cornwallis were fresh instructions from Carmarthen, authorising him to seek a formal interview with the king through the agency of the Prussian ministers. This resulted in an interview with Ewald Friedrich, count von Hertzberg, one of Frederick's most senior diplomats, during which Cornwallis indicated George III's desire for 'a firm and lasting alliance'. To make the proposition more attractive, he simultaneously emphasised that Britain had largely recovered from the late American war. Prussia, therefore, should have 'no doubt that England would be able to support her weight and dignity with the other powers of Europe'. Hertzberg replied that the British sentiments would be well received by Frederick II, though not to the extent of a formal alliance. Much depended on Austria and Russia, since those powers posed the greatest threat to Prussia itself. The king, however, would talk with Cornwallis at the Potsdam manoeuvres on 17 September.[89] The omens appeared promising.

The interview duly took place at Sanssouci, the king's summer palace; also in attendance was Duke Ferdinand. All three spoke in French, as was customary in diplomatic matters. Frederick II began by observing that Britain and Prussia potentially faced a hostile alliance composed of France, Austria, Spain and Russia. In 'this situation of affairs, he did not think it would be wise to give alarm to all the great powers of Europe by a treaty between Britain and Prussia'. He did not want to trigger another diplomatic revolution, as in 1756. However, he would do his utmost to prevent France from interfering in Holland, though not by force of arms. The key to Prussia and Britain's mutual security lay in detaching Russia from the other powers. This accordingly should be Britain's priority. Once that was effected, Prussia could safely join Britain in a triple alliance with Holland.[90]

The following evening Frederick II was taken ill, which prevented any further exchange. Though the diagnosis was gout, Cornwallis doubted that the Prussian king would survive the winter. He had in consequence to be content with a short note from Frederick II, regretting his inability to see him again before his departure.[91] Since the mission had gone as far as possible, Cornwallis set off for the final manoeuvres at Magdeburg, before making a stop in Hanover, to inform the ministers of George III's electorate about the recent talks. Here he received news of the death of an old schoolfriend, Thomas Ducie, which 'shocked' him 'beyond measure'. Though death was never far from daily life, it was still distressing when a close acquaintance was involved. All things considered, he was not quitting Germany 'with much regret'.[92]

Cornwallis should not have been disappointed at the inconclusive outcome to his mission, since the chances of success were extremely low. Nevertheless, the ministers were pleased that Frederick II was well disposed towards Britain, even though he declined any formal engagement.[93] Most importantly, Cornwallis had discovered that the heir to the Prussian throne, Crown Prince Frederick William, was 'warmly disposed to a connection with England'. This was significant, given Frederick II's failing health.[94] The groundwork had been laid for a formal treaty, which came three years later.

Less propitious was Cornwallis's verdict on York's military abilities. Despite four years in Germany, York's conduct did not give grounds for optimism. 'His military ideas are those of a wild boy of the Guards' who was engrossed by 'the uniforms and promotions of that corps, about which he is vehement to excess'. His friendly disposition also meant that 'any impudent blackguard may be as familiar [with him] as he pleases', taking advantage of his good nature. Even so one could not 'help loving him'. Nevertheless, the conclusion was inescapable: York must stay in Germany to prevent him falling into the company of the prince of Wales and his dissolute entourage.[95]

Cornwallis returned home as planned at the end of October to more begging letters from Loyalists and others who had fallen on hard times. Among them was Tarleton, who wanted help in settling a bill on Drummond the banker, prompting Cornwallis to chastise himself once more for agreeing to requests which threatened his own family's welfare.[96] But he was to suffer a far worse shock regarding the latter, when he informed Ross on 3 December 1785 that 'Mary, my darling Mary, on whom you know I doted to distraction, took the opportunity of my going for two days to London to run to Scotland with an Irish ensign of the Guards' named Mark Singleton. The pair had seemingly met while Mary was visiting Cheltenham with one of her aunts.[97] Having tied the knot, the couple had returned to London and taken refuge with Singleton's father in Portman Square. The elopement soon became common knowledge in the newspapers.[98]

For Cornwallis it was a devastating and unexpected blow, which released the darkest thoughts about his future hopes and happiness. Truly 'my measure of wretchedness is nearly complete', for should anything happen to Brome he would be beyond all hope of happiness.[99] Nor was this the end of his anguish: within the week he was confronted by the death of his mother, the dowager countess. Unsurprisingly, he confided to Ross, 'I do not feel as if I should ever be in spirits again'.[100]

Nevertheless, the situation had to be faced. First, he wrote to Mary 'representing to her the profligacy of her conduct and exhorting her to repentance and future good behaviour'. However, he would 'not discard her' as many aristocratic fathers would have done in so patriarchal a society. He would in time see her and make such allowance as was proper, provided she behaved well. Mary was only entitled to £5,000 under the terms of his marriage settlement with Jemima, so he would be able 'to speak with considerable authority', as he informed Ross. The young man was reputedly of 'a good character', though Cornwallis necessarily reflected that 'as he is five and twenty, his hurrying off a child of sixteen to her utter ruin' was hardly reassuring.[101]

Cornwallis initially asked his cousin, Charles Townshend, to act as an intermediary. Slowly his anger subsided, and he promised to see Mary in the New Year. The details of the financial settlement were also completed. Singleton's father, conscious of the injury done to Cornwallis by his son, would transfer £8,000 of 4-per-cent stock to Mark, who would add to that sum by selling his commission in the army. This would produce a clear income of £400 per annum. Cornwallis would in turn provide a similar annual stipend, providing they behaved themselves. This should allow the couple to live in society, though it was difficult to know how and where they should do so. 'They seem desirous of living in the country', he informed Ross, 'but at their age I should fear that they would soon tire of it'.[102] He accepted the desirability of Singleton quitting the Guards, as it 'would probably draw the young people into expenses and company that would be improper'.[103]

Cornwallis finally agreed to meet Mary and her husband in the last week of January 1786, which he admitted was 'a good thing' to have done. Both promised economy and prudence.[104] Two weeks later he appears to have visited Portman Square, for he informed Ross: 'I have seen Mary and her husband and all the Singletons.' Nevertheless, he did not 'find much comfort' in the encounter. Another problem was the need to find Mark Singleton a suitable occupation. Since he had quitted the army and had no liking for the navy, the third option for the younger siblings of aristocratic families was a position in the Church of England. For Cornwallis this seemed eminently sensible. An additional income of £500–600 'would be a great object' for the newly weds. Singleton had been 'educated in Harrow School and afterwards at Oxford', so 'there would be no difficulty in getting him ordained'. Catherine Cornwallis, the widow of the former archbishop, agreed to approach Singleton, while Cornwallis talked to Mary.[105] Neither was successful.

Amid these domestic concerns, the matter of an appointment in India had almost been forgotten. Indeed, by mid-February 1786, Cornwallis was convinced that either Lord Macartney or Sir Archibald Campbell, currently governor of Madras, would get the post of governor-general of Bengal. But, unknown to him, Pitt and Dundas had finally decided to meet his demands regarding control of the civil and military affairs of the East India Company. This they proposed to do with new legislation before he left for India. The offer of governor-general and commander-in-chief was finally made on 22 February 1786. He told Ross: 'The proposal of my going to India has been pressed upon me so strongly' that 'I have been obliged to say yes, and to exchange a life of ease and content' for 'the plagues and miseries of command and public station'. The deciding factors had been a readiness to make him governor-general, 'independent of his council', combined with 'the supreme command of the military'. Another bonus was that Ross would accompany him as adjutant-general.[106] Despite his reservations about the task confronting him, he now had a sense of purpose to his life, which had been missing since his return from America. That at least was of some comfort.

SEVEN

Governor-General of Bengal

The affairs of the East India Company had been of concern to Britain's political classes since the end of the Seven Years' War in 1763. Despite conquering large and seemingly profitable territories in India, the Company soon found itself in financial difficulties. The reason was that as a trading corporation, it was ill equipped to govern millions of subject peoples. The situation was compounded in 1765, when the Mughal emperor in Delhi formalised the Company's conquests by granting it a 'diwani', or right to levy taxes, in the provinces of Bengal, Bihar, and Orissa (modern-day Odisha). Because the Company lacked an effective bureaucracy, the wealth of the new territories soon went into the pockets of unscrupulous employees, creating a class of super-rich British 'nabobs' like Robert Clive. The Company in contrast found that the cost of administering its new possessions quickly dissipated the diwani revenues. Bankruptcy threatened, and with it the likelihood that the Company would become a burden on the British taxpayer.[1] But other factors were also contributing to the demand for change. In an era of 'Enlightenment', the perception was growing that governments must offer subject peoples something better than mere rapine and exploitation. Even the absolute monarchs of Europe were strengthening their right to govern by affecting to be benevolent despots.

The first attempt to rectify the situation was made by North in his 1773 Act for Establishing Certain Regulations for the Better Management of the Affairs of the East India Company. First, a new office of governor-general of Bengal was created, who was to be assisted by a council of four. Second, all Company officers were to be regulated as to their personal finances. Many were to receive fixed salaries and most were hereafter banned from engaging in private trade, a major source of abuse. The giving or receiving of bribes was also forbidden, and no one was to lend money at more than 12 per cent interest, a favourite ploy for exploiting local rulers. Finally, a Supreme Court was to be established to enforce these regulations with respect to the Company's British employees.[2]

North's India Act, however, was not successful. Warren Hastings, the first governor-general, experienced difficulties with his council, where decisions were taken by majority vote. Although Hastings had been a Company servant in India for fourteen years, his appointment had antagonised many of his peers. He was also not helped by his obvious intellectual ability, a quality which was often unappreciated by a society that valued rank and birth more than knowledge and experience. His difficulties were further increased during the subsequent war with France and her ally, Tipu Sultan, the ruler of Mysore, when the Company suffered several military reverses, including the disaster to Matthews.[3] The result was widespread recognition that, in addition to a new regulating act, a governor was needed who was not a Company employee but who had political and military stature of his own.[4]

It was for these reasons that Cornwallis was seen as a potential candidate. Few blamed him for the debacle in America, where he had proved himself an enterprising commander, thus making him a fit person to control the Company's army. He was also widely recognised as someone who placed the public good above personal profit, as was demonstrated during his testimony to the Commission for Examining the Public Accounts (see above, pp. 116–17). This put him in tune with the new ethos of economic reform and administrative efficiency that North had started, and which Pitt was continuing with increasing effect.[5] Finally Cornwallis was a peer of the realm and member of the British establishment, unlike Hastings, who depended on others for patronage and the maintenance of his authority. Although the ministry had considered other candidates, none had a curriculum vitae to match Cornwallis's. This explains why Pitt endured so many rebuffs to secure his services.

The plan, as agreed on 22 February 1786, was that Cornwallis should leave England in early April to arrive in Bengal at the end of the monsoon season. This left him barely six weeks to prepare for a term of service that would last at least five years. One early concern was the making of arrangements for Brome, who was still only eleven years of age. Women rarely filled the role of guardian in so patriarchal a society, thus excluding Cornwallis's one surviving sister, Charlotte. Since William Cornwallis was often at sea, the task necessarily fell on James Cornwallis, who in 1781 had become bishop of Lichfield and Coventry. As a pillar of the church, he would hopefully provide the right spiritual and educational environment.

Mary, in contrast, was no longer Cornwallis's responsibility following her marriage to Mark Singleton. He momentarily considered asking the couple to accompany him to India, but eventually accepted their assurances of good behaviour. He accordingly agreed to honour the arrangement to supplement Singleton's income by £400 per annum, payable in quarterly instalments.[6] The rest of the Cornwallis family would informally keep a watchful eye on the couple.

Since Lichfield would also have the management of his estate while he was in India, Cornwallis asked Pitt to make some provision for his brother should he fail to return. This might best be done by securing him the more prestigious bishopric of Durham, once its elderly occupant had died. Cornwallis disapproved of nepotism in these matters, disparaging such appointments as 'jobs', but felt justified on this occasion.[7] Others in any case were not so bashful. Once news of his appointment was known, requests arrived from dignitaries of all description, seeking positions for their relatives and friends. By the time of his departure Cornwallis had received more than 300 such letters.[8] Among the supplicants was Tarleton. However, Tarleton had become a supporter of Fox, making him politically unacceptable to Pitt.[9] To almost all enquirers, Cornwallis gave a courteous refusal, explaining that only current 'servants' of the Company could be considered for a position.[10] Nevertheless, handling such applications was an aspect of the job that would prove tiresome.

Since Lichfield would be busy with his clerical duties and management of Culford Park, Cornwallis decided to engage Dr Wakeham once more to act as Brome's tutor, should his health prevent him returning to Eton. A sense of guilt perhaps induced him to explain more fully to Wakeham the reasons why he was leaving his son for a second time at a tender stage of his life. Pitt and Dundas had insisted that only Cornwallis 'could put an end to the factions' which threatened 'that most valuable part of the empire'. This had made it impossible for him to refuse the appointment. His intention was to stay no longer than five years, though Wakeham should 'tell Brome that it will be only three'. He then emphasised that he was acting solely to benefit his heir. 'I do not mean to plunder India', which was unnecessary since 'the savings of my appointment and estate will make him an independent man'. This was why he was ready to 'sacrifice my own comfort and happiness, but that is nothing. The only real distress I feel is leaving that dear boy.' Nevertheless, he trusted 'in God's mercy' that the mission would 'turn out well'. The reality was that he 'could be of no real use' to Brome while he was at Eton, whereas 'if I live, I shall return by the time he leaves school'.[11] They could then have a meaningful relationship. Such attitudes were the norm among British aristocrats.

Meanwhile, the ministry and East India Company were busy completing their side of the arrangements. Commissions were required from both the crown and Company to make the appointment official. The first one from the king made Cornwallis commander-in-chief of the royal forces in the East Indies.[12] A second from the Directors of the Company placed him in charge of its troops there.[13] The third, also from the Directors, appointed him governor-general 'of all our affairs in the Bay of Bengal and other provinces and places belonging to the Company in the East Indies'.[14] However, his authority in practice would be limited to Bengal, except for relations with foreign powers. The two smaller presidencies of Madras and Bombay were too distant to be administered directly from Calcutta. They would, consequently, retain their own governors and councils.

The ministry's other principal task was to pass legislation to meet Cornwallis's terms for serving in India. The 'Act to Explain and Amend Certain Provisions' incorporated two key articles. The first stated that the governor-general of Bengal, or the governor of the subordinate presidencies of Madras and Bombay, could 'in extraordinary circumstances . . . have discretionary power to overrule the decisions of their respective councils'. The second stated there should be no obstacle to the Company appointing a governor-general who was also commander-in-chief of its forces.[15] The *Morning Chronicle* had earlier noted that these were extraordinary powers, which would not have been entrusted to anyone but Cornwallis.[16] However, the only criticism in Parliament came from Philip Francis, a former Bengal Council member, who suggested that the new appointee would be too busy with the civil administration to control simultaneously the Company's military arm. He elicited little support.[17]

By early April arrangements were sufficiently advanced for Cornwallis to take the oath of office. He did this in a ceremony at East India House, after which the

Directors hosted a lavish dinner, attended by Dundas and the Board of Control.[18] In keeping with the spirit of economical reform, Cornwallis informed his employers that he would only take his salary as governor-general, waiving the stipend of commander-in-chief. He would, however, still be handsomely remunerated, receiving a salary of approximately £25,000, perhaps £2.5 million in today's terms.[19] He was also to be made a knight of the Garter, becoming one of just twenty-seven members of this most exclusive chivalric order.

The following week, on 12 April 1786, Cornwallis received his instructions from the Court of Directors. These covered twenty pages and contained eighty-seven discrete articles. They were to be the guiding principles for Cornwallis's governance over the next seven years. Amidst the detail were three key tasks, which were necessary to meet the requirements of the 1784 India Act. The first was the restoration of the Company to financial health. The strictest economy, therefore, was to be practised to offset the decline in the Company's receipts from the diwani, which were now £1 million less than in 1766. This would mean avoiding wasteful expenditures, streamlining the bureaucracy, and eliminating fraud and corruption. But the Company's financial health also required better ways of collecting the revenue, which placed less reliance on tax farmers, whose rapacity undermined attempts to improve the land and create prosperity. The guiding ethos of the Company's governance was to be one of enlightened self-interest rather than mere exploitation. 'It is entirely our wish that the natives may be encouraged to pursue the occupations of trade and agriculture, by the secure enjoyment of the profits of their industry.' General prosperity should then yield higher tax receipts without burdening the producers.[20]

The second task for Cornwallis was the provision of a more dependable income from the diwani, which varied widely from year to year. The Directors believed this could not be secured by mere improvements to the collection of taxes or elimination of abuses, valuable as they might be. The problem was that the landed zamindar class held their properties at the pleasure of the Mughal emperor, which created uncertainty about who owned the land and what constituted a 'fair revenue'. The solution, the Directors believed, was to confirm the zamindars as the freehold owners of the land, since European practice showed that 'hereditary tenure' was the best security for the payment of such taxes. Once the jumma, or gross amount, had been agreed, the Directors thought this should be made permanent to avoid the disruption of annual settlements. The landowners and subordinate cultivators would then know what was expected of them, giving them confidence to improve their holdings. A fixed settlement would also eliminate the scope for corruption by the Company's employees.[21]

The third key task in Cornwallis's instructions was an overhaul of the civil justice system. As Pitt's India Act noted, 'diverse complaints' had been made by the inhabitants about 'being unjustly deprived of their lands'. 'The principles and honour' of Britain clearly required such complaints to be investigated and 'effectually redressed'.[22] How these issues were addressed was largely left to the new governor-general and his council.[23]

Despite the fullness of these instructions, the inner group of the Directors, known as the Secret Committee, added a couple of confidential directives. Most important was a review of the Company's 'investment' policy. Since the granting of the diwani, the Company had used its surplus revenues to purchase Indian goods for sale in Europe. Over the years the quality of these products had declined while prices had risen. The Secret Committee believed that members of the Bengal Board of Trade, who oversaw the Company's commercial operations, were paying extravagant prices for inferior goods, while keeping the best products for themselves as private traders. Cornwallis was accordingly to investigate such malfeasance, and, where appropriate prepare suits in equity, so that the perpetrators could be sent home and prosecuted. But to ensure better-quality goods at competitive prices, Cornwallis would need to investigate the true costs of production, not just the Company's methods of procurement.[24] This would be no easy undertaking.

Cornwallis was the first governor not to have been an employee of the Company. This brought both advantages and disadvantages. Unlike Hastings, Cornwallis had no obligations to former colleagues or jealous subordinates to contend with. On the other hand, he had no knowledge of the country, its languages, or the office he was to hold. However, he did not want for advice, not least from Hastings himself. The former governor-general had recently returned from India and readily outlined for his successor the structure of the Bengal government, its sources of revenue, and system of justice. He also enlightened Cornwallis about the native powers with whom he would have to deal, notably the Maratha Confederacy headed by the peshwa of Pune, the nizam of Hyderabad, Tipu Sultan of Mysore, and the decrepit

Mughal emperor in Delhi, now a captive of the Maratha warlord Mahadji Scindia.[25] Lastly, he alerted Cornwallis to persons he might trust, while acknowledging that the new appointee must make his own judgements concerning personnel.[26]

The new governor-general was originally to have travelled on a warship, as befitted his status. When the allocated vessel proved unseaworthy, however, Cornwallis decided to take passage on the Company's packet ship, the *Swallow*. As always, he was anxious to start his assignment and was not fussy about how he got there. The packet at least had the advantage of speed. However, delays in producing his commissions meant that he only left London near the end of April. Accompanying him were his personal staff, or military 'family', consisting of Ross, now a full colonel, Captain Henry Haldane, and Cornwallis's nephew, Lieutenant Charles Madan, whom he had taken under his protection at the request of his sister Charlotte. Awaiting them at Portsmouth was John Shore, a senior Company servant of sixteen years' experience, who was returning to India after leave. The intention was that Shore would help Cornwallis with revenue matters until a vacancy occurred on the council.[27] The two men soon established a rapport during the four-month journey, allowing Shore to brief the new governor-general on the tasks awaiting him.[28] He was to prove an invaluable colleague.

Cornwallis and his party boarded their ship on 30 April, though contrary winds detained them until 6 May, when the *Swallow* finally emerged from Spithead into the English Channel.[29] The route took them across the Bay of Biscay and down the west coast of Africa to Saint Helena, where a stop was made to take on water. After this the ship rounded the Cape of Good Hope before heading directly for India. Such a journey could take six months or longer, but Cornwallis was able to report to the Directors on 21 August that he had reached Fort St George in Madras, having enjoyed 'a most expeditious passage'.[30]

Apart from stretching his legs, a stop at Madras gave Cornwallis a chance to acquaint himself with this important, albeit smaller, presidency. He was also able to renew his friendship with its governor, Sir Archibald Campbell, a colleague from the American war. In the 1760s Campbell had been chief engineer at Calcutta, with responsibility for the rebuilding of Fort William, the Company's headquarters. Campbell was hence able to give Cornwallis useful information about the Bengal military establishment. His wife, Lady Amelia, also provided Cornwallis with various medical remedies.[31] Health was necessarily a constant topic for Europeans in a tropical climate.

The *Swallow* finally sailed up the Hooghly River to Calcutta on 12 September 1786, though the last few miles had to be traversed in a smaller boat. Dominating the flat terrain was Campbell's Fort William, a massive stone structure, well calculated to overawe all who saw it. Flanking the fort on three sides were government offices and the residencies of the principal officials, all built of stone in the Georgian style. To the rear was a promenade and small park, where the Company's European employees took their exercise. Finally, to the north lay the native town, a jumble of small dwellings, dark alleys, and open sewers, home to some 200,000 inhabitants.

Waiting on the steps by the fort were two members of the council, Charles Stuart and John Stables, who conducted Cornwallis to Government House. Here he was greeted by Sir John Macpherson, the acting governor-general. Macpherson had already written to Cornwallis, while at Madras, that everything was ready for his reception, including his living quarters. However, he suggested that Cornwallis might prefer accommodation in the garden house, which would be both cooler and quieter. He also advised Cornwallis to avoid temporarily 'the numerous invitations and attentions' that engulfed newcomers. The cooler season was shortly expected, giving him time to become acclimatised and better able to deal with such matters.[32]

However, Macpherson was mistaken if he thought that Cornwallis would opt for a leisurely induction to his new role. Once he had taken the oath of office and read his instructions to his fellow councillors, Macpherson, Stuart, and Stables, he instead immediately assumed control of the government. At their first meeting on 18 September Cornwallis admitted his diffidence about embarking 'on the very arduous undertaking of the government of this country'. Nevertheless, he was greatly encouraged by the promises of support which he had received from his colleagues. He then acknowledged the 'assiduity of the late government in conducting the important business of reform'. Hopefully they would all remain 'motivated by the same principles', since 'the greatest benefits' could only be secured 'from a unanimous council and a vigorous government'.[33]

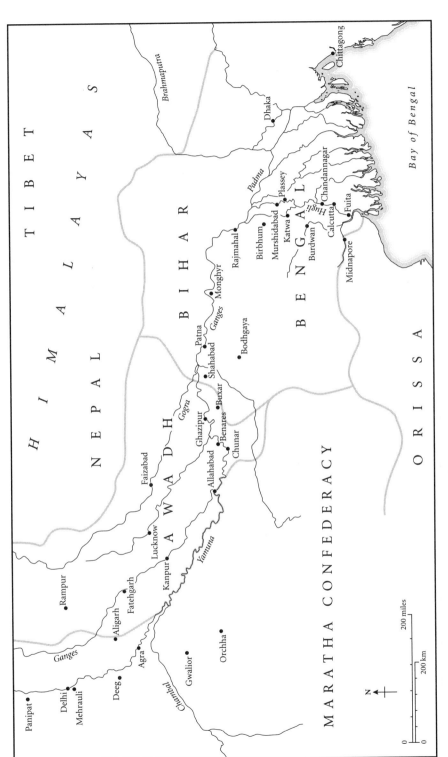

Map 4. Northern India: Bengal and the Ganges Hinterland.

Nevertheless, as Shore later commented to Hastings, Cornwallis's 'situation was uncomfortable' for the first few months.[34] The reasons were not hard to find. First, the instructions of the new governor-general were implicitly critical of the outgoing administration. Second, Cornwallis's appointment was a severe disappointment both to Macpherson and to General Sloper, who was angry at having to retire as commander-in-chief, despite being in poor health and the offer of a handsome pension. Macpherson too resented his supersession. He had lobbied hard to become governor-general himself, and continued to hope that his friends in England would ensure his eventual succession should Cornwallis succumb to the climate. In the meantime, his tactics were to appear accommodating, while doing everything possible to protect his interests. He had already written ingratiating letters to Cornwallis, justifying his conduct and that of his subordinates. He stressed in particular the need to retain the good opinion of the officers of the army. This could best be done by ensuring that they were 'unaffected by any economical orders which the Board of Control may have sent by the *Swallow*'.[35] This was a clear incitement for Cornwallis to ignore his instructions.

Two immediate problems faced the new governor-general, as he informed Dundas on 17 September 1786. The first was an agreement by Macpherson to send three battalions of native sepoy troops to assist the peshwa of Pune, who was at war with Tipu Sultan. Such assistance clearly breached the 1784 India Act, which prohibited the Company from making 'any treaty guaranteeing [the] possessions of the Indian states'.[36] Although Macpherson defended the measure as necessary to prevent the peshwa allying with France, its illegality was indisputable.[37] Since the troops had not yet departed, Cornwallis was able to resolve the situation diplomatically, by explaining to the peshwa's chief minister, Nana Furnuwees, that such a commitment was incompatible with the British constitution. Luckily the Company's representative at Pune, Charles Malet, was a man of ability, well able to smooth things over.[38]

The second, though less obvious, breach of the 1784 Act concerned another Indian prince, the nizam of Hyderabad. Sloper, with Macpherson's concurrence, had dispatched one of his officers, Captain William Monson, to act as a military aide to that monarch, who like the peshwa was at war with Tipu. But as Cornwallis commented to Sydney, the sending of a regular officer to serve in the nizam's army was effectually 'taking part in the war as if we had sent him 10,000 men'. Monson was thus ordered to re-join his regiment immediately.[39]

The incident was embarrassing because Monson was well connected with both the civil and military branches of the Bengal government. It was now that the value of Shore's presence on the voyage to India became apparent. As James Grant later reported from London, everyone in Calcutta had been astonished 'to find [Cornwallis], a stranger just upon [his] arrival, so perfectly well informed about the situation of the Company's affairs' and those with whom he was dealing.[40] His position was further strengthened by his obvious honesty, sense of purpose, and approachability. Even in these first few weeks Shore noted that Cornwallis was not only 'manly, affable and good natured', but possessed of excellent judgement and capacity for business. He was also in good health, a vital element for those wishing to implement change.[41] He would not be easily deterred from the task in hand.

Despite these teething problems, Cornwallis immediately began to address the central aim of his mission, that of restoring the fortunes of the East India Company in Bengal, its most populous and profitable territory. An inspection of the Company's accounts, therefore, was one of the first things he undertook. The Directors were expecting Bengal to produce in the next financial year a profit of 105 lakhs of rupees, approximately £1,050,000 sterling, close to what had been achieved in 1783–84. However, the figures showed that revenues had declined in the past two years to just 77 lakhs (£770,000).[42] Even worse, the latest returns convinced Cornwallis that the yield for 1786–87, after financial support had been given to the Madras and Bombay presidencies, would be only 46 lakhs (£460,000).[43] To meet its target the Company must either massively reduce its costs, improve its revenues, or procure its investment in Indian goods more efficiently.

In time Cornwallis adopted all three strategies. However, for the moment he resolved to concentrate on the management of the Company's 'investment' whereby the diwani receipts were used to purchase Indian goods for shipment to Europe. The proceeds from these sales in turn met the expenses of the Company in England and the payment of dividends to its shareholders. The principal exports were fine muslins, silk cloth, and raw silk, the latter for manufacture back home. Other commodities included saltpetre and indigo.[44]

Since commerce was a field in which Cornwallis had little experience, he asked Charles Grant, one of Stuart's personnel in the commercial department, to review the subject and make recommendations. Cornwallis's preliminary enquiries revealed that two systems had been variously tried for preventing such deterioration. One was the agency method, whereby the Company's own personnel directly supervised the producers. The other was the contract system in which production was left to the local 'dadney' merchants, which had been the custom before 1765. Grant was accordingly to give his opinion on their respective merits.[45]

Grant responded eleven days later with a detailed history of the Company's operations and methods of securing the 'investment'. Until 1750 it had been procured largely through contract with local producers, as befitted a purely commercial concern. However, a decline in quality had led to the merchants being substituted by Company servants, acting as agents. Under this system, Company officials advanced money to the silk and muslin weavers who then produced their goods at an agreed price. To protect the Company's monopoly the weavers were prohibited from dealing with third parties. Unfortunately, the agency method also revealed problems concerning price and quality. In 1773 Hastings consequently returned to using native contractors, though the agency system was not entirely abandoned. Perhaps unsurprisingly, Grant's analysis indicated that there was no perfect system for securing the 'investment'. Both had their drawbacks.[46]

Given the importance of the subject, Cornwallis determined to seek further advice, since Grant had previously been a private trader himself and might have personal interests to protect. He consequently gave similar instructions to John Taylor, the agent at one of the Company's 'aurungs', or factory workshops. Like Grant, Taylor first reviewed the previous modes of operating, either through Company servants acting as agents or native contractors undertaking the whole responsibility. On balance he preferred the practice of the last four years, whereby the Company invited native contractors to make sealed bids after public advertisement. Experience suggested that this method secured the best products at the lowest price.[47] Although Taylor's figures contained some discrepancies, Cornwallis decided to follow his advice and opt for a contract system which was 'open to the fairest bidder', and not just favoured insiders. Agencies were accordingly to be abolished except for the salt and opium monopolies, where it appeared advantageous to keep production in the Company's hands.[48]

While familiarising himself with the Company's accounts and methods of production, Cornwallis realised that its finances were not helped by the cost of borrowing. In 1785 Macpherson had been instructed to repatriate much of the

Company's Indian debt to England to secure a lower rate of interest. The scheme had not worked: few creditors wanted to see their income reduced. Another difficulty was that the Company frequently met deficits in its income by issuing short-term paper certificates or bonds. Any delay in redeeming these inevitably led to their being discounted, necessitating an even higher rate of interest to make the next issue acceptable.[49] The interest rate currently was 8 per cent. In this dilemma, Cornwallis sought help from the General Bank of India, which had been recently formed by a group of retired expatriates. As an experiment, the bank agreed to lend the government 2 lakhs of rupees (£20,000) every week for ten weeks, while the Company in return deposited its daily revenues by way of repayment. The hope was that the short-term debt would be paid off more quickly and at less cost, since the bank charged a lower rate of interest than that on the certificates.[50] Using the bank in this way also promised to lessen the Company's reliance on Indian sources of credit, which appeared demeaning for a sovereign power.

Although Cornwallis's central task was to restore the Company's finances, he recognised that this could only be achieved in conjunction with his other responsibilities as governor-general. More professional, honest personnel were required in the commerce and Revenue Boards. Justice too would be an important arm in the improvement of administrative standards, for until malfeasance and corruption were removed the Company could not prosper. Bad practices were rampant everywhere, as Cornwallis constantly discovered. One early example concerned the engineer corps, who were responsible for military works and other buildings used by the Company. An inspection of their accounts revealed that they charged a commission of 10 per cent for their own benefit on all construction. As its officers were all salaried, Cornwallis immediately raised the impropriety of the practice. The chief engineer, Colonel Thomas McCall, responded that the corps was composed of professional men, unlike the local builders, who were mere adventurers. He also argued that charging a commission was the only way of providing for their retirement. However, he conceded that abuses existed which needed correcting.[51] Another early reprimand was that issued to Edward Hay, the secretary to the council, who, Cornwallis discovered, had an interest in a local bank.[52] In future Hay and his staff must abstain from all activities other than those necessary for the performance of their office. This was essential to avoid conflicts of interest.[53]

Despite the pressure of business, Cornwallis maintained an extensive correspondence with his family and friends, though communication was necessarily intermittent.[54] A one-way journey by sea round the Cape normally took from four to six months, while the more direct overland route between the Mediterranean and the Persian Gulf via Aleppo and Baghdad was subject to disruption by banditti and unsympathetic Turkish officials. Although peace in Europe meant that travel by sea was relatively safe, sailings were necessarily constrained by climatic conditions, especially the need to avoid the monsoon season. Packet ships in consequence only sailed every six months, and the Company's merchant Indiamen were no more frequent.

Cornwallis wrote his first letters home a few days after arriving at Calcutta. To Brome he stressed that he was always thinking of him and was concerned for his well-being. Providing Brome remained in good health, 'I am sure everything else will be right.' He emphasised the importance of their correspondence: 'You must write to me by every opportunity, and longer letters than I write to you, for I have a great deal more business every day . . . and I never get a holiday.' He concluded by describing his first ride on an elephant. He had not been impressed, since sitting in a wicker basket created the impression of travelling in a cart.[55] In a second later letter three months later, Cornwallis was more jocular, especially on the topic of his recent award of the Garter, not doubting that Brome would be amused at the thought of the blue ribbon adorning 'my fat belly'. But Brome could be assured that Cornwallis had 'neither asked' for the award, 'nor wished for it'. It was sufficient ambition for a man 'to have his name transmitted to posterity for eminent services . . . to his country and to mankind'. Nobody cared whether John Hampden, the duke of Marlborough or James Wolfe were knights of the Garter. His fervent hope was 'that God may bless you and preserve you to be my comfort', for this was 'almost the only prayer of your truly affectionate father'.[56]

To Lichfield, Cornwallis naturally adopted a more adult style. In his first brief letter, he expressed his determination to live frugally so that he could remit money for his family in England. The Company had arranged to pay half his salary in cash and half in Company certificates. The latter were currently trading at a discount of 13 per cent.[57] Two months later he wrote again more discursively. The weather was cooler and he remained in good health. Bengal bore a peaceable aspect, making him 'believe that by strict economy and rigid integrity the affairs of the East' could be rectified, 'unless some unforeseen misfortune should occur'. Nevertheless, being governor-general was intrinsically disagreeable, since he was 'obliged to do many things that appear very hard', thereby making enemies. He was also disconcerted by his continued inability to remit money to Lichfield, as he had earlier promised. The problem was that his certificates could only be sold at a great loss while the gap between their issue and redemption at par by the Company was fourteen or fifteen months. Meanwhile, expenses were ever present, not least for his household, where considerable quantities of claret were daily consumed at dinner. He had already had to order another thirty casks from his supplier in England.[58]

During these first few months, Cornwallis had been quietly executing the Secret Committee's directive to investigate the activities of the Bengal Board of Trade, especially regarding silk. According to William Hickey, a local lawyer, much incriminating evidence was being secured through secret agents.[59] In reality most of it was obtained from the board's own papers by Jonathan Davies, the advocate-general, who was proving a formidable ally in the battle to root out corruption.[60] His investigations clearly showed that the 'grossest frauds' had been committed due to Macpherson's laxity. Any pretensions by the former acting governor-general to effecting economy and good practice had been at best a delusion.[61]

Davies accordingly set to work preparing bills in equity or indictments against several members of the Bengal Board of Trade.[62] These allowed Cornwallis to announce in mid-January 1787 their suspension from office pending legal action.[63] Their removal then raised the question of who should succeed them. Among the possible candidates was Charles Grant.[64] Initially his appointment appeared questionable, because of his previous connections as a silk contractor and acknowledgement that, during his early years in India, he had lived in a society where 'many reprobated things' had been done. However, he had subsequently undergone a religious conversion and after his appointment he quickly proved a classic case of the poacher turned gamekeeper.[65] Within twelve months Cornwallis was telling the Directors that Grant's conduct at the Board of Trade had shown him 'to be one of the most able and valuable men in the service'.[66] The Company came to think so too, making him a director in 1795 and chairman ten years later.

But even at this early stage, Cornwallis was opposed to any large-scale purge of the Company's personnel. He told the Secret Committee on 23 January 1787: 'I have the highest opinion of the integrity and ability of many of the Company's servants upon this establishment.' If others had failed the Company, it was 'more from want of fortitude to resist the contagion of example than from total depravity of character'. Leniency, therefore, might be the best policy, since 'the prevention of future abuses' was more important than punishing past misdemeanours. Hopefully the current prosecutions would suffice.[67]

Much of Cornwallis's governorship in these first months had been spent assessing the Company's situation as the prelude to implementing the reforms required by the Directors. Progress had not been helped by difficulties with his council and the military establishment. However, as the New Year opened Cornwallis could look forward to improvement in both departments. Sloper was too ill to dispute his recall, while Macpherson realised that his reputation in Calcutta was seriously compromised. As Shore commented to Dundas: 'never was any administration so thoroughly despicable as his', in showing 'a total want of energy, dignity and common sense'.[68] If Macpherson was to advance his cause to be reappointed as governor-general, he would have to do so elsewhere.

Sloper was the first to depart at the end of December 1786. Since he had not been charged with wrongdoing, Cornwallis felt obliged to make the customary eulogy on his departure, though it went much against the grain, knowing that he would shortly have to do the same for Macpherson.[69] But distaste turned to anger when he learnt six weeks later that Sloper had sanctioned the raising of a regiment by his son for service with Asaf-ud-Daula, the nawab wazir of Awadh (Oudh). Since the nawab wazir was a dependant of the Company, there had been no breach of the 1784 India Act. However, Sloper's son had received £8,000 without enlisting a single officer or private. The stench of fraud was hard to disguise, making Cornwallis lament his earlier generosity to the father.[70]

Macpherson finally left Bengal in early February 1787 aboard the packet ship *Berrington*, bound for the Cape of Good Hope, where he proposed to stay some time for the benefit of his health.[71] The real reason was that he could still receive his salary as a member of the council if he stayed on the Indian Ocean side of the Cape.[72] Nevertheless the two men parted amicably, for as Cornwallis acknowledged to

Dundas, he felt obligated to Macpherson for his good humour, even though he was 'unfit to be the Governor and very tiresome in business'.[73]

The departure of Macpherson now opened the way for Shore's appointment to the council. Earlier, Shore's chronic ill health had led Cornwallis to fear that he might have to leave India. If this should happen, he told Dundas, it would 'be a most serious public loss, and to me a greater disappointment than I can describe'.[74] Fortunately, his health was much improved by the end of 1786.[75] Since Stables, the fourth member of the Council, had also decided to go home, Cornwallis could look forward to a harmonious executive, as the only other councillor, Charles Stuart, appeared to be 'an honourable, good-tempered man, perfectly well disposed to me, and zealous for the public good'.[76]

Cornwallis immediately placed Shore at the head of the Revenue Board, since he was familiar with that department and had long wanted to reform it.[77] His appointment also conformed with the Company's wishes. Stuart in consequence would remain in charge of the commercial department, which included the Board of Trade. Cornwallis made these arrangements seemingly unaware that Stuart thought that he should have been appointed to the Revenue as the senior councillor.[78] Cornwallis attempted to appease Stuart by giving him more control over appointments, but it was to be the start of an uneasy relationship.[79]

EIGHT

Setting the Agenda

Within weeks of Cornwallis's landing Shore observed that the new governor-general had 'a degree of application to business beyond what you would suppose'.[1] Cornwallis himself ascribed his administrative effectiveness to a routine which ran like 'perfect clockwork'. The day began, he told Brome, at dawn with an early morning ride 'on the same road and [of] the same distance'. The entire morning was then devoted to business until noon when 'almost exactly the same portion of time' was spent 'every day at table'. However, according to Hickey, who had befriended Cornwallis's aide, Captain John Apsley, dinner was served with 'scrupulous exactness' at 3 p.m. in the cooler months, and at 4 p.m. during the summer. The duration was always two hours.[2] Apart from being the main meal of the day, dinner at Government House was a time when matters could be discussed informally during the hottest part of the day. It was also a chance to oil the machinery of government by inviting to dine those whose good opinion Cornwallis wished to cultivate. Towards sunset he took a ride in a phaeton (a small open carriage) before spending two hours on official letters and papers. About nine he would be joined by Ross, Haldane, Apsley, and Madan for an hour, to eat fruit and biscuits before retiring for the night. He concluded by telling Brome: 'I don't think the greatest sap [drudge] at Eton can lead a duller life than this'.[3] The contrast with his life in England, let alone America, could not have been greater.

Office mornings were normally spent with Company officials and others seeking direction on public matters. Anyone desiring a private audience was advised to appear on a Tuesday or Thursday, but only after making a written submission, to ensure that Cornwallis was properly briefed.[4] The morning was also the time when he customarily received 'such petitions as the natives have to present to him', though not before Ross or other aides had directed them 'to the proper office where their business is to be transacted'. Personal audiences were not generally granted to Indians, though members of the educated upper classes might do so with the assistance of Mr Cherry, the Persian translator.[5] Shore later observed that the Indian inhabitants always acknowledged Cornwallis's good intentions. However, 'the mode in which he conveyed' his decision 'was not always what they themselves would have chosen'.[6] Unlike his predecessors, Cornwallis spoke no Persian, Urdu, or Bengali, which made conversation inevitably stilted.

The reception of foreign dignitaries naturally required different procedures, though the protocols for such visits were often unclear. In early January 1787 Cornwallis received a visit from Haidar Beg Khan, the chief minister of the nawab wazir. Since the nawab wazir was a dependent prince of the Company, Khan could not be accorded the same status as the envoy of an independent ruler. Cornwallis sensibly turned for advice to those 'more versant in eastern ceremony', not least regarding 'the number of guns to be fired as a salute'. He eventually settled for the dispatch of an aide to greet the minister, after which he would be offered breakfast with Cornwallis in Fort William.[7]

Inevitably many matters of minor importance were also referred to Cornwallis for a decision. Company regulations required all employees to obtain his permission before marrying. This included confirmation by the minister performing the ceremony.[8] But wherever possible Cornwallis tried to delegate routine matters to subordinates, telling the adjutant-general shortly after his arrival not to consult him about the deployment of every sepoy guard.[9]

Though Cornwallis worked a seven-day week, he necessarily spent time socialising at official engagements and public entertainments. Shore, a similar workaholic, noted in early 1787 that there were 'balls every week', though Shore had only been to a private one 'given by Lord Cornwallis'. He had also not 'yet attended one play'.[10] Other senior members of the administration were not so abstemious; Stuart organised a concert one evening which included an outdoor supper. But Cornwallis generally limited his appearance at these functions, unless it was an official event to celebrate the monarchs' birthdays or the start of the New Year, when he entertained in style. One such function was sufficiently elegant to merit comment in the London newspapers.[11]

One reason for refusing private invitations was to prevent undue familiarity by subordinates. He was undoubtedly strengthened in this resolve after an early dinner party organised by William Burke, the paymaster of the forces. Hickey noted that the new governor-general was a man of 'engaging manners and great affability'. However, after 'a cheerful dinner', at which a good deal of wine was consumed, Cornwallis called for his carriage, whereupon Burke protested vehemently at so premature an end to the proceedings. 'His Lordship remonstrated [that] . . . he had already drunk too much, indeed more than he had done for years; that having much business of importance to attend to, he must not run the risk of incapacitating himself.' Burke inevitably had to release his guest, but only after Cornwallis agreed that Ross and Haldane should remain. He then drove off 'alone without any trooper or even a single servant behind the carriage'. Hickey noted that, 'after his escape', Cornwallis never dined away from home except with the chief justice or someone of similar gravitas.[12]

Nevertheless, Cornwallis entertained generously, as Hickey noted when dining at Government House, where he hosted daily between twenty and twenty-five persons, during which the bottles of claret were in constant circulation. 'If anyone inadvertently stopped their progress . . . His Lordship instantly attacked the defaulter to "pass the wine".'[13] However, one festivity which he abandoned was the annual Christmas dinner and ball. In his view the day ought to be celebrated as a purely religious occasion rather than in 'feasting and mirth'. He particularly objected to dancing. So began a tradition of not holding any public dinner or entertainment in Calcutta on Christmas Day.[14]

Cornwallis's social life was complemented by membership of several clubs and societies. One, established in 1790, was for Eton alumni living in Calcutta. However, the most notable outside organisation was the Asiatic Society which Sir William Jones, a judge of the Supreme Court, had established in 1784 under Hastings's patronage. The society's purpose was to advance knowledge of Indian culture. Hastings and Jones believed that India had once enjoyed a golden age, before it had been lost through corruption. Cornwallis was not entirely convinced by these arguments. Nevertheless, he recognised that such knowledge would allow a more enlightened administration of the Company's responsibilities to the indigenous inhabitants. He readily agreed, therefore, to become patron of the society and made a point of attending Jones's principal lectures.[15] It was for similar reasons that he later supported Jonathan Duncan's proposal to establish a Hindu College in Benares (modern-day Varanasi) for 'the preservation and cultivation of the laws, literature and religion of that nation'. Such institution, located at the centre of the Hindu faith, might better reconcile Indians to British rule and help in the administration of justice.[16]

With a more congenial council in place, Cornwallis could now resume his mission of restoring the Company's financial health. So far, he had investigated the contract and agency systems in an attempt to improve its commercial activities. Now, in early 1787, he decided to inspect the methods for collecting its revenues. The need to do so was emphasised by another inspection of the Company's accounts, which revealed that the Bengal Treasury was haemorrhaging money to support the Madras and Bombay presidencies.[17]

The Company in Bengal had three main sources of revenue: the yield from the diwani; the income from certain monopolies like salt; and the revenues from internal customs, or the 'sayer' duties, as they were called. The diwani was the most profitable of these, and since 1765 had been the main source of income for the Company's investment. As the annual yield had proved unreliable, Cornwallis's instructions of 12 April 1786 directed him to conclude a fixed permanent revenue settlement with the native landowners.[18] But before undertaking any such step, he recognised that more information was required about the workings of the diwani system under the Mughal emperors. This was a matter for Shore and his colleagues at the Revenue Board.

Accordingly, within days of his appointment, Shore issued a circular letter, dated 20 February 1787, requiring the Company's tax-collectors in the thirty-seven revenue districts to prepare the necessary materials for 'concluding a settlement for a long term of years'. However, implementing such a scheme, Cornwallis advised the Directors, would take time, even with Shore's 'uncommon abilities and experience'. A year would likely be necessary to ensure 'a due regard to the cases of individuals, and to the just rights of the Company'.[19]

The first to respond was Robert Bathurst, the collector for Burdwan (modern-day Bardhaman) district. He explained that much of the diwani tax-collecting was done by the native landholders who extorted as much as they could from their inferiors without necessarily forwarding the proceeds to the government. Hence, the zamindars (the largest landholders) taxed the aumils (the lesser renters) and they in turn levied what they could from the talukdars (the large farmers). At the end of this chain of extortion were the peasant raiyats, who constituted the mass of the population. Levying a fixed sum from these different classes, Bathurst agreed, would be highly beneficial, clarifying what the government could expect, while protecting the luckless raiyats from even greater exactions. He would accordingly send the required information 'with as much dispatch' as was possible.[20] But he too cautioned about the size of the task. This was confirmed by the discovery that the zamindars were committing even wider frauds than previously thought, as Cornwallis informed Dundas on 17 May 1787. In these circumstances it might be prudent to limit any settlement initially to ten years, rather than making it immediately permanent.[21]

While enquiring into the Company's tax revenues, Shore also considered the structure of the Revenue Board itself, with a view to reducing costs in accordance with Pitt's 1784 India Act. Shore's investigations quickly showed that considerable economies could be achieved, most importantly by reducing the number of revenue collectors, who were responsible for securing payment of the diwani in each district. Macpherson had previously attempted to do this in compliance with Pitt's Act. However, he then reversed the policy following protests by those being made redundant. As a result, the number of collectors and their staff actually increased.[22] With Cornwallis and Shore in charge, no such remission would be allowed. From March 1787 the number of collectors was reduced from thirty-seven to twenty-four, based on the calculation that every district should produce revenues of at least 5 lakhs of rupees (£50,000). The surviving districts too were not exempt from substantial pruning of their staffs, resulting in 'many civil servants' being 'totally unprovided for and in great distress', as Cornwallis informed Dundas. The Directors must consequently refrain from 'sending out any writers', meaning administrative personnel, until those displaced had found new positions.[23]

One effect of the reductions was a rapid change of attitude among those still employed. Robert Potts, at Murshidabad, quickly assured Cornwallis that he had never retained monies due to the government, nor shown partiality to anyone soliciting favours, and he challenged anyone to accuse him of 'a single act of venality, oppression, indelicacy or disrespect'.[24] His assertions of innocence did him no favours, since the evidence was too strong to the contrary. Archibald Seton, the collector for Calcutta, tried a different tactic to save his skin. He explained that he had merely followed the practice of his predecessors in taking fees. Would Cornwallis give him guidance on how to act 'in the light of recent parliamentary legislation on India'?[25] This proved a more effective way of averting Cornwallis's displeasure, given his inclination to avoid the wholesale dismissal of officials who had merely conformed to the previous culture of the Company. The key thing was that they now realised that new standards had been established for the conduct of public business, which must be observed.

However, to make the Revenue Department more efficient required not only the dismissal of redundant or corrupt staff, but also the appointment of better qualified persons. Cornwallis had made a significant start on first taking office in refusing to make appointments solely on the basis of personal patronage. Candidates now had to be of the right age and ready to serve an apprenticeship before attaining positions of responsibility. This in itself was something of a revolution, as Shore commented to Hastings. The result was a new sense of 'vigour, consistency and dignity' in Government House. 'The system of patronage which you so justly reprobated and which you always found so grievous a tax, has been entirely subverted.' The council, 'relieved from the torture of private solicitations', now had 'more time to attend to their public duties'. The expenses of government were also being 'kept within their established bounds' by the reductions in personnel. Of course, this meant that Shore could 'no longer gratify his own friends', since he was 'precluded from making any solicitations but such as are warranted by the strictest propriety'.[26]

Even so, some personal favours could not be denied. In the middle of 1787 Cornwallis received a request from Queen Charlotte regarding a Mr Ritso, who had arrived in Calcutta without the Company's permission. This breached Article 23 of the 1784 India Act, which prohibited all appointments other than those from its own personnel.[27] Initially, Cornwallis attempted to resist the application, telling Sydney there was 'too much at stake': he could not abandon 'the only system that can save this country, even for Her Sacred Majesty'.[28] Nevertheless, he eventually found it diplomatic to offer Ritso a position in the council office, though on a very modest monthly salary of 250 rupees (£25).[29] Others were not so lucky, as a Mr Burton discovered when he arrived contemporaneously with Ritso. What surprised Cornwallis was Burton's feigned ignorance that he required the Company's permission to come to India, since his brother had previously been sent home for that very reason.[30] But Cornwallis was even more annoyed by another fortune-seeker, who pretended he had come with Cornwallis's consent. 'After having refused the earnest entreaties of many of my nearest relations and best friends', was it probable 'that I should have given you such a preference?' Unless the young man immediately returned to England, Cornwallis would be under the necessity of forcing him to do so.[31]

Although Cornwallis favoured leniency regarding past misdemeanours, some offences were too serious to overlook. By August 1787 the case against six of members of the Bengal Board of Trade was sufficiently proven for them to be formally dismissed as the prelude to legal proceedings.[32] Action was also pending against several merchants dealing in fine muslins at Dakha, Bengal's second most important centre of commerce, where John Kennaway, one of Charles Grant's officers, had uncovered a 'maze of evils'. Particularly disquieting was the contractors' treatment of their weavers, who were not only kept in a state of 'total dependence', but were forced to work for 24 per cent less than what they were reputedly paid. Unsurprisingly, the quality of their goods had deteriorated.[33]

Kennaway's investigations raised the issue once more of how the Company could best conduct its commercial business, whether by contract with native merchants or by employing its own personnel as commercial agents. Following his discussions with Grant and Taylor, Cornwallis had been inclined to favour the contract system (see above, pp. 143–4). The revelations from Dakha now convinced him that the agency system was preferable, since it was 'impossible to make advantageous contracts without authorizing the oppression' of the weavers. Apart from considerations of humanity, Cornwallis was convinced that 'it can never tend to the general interest of any government to oppress its subjects'. But the agency system too had its drawbacks, not least that of finding suitable personnel. It was essential, therefore, that Grant found 'some good young men in the commercial line'.[34]

Unfortunately, this was no easy task, as Grant noted when looking for replacements for the Board of Trade.[35] The problem was that there was no recognised system of appointment other than that of personal recommendation. A civil service commission to oversee entry by competitive examination was still sixty years away. Seniority of course remained one method of making appointments, except that could limit the advancement of talent. On the other hand, experience was equally important. It was for this reason that Cornwallis, with the council's agreement, determined in July 1787 that collectors of the revenue in future, unless of exceptional merit, should not be appointed without the benefit of twelve years' experience.[36] But this did not solve the conundrum of whom to choose among those of equal service. The governor-general and council still had to rely on their own judgement or that of trusted colleagues to fill such positions.

Another key to improving the calibre of the Company's servants, Cornwallis believed, was proper remuneration. Only this would secure able people and remove the danger of corruption. He felt such a requirement was particularly applicable to the office of collector, whose powers now included that of magistrate for their respective districts. This change had been included in Cornwallis's instructions of 12 April 1786, as a way of improving the administration of the civil law. But Cornwallis considered the salary issue so important as a general principle that he wrote several further letters on the subject, both to the Directors and to Dundas. He told Dundas: 'I am doing everything I can to reform the Company's servants, to teach them to be more economical in their mode of living, and to look forward to a moderate competency'. However, 'if all chance of saving' for their return to England was removed, unless they acted dishonestly, 'there will be an end of my reformation'. The former practice of paying small salaries and allowing Company personnel to provide for themselves in other ways had led to the abuses that were now condemned. Admittedly, better remuneration would involve additional expense, yet, as Cornwallis pointed out to the Company, he had already made savings on 'various contracts, upon remittances, balances, and jobs of different kinds', which were many times the value of the salaries that the Directors seemingly opposed. It would be money well spent if they wanted to be served by more dedicated and honest personnel.[37]

Clearly, much still had to be done to establish an honest, efficient bureaucracy. Many collectors continued to be involved in trade, courtesy of their relations or friends, though Cornwallis was determined to 'make an example of the first offender' found breaking the new rules.[38] But, as he wearily conceded to the Directors the following year, his former profession as a soldier had ill prepared him for such investigative tasks.[39]

Busy as Cornwallis was managing the Company's civil affairs in Bengal, he also had to supervise its military establishment and corps of British regulars in the three presidencies. Together they constituted one of the largest armed forces outside Europe, with a peacetime strength of 70,000 men. Of these, the king's troops comprised one cavalry and five infantry regiments, with a nominal strength of 5,900 men, though they were 2,000 short of this figure. The Company's nine British regiments had a formal establishment of 6,000 men, but they too were a third under strength.[40] Both corps had substantial artillery complements, amounting in total to 2,500 men. This meant that by far the most numerous corps available to the Company were the sepoy native troops, who were organised into seventy-five infantry and cavalry battalions, totalling approximately 55,000 men. All were up to strength.[41]

Although a reform of the Company's army was not officially part of Cornwallis's remit, it was high on Dundas's agenda. He had three principal reasons. The first was the disproportionate number of sepoys, whose loyalty might one day be questioned. The second was his belief that a private military force was contrary to the British constitution, given the country's traditional abhorrence of standing armies. His third objection was that having two separate establishments led to friction and the ineffective use of resources. Dundas believed that most of these problems could be solved by merging and strengthening the two British corps, leaving the sepoys as they were, except that they too would be under the crown's control.[42] But what did the new governor-general think?

Cornwallis certainly found much to dislike about the existing establishment, as he reported to the duke of York shortly after arriving in India. The royal regiments appeared to be in a commendable state, despite the climate and want of recruits. The Company's artillery was also praiseworthy, while the sepoys were physically equal to the best infantry of Europe, and seemingly capable of great endurance, if disciplined properly. Regrettably, the Company's 'European infantry, on whom the defence of these valuable possession may one day depend', were 'in a most wretched state', both as to their physical condition and discipline. One problem was that the officers lacked career incentives. Promotion was by strict seniority, while the most lucrative posts went to those with influence. Merit consequently went unrewarded. Finally, the officers, lacking any provision for their retirement and weakened by the rigours of a hot climate, all too readily engaged in private commercial activities that were repugnant to a professional soldier.[43] The conclusion was inescapable, as he informed Dundas in November 1786: 'The army is in a most shocking state, and will require my utmost exertions.'[44]

The question was where to start, since by February 1787 Cornwallis doubted the efficacy of Dundas's proposed merging of the Company's European troops with the regulars. He was inclined instead towards measures to improve the existing corps. First, if the Company could enlist men in England in the same manner as the regular regiments, under the terms of the Mutiny Act, a better quality of recruit might be obtained. Currently recruitment was left to crimps, or private agents, who enlisted society's rejects whenever a Company ship was about to sail for India. Second, if an equality of rank between the officers of the two forces could be agreed, the existing jealousies should subside. This might be achieved by making the date of an officer's commission the key to determining seniority when men of equal rank were serving together.[45]

But other matters needed to be addressed, if the Company's European forces were to be effective. One was absenteeism, because their officers were often allowed inordinate leave in England. This was exacerbated by the rule that promotion must be by seniority, as the recent case of a Captain Brooke demonstrated. Brooke remained in England for twelve years, only to return to India as a lieutenant-colonel.[46] Such conduct was naturally destructive of morale among those officers who had remained at their posts. Cornwallis accordingly suggested to Dundas in early March 1787 that those going home on leave must return within three years and then only on the rank they were entitled to, had they stayed in India.[47]

So far Cornwallis had limited his discussion of these issues to Dundas. However, the defects seemed so serious that he decided to raise them directly with the Company itself, outlining his proposed reforms to remedy the situation. In a long letter dated 18 August 1787, he informed the Directors that only their artillery matched the standards of the regulars. Otherwise, he had good reason to believe that both 'in quality of men, as well as in discipline', the Company's European forces were 'extremely inferior' to those of the king. The danger was that 'without a large and well-regulated body of Europeans, our hold on these valuable dominions must be very insecure'. Relying on the sepoys could not be wise in the long run, since even the most enlightened government was unlikely to retain 'the willing obedience of so vast a body of people, differing from ourselves in almost every circumstance of laws, religion and customs'.[48]

The royal forces, in contrast, were in a good condition, except for their depleted ranks. The most contentious issue was that of officer promotion, because vacancies through death or resignation had to be referred back to London for the king to decide. This normally took fifteen to eighteen months, creating much frustration. Cornwallis assured the king's military secretary, Sir William Fawcett, that he had no wish to control military patronage. Nevertheless, the authorities must realise how discouraging it was for the existing personnel, when posts remained unfilled for long periods. At the very least Cornwallis should have authority to fill positions temporarily.[49] The sense of this proposal was duly recognised, though it took two years to implement.[50]

Another of Cornwallis's military duties was the reviewing of courts-martial proceedings. He found some verdicts astonishing, especially when one court accepted a plea of intoxication in mitigation of a soldier's misconduct. Such reasoning was contrary to universal practice and would 'destroy civil society' if allowed to continue. Individuals must be responsible for their actions. The president of the court was accordingly to inform his colleagues of their aberration and of the need to reject such pleas in future.[51] But Cornwallis was equally appalled by a verdict in Bombay, where an ensign had assaulted two Indian merchants when they requested the payment of a debt. The subsequent court-martial had simply dismissed the charge because the defendant was a British officer. Cornwallis promptly pointed out to the governor in Bombay that the court's action was equally 'incompatible with the true principles of military discipline', as with the dictates of 'morality and justice'. Such verdicts would injure 'the interests of the Company and the credit of the [British] nation with the natives of India'. The governor, consequently, was to charge the members of the court for 'refusing to administer justice according to the articles of war'.[52] Common humanity also led him to recommend that Campbell ameliorate a sentence of 2,000 lashes on one delinquent at Madras. Such punishment was absurd in any country, especially in a climate like India's.[53]

Before leaving England, George III had instructed Cornwallis to establish a botanical garden in Bengal, similar to the one that had been created in the West Indies on Saint Vincent. The king's plan was to exchange the flora of the two regions for the benefit of both, as the French had recently attempted to do. The scheme was supported by the eminent botanist Sir Joseph Banks.[54] Accordingly, shortly after his arrival Cornwallis appointed Colonel Robert Kyd to take charge. Early in 1787 Sir George Yonge, the secretary at war, informed Cornwallis that the king had commissioned an armed merchantman, HMS *Bounty*, under the command of Captain William Bligh, to sail to the East Indies to collect breadfruit plants. On its way back the vessel would collect other specimens from India, before sailing for Saint Vincent, where the breadfruit were to be grown for the feeding of slaves. The *Bounty* would then sail eastwards once more, carrying suitable plants from the West Indies for cultivation in Bengal.[55] By the time this news reached Bengal in September 1787, Kyd had not only started the king's botanical garden near Calcutta, but successfully imported mango plants from Penang, suggesting that Cornwallis should sample the fruit. He had also received some 'gummatty' trees, which produced a substance from which the 'most elastic and durable cables' could be made.[56] Cornwallis's response to this information was not recorded, nor was his reaction to the failure of the *Bounty* to appear. Other more important matters had interposed.

During Cornwallis's stay at Madras on his arrival in India, Campbell had talked about the value of a visit he had made to the interior of his presidency. This prompted Cornwallis to consider a similar journey along the Ganges to the Awadh frontier stations of Kanpur, Fatehgarh, and Lucknow.[57] Several objectives might be served thereby. It would enable him to ensure that the regiments in the interior were fit for service. He could also inspect the condition of Benares, where complaints had been received about the Company's resident or ambassador, a Mr James Grant.[58] Lastly, it would be an opportunity to discuss with the nawab wazir the defence of Awadh and its future relationship to the Company.[59] His plan was to set out in early August 1787 and to return by the New Year.[60]

The timing seemed propitious for such a project. Peace had been concluded between the Maratha Confederacy and Tipu Sultan, while Mahadji Scindia, the most likely threat to British interests in the north, was having difficulty paying his army.[61] But first Cornwallis had to settle arrangements for the government in Calcutta during his absence. Stuart, as the senior member of the council, would expect to be in charge. Cornwallis was anxious to avoid this, given their already uneasy relationship. His solution was to make each councillor responsible for his own department, reporting to him individually rather than collectively as a governing body.

Cornwallis was in good spirits when he left Calcutta on 29 July 1787 for his 2,200-mile round trip. One reason, he told Lichfield, was his continued good health, though the 'prickly heat' of the Bengal summer had given him itchy hands, which cooler weather would hopefully alleviate. Another cause for optimism was his sense that he carried with him the 'approbation' of the whole settlement. He admitted this might be vanity. Nevertheless, it was 'not only the cry of triumph from the honest part of the service' that he could hear. 'The delinquents' too were asserting that they would 'not have lost their characters' had they been fortunate enough to have served their whole time under a government like Cornwallis's. The improving credit of the Company also induced a sense of optimism, since the diminishing discount on the Company's certificates benefited him financially. Lichfield, therefore, should have no hesitation in purchasing Wordwell, a small estate adjoining Culford Park, which had come on the market.[62]

A week later Cornwallis reached Benares, his first major stop. Correspondence about the abject state of the province had caught his attention in March 1787, suggesting 'the grossest corruption and mismanagement'. However, he preferred to suspend judgement until he could see for himself.[63] Much of the controversy centred on the accusations of the rajah of Benares that Grant, the current resident, had misused his position to control the city's trade.[64] Initially Grant claimed he was innocent and even deserving of promotion to the Revenue Board.[65] Yet the more he protested the more incompatible his position appeared. The evidence showed that he had not only extorted money from the rajah, but also established monopolies in the manufacture of opium and refined sugar, 'all to the great injury of those branches of commerce'.[66]

The complaints of the rajah soon convinced Cornwallis of the need for action, both to avoid further harm to the prosperity of the city and to improve its revenues. Not only was Grant to be dismissed, but his successor was to be 'restricted to a fixed and specific allowance' to prevent similar extortion in the future. Cornwallis took this action with some confidence, believing that he had found in Jonathan Duncan, a Company servant since 1772, someone who was eminently qualified for promoting 'the true interest and happiness of the rajah' and its inhabitants. Benares was 'a great place of pilgrimage and its management to a flourishing state would acquire for the Company a reputation in all Hindustan' [India]. Duncan was accordingly to make appropriate recommendations for regulating its commerce and the administration of justice.[67] Cornwallis already had him marked for even greater responsibility.

Shortly after leaving Benares, Cornwallis heard from Campbell that Tipu Sultan was planning to invade Madras with French help. Should this happen, it was essential that the Maratha Confederacy be aligned in support.[68] But despite Campbell's certainty about the danger, Cornwallis doubted that the French at Pondicherry had authority to open hostilities, or that Tipu would be rash enough to strike alone. Nevertheless, it was right to take precautions, even though such measures would undermine Cornwallis's efforts to restore the Company's finances.[69] In the event his scepticism was merited. Tipu remained in Mysore, though his ultimate intentions were obscure. Cornwallis had wanted to open a dialogue with him on first arriving in India, and proposed to do so 'at the first opportunity'.[70] In the meantime, proper precautions were to be observed, in case Tipu made a pre-emptive attack.

Cornwallis's next stop was Allahabad, the capital of Awadh province. Here he was welcomed by the nawab wazir Asaf-ud-Daula. Awadh had become a dependency of the Company following the Battle of Buxar in October 1764. Subsequent treaties made the Company responsible for defending the province, while the nawab wazir controlled its internal administration. This included levying the taxes to pay for the costs of the British garrison.[71] The arrangement had not worked well for either party. The reason, Cornwallis believed, was that the current agreement allowed 'rapacious individuals' to exploit the nawab wazir 'to the great prejudice of the Company' and its investment. The problems were exacerbated by the Nawab's indifference to commercial matters. This was especially true of customs duties, from which he exempted many traders, resulting in 'the most scandalous frauds and oppressions'.[72]

Prior to his visit, Cornwallis had dispatched a trusted revenue officer, George Barlow, to investigate. Barlow's findings indicated that the current system was indeed of little value to the Company and its investment. It would be better for both sides if a new treaty was concluded, allowing commerce to move more freely along the

Ganges and thereby benefiting the whole region. Though duties would still be levied, the trade should be conducted at fixed published rates rather than under the current random extortions. The consequent 'affluence which the treaty would afford to the merchants' of both parties would surely be of more value than the current agreement, which allowed the Company to purchase 'a few cloths for their European investment'.[73] Barlow's proposals for a freer trade were a testimony to the increasing influence of Adam Smith's *Wealth of Nations*.

Cornwallis readily agreed to Barlow's ideas, telling Dundas enthusiastically of their author's abilities and those of his colleague, Thomas Law.[74] He accordingly used his visit to Allahabad to start negotiations for a new treaty. He began by repeating what he had previously written in April: that he wanted to restore the relationship to what it should have been after Buxar, whereby the Company defended the province while the nawab controlled its internal management. The Company's interests thereafter would be limited to the receipt of 50 lakhs of rupees (£500,000) for the garrisons at Lucknow and Fatehgarh.[75] As part of this new disengagement, the Company would not seek any investment from Awadh. Instead, a commercial treaty should be negotiated, establishing 'a free trade' to the mutual benefit of both. But to achieve the desired improvements, it was essential that no special privileges or exemptions were given to any private individuals, since these encouraged monopolies to the disadvantage of everyone else.[76] Cornwallis was hopeful that his talks with the nawab wazir and his principal minister, Haidar Beg Khan, would now open a new era in relations between the two.

Cornwallis then left Allahabad for Lucknow, still in the company of the nawab and Haidar Beg Khan. Along the way he commented on the desolate condition of the country and the obvious disorder in its governance. When he mentioned this to his companions, the nawab replied that 'he had no real interest in being economical' while the British undermined his authority and that of his ministers. After Cornwallis had again assured him of the British wish to limit their presence, he became more positive, promising to apply himself 'to the encouragement of agriculture' and the revival of his country's commerce. He would also retrench his expenses by dispensing with many 'superfluous articles of expenditure', including 'his own useless rabble of troops'. Cornwallis had seen enough of the nawab wazir's character to doubt his sincerity, though he was hopeful that Khan, a man of ability and sense, would steer his master in the right direction.[77] But even Khan seemed suspicious of British intentions, constantly observing that 'whoever has been stung by a snake is frightened when he sees a rope'.[78] Though sincere in his intentions, Cornwallis was unable to appreciate the effect created by the disparity in power between the nawab and himself, or how intimidating the Company's presence was in the Ganges hinterland.

Throughout his progress Cornwallis had reviewed the various garrisons. However, his most important inspections were at Kanpur and Fatehgarh, at the edge of the Company's territories, where two brigades were based. Here he reviewed both the regulars and the Company's troops as they performed their manoeuvres to assess their discipline and coordination. These confirmed to him that the regulars were well disciplined and zealous, though he suggested a few points for improving their performance. Essentially the officers should avoid all intricate formations, concentrating instead on marching in line and column, wheeling to the left or right as required.[79] These were the manoeuvres that won battles.

The state of the Company's British troops was another matter. 'I did not think Britain could have furnished such a set of wretched objects', was his verdict to Dundas. He doubted whether the Company's six battalions could provide men of sufficient quality to complete one serviceable corps. Clearly the matter of recruitment must be addressed, as he had previously recommended. If the British possessions in India were worth preserving, 'do not let us sacrifice them to the jobs of crimps, or to the trifling jealousies and punctilios about King's and Company's troops'. The Company must be allowed to recruit, like the regulars, under the terms of the Mutiny Act, which required all enlistees to be properly examined by a doctor and placed under martial law once they had affirmed their willingness to serve before a magistrate.[80]

While at Fatehgarh Cornwallis was reminded of the need to prevent profiteering by the Company's military officers, which was almost as endemic as formerly among civilian employees. Opportunities for private trading were especially available in the military bazaars, or markets, which supplied the troops with food and such personal items as the regulations allowed. Unfortunately, the bazaars also provided a cover for other forms of commerce. Cornwallis had already alerted the Directors about the need to regulate the operation of these markets.[81] Now he discovered that Captain Thomas Blair, a relative of the commanding officer at Fatehgarh, Colonel Blair, was deeply involved as a private trader in the shipment of indigo to Britain. Initially Blair claimed to have purchased the crop as a way of remitting his salary to England. But further investigation revealed other transactions in rum and saltpetre. Since Blair openly acknowledged his conduct, he escaped with nothing more than a reprimand, though his chance of promotion was severely compromised.[82] It was a warning to other officers to avoid such activities in the future.

With October almost over, it was time for Cornwallis to return to Calcutta. The journey home was relatively uneventful, except for the evidence of widespread hunger caused by earlier flooding, which had ruined many crops. The council in Calcutta had purchased supplies to feed 25,000 inhabitants daily for several months. However, this only sufficed for the immediate vicinity of the city. Elsewhere the inhabitants were too weak to search for food and simply died along the road. 'I seldom rode out of a morning', he told Lichfield in early November 'without seeing three or four dead bodies and several dying'.[83] Yet without a network of storehouses, the government could do little to alleviate the distress.

Cornwallis finally reached Calcutta early in December after journeying some 2,200 miles. He was generally in good health, as he informed Lichfield, though his want of exercise while travelling by boat had caused varicose veins to swell on his arms and legs. Fortunately, these had receded now that he was back to his old regime. His finances too were continuing to improve, since the interest on his certificates promised enough income to live comfortably without touching his salary.[84] This reinforced his previously expressed desire to acquire another estate adjacent to Culford Park, to prevent its acquisition by eastern 'nabobs' like Clive. 'It is a hobby horse', he admitted to Lichfield, but one 'I have a right to be indulged in'. Please 'lay aside all prudence' regarding the cost of its purchase. The news that Mary had turned her life around also gave him 'great comfort'. 'She has a good understanding and after the danger of the first few years [of child birth] is over, I should hope she will be safe.'[85]

After discussions with Shore and Stuart, Cornwallis sat down to write his first full end-of-year report to the chairman of the East India Company, Sir John Motteux. He had reason to be pleased. In pursuit of his remit to restore the financial health of the Company, he had been 'a most rigid economist'; he had abolished sinecures, ended jobbing agencies, terminated improper contracts, and prevented large sums of money being siphoned off through inflated charges. Everywhere he had been unremitting in hunting out fraud and abuse. The proof of this was that for the first time, yearly expenses were less than estimated. As to the list of prosecutions, Cornwallis repeated his request for leniency, since many honourable men had unintentionally erred due to the laxity of their superiors. His only real disappointment was that the Company's investment would be less than hoped, because of the previous poor weather. Nevertheless, he was confident that the yield next year would be much improved, hurricanes and famines permitting. He concluded with a plea for the Directors to support Campbell, who was at odds with his council. His retirement would cause Cornwallis real concern, believing it 'might be attended with the most fatal consequences'.[86]

Shortly after his return to Calcutta, Cornwallis was greeted with the news that Duke Ferdinand of Brunswick had advanced into Holland with a Prussian army to pre-empt French intrigues against the Dutch ruling family. Cornwallis immediately wrote the duke a congratulatory letter, warmly remembering their campaigning together during the Seven Years' War and more recent re-acquaintance at the Prussian manoeuvres. Like most British officers, Cornwallis believed that service in Europe was where true glory lay, and he was genuine in affirming that he would gladly sacrifice 'all the dazzling situations' of Asia 'for the honour of attending' his former commander.[87]

Less pleasurable was his reading of Tarleton's recently published *History of the Campaigns of 1780 and 1781, in the Southern Provinces of North America*, which he described to Lichfield as 'a most malicious and false attack'. Clearly Tarleton had taken offense at not being offered a position in India. The truth was that Tarleton had approved 'several of the measures which he now blames', especially the events surrounding Ferguson's defeat at King's Mountain (see above, pp. 70–1). Cornwallis admitted he was foolish to be vexed by such things, 'yet it touches me in a tender point'.[88] Tarleton had been like a son to him. However, his erstwhile subordinate received few plaudits from professional colleagues. Fawcett contemptuously dismissed the 'renegade Tarleton's miserable history', noting that Lieutenant Mackenzie of the 71st Highland Regiment had severely castigated him in a pamphlet which met with 'general approbation'.[89] Though Cornwallis was not naturally vindictive, he probably smiled on hearing that Tarleton had been blacklisted at Brookes, the London club.[90] Here at least was some justice.

NINE

The Programme Gathers Pace

Cornwallis entered 1788, celebrating his fiftieth birthday. For most men this was a time for reflection on their lives and approaching retirement. The likelihood is that he barely noted this milestone, other than having dinner with his aides. To ensure the success of his mission, he had much to do in the next three years.

Much of Cornwallis's first eighteen months as governor-general had been spent eliminating corruption and inefficiency in the Company's administration as the prelude to creating a new culture of honesty and service. He had been sufficiently successful for the talk in London to be that 'fortunes' were no longer 'to be made in India; and that gentlemen in their present situations cannot afford to live in the expensive way they formerly did'.[1] Nevertheless, many challenges remained if he was to consolidate what had been achieved. He accordingly began 1788 by setting aside one day each week for making 'a minute investigation of the different offices and establishments'.[2] The hope was that by May 1788 he and his council colleagues would have established the responsibilities of each official, allowing wasteful duplication to be excised in the interests of economy and efficiency. An early example of what could be achieved was the merging of the accounting functions of the revenue and commercial departments under William Larkins, the new accountant-general, a man recommended by Hastings for his diligence and ability.[3]

The review was eventually completed in November 1788, when Cornwallis explained more fully to the Directors what he and the council had been doing. 'The fundamental objects of our plan were to curtail all unnecessary expenses', and to establish 'useful rules for simplifying and facilitating' the dispatch of 'public business'.

In pursuit of these objectives, they had abolished useless offices and reduced unnecessarily large establishments. Moreover, to prevent such abuses in the future, 'the heads of offices were required to lay before the Board' details of what they believed were 'indispensably necessary for carrying on the business' of their departments. This included 'specifying the duties' of and appropriate 'salaries for each individual'. He also reaffirmed how essential it was, 'for the perfection of the system, to allow liberal salaries to the heads of responsible offices'. Only then could 'all perquisites and emoluments' be abolished, thereby preventing conflicts of interest. To enforce the regulations, a new post of civil auditor had been created, whose remit was 'the regular examination and check of all expenditures in the civil departments'.[4]

Cornwallis had not waited for approval from the Directors before beginning these reforms, since they were required by the 1784 Act. Nevertheless, the extent of their implementation still had to be approved by the Company. He could only plead that the Directors consider his plans as positively as possible. Apart from economy and efficiency, the scheme should 'establish a powerful check' against malpractice, by exposing officials to constant observation, both in India and at home.[5]

Despite the changing attitudes to appointments, Cornwallis continued to be solicited by powerful patrons, seeking preferential treatment for their relatives and friends. The most persistent offender was the prince of Wales, who in March 1788 requested Cornwallis to promote one of his protégés in India, a Mr Treves.[6] Cornwallis replied that Treves was attentive to business, but as a junior officer could not expect to be handsomely paid. 'The times for making rapid fortunes in India are past and it will now be only by industry and economy over a course of years that a servant of the Company ... will be enabled to return with a competency to his native country.' Many of Cornwallis's best friends and relatives would feel hurt if he was to break this rule, even for the heir to the throne. Only by selecting the best instruments could the 'national honour and interest' be promoted.[7]

While reforming the Company's bureaucracy, Cornwallis also had to contend with renewed threats to its finances and commercial activities. As he informed the Directors in early January 1788, the recent crop failures and loss of life had been so great that some reductions would be necessary in the diwani. Numerous appeals for relief had already been received. The Revenue Board would naturally investigate scrupulously every request to prevent unfounded claims. Unfortunately, it was not only the landowners and raiyats who were affected. The floods had also damaged the cultivation of raw silk and the production of indigo, which was difficult enough in the latter case, given the native prejudice about growing it.[8]

There was little that Cornwallis could do but wait for the crops to recover sufficiently to produce enough revenue for an investment of 80 lakhs of rupees (£800,000). Nevertheless, concern for the Company's profitability led Cornwallis to reopen the question of how best to secure the investment, whether by contract or by agency. His continued uncertainty led him in June 1788 to launch a formal experiment of both systems, so that he could make a more thorough comparison, and thereby finally prove which was best for procuring the Company's investment.

By early November 1788 he believed he had a definitive answer, though proving the superiority of a reformed agency system to one of contract had not been easy, following two years of inundations, tempests, and drought. But unlike previous trials, the council had this time established 'strict and detailed methods' to prevent former abuses distorting the results. The key had been better paid Company servants, operating in a new ethos of transparency and honesty. 'The quality of the most valuable fabrics', in consequence, had improved, helped by 'a general spirit of attention and exertion'. Indeed, everything indicated that the commercial department was now 'furnishing the investment intelligently and attentively at fair cost, without any charge upon it but what has been actually expended and [was] necessary'.[9]

While reviewing the progress of the Company's commerce, Cornwallis noted one cause for concern. Bengal produced the finest cotton muslin cloth, which accounted for over half of the annual investment. However, the supremacy of India's producers was being challenged by British manufacturers using powered looms, though Cornwallis believed that qualitatively the machines were no threat to the nimble fingers of millions of Bengalis. Nevertheless, he thought the Directors should pay more attention to the cultivation of raw silk, which despite the recent flooding had the potential to become a staple export. The same was true of indigo, which could hopefully be cultivated on waste lands, of which there were large tracts. But greater attention was required to improve the quality of locally grown indigo, whose true potential could not be realised without more investment in buildings and equipment.[10]

One argument that Cornwallis necessarily rejected was Adam Smith's assertion that monopolies like the East India Company strangled economic activity, damaging ironically both the holders of the monopoly and the peoples subject to their exploitation.[11] Subscribers to Smith's views were arguing that the Company should abolish its commercial establishments and open India's commerce to all. Calcutta would then overflow with goods, saving the Company the trouble of producing them. Cornwallis was certainly familiar with Smith's ideas, not least because Ross had visited the economist in Edinburgh a few years earlier with Balfour.[12] But Cornwallis was not convinced by such arguments. Multitudes of European adventurers would flock to the interior, luring the weavers into unsustainable obligations and oppression. Although wages might rise, Cornwallis believed the workers would be better protected by the Company's more humane regulations, instituted following Kennaway's investigations at Dakha. Higher wages would certainly undermine the Company, as would higher prices for raw materials, and there would be no guarantee of quality.[13]

Although Cornwallis had no authority to explore commercial opportunities outside India, he was still alert to such possibilities. One early initiative was an attempt to make contact with the rajah of Nepal to open a market for Bengal cotton. Cornwallis's envoy, Captain Amherst, duly exchanged presents with an emissary of the rajah in April 1788, only to find that he was more interested in receiving bribes than in promoting a mutually beneficial commerce.[14] Ten months later the Nepalese had yet to say whether they would even meet Amherst.[15] Nevertheless, the initiative had one unexpected consequence. It prompted the Dalai Lama in Tibet to suggest a commercial arrangement, opening the possibility of an inland route to China. The timing seemed propitious, since Pitt's ministry was similarly dispatching an envoy from England, Colonel Charles Cathcart, to negotiate new trade agreements. China was important to the Company as a source of tea, as well as a market to sell British manufactures. However, the Chinese, by confining all contacts to the port of Canton, placed severe restrictions on commerce, their goal being to limit trade solely to their own exports.[16] The result was a substantial imbalance of payments, draining the Company's coffers in Bengal and London of specie. Opium appeared one way of redressing the balance, as the Chinese were known to consume that product, though currently they refused to allow its importation. But it soon became apparent that the Dalai Lama was acting without authority from the Chinese emperor Qianlong.[17] News then arrived that Cathcart had died before reaching Beijing. The imbalance of trade with China remained for the moment insurmountable.

Despite the failure to open a new market for opium in China, Cornwallis decided to reorganise the trade, since the contract for its production was due to expire. Although he now preferred the agency system, he decided on this occasion to leave production in the hands of contractors. Public advertisements were accordingly placed in the newspapers. However, he insisted on revising the terms, believing the raiyat cultivators had been unduly exploited under the old contract. 'The true interests of the Company' and 'irresistible claims of humanity', he told the Directors, made it essential 'to give these poor people the protection of the laws'. Hopefully, the revised terms would enable them to 'make an equitable bargain with the contractor for the produce of their labours'. He recognised that these safeguards might result in a more expensive product, but was convinced that any increase in price would be offset by the encouragement given to the raiyats to increase their output. This should then promote 'the general prosperity' of the area.[18]

One important initiative during 1788 and 1789 was a reform of the Bengal currency. Cornwallis had been considering the matter since August 1787 when he had proposed establishing temporary mints at Murshidabad, Patna, and Dakha.[19] But as he and his advisers realised, the problem was not simply one of uniform value. There was also a shortage of silver, which many attributed to hoarding by moneylenders to force up the price of gold.[20] The real reasons were rather different, as Cornwallis later acknowledged to the Directors. One was the drain of bullion from Bengal to meet the expenses of the other presidencies. Another was the remittances of 'private fortunes' by Company employees to Britain in anticipation of their retirement. The imbalance was further aggravated by the use of specie for the purchase of tea in China. Cornwallis's only answer to this outflow of money was to hope that his various initiatives would stimulate the economy sufficiently to produce an inflow of specie.[21] It did not lead him to question whether the abolition of the Company's monopoly might be the real solution.

One alternative way of meeting the specie deficit was the conversion of gold mohurs into smaller denominations. These high-value coins were used by the larger merchants and landowners, but were beyond reach of the wider population. An experiment was therefore tried in April 1788 to turn 50,000 gold mohurs into smaller coins, ranging from a half to a sixteenth in value. The re-coinage unfortunately antagonised the shroffs (money-changers), who stood to lose their commission business. Since they periodically provided credit to the government, the programme had to be suspended in December 1788.[22] It was a testimony to the power of the Indian banking community.[23]

Nevertheless, Cornwallis determined to persevere with re-coining the silver rupee for the benefit of the wider population. As he explained to the Directors in August 1789, the circulation of specie had been restricted by the rupee's different qualities and denominations. The only persons to benefit from this situation were the shroffs, who charged 'an extravagant batta [commission] upon almost every pecuniary transaction'. This hurt both the Company and the mass of the population. The best remedy appeared to be 'a general new coinage of all the circulating silver of the country into rupees, or subdivisions of rupees, of exactly the same weight, standard, and denomination'. To consolidate the system and strengthen the Company's control, he proposed that 'all revenue settlements' should hereafter be made in the new coins.[24] To speed matters up, he established another temporary mint at Patna. Only a lack of skilled craftsmen for the milling process could seemingly thwart a project that would bring 'so much relief . . . to the most industrious and useful part of the inhabitants'.[25]

Meanwhile, little progress had been made transferring the Company's long-term debt to England, though the number of certificates in circulation had been greatly reduced.[26] This prompted Cornwallis to enquire of Larkins whether the 8-per-cent interest on them might be reduced to 5 per cent. The accountant-general was not encouraging, arguing that an immediate reduction of that magnitude was unlikely to be successful. Indeed, the need to preserve trust in the government precluded any reduction of more than 1 per cent. However, further cuts might be contemplated every three years, providing the certificate holders were given due notice. The likelihood was that they would retain their current enthusiasm, lacking other investment opportunities.[27]

This seemed sound advice, now that the discount on the Company's bonds and certificates had almost disappeared. Cornwallis accordingly proposed that the interest on the certificates should be progressively reduced to 6 per cent, confident that they would still be popular with 'rich natives'. The reductions should then encourage further remittances of the Company's long-term debt, especially if the bonds could be exchanged at a favourable rate of 2 shillings per rupee, rather than the current 1s 11d.[28]

Despite these successes, Cornwallis remained pessimistic about the Company's financial outlook, citing the continued difficulties in the production of silk, indigo, cotton, and the high price of rice, the staple diet of most of the region's inhabitants.[29] But at least the Company's finances in Bengal had been stabilised. Although revenues remained stubbornly flat in the years 1787 and 1789, ranging between £5,619,000 and £5,689,000, the costs of government had been reduced from £3,449,000 to £3,183,000. This represented an improvement of roughly 10 per cent, the result of Cornwallis's administrative reforms.[30] Unfortunately, the performance of Bengal was not matched by that of Madras and Bombay. In 1786–87, Madras had yielded a small profit of £40,000, Bombay a deficit of £309,000. Two years later the results were distinctly worse. Madras now had a deficit of £89,000, and Bombay one of £430,000.[31]

Cornwallis could do little about the other presidencies since he was not responsible for their internal government. His own opinion was that the Company's establishment in Bombay should be reduced to an island garrison with no dependent territories to defend. Dundas, however, on hearing about this in London, quickly ruled it out. Reducing Bombay to a mere fort and dockyard would do immeasurable harm to British prestige in India, especially with the Maratha Confederacy and Tipu Sultan. After talking to 'knowledgeable persons', Dundas was convinced that if the Company obtained the city of Surat and its neighbourhood, Bombay's trade would greatly improve, given its proximity to the Arabian Gulf. The dependent territories of Tellicherry (modern-day Thalasserry) and the area adjacent to Salsette Island could then be evacuated, producing a substantial reduction in costs.[32] In the meantime Bengal would have to support its sister presidencies, however damaging to its own finances.

Although Cornwallis and Shore had achieved significant economies in the Revenue Board, they had yet to establish a 'permanent settlement' for the diwani, despite it being a key article in Cornwallis's original instructions of 12 April 1786. The delay was not for want of endeavour, since one of Shore's first actions at the Revenue Board was his order to the collectors to gather the necessary information for making such a settlement. However, as Cornwallis informed the Directors in November

1788, the documents relating to the diwani and land ownership, which were essential for making 'a settlement on permanent principles', had only recently been received from the emperor in Delhi.[33]

Another problem was the difficulty the collectors faced in getting reliable information about their individual districts. As William Brooke at Shahabad reported in early 1788, the village headmen were using 'their utmost exertions to frustrate my enquiries into the real state of the country'. The landholders considered the raiyats as legitimate 'objects of their plunder or extortion', and resented anything which threatened that prerogative. To circumvent their obstruction, Brooke had set aside land in each village to ascertain its actual produce and determine thereby what taxes the Company could reasonably expect.[34]

The ill treatment of the raiyats by landowners was one reason why so many areas previously cultivated had been abandoned. According to a former employee, the zamindars' extortionate practices had done as much to depopulate the country as the three famines he had witnessed during a lifetime in India.[35] Cornwallis recognised that reversing this pattern would be as crucial to the Company's fortunes as permanent settlement. However, great care would be needed when establishing ownership, whether the lands were cultivated or abandoned. Justice and humanity required a 'gentle and cautious plan', even for the recovery of properties that had been 'fraudulently alienated'. But, however complex the task, he was certain of one thing. The Directors must not listen to siren voices advocating a return to the former discredited system of tax farming. The 'delusion' of a higher revenue from tax farmers, he warned, would soon be exposed, while the folly and inhumanity of such a plan would both disappoint the Treasury and lead to 'the ruin and depopulation of the unfortunate country'.[36]

Cornwallis and Shore, accordingly, continued their investigations into who owned the cultivated lands, with whom a permanent settlement might be negotiated. Superficially there were three competing classes. At the top were the large landowners or zamindars. Next in rank were the smaller landholders, the aumils and talukdars. At the bottom were the peasant raiyats. In reality a multiplicity of ranks existed, with up to four classes of zamindar in many places, and similar subdivisions among the talukdars and raiyats.[37] Hastings, who had looked into the question of a permanent settlement, concluded that the zamindars were originally tax farmers who had collected the diwani for the Mughal emperor. In the course of time their positions had become hereditary. Others queried this, notably Shore, who believed that the zamindars had always been 'the hereditary proprietors of the soil'. The uncertainty over their status had arisen because of the rapacity of the Mughal sovereign, who 'claimed what portion of the rents he pleased, thus leaving the zamindars at his mercy'.[38]

These uncertainties momentarily led Cornwallis to consider Thomas Law's 'mukarari' plan for the imposition of a fixed quit rent. This retained nominal ownership of the land in the hands of the Company, while providing the holder with long-term security. However, he assured the Directors that he would be guided by Shore.[39] In reality, Cornwallis was already convinced by Shore's arguments that the zamindars were the key to implementing any permanent settlement based on landownership. It was also the view of the Directors, who had stated in Cornwallis's original instructions that the best way of securing such settlement was through 'hereditary tenure'. Agreements 'in all practicable instances', therefore, 'should be made with the zamindars'.[40] Cornwallis was naturally sympathetic to such a conclusion. Like all his class, he believed that the landed classes in Britain, especially the aristocracy, brought stability to society, acting as a balance between the executive power of the king and democratic tendencies of the Commons.

Many details, however, still had to be settled, as Brooke noted in May 1789 at Shahabad. One was the size of the jumma, or total revenue to be raised annually through the permanent settlement. Another was the need for regulations to prevent the zamindars from oppressing their raiyats.[41] Nevertheless, Cornwallis believed sufficient progress had been made by August 1789 for him to give the Directors a generally optimistic assessment. In carrying out this task, the labours of Shore had been prodigious, despite his precarious health. But 'the outlines of the plan now proposed, are well calculated to secure and even increase your revenues'. Most importantly they should help reverse the long decline in agriculture and internal commerce, which must 'be in a great measure attributed to our former systems of government'. The 'certainty which each individual will now feel of being allowed to enjoy the fruits of his own labours' would provide the necessary incentives 'to exertion and industry'. The accumulation of wealth should also produce 'a regular graduation of ranks', which was essential for the maintenance of civil society. However, the complexity of the operation made it advisable to limit the settlement initially to ten years, though he proposed to add a clause that it would become 'perpetual and unalterable', if the Directors agreed.[42]

Although Cornwallis's letter of 2 August 1789 gave an appearance of unity in the Bengal administration, it concealed an important difference between the principle authors. While Shore argued for a trial period of ten years to see how the system operated, he opposed any mention of permanency, believing it would circumscribe the Company's ability to secure additional income in the future. Cornwallis, on the other hand, believed it essential that the landowners knew about the Company's desire to make the settlement permanent. In a minute for the council, he acknowledged Shore's mastery of the subject and his immense labours. Nevertheless, he could not accept omitting all reference to the Company's ultimate plan for a permanent settlement. Such a delay, he felt, would be fatal to its success, since the zamindars would still not know what demands would eventually be made of them. In the meantime, they would remain in effect mere tax farmers, without proper title to the soil, making it unlikely that they would improve their estates, let alone re-cultivate the abandoned lands. But while he affirmed his belief in the hereditary principle, Cornwallis had robust views about the role of the market. Those landowners who did not seize the new opportunities would lose their estates through bad management, as happened in England. Their properties could then be sold to the 'most frugal and thrifty class of people, who will improve their lands', thereby promoting the general prosperity of the country. Consequently, it was 'immaterial to government what individual possesses the land, provided he cultivates it, protects the raiyats, and pays the public revenue'.[43]

Cornwallis hoped that the instructions regarding a permanent land settlement could be issued in February 1790, to pre-empt any subsequent change in London. Shore was about to return to Britain, and Cornwallis feared that he might sway the Directors into accepting a ten-year introductory period with no commitment to permanency. To ensure that his view prevailed, he wrote privately to the chairman of the Company, Nathaniel Smith, expressing his concerns: 'I can assure you that I have not taken up these opinions lightly, that I have spared no pains in examining the merits of them, and that the generality of the most eminent men in the revenue line agree with me.'[44] Among those supporting him were Duncan, Barlow, and Law.[45]

As the February deadline approached, Cornwallis once again reviewed his differences with Shore, now that he was on his way to England, after boarding a ship in late December 1789. In a further minute to the council, he noted that the former head of the Revenue Board doubted that a permanent settlement would ever be advisable, since it would tie the hands of the government and render it unable to respond to future circumstances. But Cornwallis remained adamant that 'a fixed and unalterable assessment' of land revenues was best calculated to promote the 'interests of the Company and of the British nation, as well as the happiness and prosperity of the inhabitants'. Permanency would release the proprietors from the constraints of the Mughal system and encourage them to manage their estates more efficiently. It might even persuade them to be more generous to their raiyats. Cornwallis felt so justified in his stance that he ordered the Revenue Board to implement the ten-year settlement wherever possible without delay, informing the zamindars simultaneously that the rate of the ten-year jumma would become permanent, once the Court of Directors approved it.[46] It was a bold stroke, though only time could show whether it was the right one.

During the discussions on the permanent settlement, Cornwallis noted that procedures would be required to resolve disputes between the raiyats and their landlords, since it was essential that the whole population enjoyed the benefits of living under known and enforceable laws. Some such system was in any case necessary to conform to the 1784 India Act, which required the Company to settle indigenous grievances by taking 'such measures for their redress as shall be consistent with justice and the laws and customs of the country'.[47] However, the need to return the Company to profitability had necessarily taken priority during Cornwallis's first eighteen months in India. Not until March 1788 was he ready for even a preliminary assessment of these complex issues.

Cornwallis realised that judicial reform could not be accomplished simply by introducing English common or statute law. India's customs and history were too complex and inapposite for that. What was required was a judicious marrying of English legal principles and processes with the customs of Hindu and Islamic law.

The difficulty was that the latter were largely inaccessible to Europeans, being written either in Sanskrit or Arabic. A start had been made by Hasting in translating some aspects of the civil law, but the work was far from complete.[48] This meant that the Company's law officers remained heavily dependent for guidance from native court officials, notably the pandits (Brahmin scholars) and maulvis (Muslim teachers). This made it difficult for European judges to assess the reliability of their interpretations.

It was at this point that Cornwallis received a proposal from Sir William Jones, one of the Supreme Court justices and founder of the Asiatic Society. He suggested not only a translation of the Hindu and Islamic laws on contract and inheritance, but also the creation of digests containing the opinions of leading pandits and maulvis. Jones had arrived in India in 1783 with a remarkable knowledge of both European legal systems and of Indian literature and philosophy, including fluency in Persian and Arabic.[49] Like Cornwallis, Jones believed that the people of Bengal should retain as far as possible their own laws respecting their social and religious customs. But to execute his proposal he would need several such scholars and teachers, plus clerks to translate the original works from Sanskrit and Arabic. Provided he received such assistance, Jones believed he could provide the Company in a few years with a comprehensive civil code, similar to that compiled under the Roman emperor Justinian.[50]

Cornwallis immediately recognised the value of Jones's proposal and promptly authorised him to hire the necessary staff.[51] It proved to be the start of a remarkable partnership between the two men, who were socially and ideologically of very different backgrounds. Jones was from a middle-class Welsh family, and had earlier in his career supported the Whig demand for parliamentary reform and American independence.[52] Their new relationship was a demonstration of the governor-general's ability to accommodate differences in the pursuit of a common objective.

The support of Jones also encouraged Cornwallis to consider changes to the criminal system, though it was not until the following year that he began to address the issues. As he observed to Dundas in March 1789, the current system was 'oppressive, unjust and beyond measure corrupt'. Criminal matters were still handled by the Nizamut Adawlut courts of the old Mughal Empire, meeting in Murshidabad, though cases involving Europeans were referred to the Supreme Court in Calcutta.[53] To European eyes, there were a number of objections to the current arrangements. Most importantly, the system was based on Sharia law, a legacy of India's conquest by Muslim rulers. This seemed inappropriate when four-fifths of the population were Hindus. Another objection was that the Islamic code only defined a small number of crimes. Two of these, blasphemy and apostasy, mainly concerned Muslims. The remaining crimes, which applied to the whole population, were limited to unlawful intercourse, drinking alcohol, theft, and highway robbery. Most other offences under Sharia law were left to the victims or their families to settle, either by blood feuds or payment of compensation.[54] Such license threatened both anarchy and a denial of justice in European eyes. Only the state was properly equipped to ensure impartiality and the maintenance of order.

To remedy these defects, Cornwallis decided to start with procedural rather than substantive changes to the law. His starting point was the appointment of several judges from the Company's senior personnel to replace the existing Mughal courts, who would sit in Calcutta rather than Murshidabad. However, the new judges would also go on circuit twice a year to hear cases in the various districts, similar to the practice in England. Such a plan would be expensive, he told Dundas, 'yet whilst we call ourselves sovereigns of the country, we cannot leave the lives, liberty and property of our subjects unprotected'. It was a project that he had 'much at heart'. Happily, Jones had generously promised 'his cordial assistance'.[55]

Four months later Cornwallis acknowledged the difficulties of the task which he had undertaken, and the 'great caution' that would be necessary 'in endeavouring to reform so delicate a branch of the civil government'. Nevertheless, 'the principles of humanity, and a regard for the honour and interest of the Company and the nation' compelled him to end 'the cruel punishments of mutilation, which are frequently inflicted by the Muslim law'. Action was also desirable 'to restrain the spirit of corruption which so generally prevails in native courts', whereby wealthy offenders could generally 'purchase impunity for the most atrocious crimes'. For this reason, he thought that 'all regulations for the reform' of justice 'would be useless and nugatory, while the execution of them depends upon any native whatever'. If that proved impractical, at the very least it would 'be indispensable for the good government of this country that . . . two or three respectable Company servants should be selected to act as superintendents of the criminal trials'. They too should have liberal salaries to remove any temptation to profiteer from their offices.[56] That was one expense that could not be avoided.

Before making any decision, Cornwallis realised that he needed more information about the workings of the existing system. Accordingly, he asked the collectors in August 1789 to answer a series of questions. Among his queries was the length of time between the commitment and sentencing of prisoners; their treatment while in custody; the uniformity of penalties for robbery and murder; the qualifications of those employed in the administration of justice; the impact of Islamic law as applied to criminal cases; and the most effective means of reforming the police.[57] Sorting through such materials would clearly be a task stretching into 1790.

One other legal matter to engage Cornwallis's attention during 1788 and 1789 was child slavery. He had been advised shortly after his arrival about the barbarities practised on children in Calcutta and its neighbourhood.[58] The issue resurfaced with the receipt of an anonymous letter in November 1788 about 'the inhuman trade . . . of sending to Mauritius and the Capes, freeborn children of this country'.[59] Cornwallis was especially appalled because the traffic was being carried on by Europeans, notably the Portuguese, at a time when the slave trade was being condemned in Britain by reformers like William Wilberforce. Cornwallis had witnessed the inhumanity of slavery while in America and needed no reminder about its reprehensible nature. Accordingly, he informed the Directors in August 1789 that he had issued a proclamation that anyone living under the Company's protection who was convicted of engaging in such 'barbarous traffic' would suffer 'exemplary punishment'.[60]

On the wider question of slavery there was little that Cornwallis could do. The practice was sanctioned by both Hindu and Islamic law and was widespread in Britain's overseas territory. However, he told the Directors in August 1789 that he was considering a scheme for 'the abolition of the practice under certain limitations'. In the meantime, 'some rules and regulations' might be composed 'to alleviate . . . the misery of these unfortunate people'. Inevitably the interests of private property and the 'feelings of the natives' had to be considered. Cornwallis might issue edicts from his office, but knew that implementing them was another matter, even with a relatively efficient bureaucracy. The idea of abolishing slavery in India was in any case a measure before its time.[61] Owning slaves was only criminalised in 1861 and was never completely eliminated from India during British rule.

While maturing his plans for a permanent revenue settlement and the reform of the judiciary, Cornwallis was not without challenges of a more personal nature. Given the initial problems with his council (see above, pp. 142–3), he had enjoyed better relations than he might have expected. Macpherson's delay in reaching England meant that for almost two years the council in Calcutta consisted simply of Cornwallis, Shore, and Stuart, thus guaranteeing Cornwallis a majority. Cornwallis was not pleased, consequently, on learning in November 1788 that a former commissary-general of Bengal, William Murray, was about to return, claiming the right to sit on the council. Murray was one of those officers who had left India as a captain only to return a full colonel, despite lacking military experience. Cornwallis knew from gossip that Murray had an unsavoury reputation for pursuing personal gratification, while claiming credit for reforms that were never properly implemented. In his view Murray's position as commissary-general should have been forfeited because of his long stay in Europe, while his claim to a seat on the council was surely invalid under the terms of the 1784 India Act.[62]

Cornwallis for once vented his anger on Dundas, not least because Murray was an associate of Macpherson. His return, therefore, was certain to be construed as a sign that the former acting governor-general was in the ascendant, undermining public confidence in the reforms of the past two years. To scotch such rumours, Dundas should have told Macpherson that he would not be returning to India under any circumstances. Indeed, he should be grateful at not being prosecuted, as his misdemeanours were worse than anything now being levied against Warren Hastings. Since his meeting with Cornwallis, Hastings had been impeached in the high court of Parliament for committing various alleged crimes while governor-general of Bengal.[63] It was to prove a lengthy affair.

But Cornwallis was angry with Dundas for another reason. The news of Murray's impending arrival in November 1788 coincided with reports from London that Cornwallis had become engaged to a Miss Philpot, the daughter of a Company official. Had Dundas bothered to investigate he would have discovered that the story emanated from Macpherson, who had been asserting that it was 'very likely to be true from the attention which Lord Cornwallis had shown to the lady before he left Bengal'. Cornwallis was incredulous that Dundas should believe that, at the age of fifty, he 'had forgotten his responsibilities and grey hairs and rheumatism and married a girl of sixteen!'[64]

In his eventual reply, Dundas first dealt with the issue of Macpherson. He pointed out that Cornwallis had never provided evidence to impeach the former acting governor-general. In any case it was a matter for the Company to decide.[65] As to Murray, Dundas agreed that he had no right to sit on the council, which the Directors would confirm in their next letter.[66] Regarding Miss Philpot, he could not recall who had mentioned the story. He simply remembered that the young lady was an 'old acquaintance and particular friend of the late Lady Cornwallis'. Dundas had subsequently dined with James Grant and other friends, where the topic 'became naturally the subject of conversation', resulting in a guinea bet between them. But the gossip had quickly subsided and had done no harm to Cornwallis's character or reputation. Pitt for one had never mentioned the story.[67]

Cornwallis was not entirely mollified by Dundas's eventual response, given the numerous letters of congratulation that arrived from Britain about his impending nuptials. At least Brome and his immediate family had not accepted the report, despite it being 'talked [of] all over the town'.[68] Of one thing Cornwallis was certain, he told Dundas: Macpherson had fabricated the story as part of 'a concerted design' to suggest 'that your Indian affairs were in a very bad way, and in great want of some able assistance'. Happily, he could now laugh at what had happened.[69]

Despite Cornwallis's vehement denial that the story had any substance, it had enjoyed some credence in Calcutta, where Hickey and his circle daily expected an announcement, until Miss Philpot unexpectedly declared her affections for a different suitor. Ten years had passed since Jemima's death had deprived Cornwallis of female companionship and the pleasures of an intimate relationship. Although the memory of Jemima, his social position, and conventional morality prevented him from taking a mistress in India, like many Company employees, the chance of a new relationship with a young lady known to his mother might well have stirred romantic thoughts, until brutally extinguished by her choice of someone else. His anger and humiliation at the story's spread in these circumstances would be understandable.[70]

Although the threat of Murray had disappeared, Cornwallis remained concerned about the council's composition, given that Shore might return to Europe for health reasons. Cornwallis had first raised the issue in November 1788, in the hope that Duncan might succeed Shore as the most able person in revenue matters. A council composed of Duncan, Charles Grant, and Larkins would be best. However, Grant also wanted to return to Britain, while Duncan's appointment was likely to be rejected on account of his youth. In these circumstances, it was essential to avoid the appointment of another Stuart, 'the weakest man I ever met with in any public station', who 'would do more harm in the government in six months than I have been able to do good in six years'.[71]

The composition of the council, accordingly, remained constantly in Cornwallis's mind, prompting him to warn Pitt in August 1789 that unless governors and councillors were 'well chosen, things cannot prosper'. Shore had by this time determined to return to Britain by the end of 1789 because of his continuing poor health. Should Cornwallis die or be incapacitated after his departure, affairs would then fall into the hands of Stuart and Peter Speke, a senior employee, whom the directors had earlier nominated as Macpherson's successor on the council. Together they would surely ruin the country, just as Macpherson and Sloper had previously.[72] He reinforced this message in a letter to Dundas. Speke was 'in his private character a worthy honest man, but very weak and open to the solicitations of individuals to support their most ruinous jobs. He was also totally unacquainted with all the business of this country, except making silk.'[73] It remained important, therefore, that Cornwallis's own successor was someone of ability, for without such an appointee 'all laws, regulations and orders are perfectly nugatory'.[74]

Cornwallis had raised the appointment of his own successor at the same time as discussing a replacement for Shore. He was now approaching the half-way point in his five-year term. Since an exchange of letters normally took between nine and fifteen months, his mentioning the subject at this point was understandable, if he was to return home in January 1791. Although he was in good health and confident of completing his term, he nevertheless told Pitt: 'My time of life, and many other weighty considerations, render my longer continuance in India impossible.'[75] Brome was again unwell, and his future needed to be settled before he left Eton. These were matters best handled in person rather than through intermediaries, however conscientious Lichfield had been.

Who might that successor be? One possibility was William Medows, whom Cornwallis had known in America and who had recently been installed as governor of Bombay. Unfortunately, Medows had begun his tenure badly by nominating regular officers to posts which belonged to the Company's personnel.[76] Without wishing to appear presumptuous, Cornwallis confessed to Pitt: 'I really do not know where you will find governors.' Dundas's idea of appointing senior officers was 'a good one so long as the military men can be found who are fit for it; but from my knowledge of the army, I cannot encourage you to suppose that it will furnish you with extensive choice'. Part of the problem was the immensity of the job. Cornwallis himself had enjoyed the assistance of the indefatigable and knowledgeable Shore. Even so he had been compelled to give his whole time to business and still had 'much to learn'. It might be best, therefore, if Pitt and Dundas selected one of their more able civilian friends. The candidate should have a good constitution and not be much above thirty-five years of age. To ensure that he behaved honourably to the ministry and the country, 'he must divest himself of every idea of patronage'.[77]

One consequence of Shore's departure for Britain in December 1789 was that Stuart renewed his claim to the Revenue Board, which Cornwallis felt obliged to accept this time.[78] The Directors eventually named William Cowper, another long-serving Company official, as the fourth member of the council, despite Dundas's pleas on behalf of Duncan. The appointment was surprising: Cowper had nearly lost his eyesight and done little business in the preceding two years.[79] It made it even more imperative for Cornwallis that the next governor-general be someone who was sympathetic to his policies and prepared to defend them.

The completion of the permanent settlement was not the only project to stall during 1788 and 1789. The same fate appeared to await the reform of the Company's military establishment, despite Cornwallis's early reports about the poor state of its European corps and excessive dependence on the sepoys. Since the Directors declined to respond to Cornwallis's proposals of August 1787, Dundas and Yonge, the secretary at war, determined to press ahead with the scheme to strengthen the European military establishment in India. They proposed to effect this by a partial fusion of the Company's European forces with those of the king. Their plan was to raise 5,000 recruits in Britain for the creation of several new regular regiments. The officers for these corps would be chosen from both services, though all would receive a royal commission, which Dundas believed was 'the great object' of the Company's military establishment. Once a precedent had been established, the Company's remaining battalions could be similarly disbanded.[80] To ensure equality of treatment, Company officers selected for a commission would receive the same rank as that which they currently held, while regulars with enhanced brevet rank would lose that privilege. Apart from some cavils from the Directors and the Whig opposition, Dundas expected little opposition to the scheme.[81]

By the time Cornwallis received this news in March 1788 he knew that Dundas's plans were seriously flawed, since they took no account of the 400 officers serving in the sepoy battalions, who in general were the most deserving in the Company's army. They also enjoyed the greatest emoluments. This made the command of sepoys popular with the officers in the Company's European corps, since it was the surest route to commanding a battalion. In contrast, any officer joining the regulars 'without interest or connection . . . could not expect a regiment in twenty years', making it certain that few would avail themselves of such an opportunity.[82]

Nevertheless, Dundas and his colleagues determined to proceed with their proposals to create four new regiments, in the belief that they would meet without serious opposition.[83] Their optimism quickly proved misplaced. For the Directors, the scheme threatened a loss of patronage if commissions were issued by the king. Even worse, they feared that the practice might be extended to the civil administration of the Company, further weakening their power. They also believed that many of their officers might be unjustly overlooked, creating a strong sense of grievance.[84] The Directors were sufficiently defiant to declare that they would not meet the cost of the new regiments once they arrived in India, forcing Dundas to pass a special act of Parliament compelling them to do so.[85]

However, the opposition of the Company's officers was not so easily overridden. A group of them on leave in Britain quickly formed a committee to lobby against the plan, recognising it to be the prelude to the disbandment of their corps. News of their proceedings then led in early 1789 to meetings of dissident officers in India itself, amid calls for the formation of a similar coordinating committee in Calcutta.[86] As Colonel White, the station commander near Patna, explained to Cornwallis, the officers had devoted their lives to the Company, knowing that few of them would be able to return to their native country. Now their way of life appeared in danger and their anxiety was not allayed by the knowledge that the Company's charter would shortly have to be renewed, threatening even more radical change.[87]

Cornwallis was sympathetic to White's arguments, especially the need to ensure that the officers could eventually return to Britain, since he was against their settling in India once retired: 'It ought to be part of the political system for the management of India to discourage and prevent European officers from colonising and settling in this country.' The danger was that once they relinquished 'all thoughts of returning to their native country, they will soon become indifferent, or perhaps . . . even hostile to its interests'.[88] That surely had been the lesson of British settlement in America.

By this time, the four new regiments had arrived in India. As Cornwallis had predicted, few of the Company's officers sought commissions to serve in them, leaving Dundas's plan in tatters.[89] Cornwallis could merely repeat his more limited proposals of February 1787 for a better supply of recruits, and modification of the practice of promotion by strict seniority. The latter was essential if the Company's best officers were to have a chance of demonstrating their talents before reaching superannuation.[90] The reform of the Company's European corps was to perplex Cornwallis and the ministry for many years to come.

The sepoy regiments in contrast required few changes in their composition. The rank and file had been largely recruited from high-caste Hindu families in rural Awadh, Bihar, and Benares.[91] This instilled an *esprit de corps* which Cornwallis was anxious to preserve. It was for this reason that he blocked any attempt at religious conversion, as he explained to his old schoolmate, Shute Barrington, now bishop of Salisbury. The 'fidelity and affections' of these corps had been secured 'by an unremitted attention not to offend their religious scruples and superstitions'. All this might be put at risk by the 'imprudence or intemperate zeal' of even one missionary. The fear of losing caste, in any case, was so strong as 'to bar any material progress in the propagation of the Christian religion'.[92]

Cornwallis's dislike of missionary activity was paralleled by his opposition to the teaching of English to Indians. He feared that it would undermine the need for the Company's personnel to speak the native languages, which was essential if they were to avoid undue dependence on native interpreters. It would only be sensible were it 'possible to make English the universal language throughout our extensive territories', and that seemed unrealistic.[93] The Company's responsibility to Indians extended no further than providing them with a government that was firm and just. Beyond this, Cornwallis felt that the anglicisation of Indian society, religion, and culture was neither desirable nor necessary. It was an attitude that was to differ sharply with most nineteenth-century notions of Britain's imperial mission.[94]

Although Cornwallis was not responsible for the internal management of the other presidencies, he had known since early 1788 that Campbell was at odds with the Directors and wanted to retire. The rift had first surfaced in the summer of 1787, when a new council was appointed which led to the removal of a close friend of Campbell.[95] Cornwallis was naturally alarmed by these developments, given his respect for Campbell and the importance of Madras, should war break out with Tipu Sultan and the French at Pondicherry. His only hope was that Campbell might be replaced by Medows once the latter had proved his competence at Bombay.

Campbell eventually left for Europe in February 1789, leaving John Holland, a former Company freight manager, and his brother Edward temporarily in charge at Madras. Campbell's departure immediately raised the thorny issue of rank between the Company's forces and those of the crown, which were commanded respectively by Brigadier-General Matthew Horne and Colonel John Floyd. The position was complicated, because Horne's rank of brigadier-general was a local brevet arrangement and not part of the Company's official establishment.[96] This meant that Floyd could claim seniority.[97] Since Cornwallis's powers for dealing with the Madras Presidency were uncertain, he decided to leave Horne in charge, subject to the directions of the civil government. But as an interim measure he sent the more experienced Colonel Thomas Musgrave to take charge of the regulars. Hopefully the appointment of a new governor would alleviate the problem.

Initially, Cornwallis felt no cause for alarm, since Musgrave had been given strict orders to co-operate with Horne in the defence of the presidency. No immediate threat was in any case apparent. He was therefore surprised in June 1789 to read in the newspapers that two battalions of sepoys under Colonel Charles Stuart had been dispatched on an undisclosed mission to the interior. What astonished Cornwallis was the lack of any official notification to him about so sizeable a deployment. In his most imperious tone, he reminded Horne that it was his 'indispensable duty as commander-in-Chief of all the forces in India, to superintend the conduct of all officers, both in the King's and Company's service'. He certainly could not be content 'with vague newspaper accounts'. Horne was accordingly to send immediately all the relevant correspondence, detailing the size, purpose, and progress of the expedition, so that Cornwallis could assess its necessity.[98]

Cornwallis assumed that Horne had momentarily forgotten his subordinate position. He was consequently surprised when Horne apologised, stating that he knew nothing about the expedition other than that it was to quell some disturbances for the nawab of Travancore. After selecting the sepoy battalions and nominating Stuart to the command, he had been excluded by the Holland brothers from any further involvement. He had certainly intended no disrespect to his commander-in-chief.[99]

Soon Cornwallis had other reasons for concern, when he learnt that the officers at Madras had been making loans to the zamindars and other prominent Indians, using their public positions to enforce their private interests. This malfeasance had only emerged during a court-martial. Cornwallis quickly informed Musgrave that such practices were highly improper and must be stopped.[100] He simultaneously informed John Holland of the ban and of the need to extend it to every branch of government.[101] But within weeks Cornwallis received anonymous information that the Holland administration was committing similar irregularities concerning the nawab of Arcot's debts.[102] Nevertheless, Cornwallis was uncertain what to do, given his limited authority over the other presidencies. Only the arrival of a new governor at Madras could seemingly remedy the situation.

During this middle period of his governorship, Cornwallis continued to cherish news from home, especially reports about Brome, who suffered from heavy colds in the spring of 1788 and again in early 1789. Fortunately, warmer weather on the latter occasion produced a full recovery, as one of Cornwallis's Townshend relatives confirmed. Brome 'could not look better. He does not promise to be tall, but he promises to be stout and healthy, a fine colour.'[103] Such reports sharpened Cornwallis's anticipation of their joyful reunion in the late spring or early summer of 1791. 'God bless you, my dearest Charles, may you be as well and as happy as I wish you, and you will not desire any more.'[104] Excess was as ever to be avoided.

An important concern for Cornwallis during 1789 was the state of the king's health, following his apparent derangement the previous December. This had produced a political crisis in Britain, with the prince of Wales demanding to be made sole regent so that he could appoint a new government headed by his friends in the Whig party. The news in August 1789 that George III had recovered hence brought great relief to Cornwallis, given his distaste for Wales and his companions. To mark the event, he arranged a concert and supper for the 'whole settlement', which he described to Brome in one of his letters.[105] The army began the proceedings with a *feu de joie*, though the accompanying fireworks were extinguished by a violent downpour. The supper, however, proved a very good one. Finally, 'seven of the finest ladies' in the settlement and 'twelve gentlemen sang Handel's coronation anthem', bringing the event to a close, though some of the gentlemen 'who stayed late . . . were nearly extinguished by the claret'.[106]

Despite the celebrations, the king's malady and consequent regency crisis was not without its impact on Cornwallis, since it led to an estrangement with Lord Rawdon, who like Tarleton had become a supporter of the prince of Wales. To Cornwallis, the prince's conduct amounted to the treacherous desertion of the country's 'poor sick King, whose crown would have been torn virtually from his head' had the scheme succeeded. Cornwallis felt 'it the duty of a friend' to tell Rawdon his 'sentiments', believing their friendship would survive their political differences.[107] It proved otherwise. He was similarly saddened by the conduct of the duke of York, who had joined his brother in the demand for an exclusive regency. Cornwallis could forgive York's excesses, he told Richard Grenville, yet the want of feeling for his father had 'made me lament that I was ever acquainted with him'. It reinforced his former resolution 'to treat princes with respect' whenever he should be 'unlucky' enough to meet them, 'but never to form any connection or associate with them'.[108]

More pleasurable for Cornwallis was contemplation of his plans for improving the manor house at Culford Park, which had not been altered since its acquisition in 1660. The question was whether to repair the structure or substantially rebuild it.[109] He eventually left the decision to Lichfield, stipulating that in the latter case, the Singletons, who were in residence, were to receive £200 a year to find temporary accommodation elsewhere. The cost of the project prompted him to reassess his overall worth. He was planning to give Mary an inheritance of £20,000. He also wanted to set aside £10,000 for the purchase of a more permanent residence for himself in London. After these outlays, he calculated that his net worth would be between about £70,000 and £80,000 on his return, which, when added to his Suffolk estates, would yield an income of £8,000 a year. This would surely suffice for his retirement and the needs of his heir, for if any future Lord Cornwallis could not live on that sum, £12,000 a year was likely to prove equally insufficient.[110]

One other reason for personal contentment was the arrival in September 1789 of William Cornwallis, now commodore of the navy's East Indies squadron. His presence in Calcutta would be limited since he had orders to establish a naval facility in the Andaman Islands or Straits of Penang to protect the Company's trade route to China.[111] Cornwallis thought him less shy than before, happy with his daily diet of four glasses of claret and a slice of mutton.[112] Hickey was less impressed, noting that he was very quarrelsome and quite 'unlike his brother in both manner and person'. After insulting everyone for three weeks, he mercifully sailed for the Andaman Islands.[113]

As 1789 came to a close Cornwallis could reflect that he had a good chance of completing his mission by January 1791, thus allowing a reunion with Brome in the summer of that year. 'When you consider that your father is this day fifty-one and that he has had a full share of the fatigues and cares of this world, you must of course be prepared to see a grey-headed fellow', probably with spectacles, since he had difficulty reading by candlelight. Yet he had no reason to complain. The climate had not been unkind to him, and he had every confidence of surviving his last year intact.[114] But unknown to Cornwallis, Tipu Sultan was about to come between him and that eagerly anticipated reunion with his son.

TEN

An Unwelcome War

Tipu Sultan and his father, Haidar Ali, had posed a threat to the interests of the East India Company since the 1760s. To the British, Tipu and Haidar were cruel tyrants who would go to any lengths to expand their dominions. They were also usurpers, who had overthrown the ruling family of Mysore, though they had remarkably spared the lawful heir by keeping him in genteel confinement.[1] Their real crime was a readiness to ally with the French, which they had done in two wars against the Company. The Second Anglo-Mysore War (1780–84) had been especially difficult, with the ravaging of the Coromandel Coast, the defeat of General Matthews, and the near capture of Madras. The Company only retained a presence in southern India because of divisions among its opponents. The view was widespread among the British that they had unfinished business with Tipu: one or the other must prevail.

For Tipu of course it was the British who threatened the peace of southern India. Now forty years of age, he was at the height of his powers, having shown himself to be a talented general as well as a ruler who recognised the need for initiatives at home. Indeed, to many modern scholars he represents a charismatic Indian nationalist who challenged the imperialist order, using French instructors to modernise his army and European techniques to manufacture weapons. In reality, Tipu had rather less visionary notions. If he did have an ideology, it was that of a Muslim ruler, as he had demonstrated during his recent struggle with the nizam of Hyderabad when he appealed for Muslim support from the Nizam's army.[2] His eventual aim was to make his family the predominant dynasty of southern India. Hence any opportunity for expanding his dominion was something to be seized, with

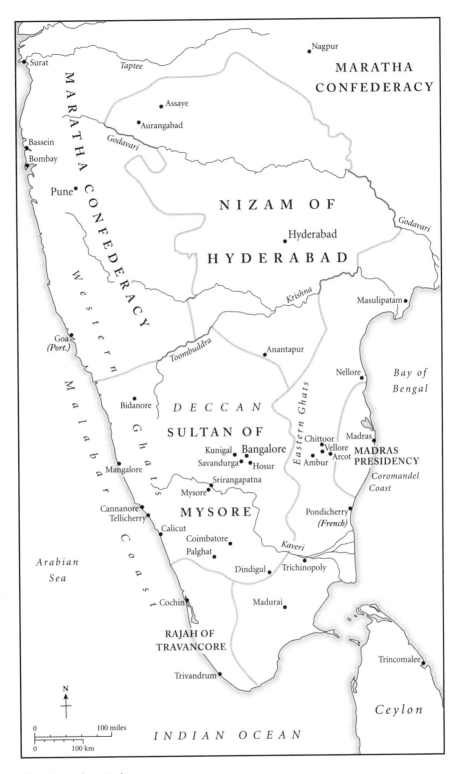

Map 5. Southern India.

or without French assistance. Rather than being a modern nationalist, Tipu was closer to the model of a feudal warlord.[3]

The trigger for war this time was the rajah of Travancore's purchase in 1789 of two Dutch enclaves along the Malabar Coast, which Tipu immediately claimed as rightfully his. The situation was dangerous because the rajah was an ally of the East India Company. Cornwallis, however, was anxious not to exacerbate the situation. He accordingly directed the government in Madras to ask Travancore to return the islands to the Dutch, pending further investigation. He also wrote to Tipu suggesting the appointment of a commission to establish ownership of the islands. However, the Holland brothers neglected to forward Cornwallis's letter, leaving Tipu with the impression that the British were indifferent about the dispute.[4]

With this false sense of impunity, Tipu decided to punish the rajah by attacking his defensive lines a few miles north of Cochin (modern-day Kochi). The Holland brothers, surmising that Tipu's aims were limited, decided to make no response.[5] Cornwallis, nevertheless, felt that the Company must act, given Tipu's failure to reply to his conciliatory plan for an enquiry. An ally had been attacked, and any failure to help the rajah would look like pusillanimity to other rulers.[6] The time for a showdown with Tipu seemed opportune, as the French had recently moved their military establishment from Pondicherry to Mauritius, and were thus in no position to help him.[7] The one disadvantage was that the war would disrupt Cornwallis's efforts to mend the Company's finances. Hopefully the conflict would be short, given the relative preparedness of the army.[8]

When the news of Tipu's assault on Travancore arrived, Cornwallis's first thought was to take command himself, given the want of leadership at Madras. The previous war had witnessed endless disputes between the military and civil authorities and it was imperative that this did not happen again. He acknowledged that combining the offices of governor-general and commander-in-chief at Madras might appear irregular. However, Article 36 of the 1784 Act allowed him to suspend one of the smaller presidencies, should his instructions regarding the defence of the Company's territories be wilfully ignored, which the Holland brothers had clearly done.[9]

In the event no such action was necessary on Cornwallis's part, since word arrived that Medows was expected shortly at Madras as the new governor and commander-in-chief.[10] The scourge of a divided command had been avoided, though Cornwallis acknowledged to Dundas that if he had been free to follow his 'own private inclinations', he would have 'taken the field against Tipu', instead of remaining in Calcutta with the 'constant drudgery' of administering Bengal. The departure of Shore and Charles Grant during 1789 meant that he received 'very little official assistance' from his council. He would still go to Madras if it appeared to benefit 'the public service'. However, by early February the military situation had improved with the news that Tipu's attack on Travancore's defensive lines had been repulsed, making a hasty journey to Madras unnecessary.[11] Yet it was still 'a melancholy task', he confided to Lichfield, 'to see all the effects of my economy, and the regulations of the finances, *which cost me so much labour, destroyed in a few months*'. But he concluded philosophically: 'I am pretty well inured to the crosses and vexations of this world', so long as 'my conscience does not reproach me with any blame'.[12]

From the start, Cornwallis recognised that it would be prudent to seek assistance in the forthcoming campaign against Tipu. Allies might lighten the burden of the conflict and make the action against Tipu less threatening to the other Indian states. Two obvious candidates presented themselves, namely the peshwa of Pune and the nizam of Hyderabad, who had both sought help from the Company during their recent inconclusive war against Tipu. Cornwallis had not pursued the matter, partly for reasons of economy and partly because the India Act of 1784 prohibited any treaty likely to involve the Company in the territorial concerns of another state. However, this restriction no longer applied, as the Company had been forced into a defensive war by an attack on one of its allies. Not that an alliance was assured, since the peshwa and the nizam had previously been allies of Tipu during the Second Anglo-Mysore War, when a British defeat seemed likely. Self-interest would be their motivation.[13]

On the first news of Tipu's attack against Travancore, Cornwallis accordingly ordered the British representatives at Pune and Hyderabad, Charles Malet and John Kennaway, to begin negotiations for an alliance. As an incentive he proposed that all three powers should have an equal share of any territory captured from Tipu. In return the peshwa and the nizam were to provide a suitable corps to co-operate with the Company's army. Most desirable would be the provision of cavalry, since the British lacked strength in that department.[14]

After this Cornwallis addressed the misdeeds of John Holland and his council at Madras, whose conduct had been criminal if not treasonous. Holland had twice ignored Cornwallis's orders to prepare for military action should Tipu disturb the peace. He had also refused Musgrave's request to purchase draft bullocks for transporting the artillery and provisions, one of the most necessary measures in any Indian war. The Madras army in consequence would be unable to exploit Tipu's recent repulse at Travancore.[15] But this was not all, for in early March Cornwallis learnt that the Holland brothers had tried to undermine the negotiations of Malet and Kennaway at Pune and Hyderabad.[16] To complete their catalogue of misdemeanours, the evidence showed that the Madras council had accepted bribes from the creditors of the nawab of Arcot to ensure that he paid the interest on his debts punctually. The stench of corruption and even treason was everywhere.[17]

Consequently, Cornwallis's first act was to suspend Holland and his brother from their posts, since 'such flagrant and disgraceful peculation [embezzlement] ought not to go unpunished'.[18] Clearly everything depended on the arrival of Medows, who, in addition to his military duties, would have to inquire into the misdeeds of the suspended officials and find replacements for them.[19] The abilities of the new governor were going to be fully tested, and soon.

Preparations, meanwhile, continued in Calcutta for fielding the largest possible army against Tipu to ensure a decisive outcome. The weakness of the forces at Madras meant that a considerable reinforcement from Bengal was needed. Six sepoy battalions under Colonel Cockerel were accordingly to march overland (as Hindu soldiers were reluctant to travel by sea), while the artillery and other European detachments simultaneously proceeded by ship. A separate corps under Major-General Robert Abercromby was also to march from Bombay to enter Mysore through the mountains of the Western Ghats.[20] Progress was also being made on the diplomatic front at Hyderabad, whence Kennaway was able to report in late March 1790 that draft articles for an alliance had been agreed with the nizam. Territories acquired through the war would be divided equally between the allies, while none of the contracting parties were to make a separate peace. Any gains would be protected by a defensive alliance, to deter Tipu from attempting their recovery.[21] Similar arrangements were also being fashioned by Malet with the peshwa in Pune, allowing a formal alliance between the three powers to be signed by the end of May 1790.[22]

Although the contributions of the Company's new allies remained uncertain, Cornwallis now had no doubts about the ultimate success of the war, even if the hostilities were more protracted and expensive because of the Holland brothers' misdemeanours. But he was uneasy about Medows's plan of campaign, as he informed Dundas. Cornwallis's preference was for a westward advance into Mysore from the Coromandel Coast, since this would allow Medows to join the forces of the peshwa and the nizam on their southward march. It would also facilitate a union with Abercromby advancing from the north-west. However, at the end of March 1790 Cornwallis learnt that Medows had 'adopted Musgrave's plan of operations . . . to invade Tipu's country' from Trichinopoly (modern-day Tiruchirappalli) in the far south, leaving the rest of the Company's forces on the defensive. Apart from making co-operation with the peshwa and nizam difficult, the decision to take a southern route ignored the fact that the monsoon season around Trichinopoly was different to that in Mysore. An army using the southern route might find itself immobilised by the rains, leaving Tipu's cavalry free to ravage the Coromandel Coast with impunity.[23]

But Cornwallis had other objections too, as he now advised Medows. The absence of any plan for joining the forces of the Maratha Confederacy and Hyderabad might result in their not appearing at all, since both powers appeared reluctant to confront Tipu without the reassuring presence of the Company's troops. Musgrave's southerly route would also take longer to execute, reminding Cornwallis of Howe's advance on Philadelphia in 1777 via Head of Elk, which had lost two months in consequence (see above, pp. 33–4).[24]

At least Tipu would receive no support from France. The Irish-born Thomas Conway, the new French commander at Pondicherry, had assured Cornwallis on the first outbreak of hostilities that he had no treaty with Tipu and that his orders were to observe neutrality.[25] He lacked the means in any case to intervene, following the revolutionary upheavals in France, which were depriving its colonies of supplies and money. The revolutionary fervour was even affecting the French factory at nearby Chandannagar, where the inhabitants were building fortifications in breach of France's treaty obligations with Britain. Since their actions had no official sanction and posed no threat, Cornwallis left it to Conway to settle what would hopefully remain an internal French matter.[26]

Cornwallis had become aware of the disturbances in France in early 1790, after receiving letters about the storming of the Bastille and the plight of the aristocrat émigrés. The news was difficult to comprehend at such a distance. As Charles

Townshend commented: 'Who could have expected to see so soon a King of France led in triumph by the mob of Paris, and forced . . . to thank God for his own humiliation'. Equally astonishing was that, while Lafayette threatened to depose his own monarch with 50,000 militia, George Washington was celebrating the recovery of George III from his recent illness. Townshend could not hide his glee that the House of Bourbon was now paying the price 'for the support which they gave to the Americans'.[27] Cornwallis readily agreed, though, as he informed the duke of York, he believed the most important consequence of these convulsions was that 'our tranquillity in Europe is not likely to be soon disturbed by that late powerful and restless neighbour'.[28]

Meanwhile, the military situation in southern India remained frustratingly static as Medows and Musgrave struggled to assemble their army. The more Cornwallis learnt about the situation the less he liked it. But when he suggested the need for stricter regulation of the supply services, Medows replied testily that if he tried to root out every rogue commissary, jobber, and embezzler, nobody would be left to undertake the business. To Cornwallis, this was unacceptable defeatism. He believed there were always more honest people than villains in any well-managed government. A start should be made with the quartermaster-general's department. Even if the current bullock contract was a bad one, the situation could still be alleviated if proper officers were appointed to execute it. One thing was certainly clear: the situation could not be remedied while the officer currently holding the position of quartermaster had a one-third share of the business. He must decide whether he wished to remain quartermaster-general or bullock contractor, for he could not be both. 'I saw too plainly the effect of such a union [in the American] war; and how four or five of our harpies at the heads of the public departments used to divide poor John Bull's money' the moment it arrived at New York. Although he still believed in the honesty of Madras's former governor, it was clear that he had not been so scrupulous about his associates. Campbell forgot 'how little consequence it was to his country whether he plundered it himself or suffered others to do it'.[29]

The failure of the southern army to advance meant that neither the forces of the Maratha Confederacy nor those of the nizam of Hyderabad appeared ready to advance, as Cornwallis feared.[30] Even worse, the delays prompted Tipu to send envoys to Pune and Hyderabad to create jealousies and undermine the alliance.[31] The danger remained that the rainy season would immobilise Medows's forces at the southern end of the Ghats, allowing Tipu to attack elsewhere.[32] Moreover, expenses were certain to rise, whether the army was in the field or in camp.[33] Cornwallis once again contemplated taking command, but then reflected that leaving Stuart and Speke in charge would ruin Bengal.[34] It was an invidious dilemma.

By the end of May 1790 Cornwallis had done everything possible to forward the campaign against Tipu. He could accordingly direct his attention once more to local matters, where three important tasks remained, if he was to fulfil his remit to the Company and the Board of Control. One was the completion of a permanent land settlement; the second was a reform of the judiciary; and the third was the merging of the two military establishments. But Dundas had recently added a fourth task, by asking Cornwallis for his advice about the terms on which the East India Company's charter might be renewed. This expired in 1793. The ministers were contemplating radical changes, whereby the crown would control both the civil and military machinery of government, leaving commerce as the Company's sole responsibility. However, before proceeding, they wished to ascertain Cornwallis's views.[35]

Cornwallis quickly noted several 'weighty objections' to the ministerial plan. In the first place he believed that the Company would be bankrupted by the scheme, since it would no longer be able to protect its commercial interests. He could also not see much advantage in placing the civil departments under the crown, since any extension of patronage was certain to bring a torrent of abuse about ministerial influence, as had happened in 1783 during the debates over the Fox–North India Act. Perhaps the Court of Directors could be made more responsive to the government's concerns if their numbers were reduced. But there were two areas where he agreed that the government's hand should be strengthened. The first was in senior appointments. In future the crown should select all governors-general, councillors, and commanders-in-chief in the three presidencies. Second, the Company's European troops must be merged with those of the crown, leaving the sepoys as a separate local force under the Company's direction. He was still unsure how that was to be effected.[36]

Cornwallis then addressed once more the issue of opening India's trade to British subjects, as advocates of Adam Smith's views continued to demand. He personally could see no objection to liberalising the export of British goods to India. But he was adamantly opposed to giving the same advantage regarding Indian exports to Britain, believing it would entice 'desperate speculators' who knew nothing about the country or its customs. He thought it much better to keep the present closed market, which gave the government a customs revenue and the Company a profit. If the current yields for 1787 to 1789 were not as high as anticipated, this was because the 'investments of the last two years had been made under every possible local disadvantage' due to the climate. Political turmoil in Europe had also not helped. However, Cornwallis admitted that the 'multiplicity of affairs' had not allowed him much 'time to reflect deliberately upon this extensive subject'. The problem was that 'there are but few people here of comprehensive views and abilities, with whom I can examine and fully discuss the various objects which ought to be included in so important a plan'.[37] No one had yet emerged to replace John Shore.

The sense of Cornwallis's views about not imposing a radically different charter on the Company were readily accepted by Dundas when he received them in London.[38] Cornwallis, meanwhile, had returned to the completion of his plans for a permanent settlement with the landed classes. A week after writing to Dundas about re-chartering, he was able to tell the Directors that the necessary details for a ten-year settlement were almost complete for Benares, Bihar, and Orissa, and that instructions had been given to the collectors in Bengal to implement the same system.[39] However, Stuart at the Revenue Board still questioned the hereditary rights of the zamindars and talukdars.[40] Many collectors were also experiencing continued difficulty obtaining the necessary documents from the zamindars for completing a settlement.[41] After repeated obstruction in the Burdwan district, Cornwallis ordered Lawrence Mercer, the collector, to inform the offending rajah that he would be arrested unless he ceased his obstruction. Moreover, Cornwallis would tear up any petition on the matter and imprison the person 'who should dare to present it'.[42] Hopefully a firm stance now would enable the project to be completed.

Differences about the rights of the zamindars and talukdars were not the only issue dividing the council, for Stuart next complained about Cornwallis's sudden decision to abolish the sayer – or internal customs – duties without first informing him.[43] After a tense disagreement in the council, Cornwallis sought to defuse the situation in a personal letter to Stuart. He believed, he wrote, that certain 'designing persons' had exploited Stuart's 'open and easy disposition to infuse jealousy and dissatisfaction' on account of an alleged 'want of communication and confidence'; that Cornwallis, in short, had not 'looked for his assistance in the same manner' as he had with Shore. However, Cornwallis pointed out that since his arrival, Stuart had never shown any 'inclination to enter into the details of business', which Cornwallis surely had a right to expect. 'We live at a great distance from each other and rather than coming to Government House, four times out of five when I have asked the favour of your company to dinner, you have declined the invitation.' Cornwallis personally bore no enmity to Stuart, and could only hope that he would guard against those 'who think they have an interest in separating us'.[44]

Portraying Stuart as the dupe of others was not a tactful comment to make about his most senior colleague on the council. Cornwallis had also unfairly discounted Stuart's reservations about the rights of the zamindars and talukdars, which were not entirely misplaced. Nevertheless, in his reply to Cornwallis Stuart acknowledged 'the candid and polite manner' in which the governor-general had explained himself. He admitted he had long felt 'reason to complain', having 'frequently been surprised to find the intentions of government . . . publicly known and talked of long before I received the slightest information of such designs'. The recent suspension of the sayer duties was one such instance, which had led him to speak as he had in council. That would not have happened had Stuart received timely notice of Cornwallis's thoughts, though he admitted that there were people who were ready to sow dissentions between them. But Stuart would never be a party to them.[45]

The issue that had ostensibly caused the contretemps between Cornwallis and Stuart initially concerned the collection of the sayer, which had previously been performed by the zamindars. Thomas Law, who was now a member of the Revenue Board, believed that once the zamindars' ownership of the land was confirmed, they ought to lose the right to collect these duties, which should be done by the government.[46] However, Cornwallis was also challenging the utility of such duties, which were randomly levied 'on every article of commerce and necessary of life'. Here he agreed with Smith's advocates that an untrammelled internal commerce would greatly benefit ordinary Bengalis. The loss of revenue to the government would be trifling and could be easily recouped by an excise on spirituous liquors.[47]

In between managing the war effort, pacifying Stuart, and dealing with the Company's re-chartering, Cornwallis had resumed work on his ideas for a reform of the criminal justice system, which he had temporarily suspended in August 1789 to await the collectors' answers to his questions.[48] The first replies had been received in February 1790. Nevertheless, with so many other preoccupations, he had 'not yet been able to reduce my proposed regulations sufficiently into form' for submitting them to the board, as he informed the Directors on 19 April 1790. But one thing at least was clear. The need to reform 'the present wretched and corrupt system' of 'criminal justice' was as urgent as ever, in order to remedy those evils 'which have been so ruinous to the honest and industrious inhabitants of this country and so disgraceful to our Government'.[49] His intention was that the draft articles should first be checked by Sir William Jones. In the event he only submitted his regulatory outline in November 1790, when Jones was entirely complimentary: 'I read them all with my pen in hand, intending to write without reserve all objections that might occur to me'. However, 'I found nothing to which I could object.' His one substantive recommendation was that the pardoning of offenders should be transferred to the governor-general and council, rather than remain the responsibility of the circuit judges. Otherwise, 'I think the whole minute unexceptionably just, wise, and benevolent.'[50]

With such encouragement, Cornwallis presented his seventy-one-page minute to the council without further delay. First, he reviewed the existing system, remarking that although 'the regulation of justice in criminal cases' constituted 'one of the most important requisites of good government', its administration had never received proper attention, either from the Mughal emperors, Hindu rajahs, or Company officials. He then summarised the responses of the collectors to his nine questions. These indicated two areas where reform was required from a European perspective: first, defects in Islamic law which appeared contrary to natural justice; and second, failings in the court system for trying offenders.[51]

Regarding the Islamic law, he proposed that homicides should be determined by 'the intention of the criminal rather than the mode of the crime'. Currently strangling, drowning, poisoning, or the use of a club, where no blood was shed, were not deemed capital offences. Second, the practice of allowing victims or their relatives to pardon an offender should be abolished, since it permitted the perpetrators of many notorious crimes to buy their freedom. Third, Cornwallis proposed to eliminate the amputation of limbs and other cruel mutilations, to prevent the recurrence of a recent case in the Burdwan foujdary (district criminal court), where fifteen prisoners were to lose both their right hand and left leg.[52] Instead he proposed a table of equivalent punishments, substituting, for example, fourteen years' hard labour for the loss of two limbs. Finally, non-Muslims should be able to testify against Muslim defendants on an equal basis.[53] Cornwallis acknowledged that the Muslim community were likely to object to the changes. However, their most revered texts and teachers often disagreed about the correct interpretation of the Prophet's intentions. Most existing laws in any case would remain unchanged.[54]

The second area for reform was the court system. Cornwallis repeated his view that the procedural failings of the old Nizamut Adawlut courts of Mahomet Reza Khan, the last representative of the Mughal emperor in Bengal, were too notorious to merit any defence. His first proposal therefore was that the chief criminal court at Murshidabad should be replaced by the governor-general and council, sitting as a court of appeal, with suitably qualified pandits and maulvis to advise them on Hindu and Islamic practice. Second, the foujdary courts should be superseded by four new circuit courts, as he had earlier suggested to Dundas in 1789. Each court would be presided over by two Company judges, who would also have pandit and maulvi advisers, plus a registrar to keep proper records. The bottom or third tier of the criminal justice system would remain in the hands of the collectors, empowered as magistrates for dealing with petty crimes, while committing the more serious offenders to the circuit courts. However, cases involving British subjects and other Europeans would continue to be handled by the Supreme Court in Calcutta.[55] Racial integration of the justice system was not part of Cornwallis's agenda.

Although Speke asserted that the removal of the Nizamut Adawlut courts from Bengali control amounted to an unwarranted assumption of power, the other members of the council agreed with Cornwallis that they had sufficient authority to do this under the existing acts of Parliament.[56] However, a final decision on the proposed reforms necessarily required approval by the Directors in London, not least because the expense would be considerable. Nevertheless, Cornwallis believed it would prove a false economy not to implement the reforms, even in the middle of a costly war. To ensure that his proposals were properly considered, he took the precaution of forwarding a copy of his minute to Dundas.[57]

One thing that escaped discussion was the wisdom of replacing native judges. The assumption was universal that only British judges could ensure a uniformly impartial system that rose above the conflicting values of Muslims and Hindus. Such views were typical even for liberals like Jones. Writing to Arthur Lee, the American Patriot, Jones had commented in October 1786: 'Your observations on the Hindus are too just; they are incapable of civil liberty; few of them have any idea of it and those who have do not wish it.' The deplorable though necessary conclusion was that the peoples of India must 'be ruled by an absolute power'. The one consolation for those, like Jones and his correspondent, who cherished liberty was that 'the natives themselves . . . are happier under us than they were or could have been under the sultans of Delhi or petty rajahs'.[58] Such attitudes would remain largely unquestioned by Europeans until the twentieth century, however much they have subsequently been condemned.

As autumn approached Cornwallis's thoughts once again turned to the southern campaign, having heard nothing from Medows for two months. The last news from Medows was that he had occupied the fertile countryside around the town of Coimbatore, but did not expect to pass through the Ghat Mountains into Mysore before January 1791. This want of information was irksome because Cornwallis, as commander-in-chief, was ultimately responsible for the campaign's outcome. He was not alone in his ignorance. Abercromby too was awaiting instructions, as were the nizam and the peshwa. This led Cornwallis to urge Medows once more to change his plan. Because the southern campaign was currently stalled, he suggested that Medows prepare depots for an ascent of the Ghats from the Coromandel Coast. He should then transfer his army thither, leaving behind only enough troops to hold Coimbatore, as he would not have the resources for two offensives.[59]

Cornwallis was prompted to renew his suggestion of an alternative approach because he had received intelligence that the passes through the Eastern Ghats were lightly guarded. Perhaps a preliminary advance there might yield valuable results.[60] Three weeks later it appeared that Medows might be acting on his advice, for which Cornwallis was duly complimentary. Nevertheless, he could not refrain from adding that people were talking in Madras as though Musgrave was in command. Medows must be more forceful in asserting his authority.[61] These sentiments were hardly calculated to improve Medows's morale. Unsurprisingly, he began to talk about returning to Europe – limiting his stay as governor-general in Calcutta, should he be appointed to the role, to just twelve months. Such sentiments horrified Cornwallis. For the last eighteen months he had viewed Medows as his likely successor. Medows must surely realise that no one could establish a reputation in so short a time. Hopefully, he would reconsider his situation and commit himself to staying at least as long as Cornwallis had in Bengal.[62]

Nevertheless, for the moment Cornwallis had to accept the plan of Medows and Musgrave to advance from the south, given their confidence that the troops could ascend the Eastern Ghats from Coimbatore with less difficulty than supposed. They also believed that there was a good road leading directly from Coimbatore to Seringapatam (modern-day Srirangapatna), Tipu's capital.[63] But appearances proved deceptive: within a week, Cornwallis learnt that Tipu had descended from the Deccan Plateau and surprised a corps under Colonel John Floyd, forcing him to retreat with the loss of his artillery.[64] Most disturbing was a despondent letter from Medows asking to be relieved of his command, as he felt unequal to the task facing him.

Medows's request stunned Cornwallis, coming as it did from a man for whom he had 'always entertained the greatest esteem', a man who 'stood high in the opinion of the British nation'. Now that same man was proposing to 'sacrifice not only the interest of the public but his character as an officer'. Even the lowest ranks knew the disgrace an officer must suffer, if he quitted 'his station in time of war, merely to gratify his own inclinations'. Cornwallis could only reaffirm his own principles: 'No considerations of a personal nature, either regarding myself or any other individual, shall induce me to swerve from the line, which I have hitherto so steadily pursued' of serving king and country. Medows should do the same. Nevertheless, Floyd's recent setback made it inevitable that Cornwallis would be expected to 'take an executive position in the conduct of military operations'. Hence, unless Medows's advance through the Ghats brought a speedy and decisive outcome, Cornwallis would join him in December at Madras, 'when I trust that our united efforts in the cabinet and in the field will soon bring the contest to an honourable termination'.[65]

In his public dispatches, Cornwallis tried to protect Medows and Musgrave.[66] Privately he was scathing of both, telling Lichfield that they were highly 'reprobated'. Their mismanagement meant he would have to take command himself, travelling to

Madras on a ship which should otherwise have carried him to 'a happier port' in Europe. In prospect was a zero-sum game, since he would get no credit for defeating Tipu, but incur eternal disgrace if he was unsuccessful.[67] The reality was that Tipu 'by his rapid and well-concerted marches' had effectually destroyed Medows's campaign. Regrettably, the consequences did not stop there, as he informed the prince of Wales. At stake was Cornwallis's programme for reforming the East India Company. So far, 'everything in Bengal has succeeded to the utmost of my wishes: the permanent settlement of the land revenue is nearly completed; vexatious duties that brought little to the government and oppressed the people are now abolished; [while] the gross abuses and corruptions in the administration of the criminal justice will be corrected by the regulations' that he had recently proposed. 'If the restless ambition of Tipu had not intervened, I could have executed my original intention of embarking for England in January next . . . leaving the Company's affairs in excellent order, and the country in a state of happiness and prosperity little known in the Asiatic world.'[68] Now this was all in jeopardy.

Among the first to know of Cornwallis's decision was Malet, who was to assure the peshwa's court at Pune that, despite the recent setback, the Company still intended to invade Mysore and reward the peshwa for his support. The difference was that Cornwallis would now direct operations himself, assisted by further reinforcements from Bengal.[69] Cornwallis still had to persuade the council that he should take command at Madras. He had in the past been dubious about leaving his colleagues in charge, but this had changed following the resolution of his differences with Stuart. He was now more confident that the council would continue 'the measures for the internal government of Bengal', which he had initiated. But to ensure this happened, his colleagues were to send him regular reports of their proceedings during his absence. He would in turn write with 'as much punctuality and expedition as the nature of the service' would allow, receiving 'their advice and suggestions with all the attention and deference which is due to private friends and to the acting members of the supreme government'.[70]

The response of the council was uniformly in favour of Cornwallis's proposal. He was especially pleased with Stuart's reaction, as he informed Dundas. Stuart had given him the strongest assurances that as head of the council he would 'do nothing without consulting the official people' in whom Cornwallis principally confided.

This confirmed Cornwallis's belief that 'no material mischief' would happen during his absence. However, it would be reassuring if Dundas could finally secure the appointment of Duncan to the council. As to the war, Cornwallis remained confident that it would end successfully, despite Tipu's recent victory. He would be taking with him the 73rd Foot Regiment, another 1,200–1,400 sepoys, a regiment of cavalry, and 1,000 bullocks for hauling the artillery.[71] Hickey noted that the Sepoys were ready to 'surmount their long-established prejudices' against travelling by sea because of 'their extraordinary respect for Lord Cornwallis'.[72]

Before his departure, Cornwallis wrote a longer than usual letter to Brome, lamenting that they would not meet as expected next summer. Instead of 'embracing you and Mary, and enjoying the society of my nearest relations and best friends, my duty to my country obliges me to go to Madras, in order to take the field against Tipu Sultan', who had 'proved a more formidable enemy' than expected. As to Brome's future, Cornwallis always intended that he should stay at Eton until Christmas 1791, when he would be seventeen years of age. Even then he would be too young to 'lay aside all thought' of improving his mind. The question was whether he should go to university or attend a foreign academy to learn French and perhaps German. As to a future career, Cornwallis was against his going into the army, doubting that Brome had the necessary physique. 'I earnestly exhort you not to do it, unless you feel a decided and insuperable inclination for that profession.' Should that be the case Cornwallis would give his consent, 'for it is your happiness and not my own that I am to consider'. But Brome should understand that soldiering was 'a thorny path, full of disappointments', as Cornwallis could attest, bringing 'years of heartaches for moments of gratification'.[73]

At a final meeting with the council on 3 December, Cornwallis expressed his confidence that Bengal would be well managed during his absence, being in the hands of colleagues for whose 'principles and public spirit I have the highest respect'. With these formalities concluded, the following day he boarded his yacht for Diamond Harbour, where the frigate *Vestal* waited to carry him to Madras.[74] Despite the public acclaim, he departed, as he confessed to Lichfield, 'with a head full of care, and an aching heart'.[75]

ELEVEN

Clipping Tipu's Wings

The journey southward proved mercifully short. The *Vestal* arrived at Madras just seven days later, on the morning of 13 December 1790. Here Cornwallis's first task was to confirm to Medows his intention to abandon the plan to enter Mysore from the south. His reasons were essentially the same as before. Most importantly, any advance from Coimbatore must use either the Gajalhatti or Kaveri Falls passes. The first was strongly fortified and the latter required multiple river crossings. Second, such a route would be difficult to support from Madras. An advance on Hosur and Bangalore from the Coromandel Coast, in contrast, would force Tipu to defend these key locations, providing the chance for a decisive battle. It would also offer a shorter and more secure communication via Ambur and Vellore, where large magazines were already established. Finally, that route would provide a protective shield for the forces of the peshwa and the nizam on their southward march towards Tipu's capital, Seringapatam.[1]

Medows was accordingly to abandon his present positions, except for keeping garrisons at Dindigul, Madurai, and Trichinopoly. As to Coimbatore, Medows could either evacuate it or leave a garrison capable of resisting artillery for a month. His army was then to march in two divisions to Vellore, 80 miles west of Madras, though the two corps were to remain within 30 miles of each other, so that they could reunite in an emergency. At Vellore they would be joined by Cornwallis with the Bengal reinforcements for the advance on Bangalore.[2]

Cornwallis's next letter was to Abercromby, informing him of the recent change of plans and that the Bombay army should begin its campaign by attacking Cannanore (modern-day Kannur) on the Malabar Coast. Here Abercromby should attempt to enlist the support of the Hindu Nair people, who were in revolt against Tipu. After this Abercromby was to find a pass through the Western Ghats into Mysore itself. However, he was not to advance on Seringapatam until he was sure of support from Cornwallis's army.[3]

Cornwallis had started his own preparations well before leaving Bengal. Among his first actions was the dispatch of Captain Alexander Kyd to gather intelligence about the passes into Mysore, the state of the roads, the surrounding countryside, and anything else likely to assist or impede an army.[4] He had also sent Lieutenant George Robinson, the military auditor, to assess what funds would be needed. Robinson was in addition to check on the ordnance, camp equipage, and provisions, as well as the draught cattle likely to be required. The Madras government had strict instructions to assist him.[5]

For the next few weeks Cornwallis's life was one of total immersion in business. Apsley, his aide, wondered how he could endure such fatigue, 'being night and day in conference with natives of rank and abilities, endeavouring to obtain information', while 'writing and receiving dispatches to and from the army'.[6] The multiplicity of business led Cornwallis to advise Abercromby that he was unlikely to advance from Vellore before 10 February 1791.[7] Another impediment was the failure of the reinforcements from Bengal to arrive. Even at the end of January many vessels were still missing. The reason for their delay was contrary winds, rather than a want of effort in Calcutta. 'Stuart is doing vastly well', Cornwallis reported to Dundas, while Cowper, whom he had opposed for promotion, was consulting Cornwallis's' trusted officials on all important points.[8] Another person to exceed Cornwallis's expectations was Murray, who as commissary was in charge of forwarding supplies: 'Your zealous exertions in the very disagreeable and troublesome task, which you were so kind as voluntarily to undertake', were greatly appreciated.[9]

One concern was the report of tension between Pune and Hyderabad, which suggested that the two courts might not co-operate. However, on 11 January Kennaway reported that the nizam's chief minister was to meet the peshwa's envoys to discuss a joint invasion of Mysore. Cornwallis's advice that a union of their forces was the best defence against Tipu was seemingly having effect.[10] Time was pressing, for as Cornwallis informed Kennaway, he now hoped to advance by 20 February. Would the nizam provide a body of cavalry in support? Kennaway was also to inform Hyderabad of a recent attempt by Tipu to detach the British from the alliance, as Cornwallis believed that honesty was the best way of building trust. Kennaway was accordingly to reassure the nizam that 'no consideration shall ever induce me to abandon allies who are faithful to us'. Equally, no attempt would be made 'to gain advantageous terms for ourselves' without securing proper compensation for Pune and Hyderabad.[11] Similar undertakings were being given at Pune, where Malet urged the peshwa's chief minister, Nana Furnuwees, to seize the opportunity for 'personal fame and national renown' by expediting the progress of their renowned commander, Haripant Phadke, or 'Harry Punt', as the British called him.[12]

By the middle of February, the army at Vellore, now united under Cornwallis's command, was ready to begin its march through the Eastern Ghats. Several routes beckoned, and Cornwallis only ascended the Mugli Pass west of Chittoor at the last moment, a manoeuvre which caught Tipu by surprise.[13] The advance, therefore, was unopposed, allowing the heavy artillery and stores to reach the open countryside of the Deccan Plateau without interruption. Bangalore, the immediate objective, was 110 miles to the west, a march of six to ten days. Ascending the Eastern Ghats meant the advent of cooler weather, which was a great comfort to Cornwallis. Even so the temperature rose from 19°C at five in the morning to 35°C or above by early afternoon. Fortunately, the health of the troops had not been affected. Since he had little time to write private letters, Cornwallis asked Lichfield to give his love to the children, commenting that Brome would have enjoyed seeing the elephants pushing heavy cannon over 'bad roads with their forehead and their trunk'.[14]

After a few days spent on the plateau to reorganise and recuperate, the army resumed its march on 23 February. Before the start of the campaign, Cornwallis had rebuked one of Tipu's commanders for committing outrages against the civilian population. 'Whilst the English troops abstain from all violence against defenceless people', Tipu's line of march was customarily marked by burning villages and the mangled corpses of raiyats.[15] Now, ironically, he found himself issuing general orders condemning 'the shocking and disgraceful outrages' that his own troops had perpetrated on the first stage of the march. As in America, such conduct, if left unchecked, would 'defeat all our hopes of success and blast the British name with infamy'.[16] The twin scourges of looting and violence to civilians were ever present when British troops campaigned in a foreign country.

1. Cornwallis's grave demeanour suggests that his responsibilities as a newly promoted twenty-two-year-old lieutenant-colonel of the 12th Foot Regiment were uppermost in his thoughts. Here he is seated in his regimental uniform, contemplating an imminent return to active service in the allied army of Duke Ferdinand of Brunswick towards the end of the Seven Years' War.

2. The Reynolds portrait admirably captures the poise and elegance of Jemima Countess Cornwallis (née Jones), with just a hint of the playful spirit that captured Cornwallis's heart. Her early death was to be an enduring sadness for him, explaining his constant restlessness and wish to be employed on public service during the rest of his life.

3. Though now a major-general, Cornwallis still kept his uniform as colonel of the 33rd Foot Regiment, which he wore at regimental functions when not on active service.

4. Wearing the green uniform of the loyalist British Legion, Banastre Tarleton has dismounted from his horse and is about to draw his sword to continue the battle on foot. The picture captures both his youthfulness and ruthlessness, as he stares fixatedly on vanquishing the enemy.

5. The portrait is suggestive of a genial character, far different from the prickly personality lurking beneath, as Cornwallis discovered while serving in America. Here Henry Clinton is dressed in the uniform of a lieutenant-general, wearing the insignia of the Order of the Bath.

6. Archibald Campbell served, like Cornwallis, in America, though this portrayal shows him ten years later when governor of Madras, suggesting the effect that India's climate could have on Europeans serving there. He died within two years of returning to Britain, aged fifty-two.

15. Like George III, Cornwallis held regular receptions for local dignitaries. By now his large paunch had become a regular feature of cartoons about him. Here he is seen receiving a succession of sycophantic guests, pointing out his Garter star to one attendee. In the foreground Colonel Alexander Ross and another senior military officer hold an animated conversation. No Bengalis appear to be present.

16. The forbidding walls of Fort William and the severe architecture of Government House inside provided the first glimpse of Calcutta for new arrivals. Even for Cornwallis, the fort and its associated buildings were a stark testimony to the East India Company's power and dominance in the region.

17. East India House was another reminder of the power and wealth of the East India Company, being one of the largest and most impressive buildings in London.

18. The print shows the courtyard as it is today and as Cornwallis would have known it, with the state apartments on the left opposite the Bedford Tower to the north, the latter being flanked by the imposing arches of the twin main gates. It was at one of these that Cornwallis was fired upon after failing to answer a sentry's challenge.

19. William Pitt is shown speaking to the House of Commons in St Stephen's Chapel at the Palace of Westminster, where debates were held before 1834. Pitt was famed for his oratory and the members are clearly attentive, perhaps having just received news about the outbreak of war with Revolutionary France.

20. This aerial view provides a classic example of an eighteenth-century fort, built on Vauban's principles, with protruding redoubts at each corner to enfilade any attempt to scale the walls. Combined with batteries on the opposite bank, the structure was well calculated to prevent an enemy reaching London via the River Thames.

21. Henry Dundas was the one member of Pitt's cabinet with whom Cornwallis felt at ease. He was also the only minister to keep Cornwallis informed while he was in Ireland and feeling beleaguered by the twin tasks of ending the 1798 rebellion and securing a political union of the two kingdoms.

22. By this time the duke of York had become commander-in-chief of the British army and a key adviser to the Pitt ministry. His genial personality made him, in Cornwallis's opinion, too easily manipulated by unscrupulous companions, prompting him to make misguided decisions on critical issues.

23. Cornwallis is depicted here as the victorious proconsul, wearing the Garter star and uniform of a lieutenant-general. In the background an Indian prince and his entourage make their way towards Calcutta on ceremonial elephants. Cornwallis's continued difficulty controlling his weight is not disguised.

24. Sculptor Charles Rossi depicts Cornwallis here in the guise of a Roman general. Beneath him on the left sits Britannia with her trident and shield, to the left reclines the figure of the Ganges River god, while in between them stands Columbia. The three figures collectively provide an allegorical allusion to Cornwallis's service in America, India, Britain and Europe.

The army reached Bangalore on 5 March, where the engineers carried out a preliminary inspection of the city's defences. While this was in progress, Floyd, in charge of the cavalry, mistakenly attacked what he thought was the enemy's rearguard, only to discover he was engaging Tipu's main force. The result was the loss of 200 men and 300 horses. Nevertheless, Cornwallis determined to commence a siege, despite the strength of the garrison and the nearby presence of Tipu. The town itself was secured on 7 March, after which resources were directed against the main fort. This was finally captured during a night attack on 21 March, in which as many as 2,000 in the garrison were killed or wounded and fifty pieces of ordnance captured. British losses were modest in comparison, amounting to just 100 Europeans and thirty sepoys.[17]

After putting Bangalore into a state of defence, Cornwallis advanced once more on 28 March for a union with the nizam's forces. A large convoy was approaching from the coast, with vital supplies for the investment of Seringapatam. Caution was essential, since Tipu was clearly awaiting another opportunity to strike a blow. On the afternoon of 6 April Cornwallis was consequently astonished to find that the officer supervising the army's next encampment, Major Peters, had neglected to secure some heights overlooking a road that led directly to Tipu's camp. This was unpardonable neglect. Only the want of time prevented him from calling the officer to a more rigorous account for his conduct.[18]

Despite the capture of Bangalore, the timetable for a successful outcome before the monsoon season was beginning to slip. Abercromby had reached the head of Kodagu Pass on 26 February with a force consisting of 2,100 Europeans, 3,000 sepoys, and 700 Travancore irregulars, plus artillery.[19] However, he warned Cornwallis on 6 April that the monsoon season would arrive in late May, making the Western Ghats impassable and further operations inadvisable. If Cornwallis was unable to reach Seringapatam shortly, Abercromby would have to retreat.[20]

One reason for the lack of progress was the failure of the nizam's cavalry to appear to reinforce Floyd's depleted corps. That mishap had made Rajah Teige Wunt, the nizam's commander, even more fearful of meeting Tipu in the field. Only after Cornwallis had sent a stinging rebuke was a junction eventually made.[21] He may have regretted being so peremptory. When the nizam's 16,000 horsemen finally arrived on 13 April, they were clearly 'defective in almost every point of military discipline'. Nevertheless, the men were well mounted and Cornwallis resolved to continue his advance on Seringapatam, as he informed the Directors on 20 April 1791. He was still anxious to avoid a protracted war which would ruin the Company's finances. Hopefully, the Maratha Confederacy would appear in time to allow the army to conclude matters before the monsoon season arrived. The capture of Seringapatam would in these circumstances be an 'ample reward'.[22]

The army eventually began its final advance on 3 May 1791 with the nizam's cavalry, five regiments of sepoy cavalry, six royal regiments, seventeen sepoy infantry battalions, and a 'respectable corps of artillery', totalling some 60,000 men. As Cornwallis approached Seringapatam, he asked Wunt to deploy his cavalry to prevent reinforcements reaching the city, fearing that he might otherwise linger in the army's rear, consuming provisions without making any contribution to the campaign.[23] But despite these orders, Cornwallis was mortified to hear that barely 200 of Wunt's men had gone out on patrol, while a numerous crowd of his camp followers had impeded the army on its line of march.[24]

Cornwallis reached the village of Arakere a few miles from Seringapatam on 13 May 1791, where he hoped to ford the Kaveri River. Here he learnt that Tipu had similarly placed his army on the northern bank, presenting an opportunity to engage him in battle, which the sultan had so far been careful to avoid. To make an engagement more certain, Cornwallis resolved to approach the enemy encampment at night and surprise the Mysore army at dawn on 15 May. His plan was unfortunately disrupted by a violent rainstorm, which allowed Tipu to withdraw into Seringapatam, though the outcome might still have been decisive had Wunt's cavalry not obstructed operations at a critical moment. Left behind by the enemy were numerous regimental colours, several brass cannon, and evidence that Tipu had suffered heavy casualties.[25]

Nevertheless, the victory was incomplete since the town's defences still had to be breached. This would require a siege. Moreover, despite Cornwallis's best endeavours at procuring supplies, he now faced a critical lack of forage and provisions. He would also have to cross the Kaveri to accomplish a junction with Abercromby, and a suitable ford had yet to be found.[26] The situation could only worsen with the start of the monsoon season. Finally, the Maratha commanders, Haripant Phadke and Perseram Bhow, had failed to appear.[27]

In the midst of these difficulties Cornwallis was contacted by Tipu proposing peace talks. However, he made no mention of the nizam or the peshwa, forcing

Cornwallis to repeat what he had previously affirmed: no talks could be started that were not tripartite on the British side, since Cornwallis was determined to honour his undertakings to the allies. Hopefully Tipu would recognise these necessary preconditions so that together they could 'prevent the total ruin' of his country and end the distress 'to which the wretched inhabitants are at present subjected'. Tipu should accordingly suggest such inducements as his opponents might legitimately expect for their exertions, which could then be discussed at a formal congress.[28] Yet despite the clarity of Cornwallis's declaration, Tipu still refused to accept it as a final answer, sending him instead a bowl of the choicest fruits. Cornwallis's response was terse this time: 'His Lordship cannot with propriety receive a present', though he would be happy to do so once peace had been re-established. He would then use 'every means in his power, to encourage and increase a friendly intercourse'.[29]

If Tipu's aim was to delay the allied advance, he was successful, since the prospects for making further progress appeared distinctly unpromising. The nizam's main army was reluctant to advance because of the lateness of the season.[30] Abercromby was in a similar quandary, being anxious to withdraw before the mountain passes became blocked. He had already decided that he must leave behind several 18-pounder iron cannon.[31] The news was enough to convince Cornwallis on 21 May that he would have to postpone the attack on Seringapatam until the monsoon season had passed. Abercromby could, therefore, continue his retreat, while the main army returned to Bangalore on half-rations. Cornwallis too would have to destroy part of his battering (siege) train of heavy cannon and mortars.[32]

But just when the situation seemed most dire, it was suddenly transformed by the arrival of the Maratha armies of Phadke and Bhow. Cornwallis reflected in frustration what might have happened had they appeared two weeks earlier. Tipu would have been forced to yield, since the Maratha brought with them great supplies of provisions to sustain a siege. Cornwallis would also have preserved his battering train.[33] Nevertheless their appearance meant that he could remain before Seringapatam for a few more weeks, despite the imminent rains, to prevent Tipu from receiving supplies. A James Gillray cartoon subsequently portrayed Cornwallis as being driven away from the city by a monsoon conjured up by Tipu.[34] The suggestion of needless caution was ill founded, as were the newspaper accusations of unbridled eastern luxury in the British camp. As Cornwallis had earlier observed to Dundas, had these critics served on the present campaign they would have known better than to voice such ridiculous sentiments.[35]

The army finally began its retreat to Bangalore towards the end of June, unmolested by Tipu, who was too weak to harass it on the march. Along the way, Cornwallis noted the lack of medical provision for the injured sepoys of the Madras Presidency. No matter what their injuries, each of these wretched men was 'squeezed into a blanket and carried by two of their comrades'. 'It is hardly creditable', he told Sir Charles Oakley, the new governor at Madras, 'that so shocking a practice could have existed so long'. Apart from its inhumanity, the practice was a false economy, since it greatly weakened morale and encouraged desertion. Wagons or carts must in future be provided for sick sepoys in like manner as the Bengal corps.[36]

Once back in Bangalore, Cornwallis immediately began addressing the problems which had undermined the recent campaign. High on his list was the replacement of Wunt as commander of the Hyderabad cavalry. Cornwallis was especially annoyed at Wunt's attempts to blame his failings on others. Although Kennaway was to observe diplomatic protocol, he should make Cornwallis's dissatisfaction clear to the nizam. In 'the refutation of so much misrepresentation and falsehood, it is necessary that you should tell the whole truth'.[37]

Plain speaking was similarly required of Malet at Pune, where he was to inform the peshwa that their treaty required all three signatories to make an equal contribution to the common objective. Throughout the campaign Cornwallis had had to pursue his operations without the assistance of Phadke, despite repeated promises of support. The other Maratha commander, Bhow, had been equally remiss in not assisting Abercromby to find cattle and other supplies. The British commanders had had in consequence to end their operations early, surrendering the advantages that should have accrued from the advance on Seringapatam.[38]

To avoid a repetition of these disappointments, Cornwallis requested both courts to have their forces ready by early October 1791. Early indications were that the nizam was ready to comply, since Kennaway reported in mid-August that his officials were busy recruiting 'banjaras'.[39] These were itinerant merchants who carried provisions on small carts or oxen for sale to the army. Once they had disposed of their goods in the military bazaar, they would return under escort for another consignment. Cornwallis decided to follow the nizam's example and soon had agreements with several thousand banjaras, many of them former employees of Tipu. Food at least should not be a problem next time.[40]

While dealing with supply details, Cornwallis also pondered the strategic outlines of his forthcoming campaign. The main difference, he informed Abercromby, would be an earlier start in November 1791, rather than after the New Year. Otherwise his plans were similar to the campaign just ended. Cornwallis would again advance from Bangalore, supported by a supply chain based on Madras. The Bombay army was similarly to advance down the coast to approach Seringapatam from the north-west. Abercromby's main difficulty, judging from recent experience, was likely to be a lack of draught animals for hauling his artillery and wagon train. To meet this deficiency Cornwallis proposed to send him 10,000 bullocks with pack saddles from Madras. Nevertheless, Cornwallis would be glad to hear Abercromby's thoughts on the matter.[41] Two heads were always better than one.

One cause for confidence was the continued efficiency with which the war was being supported in Calcutta. Murray had already anticipated the need for another campaign, despite the successes at Bangalore and Seringapatam, and was making preparations for the supply of bullocks and other necessities.[42] Cornwallis was quick to appreciate his 'zealous assistance', affirming that his earlier opposition to Murray's return was solely because his appointment might breach the Act of 1784. Now he would have Cornwallis's full support, should queries be raised about his position as commissary-general.[43]

The break for the monsoon season meant that Cornwallis could resume his personal correspondence. Writing to Lichfield on 13 July, he reported that he was in good health, despite earlier complaints about the heat. He admitted, however, that his spirits were 'almost worn out'. If Tipu could not be reduced soon, 'I think the plagues and mortifications of this most difficult war will overcome me'. His anxiety was not eased by the reflection that he would be unlikely to leave India before January 1793. This raised again the question of Brome's future when he left Eton. If he did not wish to become a soldier, attending university might be the right course after all, given the turmoil in Europe. But if soldiering was his choice, he should go to a German academy and learn that language, 'the want of which I have often regretted'.[44]

Another domestic concern requiring Cornwallis's attention was the management of the Eye constituency, where a 'spirit of disinclination to the ancient connection with our family' had arisen. Cornwallis had two options: either to abandon the borough or try to strengthen family influence there. But despite past tribulations, Cornwallis refused to contemplate withdrawal. The right to vote in the constituency was held by the 200 householders who paid the local scot-and-lot municipal taxes, but did not necessarily own their homes. Cornwallis accordingly gave Lichfield full powers to purchase any properties for sale in Eye as a way of exerting influence.[45] It was a tactic well known to his former godfather, the duke of Newcastle.

It was during this time that Cornwallis received details regarding the improvements to Culford Park, where the decision had been taken to rebuild rather than repair. Construction had begun in February 1790 under the guidance of the architect James Wyatt. Because of his other responsibilities, Lichfield had left supervision of the project to Charles Townshend.[46] Later in the year the Reverend William Palgrave, an old clerical friend, sent Cornwallis a description of how the work was progressing. A new staircase had been installed where a small open courtyard had previously been, creating a spacious atrium under a glass roof. This had enabled the first floor to be reconfigured to increase the size and number of the bedrooms. Downstairs the former dining room and Cornwallis's bedroom had been combined to create a new library 'with every comfort and convenience'. Palgrave's only regret was the loss of some bow windows at the front of the house.[47]

In his most recent letter, Lichfield also sent accounts that the parliamentary opposition were criticising Cornwallis for provoking an 'unjust, ambitious and inexpedient' war. Their principal argument was that the alliance with the peshwa and the nizam contravened the 1784 India Act forbidding all wars of conquest. Leading the attack was John Hippisley, a former Company employee in Madras.[48] But as Cornwallis commented to Lichfield, Hippisley's time in India had been entirely devoted to making money: his speeches revealed that he knew nothing of the country's politics, history, or geography. No one had 'ever entered into a war more unwillingly' than Cornwallis, 'or would be more sincerely rejoiced to get out of it', as his correspondence would show.[49] He was right to be contemptuous, as the opposition resolutions were defeated by large majorities in both houses in favour of motions approving his conduct.[50]

Apart from preparing for the next campaign, Cornwallis again addressed the question of a successor, since Medows no longer wished to be considered for the position of governor-general. Given this vacancy, he appealed to Dundas to cajole the Directors into settling the matter. Cornwallis would of course complete the business on which he was engaged, much as he wished to depart. The key thing was to have a successor in place. Stuart had greatly exceeded Cornwallis's expectations while in charge at Calcutta, but wanted to retire, which would mean leaving the unreliable Speke in charge for six months.[51] This latter danger prompted Cornwallis to write a few days later to the Directors, reminding them of the need to avoid any temporary appointment, as had happened with Macpherson in 1785. This meant that the new governor-general should be ready to leave Britain so as to arrive 'no later in Bengal than January or February 1793'.[52]

Although the rainy season had intervened, military operations were not entirely halted, since in early August Tipu launched a pre-emptive strike against Coimbatore. Fortunately, Major William Cuppage, an experienced artillery officer, had been able to march to its relief from Palghat, leaving an extra battalion for the town's defence.[53] Tipu also tried diplomacy again, sending vakeels, or envoys, to the British camp to discuss peace terms. Cornwallis, fearing they were spies rather than diplomats, quickly ordered them to talk with the allied representatives at Hosur, well away from the main army.[54] He was right to be sceptical for he shortly learnt that Tipu was making separate proposals to the nizam as a co-religionist and former ally of his father Haidar Ali.[55] When the vakeels refused to go to Hosur, Cornwallis told them to return to their master in Seringapatam.[56]

By the end of October 1791 Cornwallis's plans for the forthcoming campaign were almost complete. Still missing were details about fording the Kaveri River, since its crossing would be the key to a union with Abercromby.[57] It was partly for this reason that he remained unsure how to reduce Seringapatam, whether by an assault or blockade of the main fort. The intentions of the allies were also unclear, though they promised to advance when requested. News then arrived that Tipu had renewed his attack on Coimbatore. Cornwallis initially affected to be unconcerned, given its recent reinforcement by Cuppage. His attention was focused on Medows's mission to capture several forts to the east and north of Bangalore, which were vital for securing the army's communications.[58]

Cornwallis's belief that Coimbatore was not in danger was quickly proved mistaken. This time Cuppage found he had insufficient troops to rescue the garrison, and had to leave the town to its fate.[59] Cornwallis was sufficiently humbled to warn Pitt that the expectations in Britain of his impending success were too sanguine: 'It is no easy task to provide for the subsistence of vast multitudes in a distant desert, nor can it be the work of a day to subdue a prince so active and capable, possessed of such immense resources and so well served by his officers as Tipu.'[60] The sultan and his father had twice defeated British armies and a third disaster was not impossible.

Nevertheless, the work of preparation went on. Because the countryside between Bangalore and Seringapatam was barren, Cornwallis increased the number of banjaras for bringing provisions to the army to 40,000. But to keep the supplies flowing securely, one final threat remained to the army's line of advance, namely the fort of Savandurga. This was perched on top of a basalt rock, 900 feet high and several miles in circumference. While Tipu held this, no banjaras would dare pass.[61] Cornwallis had hoped to remove this obstacle in early November, but rain had slowed the delivery of men and materials from the coast. When the troops finally reached Savandurga on 2 December, the senior engineer could see no weak point for an attack.[62] However, Cornwallis was not convinced about Savandurga's impregnability, since closer inspection revealed it consisted of two forts separated by a deep gully. He accordingly ordered Colonel Stuart to begin the assault by focusing on the smaller post to the north-east. The boldness of the attack quickly overawed the enemy, as Cornwallis informed the Directors on 26 December 1791. The western fort was shortly afterwards similarly terrified into surrendering. The British did not lose a man in the actual assault and suffered only seventeen fatalities in preparation for a siege. Cornwallis was justifiably proud of the troops' achievement, believing the operation had few parallels in history, certainly none in India.[63] As a result many other smaller forts surrendered with minimal resistance, providing the army with a secure communication to

Seringapatam. The prospect of bringing this tiresome war to a happy termination had been greatly improved.[64]

But every success was invariably balanced by a setback; this time it came to the nizam's forces at one of the forts recently captured by Medows, following a surprise cavalry attack by Tipu's eldest son, Shezada Haidar Ali.[65] Cornwallis was also concerned about the tardiness of the Maratha forces of Perseram Bhow, who was to support Abercromby in his advance on Seringapatam.[66] His fears proved well founded, for in mid-January 1792 he heard that Bhow, despite repeatedly promising to join the British, had instead opted to plunder Tipu's western territories of Mangalore and Bidanore.[67] The Maratha commander asserted in justification that he had defeated one of Tipu's generals, Ali Reza Khan, and cut off the flow of enemy supplies from Mysore's richest province.[68] Nevertheless, it was clear that Bhow's diversion would make Abercromby's communication less secure and increase his difficulty in reaching the Kaveri River.[69]

Although Malet protested to the peshwa about Bhow's conduct, Cornwallis recognised that the final advance on Seringapatam would have to proceed without him, relying instead on the smaller force of Maratha cavalry of Phadke, together with the nizam's mounted troops, who were now under a new commander. As no ford had yet been found over the Kaveri, Cornwallis advised Abercromby to travel with as little baggage and heavy equipment as possible. He was confident that Tipu's weakened forces were unlikely to trouble Abercromby, even without his artillery. The army in India had too often dragged unnecessarily large trains behind it, adding to the expense and delay. Once the two armies had made contact, Abercromby was to stay on the south side of the Kaveri to complete the encirclement of Tipu's capital.[70]

The army commenced its march from Savandurga on 1 February with the British forces deployed in three parallel columns: in the middle Cornwallis placed the baggage and artillery, on the right the infantry, and on the left the cavalry. According to Major Alexander Dirom, the deputy adjutant-general, this method of advancing proved highly advantageous, since it provided a more compact and effective formation in the event of an attack. He also commended Cornwallis's decision to take a different route to Seringapatam through more fertile terrain, taking advantage of the army's experience the previous year. Finally, Dirom noted the greater use of elephants, especially for pushing wagons with their tusks at difficult points, which they did with ease, having the strength of sixteen bullocks. Previously the Company's officers thought that elephants could only live on a costly diet of rice. In reality they were readily nourished by leaves and sugar cane.[71]

The allied forces reached the vicinity of Seringapatam on 5 February 1792 without mishap. Here they found Tipu's army still encamped on the northern bank protected by a thick hedge. Interspersed were strong redoubts, which in turn were guarded by small ravines, swamps, and water courses. Another series of fortifications protected the island on which the city stood.[72] Since a daytime operation would result in heavy casualties, Cornwallis determined to attack once more at night, sensing that Indian armies, lacking the discipline of European troops, were more vulnerable to surprise when they could not see their enemy. This would mean attacking before Abercromby arrived, but Cornwallis surmised that his own nineteen European and sepoy battalions were more than sufficient for the immediate task.[73]

After a thorough examination of Tipu's dispositions, Cornwallis decided to strike in three columns on the night of 6 February 1792, with an elite force of 8,700 men. Medows was to command the right wing, while Cornwallis himself directed the centre, leaving Colonel Hamilton Maxwell in charge of the left. The immediate objective of Cornwallis and Medows was Tipu's encampment, which they were to storm before crossing the seasonally low river into the city. Maxwell, however, first had to seize some heights around the Karegat Pagoda before similarly entering the town. Since the operation would take place at night, no artillery or cavalry would be necessary.[74] The Maratha and Hyderabad horse was instead to patrol the flanks and rear of the army to protect its baggage and encampment. The allies' astonishment at the speed and daring of Cornwallis's plan was only equalled by their surprise that he would lead the attack in person, and 'fight like a common soldier'.[75]

In the event the centre and left divisions were entirely successful, though Medows's corps attacked the wrong target owing to an error by his guides. Cornwallis himself spent most of the night on horseback directing operations as best he could, during which his left hand was grazed by a bullet. Later, while awaiting Medows, Cornwallis's entourage was subjected to a fierce counterattack by Tipu. Only the bravery of some heavily outnumbered sepoys saved Cornwallis from capture and death.[76] Nevertheless, by daybreak the entire north bank had been occupied and much of Seringapatam too. Although the left wing of Tipu's army remained unscathed, the rest of his army suffered heavy losses, including sixty pieces of artillery. The Company's casualties were 533, of whom 302 were Europeans and 231 sepoys.[77]

With most of the town in British hands, attention turned to the investment of the main fort. Although Tipu organised several counterattacks to relieve his beleaguered forces, none were successful. His position became even more precarious with the approach of Abercromby's army, which would allow the fort to be invested without interruption. On the afternoon of 8 February 1792, he made his first request for peace talks. Cornwallis immediately responded that Tipu must first release the garrison captured at Coimbatore before negotiations could begin. Tipu's commander there, Kamar-ud-Deen Khan, had promised to free the garrison if they surrendered the town, but had promptly incarcerated them once the gates were opened. Since the captives were scattered over a wide area, Cornwallis decided on 14 February to accept the release of two officers, Lieutenants Chalmers and Nash, as evidence of Tipu's good faith, so that 'no time should be necessarily lost in securing a safe and honourable peace'. That was the great objective 'of the Company and the British nation'.[78]

The ministry had discussed peace terms as early as November 1790. One proposal was to restore the former ruling family to the throne of Mysore. Another was for the Company to take advantage of the conflict to swap Tellicherry for Gujarat to make Bombay more economically viable. But, as Dundas acknowledged, the negotiations must not result in the indiscriminate acquisition of territory, since 'the reverse is our avowed principle', a nod to the 1784 India Act. Some ministers also thought that the elimination of Tipu might make the Maratha Confederacy too strong.[79] However, Medows's disappointing campaign in 1790 led them to recognise that the eventual terms were best left to those conducting the war.[80] The Directors thought similarly, telling Cornwallis in September 1791 that they had 'the fullest confidence' in his discretion, especially on the need to bring the war to a speedy completion for the benefit of the Company's finances. The Directors would be satisfied if he obtained terms which indemnified them for the cost of the war and provided security in the future.[81]

These sentiments accorded well with Cornwallis's own views. Although the removal of Tipu remained desirable, the conclusion of a safe and honourable peace was still greater.[82] Talks accordingly began with Tipu's vakeels on 15 February, when the allies demanded the surrender of half of his territory plus a large sum of money. Tipu's envoys quickly protested that such terms were beyond their master's means.[83] The siege preparations therefore continued, which were fully justified when Abercromby's forces were involved in a sharp engagement on 22 February, during which over 100 were killed or wounded. But any inclination by Tipu to continue the war evaporated the next day with the arrival of Perseram Bhow and the main Maratha army.[84] Under the preliminary articles of peace agreed on 23 February 1792, he was to surrender half of his lands, based on the revenues produced rather than their physical extent. The territory would then be divided equally among the three allies, according to the proximity of their existing possessions. Financial reparations of 2 million rupees (£200,000) were also to be paid, and two of the sultan's young sons given as hostages to ensure the terms were fulfilled.[85]

Cornwallis was pleased with the outcome, believing the agreement would prevent Tipu from disturbing the peace again and be far less costly than continuing the war to depose him as ruler of Mysore. He recognised that the treaty would still be criticised for being too harsh or too soft, by depriving Tipu of too much territory, or for sparing a dangerous tyrant. But, as he told Oakley, his paramount duty was 'to consult the real interest of the Company and the nation', and that was achieving an honourable peace.[86] In an attempt to soften opposition in Britain, he wrote to the prince of Wales, assuring him that the war had been both just and necessary to protect the 'honour, good faith and . . . future security' of the Company. Even Tipu's best friends in England must surely acknowledge that 'he will not be the worse neighbour for having his wings a little clipped'.[87]

A slight delay occurred before the two sons of Tipu were surrendered to Cornwallis, seemingly because of their distress at leaving home. The circumstance of their delivery on 26 February was captured by the artist Robert Home, who accompanied the army during campaign. The picture shows the two princes, one aged ten and the other eight, being received in a fatherly manner by Cornwallis after arriving at his headquarters on their ceremonial elephants.[88] Being mere children they were naturally apprehensive of their fate. Cornwallis quickly reassured them by taking each by the hand, before entering his headquarters tent. Here he showed them 'every mark of kindness and respect', as he informed Oakley, and was genuinely pleased that 'the boys seemed to entertain no apprehensions of their new father'.[89] Yet there were still problems aplenty. In the first place, neither of the hostages was Tipu's heir. Another issue was Tipu's request to pay part of the reparations in jewels. A third was his attempt to exaggerate the value of the lands furthest from his capital, while grossly undervaluing the districts closer to Seringapatam.[90] The army accordingly remained in its entrenchments ready to resume the siege, a wise precaution since Tipu continued to strengthen his defences. The uncertainty prompted Cornwallis to delay the dispatch of the treaty to Britain.[91] In reality, Tipu had no option but to comply with the terms, since his army was rapidly dissolving and was destitute of supplies. The definitive articles were finally signed on 18 March 1792.[92]

In his reports to Dundas and the Directors, Cornwallis reaffirmed his view that the peace terminating the Third Anglo-Mysore War was both honourable and beneficial, since the additional territory would help secure the Company's possessions on the Malabar and Coromandel coasts. The new acquisitions should also produce a useful revenue. He then praised the conduct of the troops, especially their courage and discipline on 6 February, singling out Medows and Abercromby for fulsome mention. Finally, he noted that his dispatches were being delivered by Captain Madan, 'whom I beg leave to recommend' to His Majesty as a deserving officer. It was a gesture which he knew would delight his sister Charlotte.[93]

Although Cornwallis exonerated Medows for the mishap on the night of the attack on Seringapatam, his failure to participate in the main assault appears to have affected his sanity. On 26 February he attempted suicide with a pistol, lodging three bullets in his body. None hit a vital organ and he soon recovered.[94] Nevertheless, Cornwallis admitted to Stuart that this 'melancholy affair' had been very distressing.[95] It was in a similar vein that he wrote to the duke of York, confessing how stressful his period of command had been: 'I would not live the last year over again for any reward that could be held out to me.' But he was comforted by the reflection that he had done his best, whatever the public thought of him as a soldier and negotiator.[96] The conflict itself had brought him no financial benefit, however much political opponents might allege about his 'avarice'. He could have benefited from the prize money taken on the capture of Seringapatam, but had waived his share for the benefit of his officers and men.[97]

With the ratification of the definitive treaty completed, the allied armies began their northward withdrawal to Kunigal, 50 miles west of Bangalore. Here they parted company on 9 April, 'with the strongest appearances of perfect cordiality on all sides'. Nevertheless, tensions remained between the nizam's minister and Phadke, prompting both to request British assistance should their disputes escalate. This was something that Cornwallis was anxious to avoid, since it contravened article 34 of the 1784 Act regarding third-party disputes. He could only promise his good offices in promoting friendship between them.[98]

Before departing, Cornwallis discussed arrangements with Abercromby for the administration of the new Malabar territories. He was keen to introduce a 'system for their future management', similar to that in Bengal.[99] His desire to extend the Bengal system led him to raise the subject once more with the Directors on 2 May 1792. Although the expense might initially increase, employing capable and honest men would soon reward the Company through increased revenues and commerce. The Directors should understand that the British presence in India would never be secure until it was 'established as an invariable rule that Company servants shall be confined to public business only'. He believed this principle should even be extended to commercial agents, something he had not advocated before.[100] The day when Company servants were primarily traders was truly over.

Meanwhile, Cornwallis found himself once again confronted by the issue of a successor. With Medows no longer a candidate, he was increasingly anxious that the Company should nominate someone else of proven ability to succeed him. He had already informed Dundas at the beginning of 1792 that he would remain in Bengal until a replacement arrived, since he was determined not to leave Speke – 'a man so wonderfully eccentric' as to be beyond all control – in charge. Even a few weeks with him at the helm might prove fatal. These fears were not abated when he learnt that Stuart's replacement was to be Thomas Graham, another long-serving revenue official. Apart from being a former bankrupt, Graham lacked any formed opinions about public matters and had a strong inclination to jobbery and intrigue. He also had connections with 'the worst black people in Bengal'. Such unsatisfactory appointments led Cornwallis to question the wisdom of renewing the Company's charter, since the present system of vetting appointments was clearly not working.[101]

The importance of able personnel was reinforced on Cornwallis's return to Madras, where he quickly discovered that Oakley was not the man he had initially assumed. Not one 'material improvement' had been made in conformity with the Bengal system, nor was there any prospect of such change. This was the consequence, he told Dundas, of the Directors giving a man who had served under the old system the task of reforming his former colleagues. It reaffirmed his conviction that the governors of Calcutta, Bombay, and Madras must not be Company servants.[102] As he had earlier stressed, such appointees must be persons 'of ability and earnest application, who positively will not job and who can say no' to colleagues without embarrassment.[103]

Prolonged office often persuades incumbents that they are indispensable for the survival of their legacy. Such was clearly Cornwallis's current frame of mind. He confided to Medows that protecting his achievements had become more important to him than anything else. 'Even my anxious desire to return to England would hardly induce me to leave Bengal without seeing my permanent successor upon the spot.' A personal handover was essential for explaining 'the object of my plans and regulations and the measures which should be adopted or persevered in' to ensure their success.[104] He might for this reason even delay his departure until early 1794.[105]

One thing he remained sure of was the correctness of the peace he had just signed. He told Stuart: 'If we had taken Seringapatam and killed Tipu', as many advocated, 'we must either have given that capital to the Maratha', a potential rival, 'or set up some miserable pageant [puppet] of our own'.[106] But he had no reason to worry about the treaty's reception in Britain, since the peace was well received by the public, prompting the award of a marquisate from a grateful king.[107] The Directors were equally fulsome, as were the lord mayor, aldermen, and common council of London. The ministry had already indicated their confidence in Cornwallis, asking him to become home secretary on his return.[108] The future looked decidedly bright for the new marquess.

Before leaving Madras, Cornwallis attempted to address the vexed matter of the nawab of Arcot's debts. The issue had been included in his original instructions of 12 April 1786, but had become more pressing following the investigations into the activities of the Holland brothers. These revealed that both the nawab and his neighbour, the rajah of Tanjore (modern-day Thanjavur), had borrowed money at usurious rates from Holland and his council, providing large tracts of land as security.[109] Since the two rulers appeared incapable of managing their finances, Cornwallis decided to place their principalities under temporary Company control to prevent permanent insolvency.[110] He was uneasy about doing so, since the nawab in particular was 'an old friend and ally of this Company'. The Madras government was accordingly to treat him with all possible 'delicacy'.[111] At least Company control ought to be less oppressive for the two populations than the rapacious governance of their rulers.[112]

While the war continued no final settlement of the Arcot debts was possible. The nawab suggested that he retain control of his country's internal affairs while the Company took responsibility for its defence. However, as Cornwallis pointed out to the Directors, there were obvious disadvantages to such a scheme, not least the nawab's inability to improve his territory economically. Much the best plan, for promoting his interest and that of the inhabitants, would be for the nawab to entrust both the defence and internal management of his country to the Company, receiving in return a fixed allowance for his family and entourage. This subsidiary arrangement should then permit a steady reduction of his debts. His advisers, however, adamantly opposed such a plan, recognising that it would lead to a permanent loss of sovereignty. Being reluctant to use force, Cornwallis then looked at various ways of limiting the demands on the nawab's purse. Eventually, a new treaty was agreed similar to the previous one, though he doubted that it would be successful, given the improvidence of the nawab and his vulnerability to court intrigues. The likely outcome was that he would again fall into arrears, resulting in a permanent dependency.[113] It was a classic case of encroachment that Cornwallis was anxious to prevent. Though sincere in his desire to limit the British presence in India, his commitment to the honouring of contractual obligations, especially financial ones, necessarily led to more interference.[114] It was a process that Cornwallis's successors, notably Lord Wellesley, adopted with enthusiasm to make most of India's native rulers dependents of the British Raj.

TWELVE

Completing the Mission

Cornwallis returned to Calcutta on 27 July 1792. Hickey noticed that he looked 'thin, ill and exhausted', not surprising 'considering the extraordinary fatigues of body and mind' he had endured during the preceding eighteen months.[1] This was confirmed by the miniaturist painter John Smart, who portrayed him shortly afterwards in a loose-fitting uniform, his face weather-beaten and lined, suggestive of someone twenty-five years older than the person depicted by Gainsborough. At the quayside he was presented with several loyal addresses. The British inhabitants congratulated him on his safe return and the glorious outcome to the war, which he had achieved with honour to friend and foe.[2] The Indian representatives, in more florid language, praised his endeavours which would secure to them 'the advantages and blessings' of his governance, especially the 'freedom and independence' to observe 'our religion and customs', and 'the perfect security of our persons and property'.[3] Earlier, a number of Cornwallis's friends had wanted to present him with a commemorative star-shaped diamond medal in token of his services, but he promptly asked Stuart to quash the idea. The time for such presentations would be on his departure for home.[4] However, he was anxious not to give offense and agreed to their commissioning his portrait for display in one of the public buildings.[5]

The most pressing task on Cornwallis's return was the need to tackle the damaging costs of the war. Encouragingly, public credit was reviving with the ending of hostilities, helped by the economies which he had initiated on his way back to Bengal.[6] Most important had been his instructions to Stuart to reduce the thirty sepoy battalions stationed in the Calcutta Presidency to their peacetime establishment.[7] Contracts for provisions and bullock trains were also terminated, so that most wartime expenses had been eliminated before he reached Calcutta.[8] Graham at the Revenue Board had earlier warned that the land revenues were likely to be smaller than previously, though the collectors' returns varied considerably. Salt sales had also been disappointing. On the other hand, the excise on liquor was improving and ought in the next ten years to compensate for the abolition of the sayer duties. But the decline in the land revenues remained a concern, though unfavourable weather was partly to blame. The danger was that a reduced harvest would make it more difficult to levy an advantageous permanent assessment for the Company.[9]

However, by the time of Cornwallis's return the situation had improved considerably. Graham's previous estimates about the excise duties had proved overly cautious, since one district was already producing as much revenue as the former sayer duties. This had been achieved by levying the duties on the output of the stills themselves, rather than through the sale of licences. The change had not only increased the revenues of government but simultaneously relieved the inhabitants 'from the most burdensome and ruinous exactions'. Cornwallis concluded with justifiable glee: 'As this measure was disapproved by Stuart and Speke, as well as my friend Shore', Dundas would readily understand 'the satisfaction I must feel at its extraordinary success'.[10]

Meanwhile, the interim decennial settlement (see above, pp. 176–7) still had to be implemented in many districts where negotiations had been 'unavoidably protracted', though Cornwallis was hopeful of finishing them shortly. He was also optimistic that improved collection would increase receipts, as a council paper suggested in late August 1792. In future the talukdars and petty zamindars would pay their assessments through bankers, thus cutting out the need for a large collecting agency. Yet it was clear that a better regulatory framework was required, since the current system still screened 'oppression and dishonesty', while discouraging 'moderation and good faith'. Although landowners must be able to collect legitimate arrears of rent, the 'tenants and cultivators of the soil should be protected from oppression and unjust demands'. Only then could the twin objectives of prosperity and healthy public revenues be achieved.[11]

Nevertheless, by the start of 1793 the financial health of the Company was indicated by the appearance of a premium on its certificates, raising Cornwallis's long-held hope that the interest on them might be reduced to 7 per cent. The demand for certificates reflected the prosperous state of domestic commerce and the availability of money for investment. The Company's own commercial concerns were certainly thriving, especially the procurement of Bengal's fine textiles. Everything led Cornwallis to believe that he would be 'leaving this country in the highest state of prosperity' at the expiration of his governorship.[12]

Apart from restoring the Company to financial health, Cornwallis still had two other projects to finish before leaving Bengal. One was confirmation that the land settlement would be permanent. The other was the completion of his plans for reforming the judicial system, which had been interrupted by the war with Tipu. As confirmation of the permanent settlement could only be taken by the Company and Board of Control in Britain, Cornwallis turned to reform of the judiciary as his next priority.

Since Jones still had to complete his work on the Hindu and Muslim texts (see above, pp. 178–9), Cornwallis decided to address what he now considered the most pressing issue regarding civil justice, namely the structure of the courts. He had become increasingly concerned about the collectors' role as magistrates, which made them both judge and jury in revenue disputes. This was clearly detrimental to judicial impartiality. Perhaps influenced by Montesquieu's observations about the separation of powers and their recent inclusion in the American constitution, Cornwallis began work in mid-October 1792 on proposals for dividing the two functions in conjunction with more general improvements to the administration of justice, 'which God knows is much wanted'. He considered the matter 'so important for the honour of the British government and for the future prosperity of this country' that he decided to send his proposals, once completed, directly to Pitt and Dundas as well as the Directors, for approval. His hope was that the changes could be implemented before his successor arrived to avoid any delay in their execution.[13]

Six weeks later Cornwallis produced a seventy-page minute on the civil law for discussion by the council. He first outlined his thoughts on the role of the Company and the British nation in India, something that had rarely been done before. Clearly 'two of the primary objects which this government ought to have in view . . . are to ensure its political safety and to render the possession of the country as advantageous as possible' to the imperial power. However, he affirmed these objectives could be best secured by ensuring that the people were happy and the country was prosperous, for 'if the people are satisfied with our government', they would 'wish for its continuance'. Like later Utilitarians, Cornwallis believed that 'a spirit of industry has been implanted in man, that in seeking his own good he may contribute to the public prosperity'. Imperial control, therefore, did not have to mean mere exploitation of the governed, since both rulers and subjects could be winners in material terms.[14]

However, for such prosperity to occur, the individual must be confident in the security of their person and property, and that required a judiciary that was separate from the executive branch of government. Indeed, 'the supreme power should divest itself of all interference' in judicial matters, except 'in the last resort'. He believed that the current defects in the justice system and the arbitrary nature of the revenue assessments accounted for 'the slow progress which the country has made towards improvement'. Poverty was rampant even among the most productive elements in society, meaning 'the landholders, cultivators of the soil, and the manufacturers'. This stagnation could best be reversed by devising arrangements that were 'calculated for all times and circumstances', thereby giving a stability to the whole. 'We should endeavour to establish a constitution for the country that will protect private property . . . even under the worst administrations'. This could only be achieved by giving the courts 'the entire judicial authority', so that 'no single member of government or any individual . . . will be able to invade the rights and property of the people'.[15] The language was similar to that of the American federal constitution, and perhaps with reason, since in September 1788 Jones had asked Arthur Lee for a copy of that document.[16] After embarking on judicial reform, Jones and Cornwallis had been close collaborators.

However, there would be no role for Indians in the higher echelons of the new system. Nothing in his six years in India had eroded Cornwallis's distrust of the Indian people. 'The problem of native agents', he affirmed, was that they would either abuse the authority given them 'to promote their private advantages', or, 'to gain credit with their employers', would 'commit the most unjustifiable acts to promote . . . the business committed to their charge'. He was especially opposed to admitting 'the natives to any participation in the legislative power' which was essential for maintaining British rule. Indians, he reminded the council, had been 'accustomed to foreign and despotic rule from time immemorial', and were 'well acquainted with the miseries of their own tyrannical administrations'. He was confident, hence, that both 'the long-oppressed Hindu, and their oppressors the Muslims' would appreciate a system of government which protected 'the greatest blessings of all human beings . . . the free exercise of their religion' and the security of their persons and property.[17] Compared to previous regimes, he believed, his system embraced 'a liberal and humane spirit' while preserving 'the interests of the British nation'. He might have added that his exclusion of Indians in the new system merely conformed to the Directors' decision in April 1791 'that no natives of India' should be given any covenanted civil or military office.[18]

Cornwallis then turned to the operation of court system itself. He noted that 62,000 cases were waiting to be heard in the Collectors' revenue courts, which defeated the purpose of justice and struck at the roots of prosperity. The delays were mostly caused by the courts' concentration on revenue cases rather than the wider concerns of the population. This again emphasised the need to separate the judiciary from the executive powers of government. Once this had been achieved, such delays should cease. He accordingly proposed to give the judicial functions of the collectors to new 'zilla', or district, courts, which would handle all civil cases, including those of the revenue. To oversee them and ensure uniformity, four new courts of appeal were to be established in Patna, Murshidabad, Dakha, and Calcutta. Each bench would have four judges.[19]

As part of his grand plan for the Bengal judiciary, Cornwallis next proposed improvements to court procedure to ensure a more effective and just outcome. No deposit was to be required from plaintiffs, who could under certain criteria prosecute government officials for wrongs committed in an official capacity. Those seeking redress could employ native lawyers to present their cases more effectively. However, such attorneys were to be licensed to ensure that they were persons of 'respectable character', possessed of a proper knowledge of Indian laws and customs. To provide a sufficient number of qualified persons, he suggested that provision be made for their training at the Islamic and Hindu colleges in Calcutta and Benares. Lastly, all laws or amendments thereto were to be numbered for cross-referencing, with a preamble explaining their purpose. They would then be translated into Persian and Bengali before being printed, to aid transparency and general understanding.[20]

At the end of his minute Cornwallis addressed the cost of the new system, which he admitted would be substantial. However, retrenchments had been made in every department of government, while the collection of revenue had greatly improved. It would be 'the greatest injustice to a people who pay so great a revenue, and from whose industry the country derives so many advantages', to deny them the benefit of good government. Failure to act would also hurt the Company, since his proposed changes were 'essential to the future security and prosperity of the British dominions in Bengal'. To do otherwise would be 'a criminal species of economy'.[21]

After further work on the regulatory framework, Cornwallis submitted his plans to the Directors in a council minute dated 6 March 1793. The document acknowledged that separating revenue collection from the administration of civil justice would mean a substantially different system. However, the merging of these two functions in 1787 had been done for administrative convenience and was clearly incompatible with the principles of equity and justice.[22] In a further letter the following day Cornwallis expressed the hope that the Directors would give their hearty approbation to his plans for judicial reform. 'The radical defects which have long prevailed . . . in the administration of civil and criminal justice to your native subjects, have been no less unworthy of the British character than injurious to your interests.' The plans now submitted were 'the result of my most deliberate consideration for several years', which he was confident would secure the lives, properties, and happiness 'of many millions of people'.[23] To Dundas, Cornwallis admitted privately a deep sense of satisfaction: once his proposals had been carried into execution, he would not only 'have secured the most important advantages to the natives', but would have 'struck at the root of the abuses which so long disgraced the British administration in India'.[24]

Cornwallis was so certain about the rectitude of what he was doing that he started implementing the reforms without waiting for authorisation, even though such changes contravened the Directors' strictures to avoid innovation.[25] However, after seven years in office, Cornwallis was confident of carrying such projects, assured as he was of the support of Pitt and Dundas. He proved correct in his surmise, though the Directors only approved the scheme after his return to Britain.[26]

In their original instructions of 1786, the Directors had directed Cornwallis, 'to lay down such rules and principles as may best conduce to the establishment of general systems'. Cornwallis now proposed to achieve this not only for the justice system, but for the wider activities of government. He accordingly began drafting regulations, both to guide the Company's officials and to inform the wider population. Forty-eight articles or codes were eventually produced. Among the more notable were the inviolability of the land settlement; the procedures to be followed by the courts; the nature and severity of punishments; the principles of inheritance under Muslim and Hindu law; the process of buying and selling property; the conduct of Company officials; the efficient keeping of records; conditions for the employment of weavers; and a regulation to codify future initiatives 'for the internal government of British India'. The articles collectively came to be known as the Cornwallis Code, though much of the work was done by Barlow at the Revenue Board.[27]

Drafting the codes proved a lengthy process and only twenty were ready by the time of Cornwallis's departure. A year later Barlow was still completing the project, though he had no doubts about what Cornwallis had devised. Apart from the benefits of enlightened government, Barlow believed the new system had removed the malaise of British political instability, which had blighted the Company's governance in the early 1780s. Bengal now had a written 'constitution' of laws to protect it from becoming the plaything of politicians at Westminster.[28] Equally advantageous was that Cornwallis's new regulatory system could be extended to the Company's other dominions, since the object of the codes was 'not to subvert local usages and customs, but on the contrary to preserve them and to ensure to the people the enjoyment of the rights and privileges they deserve'. The key thing was that 'by framing them into laws and making those laws all powerful', the danger of arbitrary government had been removed.[29] The Directors accepted the new codes at the same time as Cornwallis's proposals for the administration of civil justice.[30]

While completing his plans for the judiciary, Cornwallis continued to await news of a successor and a decision about the permanency of the land settlement. Both decisions were eventually taken by the politicians rather than the Directors.

Regarding the permanent land settlement, the arguments of Cornwallis and Shore appeared so finely balanced that Dundas invited Pitt in September 1792 'to shut himself up with me' at his house in Wimbledon for ten days to settle the question. Also in attendance was Charles Grant, a key ally of Cornwallis. After prolonged discussion, all three agreed on the desirability of a permanent rather than a decennial settlement. Dundas informed the Directors accordingly. With the charter due for renewal in 1793 the Directors necessarily acquiesced, giving Cornwallis permission to proceed.[31]

Dundas simultaneously informed Cornwallis that he had found a successor, who was none other than John Shore. Dundas admitted that the search had proved difficult and he had even considered coming to India himself. But it had been impossible to overlook Shore, given 'his talents, industry and candour', whatever his views about a permanent settlement. Most importantly, Shore would be flexible: 'He is willing either to remain for a few years at the head of the government, or to become second in council, if we think it right . . . to send out any other person from this country, or to come home again, if that suits our arrangements best.' Equally encouraging was the news that Robert Abercromby was to succeed Cornwallis as commander-in-chief with a seat on the council. This would ensure the exclusion of Graham.[32]

Dundas's letter reached Calcutta on 2 March 1793. Although Cornwallis had several times declared his opposition to the appointment of a Company servant, he informed the Directors of his 'very great satisfaction' at the news. However, he would not be boarding the first ship home. The monsoon season was approaching, and the date of Shore's arrival uncertain. He accordingly proposed to remain in Bengal until August, which would allow him to induct Shore into 'the principles of the plan', both 'for the future collection of the revenue', as well as the 'regular and efficient administration of justice in the Bengal provinces'.[33] Privately he expressed relief to Dundas, especially about the exclusion of Graham, who might otherwise have succeeded to the chief position, should there be no governor-general. 'Being so deeply interested in the success of our affairs in this country . . . I would suffer anything' rather than see him in charge 'even for a month'. That included enduring another Indian summer.[34]

It was with renewed enthusiasm, therefore, that Cornwallis returned to the remaining legal and regulatory details that still had to be settled before implementing the permanent settlement. One was the question of abandoned waste land, which the council believed still accounted for approximately 30 per cent of the cultivable acreage.[35] The Directors wanted a portion of any crops produced thereon to accrue to the Company. Cornwallis objected that such stipulation would 'greatly counteract, if not altogether damp, that spirit of industry and improvement . . . which is the great object of fixing the tax upon each estate'. It would also infringe the rights of the zamindars, since much of the waste land already belonged to them. Should the Directors require extra revenues, they could secure it indirectly from the increasing 'general wealth and commerce of the country'. But first agriculture must be allowed to flourish, since most commerce depended on its products.[36]

Another issue to be addressed, before announcing the permanent settlement, was the provision of pattas, or written documents, defining the relationship between the landowners and their raiyats. Much work had been required here, since many zamindars were reluctant to admit how many raiyats worked their lands, for fear of incurring higher taxes. Nevertheless, Cornwallis and his colleagues could assure the Directors that 'throughout the greater part of the country specific agreements have been exchanged between the landholders and the raiyats'. Where these agreements were not yet settled, 'the landholders have bound themselves to prepare and deliver them by fixed periods'. The pattas were essential to protect the raiyats, by giving them 'power to compel an adherence to the agreements' through 'appeal to the courts of justice'.[37]

The last issue that Cornwallis and the council had to address was that of the jumma, or total revenue to be raised annually through the permanent settlement. The figure was usually determined by the upper limit of what had previously been levied. The current year had been a prosperous one, suggesting it would provide an advantageous basis for calculating future levies. The time appeared propitious for finally making a declaration of permanency, not least because the landowners could start improving their properties, secure in the knowledge of what their future taxes would be. However, Cornwallis proposed that the Company should retain certain powers as 'sovereigns of the country'. Among these were the levying of future internal duties and the right to adjust the relationship between landowners and raiyats, should the latter need further protection.[38]

Four days later, 10 March 1793, Shore arrived, now elevated to a knighthood in recognition of his readiness to serve once more. As Dundas had forecast, he accepted

Cornwallis's plans without complaint.[39] He not only agreed about the plan for a permanent settlement, but, gratifyingly, would give his 'approbation and resolution to support and enforce the late domestic arrangements'. Shore was also not 'in the least disappointed' by Cornwallis's resolution to retain the government till August, offering instead 'his cordial assistance whenever I might wish to employ him'. Such complaisance inclined Cornwallis to 'retract' his previous opposition to the appointment of Company servants as governors, since Shore truly appeared to be 'an exception to my general rule'.[40]

The plan for a permanent revenue settlement was formally promulgated on 22 March 1793.[41] At last Cornwallis could contemplate returning home with his mission complete. He had one final favour to ask of Lichfield, which was to find him lodgings in London until his own residence in Grosvenor Street was ready. The location was less important than that the property be clean and tidy.[42]

One issue that Cornwallis had not been able to resolve was the reform of the Company's army, despite his long-standing belief that change was urgently needed. The outbreak of hostilities with Tipu had further delayed matters, though this did nothing to alter Cornwallis's opinions or those of the ministers back in Britain. Indeed, the war reinforced his condemnation of the Company's policy of promotion by strict seniority (see above, pp. 159, 187), which 'levelled all distinction between the indolent, incapable, zealous and able'.[43] Nevertheless, eight months after his return from Madras, he had still been unable 'to form any satisfactory plan for the Indian army' despite considerable thought. The one clear thing was that 'it cannot go on long on its present footing'.[44]

As a last resort he decided to consult a small group of senior officers. The starting premise for their deliberations was to be the 'great danger' posed 'to our Asiatic possessions' from having 'a separate provincial army of Europeans'.[45] His plan, as he explained to Abercromby, was to obtain the opinions of 'the most sensible officers' about a merger with the regulars.[46] Among those consulted was Colonel John Braithwaite, the senior officer at Madras.[47] In the event no responses were received before Cornwallis boarded his ship for home, seemingly unaware that his letter had already become common knowledge among the Company's officer corps. The consequence was a groundswell of anger for his successor to deal with.[48]

One other task before his departure was the negotiation of a treaty with the nizam of Hyderabad and the peshwa of Pune for the mutual defence of their newly acquired territories, in case Tipu should attempt to regain them. It was imperative that any such agreement did not breach the 1784 India Act. Malet and Kennaway were accordingly to take 'the greatest care . . . that no vague or ambiguous expression shall be admitted into this new instrument'. The matter could not be ignored, since both the peshwa and the nizam were seeking help in enforcing the peace terms agreed at Seringapatam. Tipu had yet to pay any reparations to either power, even though his sons would remain in custody until he fulfilled his obligations.[49]

The two hostage princes, consequently, remained at Madras under the care of Oakley and his wife. Cornwallis was genuinely anxious for their welfare, and was pleased to receive reports that the princes and their companion, General Ali Reza Khan, readily acknowledged Cornwallis's kindness and attention.[50] This prompted Cornwallis to write to Tipu in the spring of 1793 that he was anxious to release the two boys before he left India. This would give him much pleasure, not least because of 'their good manners and disposition during the period I had the happiness of being in their company'. By May, the only outstanding issue between the Company and Tipu preventing their release was the return of a few European prisoners. Hopefully these matters could be resolved by the time Cornwallis reached Madras.[51]

Although one war was over, a new one had begun in Europe, with the news in June 1793 of hostilities with France. On this occasion Cornwallis was not unduly concerned. The French military establishment in India was too weak to pose any threat. Nevertheless, precautions were still advisable, and he promptly ordered the Madras authorities to prepare an attack on Pondicherry.[52] He simultaneously arranged for the seizure of Chandernagore and all vessels carrying the French flag. French nationals were either to be imprisoned or offered parole.[53]

Cornwallis was hence gratified to learn from Braithwaite that he had already assembled twelve sepoy battalions for that purpose.[54] The news prompted Cornwallis to consider joining him at Madras. However, he advised Braithwaite on 26 June that he was not to await his arrival before commencing hostilities, as he was sufficiently experienced to conduct operations 'with judgement and activity'. Nevertheless,

Braithwaite was to avoid all 'unnecessary appointments', exerting the 'utmost vigilance to prevent waste and peculation'.[55] Everything possible should be done to prevent the Company's profitability from again being undermined by war. Not wishing to leave anything to chance, he perused French accounts of Sir Henry Monroe's siege of Pondicherry in 1778, which had taken ten weeks to complete. The key factors for the length of the operation had been Monroe's lack of heavy artillery and insufficient manpower. Accordingly, Braithwaite was not to proceed if he had any doubts about the operation. Cornwallis still hoped to join him, once he had found a suitable ship to carry him to Madras.[56] In the meantime five companies of artillery, a battering train, and twelve companies of Bengal marines were being sent in case a siege prove necessary.[57]

Cornwallis left Calcutta on 13 August 1793 without ceremony, giving the impression that he would return for a formal handover to Shore. He certainly gave no indication of doing otherwise. He reached Madras on 7 September to find that Pondicherry had already fallen to Braithwaite, assisted by William Cornwallis's squadron. Cornwallis now had no reason to delay his departure, as he acknowledged to the Court of Directors on 18 September 1793.[58] This confirmed him in his determination not to return to Calcutta. Going home from Madras would not only shorten his journey but avoid the outpouring of public esteem which he found so embarrassing. Earlier he had requested William Cornwallis to send a frigate so that he could reach Madras safely, yet had received no response.[59] Cornwallis's presumption that his brother would automatically comply had seemingly hit a raw nerve. William stayed on his ship, leaving Cornwallis to request plaintively that he would at least escort him safely out to sea.[60] The packet *Swallow*, on which he had first travelled to India, would be sailing in early October, and Cornwallis, disdaining once more all considerations of ceremony or safety, decided to take his chance with that vessel. Accompanying him were Ross, Haldane, and Apsley.[61] Only then did the commodore pay him a short visit.[62]

All this while, Shore had been waiting for news of Cornwallis's intentions. As late as mid-October 1793 he told a friend that Cornwallis had 'gone to Pondicherry to smell a little French gunpowder'. He was still not certain if he would even become governor-general.[63] At best it was cavalier treatment of a faithful deputy. Not until the day before his ship departed, on 9 October 1793, did Cornwallis finally write to the Bengal Council that he was resigning his office, leaving Shore as governor-general in accordance with the Company's instructions. Included was a fulsome testimony to the merits of his successor.[64] He also wrote privately to Shore wishing him good health and success as governor-general. He would follow Indian affairs in Britain and begged Shore to alert him to issues on which he wanted support. Cornwallis could then 'counteract any plan or resolution at home that militates against them'.[65]

News of Cornwallis's resignation was announced in Calcutta on 26 October 1793. Two days later Shore was formally installed as governor-general, as he informed Cornwallis on 10 November. He then acknowledged the generosity of Cornwallis's public testimony. In return he assured Cornwallis of his determination to 'imitate' his conduct and consolidate those improvements which he had established.[66] Shore appears to have been genuinely free of resentment over his treatment in the last six months, affirming to a confidant: 'We lived and parted upon the most cordial terms, and although my succession has been postponed, I love him as much as ever.' Cornwallis had always had the good of the Indian people in mind, even if he occasionally paid insufficient attention to the details of his policies. Everything considered, 'the country will not see his like' again.[67]

Once the resignation was announced, the wider Bengal community could show its appreciation for what Cornwallis had achieved in his seven and a half years as governor-general. On a finely scrolled parchment, the principal officers and inhabitants, headed by Barlow, expressed their profound respect for his public character and private virtue. His many eminent accomplishments were a reflection of his wise and vigorous administration which had brought prosperity to the country.[68]

Cornwallis's voyage home was not without danger, given that Europe was now at war. However, the packet ships, though lightly armed, were built for speed and could out-sail most opponents. Much of the voyage was spent discussing the reform of the Company's army with Ross. The *Swallow* reached Saint Helena in the southern Atlantic on 15 December, before setting off a few days later along the west coast of Africa. Approaching the Channel, Cornwallis faced a repeat of his return from America (see above, p. 109). A French frigate chased the *Swallow* for several hours until it reached the shelter of Torbay, where the vessel dropped anchor on the morning of 3 February 1794.[69] Informing Dundas of his arrival, Cornwallis confessed, 'my fingers are so cold that I can only tell [you] that I left Madras on 10 October and that our affairs in India were in a most prosperous state'.[70]

Cornwallis had reason to be pleased with his governorship of Bengal. Although the defeat of Tipu had not been part of his original instructions, his success had removed a major threat to the Company's fortunes in India, along with that of France. He had done so without overly extending the Company's responsibilities or dramatically changing the balance of power. As to the Company's internal administration, he had radically reformed its ethos, giving officials a higher sense of purpose than mere profit or personal gain, making merit and experience rather than patronage the key requirements for appointment and promotion. These changes, of course, were consonant with the economical reforms of North and Pitt, anticipating the later Victorian British and Indian civil service. Regarding the Company's finances, he had stabilised expenditures and balanced the budget, despite the Third Anglo-Mysore War, while the abolition of internal duties was calculated to encourage native commerce and general prosperity. In addition, the permanent settlement promised to create both social stability and the incentives for agricultural improvement, as had happened in England after 1688. Finally, Cornwallis could feel that he had brought a sense of justice and equity to the legal system, which the inhabitants of Bengal had rarely enjoyed. What had started as a limited plan of reform had blossomed into a startlingly radical system of government. The new regulations effectively gave Bengal a written constitution, which enshrined individual rights while imposing restraints on arbitrary governance. The idea that the inhabitants could sue officials for wrong doing was something previously inconceivable among the feudal states of India. The desirability of extending Cornwallis's system to Madras and Bombay seemed unquestioned.[71]

In the accomplishment of these achievements, Cornwallis was quick to acknowledge the help of others: Shore and Law in the drafting of the Permanent Settlement; Jones in the reforms to the civil and criminal law; Barlow in drafting the Cornwallis Code; and Stuart for his unexpected leadership during the Third Anglo-Mysore War. Nevertheless, it was Cornwallis who had drawn together their ideas and talents to provide a radically new vision of how British India should be governed for the benefit of all.

The verdict of historians, however, has not been so flattering. His flagship policy of a permanent settlement has incurred particular criticism. His expectation that it would create a more enlightened class of landlord, who would see the advantages to be gained of improving their estates in co-operation with their raiyats, never came to pass. Although a brisk land market developed, both old and new landowners remained indifferent to what Europeans saw as enlightened self-interest, being more akin to the absentee landlords of Ireland rather than improving owners like Cornwallis's great uncle, 'Turnip' Townshend.[72] As a result no agricultural or commercial revolution followed the implementation of the scheme, leaving Bengal's traditional staples to suffer from increasing competition with British manufacturers. The economy of Bengal in consequence continued its slow trajectory of decline, strangled by the constraints imposed on its commerce and industry by the monopolistic policies of the East India Company and the equally harmful deflation caused by the outflow of capital to Britain and China.[73] By the early 1800s the failings of the Permanent Settlement had been sufficiently recognised for it to be abandoned at Madras in favour of the existing ryotwari system, where the raiyats were declared owners of the land and liable for the payment of taxes to the government.[74]

The value of Cornwallis's reforms to the civil and criminal justice system have also been questioned. The landed classes quickly saw the value of litigation to contest government tax claims and landownership. The system became so overloaded that by 1800 there was a backlog of 160,000 cases.[75] The Company responded by restoring priority to revenue cases, further delaying the suits of others. Fees were also re-imposed.[76] Cornwallis's desire to make civil justice cheaper and more accessible had paradoxically made it more expensive, because the complexity of court procedures necessitated the employment of expert counsel. The raiyats in consequence contested few cases, being too poor to resort to litigation, while their pattas generally proved ineffective even when issued. The result was to reduce them to mere tenants at will, enjoying none of the previous communitarian customs that had protected their livelihoods.[77] In reality Cornwallis's plans were too ambitious to be successful. Like other benevolent despots, he was full of good intentions, but too remote to appreciate the requirements for implementing them.

Lastly, historians have criticised Cornwallis's exclusion of Indians from positions of responsibility. The Mughal emperors, though devout Muslims, often entrusted Hindus with high office, as did Tipu. Cornwallis's exclusion of Indians demeaned them as a people and undermined their self-respect.[78] His belief in their untrustworthiness reflected an inability to appreciate the effect that great inequalities in status and power have on human relationships. Hence, despite his grand scheme for the governance of Bengal, he lacked any vision for India's inhabitants other than as permanently subject peoples. The best that they could expect was some form of benevolent despotism, and that was far from guaranteed, as the nineteenth-century Raj revealed. Cornwallis's attitudes, of course, merely reflected generally held contemporary prejudice. European superiority over Asian peoples seemed the natural order. At least Cornwallis treated those under his care with courtesy and humanity, though his vision of a humane, well-regulated society could not succeed in a system that had been created by conquest and ultimately relied on force, since for every Company official like Cornwallis, there were probably five others who had no compunction in abusing people of colour. Nevertheless, his concern for the prosperity of the Indian peoples was remarkable by contemporary standards, however ineffective the means deployed. He was also distinctive in his opposition to imperial expansion, seeing no advantage in conquering India simply to spread British religious ideals and customs. Cultural imperialism was not one of his alleged crimes.

Historians, in consequence, can still find reason to commend many aspects of Cornwallis's period as governor-general.[79] The Bengal system of government and justice was an improvement on the feudal structures that preceded it. He had also given Bengal the framework of a sound currency. The advantages of a salaried civil service, partially independent judiciary, and government based on known laws continue to be widely recognised.[80] These were not insignificant achievements in any age.

Part III
EUROPE

THIRTEEN

Minister of the Crown

The world that Cornwallis returned to in February 1794 was very different to the one he had left in April 1786. Europe had then been at peace, with Britain and France seeking a mutually beneficial commercial treaty, inspired by the doctrines of Adam Smith. Now that same Europe was combating the horrors of the French Revolution and its Jacobin ideology, which threatened the established order in every country on the Continent, including Britain. No monarch or aristocrat could feel safe, as the stream of French émigrés to Britain testified. Flight alone had saved them from the sharp steel of the guillotine.

Cornwallis reached London on 7 February, and as before made attendance on the king and ministers his first priority. Expectations were high that he would be offered a prominent post in the government. The king had already honoured him with the marquisate. The Directors too had shown their appreciation, by giving Cornwallis (or his heirs) an annuity of £5,000 for twenty years.[1] They had also commissioned his statue for display in the courtroom, placing him alongside Robert Clive in the pantheon of the Company's heroes.[2]

The next, and most important, item in his schedule during the next few days was his long-delayed reunion with Brome and Mary, though the records do not show where or when they met.[3] Other meetings undoubtedly took place with the rest of the family, including perhaps his sister, Charlotte Madan, who had been seriously ill the previous November.[4] A meeting with his regimental agent, James Meyrick, would also have been a priority in order to ascertain the state of the 33rd Foot Regiment. The corps was currently serving in Ireland under its recently appointed lieutenant-colonel, Arthur Wellesley, the future duke of Wellington. Cornwallis would later describe him to Shore as 'a sensible man and a good officer', who would conduct himself in a meritorious manner.[5]

With these reunions and formalities complete, Cornwallis visited Culford Park to inspect the changes which Lichfield and Townshend had arranged while he was in India. Here too no record exists of his reaction to the completed work, though it is likely that he was pleased with the result. He had never been overly ostentatious or greatly interested in the details of construction. His main concern was that the house be suitably functional for someone of his rank. His stay at Culford Park was in any case limited to a few days, as he was due to testify at Warren Hastings's impeachment in Westminster Hall, where proceedings had now entered a sixth year. Cornwallis was initially scheduled to appear in early March, but a 'troublesome complaint' then intervened.[6] Eventually he gave his testimony on 9 April, as reported in *The Times*. He then affirmed that no one had ever complained about Hastings or ever charged him with any 'violence, cruelty, bloodshed and oppression'. Rather, the 'people in general respected him very much'. When asked if he had 'found any just cause to impeach the character of Mr Hastings', Cornwallis answered 'never'.[7] Edmund Burke, the chief prosecutor, then suggested that Cornwallis's inability to speak the native languages undermined the value of his testimony. To this Cornwallis replied curtly that he had conversed sufficiently through interpreters to know what Indians thought of Hastings.[8] It would be another year before Hastings was acquitted.

Meanwhile, Cornwallis's return to health allowed a grateful nation to show its appreciation. The first such honouring occurred in the House of Lords on 24 March, when the lord chancellor delivered a vote of thanks from the peers 'for the eminent and meritorious services' which he had rendered in India.[9] Equally flattering, a few days later, was the granting of the freedom of the City of London. The lord mayor and aldermen first 'paraded in state' to Cornwallis's house in Burlington Street, where they presented him with the customary gold box, suitably inscribed to commemorate the occasion. The whole entourage then escorted Cornwallis, Ross, Singleton, and Haldane back to Mansion House for a formal banquet.[10] The former lord mayor of London, Thomas Boydell, also commissioned the American artist John Singleton Copley to paint Cornwallis's portrait for display in the common council. This showed him at the height of his pomp and reputation, in his lieutenant-general's uniform, wearing the Garter star, while leaning on his baton. Fort William appears in the background, as Indian dignitaries pass by on their elephants.[11]

With these matters settled it was time to think about the future. He professed to Shore that he wished 'to remain quiet', yet admitted he could not be sure of doing so.[12] Britain was now at war with France, making it likely that Cornwallis's talents as a commander and administrator would be called upon in some capacity. As already noted, Pitt had earlier offered to make him home secretary on his return from India.[13] Cornwallis had replied while campaigning in Mysore that he would be proud to be part of Pitt's administration, but declined the proffered office, because he was uncomfortable speaking in Parliament. He rightly believed such faculty was essential, both 'to do justice to a good cause', and to defend 'his measures' and 'those of his colleagues'.[14] He may also have refused because of his dislike of political manoeuvring, which such appointments necessarily involved.

However, it was not long before Pitt and Dundas, who was now secretary of state for war, found Cornwallis a new role more in keeping with his military talents. On the outbreak of hostilities with France in February 1793, the ministry had sent the duke of York with several thousand British troops to help defend Flanders, acting in concert with the Austrians, Prussians, and Dutch, along with the Hanoverian forces of George III. But after some initial success the offensive had stalled, compelling York to retreat from his objective, the port of Dunkirk.[15] By the time of Cornwallis's return from India, the ministers were planning a new offensive and keen to involve him in their campaign plans.[16] One possibility was for Cornwallis, now a full general, to command the British troops in Flanders, though George III was certain to object to his son's demotion. The ministers consequently decided on an alternative scheme whereby Cornwallis would command the king's Hanoverian troops in co-operation with the Prussian army, leaving York in charge of the British contingent acting in concert with the Austrians. Pitt and Dundas hoped that Cornwallis's dispatch would energise the recently signed Anglo-Prussian subsidy treaty, whereby Frederick William II was to furnish an army of 62,000 for joint operations against the French.[17]

The details of the mission were completed at a meeting on 27 May in Downing Street with Pitt, Dundas, and Lord Grenville, the foreign secretary, present.[18] Cornwallis's first task was to visit York at his headquarters in Tournai near the French border to ascertain his views on the forthcoming campaign. Next, he was to converse

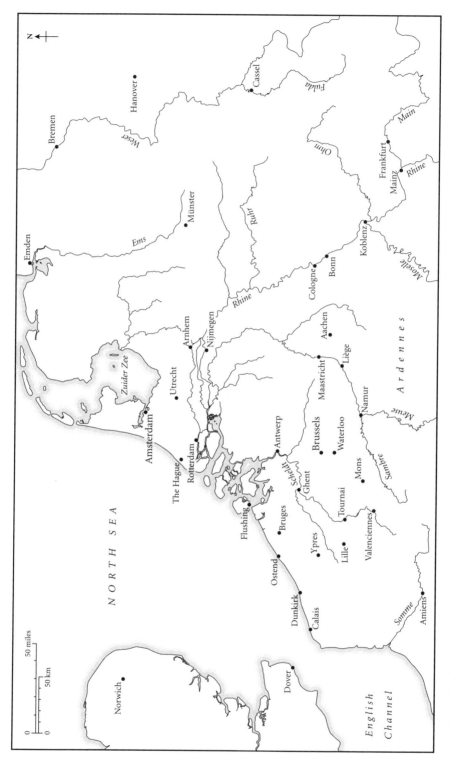

Map 6. Holland and Flanders.

with the Austrian emperor, Francis II, who had taken command of his army in Flanders. The ministers hoped that Cornwallis's diplomatic tact and military acumen would galvanise the disparate allied forces into an offensive towards Paris, though it was recognised that co-ordinating the Austrian and Prussian forces would be difficult, given their long history of mistrust. After this Cornwallis was to travel to Maastricht for a meeting with Field Marshal Wichard Joachim Heinrich von Möllendorf, the Prussian commander, to ensure that his forces advanced towards the River Meuse as part of the plan to invade France. Once those details were settled Cornwallis would take command of the king's Hanoverian troops, acting in concert with the Prussians.[19]

After naming Ross and Balfour to his staff, Cornwallis set out at the end of May, travelling by way of Ostend and Ghent to Tournai.[20] York had previously expressed his pleasure at having Cornwallis as a colleague, indicating that there would be no friction on his part.[21] However, before they could meet, news arrived that the Austrian emperor was planning to return to Vienna. No satisfactory reason was offered for his departure, fuelling suspicions that the Austrian commitment to defend Flanders was weakening.[22]

It was in these discouraging circumstances that Cornwallis reached the British headquarters on the evening of 4 June. Here he had several discussions with York, in which they agreed about the necessity of deploying the Prussian army in western Flanders, 'in preference to every other operation'. To facilitate this outcome, magazines should be established to support Möllendorf's army as it marched westward from the Rhine into Flanders. The allies should then have sufficient strength to advance on Lille, the principal fortress guarding France's north-east frontier.[23]

Thirty-six hours later Cornwallis was again on the road, this time for Brussels with a letter from York for the Emperor Francis, asking him to remain with his army to boost morale. At least he might welcome the Prussians to west Flanders for the joint offensive into France. Cornwallis reached Brussels that evening, where he received an audience with the emperor the following morning. Here he presented York's letter. Unfortunately, neither the letter, nor Cornwallis's 'earnest representations' about 'the mischievous effects which his departure' would have, 'appeared to make any material impression'. The only consolation was the emperor's assurance that his zeal for the common cause remained unabated. He was merely returning to Vienna to secure additional supplies of men and money.[24]

Cornwallis accordingly continued his journey to Maastricht for the anticipated meeting with Möllendorf and Friedrich Wilhelm, count von Haugwitz, one of Frederick II's senior ministers. The experienced British diplomat, James Harris, earl of Malmesbury, was also in attendance. The talks commenced on 11 June with Cornwallis urging Haugwitz to do everything possible to expedite the movement of the Prussian forces from the Rhine to west Flanders. The discussions, however, were inconclusive: Möllendorf was unexpectedly still at his headquarters near Mainz, 170 miles distant on the upper Rhine. Since Prussian support was essential for an invasion of France, Cornwallis decided to visit Möllendorf and 'use every means to get him to expedite his march', while simultaneously establishing 'the future operations of the campaign'.[25] The situation was threatening because the Austrians had failed to relieve the key fortress of Ypres, whose capture would undermine the allied position in Flanders, especially if the Prussians failed to appear.[26]

Cornwallis finally met Möllendorf on 20 June 1794. The outcome was not encouraging. Möllendorf was unresponsive to the idea of marching into Flanders, claiming he had no knowledge of his government's intentions regarding that proposal. Indeed, he and his staff talked repeatedly of peace, perhaps spurred by the inability of the Austrians to relieve Ypres. They argued that any forward movement towards Flanders would be dangerous, given French strength on the upper Rhine. His army therefore would be best deployed protecting Germany.[27] Malmesbury privately criticised Cornwallis for not refuting Möllendorf's military arguments about the inadvisability of a Prussian advance into Flanders. Throughout the discussion 'he was perfectly silent' and this had given 'umbrage to the Marshal'.[28] Cornwallis's reticence undoubtedly stemmed from his recognition that nothing would change Möllendorf's attitude.

Faced with this impasse, Cornwallis decided to return to Flanders to await further instructions from the ministry. Privately he advised Dundas that nothing further could be done, and requested permission to return to Britain, 'where I may perhaps render some service by talking over the business fully with you'.[29] However, he wrote this before learning that Ypres had fallen to the forces of the French general Charles Pichegru, which prompted him to return to York's headquarters.[30] Here he found York anxious for him to stay, because he distrusted the Austrian commanders, Count Clerfayt and the prince of Coburg. Cornwallis readily agreed, hoping that something might be done to redeem British credit, either by retaining part of Flanders or by withdrawing to more secure positions along the Dutch border, as he informed Pitt on 2 July 1794. But he deferred judgement on the ministry's plan to send an additional 10,000 British troops for a new offensive. The simple truth was that it was difficult to be optimistic against 'such active and numerous enemies', and with 'such wretched allies', who distrusted one another more than they hated the French. Only the need to preserve the alliance with Holland could justify further operations.[31]

It had been a chastening few weeks. Though Cornwallis had never been optimistic about his mission, he admitted to Pitt that he never imagined how it would be 'so speedily ruined'. Fortunately, York's army had successfully retreated to more secure lines by 7 July, protecting Antwerp and Namur. Cornwallis could now leave the British headquarters, since two experienced officers, Lord Rawdon (now the earl of Moira) and Sir Ralph Abercromby, Robert Abercromby's older brother, had arrived to assist York.[32] At Flushing a warship was waiting to ferry him back to England.[33]

Given Cornwallis's pessimism about further military operations, Pitt, Dundas, and Grenville decided to try diplomacy instead, sending a high-level mission to Vienna headed by Lord Spencer. Cornwallis much approved of their decision, believing it the only initiative open to them. Ross, though still a colonel, was to accompany Spencer as military adviser.[34] However, as Cornwallis feared, the Austrians continued to prevaricate. The only positive note by mid-August was a readiness to replace Coburg as one of their senior commanders in Flanders. But no successor was named and Spencer noted the Austrians remained reluctant to undertake further operations in Flanders, unless supported by a British loan and even larger subsidy.[35]

Despite this, the ministers remained optimistic, since they knew that the Austrians were sending another senior diplomat, Florimond Claude, comte de Mercy-Argenteau, to Britain. At Pitt's 'earnest request', Cornwallis agreed to remain in London, as he told Ross, though it was to his 'utmost mortification and misery'.[36] The partridge shooting season was approaching, offering him a rare chance of indulging in his favourite pastime. However, on Mercy-Argenteau's arrival events took an unexpected turn. The envoy explained that his government still wanted to continue the alliance as the best means of facilitating an invasion of France, providing financial assistance was forthcoming. The Austrians, however, had no commander in whom they had confidence. The solution, Mercy-Argenteau suggested, might lie in giving Cornwallis overall command of the allied forces, with the temporary rank of field marshal. Pitt quickly embraced the idea, telling Cornwallis on 24 August: 'I need not say how advantageous we should think it to the cause' if he undertook the assignment. George III still had to be convinced, since he was likely to resist the implied demotion of his favourite son. York too would have to be consulted. Nevertheless, Pitt believed that if the duke remained in command of the British troops, he would have the good sense to realise that 'his having the command of the whole combined army' was 'out of the question'. Hence if Cornwallis consented to undertake the mission, the whole nation would be in his debt, as the scheme offered 'the only probable chance of putting things into a good train'.[37]

Pitt did not hide the difficulties he was asking Cornwallis to undertake. Even so, Cornwallis's natural inclination was to accept dutifully the call of king and country. He accordingly replied in the affirmative. His only proviso was that he have the confidence of the Viennese court and acquiescence of York, both of which he knew were doubtful. Clearly, he would be undertaking 'the most arduous and invidious' task 'in which a man could possibly find himself'. Nevertheless, he had too much regard for Pitt and 'too much deference for [his] sentiments' to refuse. Consequently, he would await the ministerial summons, though he preferred that this be done privately rather than at one of the Cabinet dinners.[38]

In the event the scheme came to nothing, as Cornwallis suspected, because Mercy-Argenteau had exceeded his instructions. The emperor and his ministers in Vienna had no intention of entrusting the command of their army in Flanders to a British general, whatever might have happened under the duke of Marlborough during the war of Spanish Succession.[39] Cornwallis was personally relieved at avoiding an assignment that was fraught with difficulties, given the divisions between the Germanic powers. But he was apprehensive about how his conduct might be viewed by York and the king, telling Dundas: 'I conclude I am now completely ruined at St James.'[40]

With their hopes dashed for a major land offensive, the ministers turned to the idea of a coastal expedition to aid the Royalists in western France. Cornwallis was not enthusiastic, believing that Britain did not have sufficient resources for such an operation, which would require at least 20,000 regulars.[41] Indeed, he doubted that either Britain or her allies could do much to retrieve the situation, as he told Shore.

Despite the bloodshed in Paris, the French were still able to 'carry on the war with a vigour and energy that is scarcely to be conceived'. Cornwallis, like most of his contemporaries, still failed to appreciate the wellsprings of energy and ideological commitment which the Revolution had unlocked. He preferred to blame Britain's continental misfortunes on 'the incapacity and misconduct' of its commanders, rather than the ability of the enemy. Yet he could not help pondering 'how we are to get out of the war', or what effect its continuation might have 'upon the temper' of the country, faced with ever higher taxes. It was fortunate that the parliamentary opposition was so feeble and that the populace in general were seemingly supportive of the 'British constitution'.[42]

Although Cornwallis remained available for ministerial consultation, he now had an opportunity for some relaxation at Culford Park where he had spent just six days since returning from India. Among the invitees were Lichfield and his family, who had yet to see the remodelled house or additions to the Culford Park estate.[43] But Cornwallis also wanted time to set the record straight with York concerning recent events. In a long personal letter, he first reminded York that the recent situation had arisen because of his desire for a change of command in the Austrian forces. This had resulted in the dispatch of Spencer to Vienna, though Cornwallis had never been mentioned as a prospective commander-in-chief, as Ross could testify. Rather the proposal had come from the Austrian diplomats in London, as a means of filling the vacuum caused by the departure of Coburg. From the start Cornwallis had considered the plan absurd, but, believing 'it was highly disgraceful for an officer to refuse his services', he had reluctantly consented. Yet York must understand that he 'was actuated by no motives but a strict sense of the duty which I owe to my king and country'. He was not apologising, therefore, for what had happened, and hoped that York would not think he was 'base enough to have endeavoured to supplant' him 'by a dirty intrigue'.[44]

York responded gracefully, thanking Cornwallis for his 'very friendly letter'. He had too high an opinion of Cornwallis's character to think him capable of any base conduct. At such a critical juncture, the ministers were naturally 'anxious that a person of Your Lordship's military talents and reputation should not remain unemployed'.[45] However, York's days as a field commander were numbered, and ironically it was Cornwallis who facilitated this, following complaints about the condition of the army in Flanders. One such letter, from the army's camp at Arnhem on 11 November, confided to Cornwallis that the army had reached 'a critical situation'. Unless 'decisive and immediate steps are taken, God knows what may happen'. The British forces, despite some spirited actions, were now 'despised by our enemies', being without 'discipline, confidence, or exertion'. Sadly, they were 'hated and more dreaded than the enemy, even by the well-disposed inhabitants of the country'. The author, who was personally attached to York, had never spoken 'to anyone on this subject, nor would I to anyone but yourself'. Nevertheless, 'things are in such a state that I cannot avoid giving my opinion to the only one I know whose high character, reputation, and love of his country could save us'.[46]

Cornwallis never divulged the authorship of this letter, concealing it even from Ross, to whom he merely acknowledged that the writer was a 'friend' in whose judgement he trusted. The most likely candidate was Balfour, who had remained with York as a staff officer, following Cornwallis's return to Britain.[47] The letter certainly placed Cornwallis in a dilemma. He had assured the duke that he would not be privy to any intrigue and genuinely wished to avoid succeeding him as commander of the British forces. Nevertheless, the likely consequence of divulging the letter, as he told Ross, was that he would be 'pressed to undertake what no other person will attempt, and what I am afraid, cannot now possibly succeed, for discipline and confidence are not plants that will grow in a day'. Therein lay his real dilemma. Discipline and the well-being of the army were things that he could not overlook. He felt compelled, hence, to forward extracts of the letter to Dundas.[48] At least any opprobrium would fall on Cornwallis's shoulders rather than those of York's officers.

Such damaging revelations persuaded even the king that his son must be recalled, especially after Pitt explained that York's 'want of experience and of habits of detail' made it 'impossible for him to discharge all the complicated duties of his situation'.[49] The blow was softened under the guise of the duke being recalled for consultation with the ministry. Abercromby would in the meantime act as temporary commander of the British and Hanoverian forces.[50] Cornwallis had done his duty and with a clear conscience.

Although York had been recalled from Flanders, the poor performance of the army convinced Pitt that wider changes were needed in the ministry itself, if things were to improve. First, a new commander-in-chief was required to replace the seventy-eight-year-old Amherst, who clearly lacked the capacity for dealing with the crisis now facing Britain.[51] Second, the ministers were dissatisfied with the management of the Ordnance Board. The current master-general, the duke of Richmond, was not without administrative talent, having introduced several reforms in the running of his department.[52] He was also a competent army officer. But his recent tenure had met with criticism, especially his failure to provide a timely siege train for York's investment of Dunkirk during 1793.[53] Richmond was also at odds with the ministry's strategy for dealing with France, believing that Britain should concentrate on supporting the Royalists in western France. The result was his increasing absence from the Cabinet, leaving Pitt and his colleagues dependent on the ageing Amherst for military advice. The previous September the ministry had contemplated placing York in charge of the Ordnance Board.[54] Pitt now saw Richmond's removal as a way of remedying the current difficulties. He first proposed that York should succeed Amherst as commander-in-chief in Britain, with the rank of field marshal, a move which was sure to please George III. Cornwallis could then replace Richmond as master-general, giving the ministers a soldier in whom they trusted and a proven administrator to energise the Ordnance Board.[55]

Cornwallis first heard of these developments over Christmas 1794. His initial inclination was to decline the proposal, apprehensive that York would also be in the Cabinet, which would make 'the situation of an inferior military man . . . very unpleasant'.[56] But he was mistaken in this supposition, since the politicians were also against having York at their meetings. By the end of January, Cornwallis had persuaded himself that it was his duty to accept the post, especially if he was to assume 'almost the whole military responsibility in council'.[57] A bad cold then rendered him 'unfit for all society' for a few days.[58] He eventually commenced work on 11 February, after kissing the king's hand earlier that day.[59]

Because the Ordnance was critical to the war effort, the ministers initially proposed to strengthen it further, by making Abercromby lieutenant-general of the Ordnance Board in place of Cornwallis's former superior, Sir William Howe. In the event Howe remained in post. However, his ponderous approach to business determined Cornwallis to have Ross on the board, telling Dundas that he must have 'a capable friend in one of the efficient offices'.[60] When nothing happened he reminded Pitt that any 'reform to the Ordnance is very much founded on my obtaining the very able assistance of General Ross'.[61] After some rearrangement of offices, Ross was duly appointed surveyor-general in June 1795.

The patent establishing the Ordnance Board stated that the master-general was not required to attend or even secure the consent of his colleagues, having sole power in both the civil and military branches of the service.[62] However, no absentee could be effective unless he retained contact with the board, and like his predecessor, Cornwallis attended regular meetings with his colleagues. Although the board's headquarters were traditionally in the Tower of London, Cornwallis adopted Richmond's example of operating from offices at Westminster. The board's civil responsibilities included the provision of small arms and ordnance for the army and navy, and maintenance of all fortifications at home and abroad, which numbered fifty-five establishments.[63] The military branch comprised the Royal Artillery Regiment, the Corps of Royal Engineers, and the Royal Military Academy. The one area that Cornwallis reserved to himself as master-general concerned military appointments, which also required the king's consent.

Cornwallis quickly discovered that the direction of a major department in wartime was no easy matter. Within a week he was complaining to Ross: 'I am really overwhelmed with business', which was made all the more onerous by his having subordinates who were 'in perfect ignorance' of what others were doing. John Apsley, his secretary, was methodical but slow and lived 'so far off that I cannot get him early enough in the morning'.[64] Cornwallis's practice of starting early was confirmed by James Grant, who observed that an acquaintance had called several times at Cornwallis's house with important information about the French naval base at Brest, only to find its occupant absent. Seemingly, the only time to catch him was at daybreak. Nevertheless, Grant hoped that Cornwallis could attend a dinner he was arranging, since Dundas had confirmed that no Cabinet meeting was scheduled that evening. Seven of his friends would be present.[65]

The weekly Cabinet meetings were usually accompanied by a dinner, hosted by one of the members. Cornwallis's turn to entertain his colleagues first occurred on 18 March in Lower Grosvenor Street.[66] But even before his appointment, the Cabinet had been 'in great haste' for his opinion about the future deployment of the army under Abercromby, which had retreated into Holland. Cornwallis this time had no difficulty in giving his opinion, as he informed Dundas. The army should be recalled for three good reasons. Withdrawal would save considerable expense; it would strengthen the home defences; and lastly it would release forces for deployment in western France, if circumstances were propitious. Leaving the army in Holland merely endangered the troops without any compensating advantage, should the enemy threaten Britain.[67] The sense of his advice was obvious. The troops under Abercromby were withdrawn by way of Bremen.[68]

During these early days, Cornwallis faced his first departmental challenge, when Dundas requested measures to make 'the corps of artillery fit for carrying on the ensuing campaign'. Notionally an extra 1,000 men were required.[69] This was equivalent to the creation of another battalion to add to the four already in service. Cornwallis replied that no quick solution should be expected. Even if the men could be found, 'it would be impossible to train them in such a manner as to render them useful in the course of next summer'.[70] However, 300 Irish recruits, who had just landed at Chester to complete their training at Woolwich, might provide one source of manpower. Five hundred recruits might also be found by taking men from some newly created infantry regiments. A third possibility was to offer a bounty to the part-time 'fencible' companies, that had recently been raised to meet the invasion scare.[71] In the event, the king ordered the Irish recruits to be returned from whence they had come.[72] Cornwallis had instead to appeal for volunteers from the British militia, but without any compromise in standards. No recruit was to be under 5 feet 7 inches in height, though previous training was not important.[73] By the end of the year a fifth battalion had been added to the artillery in conformity with Dundas's original request.[74] Yet recognising that he still had much to learn, Cornwallis asked the officers of the horse artillery to inform him of any 'imperfections', and any 'improvements' that might be made. Light, fast-moving horse artillery on the Prussian model had only been introduced into the army in 1793, and Cornwallis was keen to know more about the corps.[75]

One important task in these first few weeks was Cornwallis's responsibility to ensure that the nation's fortifications were in a condition to withstand an invasion. Two major schemes were in progress along the Thames at Tilbury and Sheerness, the former to prevent a French attack on London, the latter to guard the naval dockyards on the River Medway. Both projects had been commissioned by Richmond on the advice of the chief engineer, Sir William Green. However, to Cornwallis's surprise, Green denied any knowledge of their progress, because he had been excluded from the drawing room in the Tower, where the details of all military works were held.[76] Cornwallis, intolerant of such departmental squabbles, quickly ordered Green to be given access, and also requested copies of various plans and drawings so that he could peruse them in more detail in his office at Westminster.[77]

Armed with this information, Cornwallis decided that his immediate priority must be to strengthen the approaches to London. On 9 March 1795 he accordingly issued orders for three discrete measures to protect the capital. The first was the building of a palisade around Gravesend, since the town was pivotal to the defensive chain guarding the capital. The second was the installation of a boom across the river between Gravesend and Tilbury, which was to consist of various vessels joined by cables, each one armed with two 68-pounder carronades. His third measure was the provision of 'two communications' to facilitate the 'passage of troops across the Thames in barges'.[78] However, Cornwallis's focus was by no means restricted to the Thames, since he simultaneously dispatched an engineer, Captain Hay, to East Anglia to see what works might be necessary there.[79]

As master-general, Cornwallis was the channel for patronage requests for places at the Royal Military Academy at Woolwich. From the start he made clear his determination to abide by the rules concerning age and suitability, no matter what rank the enquirer might hold. In April 1795 he informed Francis Napier, seventh baron and lieutenant-colonel in the army, that as applications for admission to Woolwich were so numerous, he could only admit those who had reached the designated age.[80] He answered similarly to Prince Edward, the king's fourth son, who wrote on behalf of two young men, Mr Weatherall and Mr Warburton. Cornwallis assured him that once their age had been established 'every attention will be paid to your commands'.[81] To another enquiry he affirmed that whatever the present demand for artillery officers, this still could not justify 'departure from the rules of the institution at Woolwich'.[82]

Cornwallis responded similarly to applications for more senior positions in the artillery and engineers, where it was often assumed that his authority was unlimited.

Such was the case of Major John McLeod, whom Cornwallis had previously commended during the American War. McLeod had clearly been persuaded by some 'fools' that Cornwallis could secure him the rank of lieutenant-colonel merely by intimating his wishes to the king. But as Cornwallis told McLeod, even 'if I could bring myself, in contradiction to my own sentiments and professions, to ask for it, I had not the smallest chance of obtaining it'.[83] The same strict rules also applied to the civil branch of the Ordnance. As he later told the duke of Grafton, promotion in the Ordnance was 'invariably made on regular progression from the inferior clerks, to clerks of the cheque, clerks of survey and storekeepers'. There were good reasons for so doing: 'Justice to individuals and the qualifications requisite for the superior officers in which great trust is reposed, render this order of preferment essentially necessary'. Cornwallis had only broken this rule in two minor instances.[84]

He did make one significant exception, and that was the appointment of Mark Singleton to the post of storekeeper of the Ordnance, though he first informed Pitt of his intention. He explained that his son-in-law had long regretted his lack of a regular occupation and had given Cornwallis 'the strongest assurances' that nothing would 'be wanting on his part to render himself a complete man of business'.[85] Nevertheless, the appointment breached his rules regarding promotion within the service. He likely did so to help Mary, but it was a rare exception.

Initially, the supply of arms and ordnance to the army and navy seemed satisfactory. However, in May 1795 Cornwallis and the board noted that the assembling of muskets was being delayed by a lack of wooden stocks.[86] Within weeks it was also apparent that locks and barrels were also in short supply. To meet the deficiency, the board ordered Major Thomas Trotter, an artillery officer, to visit Hamburg to see what small arms might be purchased there. Similar orders were given to another officer, Captain Miller, regarding purchases in Gothenburg or Copenhagen.[87] The results were distinctly mixed. Miller found no weapons for sale and returned home empty-handed. Trotter eventually secured 15,000 French muskets and the promise of further deliveries to a total of 50,000 weapons at 39 livres per musket. Given the continued need for muskets, Cornwallis and his colleagues had little choice but to accept the offer.[88]

Fortunately, supplies of powder appeared less problematic. The Ordnance Board had its own powder mill at Faversham, though this only supplied a modest quantity, leaving the board heavily dependent on merchant supplies.[89] The first real test came in June 1795 when York requested a reserve of 200 musket cartridges per man at the various artillery parks now scattered around south-east England. This would mean the production of 4 million cartridges, requiring 320 wagons and 1,280 horses to transport them. The ammunition would also be less secure if stored in relatively unprotected sites. Cornwallis suggested in response that it would be more sensible to keep the reserves of ammunition at Woolwich and other major depots like Portsmouth, ready 'to reinforce any particular division'.[90] However, by way of compromise, Cornwallis agreed that the board would increase its stock of ammunition at various sites as York had requested.[91]

These supply problems led Cornwallis to reconsider the method of procuring 'several species of stores' which were currently produced by the Ordnance's own workforce. He suggested that it might be 'much to the advantage of the public if contracts were issued for a limited term' to other parties, provided they offered proper security for the 'due performance of their engagements'. He hoped thereby to secure cheaper articles of similar quality and speedier delivery. Competitive tendering had worked well in Bengal (see above, p. 172) and there was no reason to suppose otherwise in Britain, where it was already widespread. It was undoubtedly one of the measures he had in mind when talking about reform to Pitt in the context of Ross's appointment. A list of the current suppliers, accordingly, was to be compiled to help decide which 'contracts should be thrown open for fresh proposals by public advertisement'.[92]

In addition to his duties as master-general, in April Cornwallis had been appointed commander of the land forces defending Essex.[93] For the next three months he resided in a summer camp at Warley near Brentwood, where the forces for his district were concentrated. Serving under him were two lieutenant-generals and five major-generals, among them old friends like James Grant and William Medows. The current plan for the defence of Britain was largely the work of Major-General David Dundas, the author of a widely used training manual. Cornwallis was not enamoured of the manual nor of its author's current defence scheme, which he thought unintelligible. Nevertheless, he was anxious that the 'camp at Warley should not appear particularly defective'.[94]

The pressure of business meant that Cornwallis spent little time during 1795 at Culford Park. When he finally visited in September, the hot dry weather meant few partridges were in evidence.[95] This was disappointing since shooting was now his main recreation. At fifty-five years of age he had become too heavy to ride most horses, making foxhunting difficult.[96] Earlier that June, he had been delighted to hear that William Cornwallis had repulsed a French fleet twice the size of his own squadron in the Western Approaches and had done so with minimum casualties.[97] Less pleasing was Robert Abercromby's report from Calcutta that the Company's army officers in India remained obdurately opposed to any changes in the service. His one hope was that Cornwallis could still devise a scheme giving 'satisfaction to all moderate men' along the lines of the paper that he had circulated before his departure from India.[98]

Meanwhile, Cornwallis saw his role in the Cabinet as one of giving technical advice, having no magic formula himself for winning the war. Strategy was a matter for the politicians to decide. On the withdrawal of the army from Holland, the ministers in any case needed no prompting to switch their focus to helping the Royalists in western France, as Richmond had wanted. Their plan was to send a corps of French émigrés from Britain to Quiberon Bay in Brittany in the hope of inducing a general uprising. During May and June 1795 Cornwallis valiantly co-ordinated the Ordnance's contribution to the scheme, despite the 'secrecy to be observed' and the uncertainty about 'the numbers and kind of service for which arrangements' were to be made. Two landings were eventually accomplished in July.[99] However, dissentions among the émigrés quickly saw the venture collapse, signalling an end to British hopes of influencing events inside France.[100] With Prussia and Spain quitting the war, it was difficult to see where any effective strike could be made.

Nevertheless, the ministers were determined to keep trying, as Dundas made clear when pressing Cornwallis at the end of July 1795 to come to London before the next Cabinet meeting: there were 'many things on which I need to converse with you'.[101] The setback in France had persuaded Pitt and his colleagues to concentrate Britain's military effort on the Caribbean instead, as a way of counter-balancing enemy success in Europe. The result was an agreement to send an expedition of 15,000 men in the autumn of 1795 to attack the French sugar islands of Grenada, Saint Vincent, Saint Lucia, or Guadeloupe, with Saint-Domingue thrown in for good measure. Cornwallis was asked to recommend a commander for the enterprise. He suggested the highly respected Major-General Ralph Abercromby, now returned from the Continent, as the best candidate from 'a melancholy list'.[102] Cornwallis's own views about the scheme are unclear, but he loyally set about ensuring that the Ordnance Board played its part. A considerable train of artillery and supply of munitions were necessary, requiring the hire of twelve transports. By the end of October 1795 three of the nine vessels were still waiting at Woolwich for their stores.[103] However, a subsequent Commons enquiry attributed the delay to the Navy Board's transport arrangements rather than any failings by 'the noble Marquess' or his colleagues.[104]

In reality, all the departments had struggled to meet the ministers' timetable.[105] But other factors had also intervened to hinder the operation. First, bad weather confined the flotilla to port. Then it was scattered by a violent storm, and forced to return to Portsmouth. Cornwallis was sufficiently dispirited to suggest that the country should give up all offensive operations for the next twelve months, using the time to restore the army to a proper strength.[106] Yet such negativity was not what his Cabinet colleagues wanted to hear, since they had to convince the country that they had a viable strategy for winning the war. Pitt was naturally conscious of his father's reputation as a war leader, and was anxious to achieve similar acclaim.[107] His aspirations were shared by Dundas and Grenville, who now constituted an all-powerful triumvirate in the Cabinet. Imperceptibly, Cornwallis found himself playing a less influential role in the direction of the war than originally envisaged, since the ministers began to seek advice from David Dundas instead, who, though no relation to the secretary of state for war, commanded the forces along the south coast.[108] The change of adviser, however, did not produce any improvement in military fortune. The expedition finally reached the West Indies in the late spring, its one success being the retaking of Saint Lucia, which even Abercromby admitted constituted a 'barren conquest'. He had, however, been well served by some excellent artillery officers.[109]

The difficulties experienced by the expedition affected Cornwallis in a more personal capacity. After the flotilla had reassembled at Portsmouth in early January 1796, the command of the naval escort was given to William Cornwallis. His ship, the *Royal Sovereign*, then became disabled. Instead of transferring to another vessel, William returned to England, leaving the command with his deputy. Lord Spencer, now first lord of the Admiralty, immediately ordered him to re-join his squadron on a frigate. This he refused to do, because he wanted to remain with the officers and crew of his currently disabled flagship, offering by way of excuse that travelling on a small frigate would damage his health.[110] Such disobedience was clearly inadmissible, and Spencer rightly ordered him to be court-martialled for disobeying orders. The dispute was embarrassing for Cornwallis, since he was on close terms with Spencer as a member of the Cabinet. His immediate reaction was to urge William to proceed as the Admiralty desired, though he admitted to Ross that he had little influence over his headstrong brother.[111] He also wrote privately to Spencer, offering to go to Portsmouth to talk with the recalcitrant admiral.[112] But it was all to no avail. The Admiralty and William persisted in their respective viewpoints, leaving a court-martial the only way of resolving the matter. The subsequent trial resulted only in a mild reprimand, much to Cornwallis's relief.[113]

Although 1796 began relatively calmly, there was no room for complacency, given the rising fears of invasion. One early test for the Ordnance concerned the supply of trained artillerymen, following a request from the governor of Gibraltar for another company to be stationed there. Cornwallis quickly warned York that the strength of the Royal Artillery Regiment was scarcely adequate to the requirements at home, let alone additional demands from overseas. Nevertheless, he conceded that the preservation of Gibraltar was essential and had consequently arranged for the immediate dispatch of a full company.[114]

The supply of muskets was also of concern, not least because the Birmingham manufacturers began demanding a uniform price well above the usual rate. This suggested a cartel and a brazen attempt at profiteering. Cornwallis and his colleagues were in no mood to comply with such opportunism. They accordingly informed the manufacturers that they would make no further purchases until they were more reasonable in their demands.[115] As a precaution Trotter was again ordered to investigate the purchase of foreign barrels and other parts to circumvent the demands of the British makers, providing they were of the designated pattern.[116] The Ordnance's stance this time proved successful, for by mid-June one of the larger Birmingham suppliers agreed not only to moderate his prices, but to increase his deliveries too.[117]

This was fortunate. In August 1796 the Ordnance received a large request for small arms and saltpetre from Portugal, Britain's oldest ally. The withdrawal of Spain from the war in 1795 and its likely alliance with France made the Portuguese fearful of being invaded. However, the demand for 60,000 muskets and 750 tons of refined saltpetre was so large that Cornwallis felt obliged to reduce it, substituting 200 tons of rough saltpetre and 12,000 muskets for the original order.[118] He took this decision, despite an offer from one of the Birmingham manufacturers to supply inferior weapons, because the board was determined 'to return again to . . . the old established pattern' of musket, commonly nicknamed the 'Brown Bess'.[119] Experience showed that it was a false economy to accept inferior weapons, whatever the emergency.

A contributory factor to the Ordnance Board's difficulties was the country's want of money, which had necessitated an emergency issue of Exchequer bills to meet the army's need. Another sign of the financial turmoil was the fall in the price of the 3-per-cent consolidated stocks to 66 per cent of their original value. Apart from the armed forces, the government also had to finance its foreign policy, since it was trying to keep the Austrians in the war by the offer of a new subsidy.[120] Confidence was not helped by domestic unrest. The country had suffered a poor harvest in 1795, sending the price of wheat and other necessities to unaffordable levels. Requests for relief from Ordnance workers had begun early in the year, starting with the labourers in the storekeeper's department at Woolwich. Despite the financial constraints, Cornwallis recognised the humanity and justice of such cries, given the 'present high price of every necessary of life', and ordered extra pay. Other pleas of hardship inevitably followed.[121]

Finally, the country had to contend with a rapid deterioration in the war. In April 1796 a French army under Napoleon Bonaparte burst into Italy, forcing Sardinia to capitulate before driving the Austrians back across Lombardy. By June 1796, only the fortress of Mantua prevented their expulsion from the region. The news led Cornwallis once more to advocate a peaceful resolution to the war. However, with France and Spain on the verge of invading Britain and Ireland, Dundas justly commented: 'You say you must have peace, I ask, how are you to get it?'[122] It was a fair question.

The threat of invasion prompted Cornwallis in August 1796 to visit the Essex coast to inspect progress on the defensive works around Clacton, which he had authorised the previous June. This revealed that there were few obstacles to a landing there and that any batteries covering the inland roads would be easily bypassed. In these circumstances, Cornwallis decided the priority must be to hold the strategic towns of Yarmouth, Ipswich, Chelmsford, and Colchester. The latter was especially important, being within marching distance of the key assembly points for defending either Suffolk or Essex.[123]

The coastal communities inevitably had different priorities. They wanted the government to strengthen the volunteer units manning the batteries. The master-general had no wish to damper local enthusiasm, but had to point out the 'many difficulties' in making such corps 'serve any useful purpose'.[124] He was accordingly annoyed to learn that his former colleague in India, William Cuppage, had detached 100 men from the Royal Artillery Regiment in Kent to supervise the volunteer emplacements along the coast, 'every one of which must be abandoned' should the enemy land there. Cornwallis preferred to keep a strong reserve of field artillery at Woolwich, which could be deployed in 'any part of the country where they may be required'. Nevertheless, as Cornwallis ruefully acknowledged to Fawcett, the king's military secretary, Cuppage was answerable to York, who was now commander-in-chief.[125] Cornwallis could only indicate what he thought best.

This set the scene for another disagreement with York, concerning the creation of a 'permanent regiment of artillery', independent of the Ordnance Board. The duke's plan in the late autumn was for the new corps to provide field artillery to each infantry regiment. York was undoubtedly influenced by the continental practice of deploying mobile field artillery in this manner.[126] However, as Cornwallis explained in response, the present horse artillery was more than adequate for current purposes. The key question was 'whether the battalion guns are likely to be better served with the assistance of a few men regularly bred and instructed in the corps of artillery', or by 'soldiers of the different regiments, who, from the dispersed state of the British army, would in many instances have but little opportunity of acquiring a competent knowledge of their business'. He continued: 'artillery is undoubtedly a most powerful arm in war, but I cannot subscribe to an opinion which has of late been prevalent . . . that everything is to be decided by artillery'. Well-disciplined infantry 'will ever be formidable in whatever country it is to act and I am persuaded must in general decide the fate of battles'. This did not mean that he was against the European practice of battalion guns, merely that they should be restricted to ordnance no heavier than light 6-pounders. He concluded by assuring York that he was not advancing these opinions to protect his own department and influence. His only wish was to assist to the best of his ability.[127]

If Cornwallis thought 1796 had been a difficult year, he was to discover that 1797 was to be even worse, starting with further heavy demands on the Ordnance Board. In early February, Lord Gordon, the commanding officer in Scotland, requested additional field artillery and muskets for the inhabitants. He channelled his request through York.[128] Cornwallis replied, contrary to his recent assurances of sufficiency, that the artillery corps in Britain was too reduced to permit the dispatch of any further detachments to Scotland. The establishment there had long been considered adequate for that part of the kingdom. The most that Cornwallis could offer was some 5½-inch howitzers, which were more suitable for field service than the 8-inch variety. As to small arms, he might meet perhaps a fourth part of Gordon's demand.[129]

These difficulties were seemingly the reason why York sent Cornwallis a series of questions about the state of the artillery parks; the number of regiments with field guns; the strength of the horse artillery; and the speed with which their brigades could be mobilised.[130] Cornwallis, in response, assured York that the artillery parks were prepared for any emergency, while the field pieces attached to the regiments had a full complement of horses. The brigades of horse artillery were also fully equipped, many having their ordnance mounted on new carriages. In addition, the Woolwich Arsenal had a number of 12-pounder cannon and howitzers ready for deployment. Finally, the Arsenal had copious supplies of cartridges and wagons to transport them, as had the principal parks and naval storehouses.[131] York duly acknowledged his pleasure at receiving Cornwallis's report, admitting it had surpassed 'what I expected'.[132]

Nevertheless, the difficulty in supplying small arms for Scotland prompted Cornwallis to defend his record to Dundas. The demand for muskets had been exceptional. During 1796 the corps in Britain had required 27,000 new muskets, the Portuguese 19,000 (including 7,000 carbines), the troops in Saint-Domingue 8,000, while another 10,000 had been shipped to Ireland. Part of the Portuguese order had been arranged separately by Grenville, much to the inconvenience of the Ordnance. Another 50,000–60,000 weapons would be required shortly for the militia, as well as 40,000 for the new regiments that were expected to be raised during 1797. This would leave 20,000–30,000 muskets in the Tower and other principal armouries for any emergency. The current shortage was partly due to the delay in paying the manufacturers, who were slowing their deliveries in response. But whatever the cause of these delays, Cornwallis acknowledged that the consequences would be fatal if weapons were unavailable for those 'willing to hazard their lives' in the service of their country.[133]

While dealing with these Ordnance matters, Cornwallis found himself unexpectedly immersed once more in the affairs of India. At the end of 1796 alarming accounts were received of officer dissatisfaction in Bengal, following the circulation of Cornwallis's confidential enquiries and publication of a plan which Dundas had concocted with the Directors of the East India Company.[134] Dundas had taken the initiative, believing that Cornwallis's own plan for the crown to control both the Company's European and sepoy corps, which he had drafted while returning from India, was too radical.[135] Nevertheless, remonstrances still poured in from every station, prompting demands for concessions from the Bengal government. These included assurances that the Company's regiments not be reduced; that the number of the king's troops in India be limited by law; and that no distinctions be made between the European and sepoy corps regarding pay and emoluments.[136]

In this crisis it seemed that only one person had the right blend of firmness and diplomacy to overcome these difficulties. Dundas assured Cornwallis on 18 January 1797 that he would go himself, but Pitt refused to release him. Hence, if Cornwallis could forgo his home comforts for one more year, he would be doing 'the greatest service to your country that ever any man had it in his power to do'. To ensure that his appointment as governor-general was temporary, Cornwallis could take his successor with him and retain the outward-bound warship to transport him home again. He would then have the distinction of having twice saved the British Empire in India.[137]

Dundas knew that this appeal to service to his king and country would be a powerful inducement on Cornwallis, who remained anxious to preserve his legacy in India. He was not disappointed, since Cornwallis immediately agreed to discuss the matter after the next Cabinet meeting. Here he argued half-heartedly that Dundas would experience less hostility in India: his role in the new regulations was less obvious, since these had been presented as though they were the Company's own policy. However, Cornwallis would 'not depart from the line of conduct' which he had 'invariably pursued throughout life, of sacrificing all private considerations of comfort and happiness to the service of the public'.[138] Four days later he was officially reappointed governor-general by the Court of Directors, though he confessed privately to Ross that his heart was aching at the thought of what he had undertaken.[139] The king noted, approvingly, that Cornwallis as usual had showed his 'upright character'; would that such qualities were 'more frequently met with'.[140]

Cornwallis, accordingly, began preparations for his departure. Among his more important tasks was the naming of his staff, though Ross would not be among them, having just become a father. 'Would to God you could be of the party; but Mrs Ross, your rank in the army' and position at the Ordnance all presented 'insuperable barriers'. Cornwallis in any case would remain master-general, leaving Howe temporarily in charge.[141]

His preparations, however, proved suddenly redundant. In early February letters arrived from Robert Abercromby and Shore informing the Directors that Dundas's regulations, with some modification, had been accepted by the Company's officers. The situation was now much quieter, though Abercromby admitted that Cornwallis's plan for merging the two forces under the crown, which he had formulated on his homeward journey, would eventually have to be implemented.[142] However, according to George Robinson, the military auditor, Shore and Abercromby had effectively surrendered 'to a factious army' almost everything originally contained in the revised regulations.[143] This was also the view of Dundas when he heard the details. Since the Directors were reluctant to act, he proposed passing a new bill in Parliament which would empower Cornwallis to carry out a more sweeping reform. Cornwallis, however, was not encouraging. With Britain and Ireland again facing invasion, it was no time to make 'speculative arrangements' for the forces in India. The reform of the Company's army would have to wait, since there were more immediate challenges to meet at home.[144] The plan to reappoint him governor-general was no longer sensible.

Cornwallis was rightly cautious. 1797 was turning into an *annus horribilis*. In February a run occurred on the Bank of England, raising the spectre of default and the collapse of the government's credit.[145] Then, in April, several mutinies broke out in the Royal Navy, starting at Portsmouth. Fears were also expressed about the loyalty of the army, prompting William Windham, the secretary at war, to bewail the Ordnance Board's practice of keeping 'all the arms of the country' in the Tower. Should the elite Guards regiments mutiny, as was rumoured, there would be nothing to prevent them from seizing the Tower, together with the Royal Mint, St James's

Palace, and the Cabinet in Downing Street.[146] To nullify the threat, assurances were quickly given to the Guards about their pay and allowances. But the Ordnance was not immune from the contagion, with an outbreak of rioting among the artillerymen at Woolwich.[147] To deal with the crisis, Pitt hastily summoned Cornwallis and York to Downing Street in the early hours of 27 May 1797, after which Cornwallis travelled to Woolwich with a detachment of the Guards to restore order. Reason fortunately prevailed without the need for bloodshed.[148] Nevertheless, the Cabinet was sufficiently unnerved to discuss the dispatch of a peace envoy to France. Grenville firmly opposed the idea, while Cornwallis was 'vehemently for' it. Nothing came of the proposal.[149]

Even as these events were unfolding, another crisis was brewing in Ireland. In December 1796 the French had dispatched a powerful expedition to Bantry Bay in the south-west of the country under General Lazare Hoche. Only bad weather prevented a landing. The episode terrified the lord lieutenant of Ireland, John Pratt, Earl Camden, especially as he distrusted his commander-in-chief, Henry Luttrell, earl of Carhampton. A more experienced general was required from Britain.[150] His request arrived just as Cornwallis was retrieving his baggage from the warship that was to have taken him to India. In a casual conversation with Dundas, he observed that as 'his services would not be useful in India, they might be wanted in Ireland'. He repeated these sentiments to Pitt, adding that 'the office he would consent to undertake was that of Commander-in-Chief'. This would keep his responsibilities 'within the limits of his own profession', for 'no consideration whatever could tempt him to accept the government of Ireland'.[151]

Cornwallis's offer was surprising, given his previous affirmations about his desire to remain at home. He may have privately been disappointed at being denied the chance to reform the Indian army. Another possible factor was a desire to escape the drudgery of the Ordnance Board and membership of a Cabinet from which he felt increasingly alienated. His colleagues had recently advocated using the French tactic of firing 'helter-skelter' when making an attack. To Cornwallis this was madness: he believed that there was no substitute for disciplined firing by platoon when engaging an enemy.[152] Hence, what better way of avoiding such ill-informed discussions than returning to active service? Dundas was sufficiently receptive to suggest that Cornwallis's baggage should be redirected to Dublin. One obstacle was whether Camden would welcome his appointment. In reality Camden was delighted at the prospect of having Cornwallis as commander-in-chief: 'Your Lordship's inclination to act with me in this country' would be 'the most flattering circumstance of my life'. He would be even more indebted if Cornwallis replaced him as lord lieutenant, though he understood his reluctance to do so.[153]

Departmental responsibility for Ireland lay with William Cavendish-Bentinck, duke of Portland, the home secretary. He accordingly invited Cornwallis on 28 May 1797 to discuss the matter in person.[154] The meeting, however had to be delayed, because Cornwallis was currently dealing with the mutiny at Woolwich. In reality he was already having second thoughts about the appointment. As Portland explained to Camden shortly afterwards, Cornwallis had become apprehensive about 'engaging in the business, unless means were taken to placate the Catholics' and separate them from the Dissenters. He believed that 'concessions little if at all short of what is termed Catholic emancipation' would be necessary. Of course, he would go to Ireland should an invasion be imminent, but doubted that he could do any good in the present circumstances, since he was convinced that 'no force or power . . . would place that unhappy people in a state of obedience and security', unless some such measure was adopted. To pretend otherwise would be dishonest.[155] The futility of trying to coerce an alienated populace was a lesson he had leant while in America.

Cornwallis seems to have taken his stance on Catholic emancipation mainly on political rather than theological grounds. His own religious convictions were those of a latitudinarian Anglican, inclining him to believe that everyone should be allowed to worship the Creator in their own manner, since religious diversity was not incompatible with British authority. This had been his position in India. The reality was that the Catholics in Ireland comprised 75 per cent of the inhabitants, making it impossible to ignore their interests.

Although the mutinies were suppressed, events throughout 1797 offered the master-general little cheer, other than the marriage in April of Brome to Lady Louisa Gordon, a daughter of the duke and duchess of Gordon.[156] Socially it was a good match, giving Cornwallis the prospect of a grandson to continue the dynasty. On the Continent, the Portuguese in August sued the French for peace, while Bonaparte first expelled the Austrians from Italy and then followed them to within 100 miles of Vienna.[157] The enemy successes further divided the Cabinet on how to respond, though by now Cornwallis had developed a strong aversion to Lord Grenville, the foreign secretary, observing sarcastically that he must have nothing to do, now that Britain had been abandoned by her allies. Hopefully, the collapse of his plans would prompt him to resign his office instead.[158] Matters failed to improve in the latter half of 1797, as he related to Ross at the year's end: 'Torn as we are by faction, without an army, without money, trusting entirely to a navy whom we may not be able to pay . . . how are we to get out of this cursed war without a revolution?' The delusions of Grenville and his circle about Britain standing alone would surely be exposed as folly.[159]

Thus, 1798 promised to be another difficult year, as he informed Arthur Wellesley, now in India with the 33rd Foot Regiment. The country had been brought to a state he had long dreaded, 'deserted by our allies, and in daily expectation of invasion, for which the French are making the most serious preparations'. Cornwallis had no doubts about the courage or fidelity of the militia, 'but the system of David Dundas, and the total want of light infantry, sit heavy on my mind'. The lack of such corps would give the French every advantage 'in a country, which is for the most part enclosed'.[160] The threat of invasion inevitably produced the usual crop of impractical suggestions. Cornwallis was particularly annoyed by the demand of George Nugent-Temple-Grenville, marquess of Buckingham that the county militia be provided with heavy ordnance. Apart from the expense, there was the impracticality of using untrained part-timers in the deployment of such weaponry. Fortunately, York vetoed the idea, but further wild schemes were inevitable, since Buckingham was clearly not the 'only wrongheaded, absurd colonel of militia'.[161]

Although Cornwallis had been marginalised in Cabinet discussions, he still had responsibility for the kingdom's fixed defences.[162] Accordingly, in April 1798 he made a short tour of Kent and Sussex to inspect the defences around Dover Castle, which he found in a better condition than expected. As to emergency measures, he was against emptying the countryside of people and livestock. He also opposed the erection of batteries at every crossroad and the flooding of low-lying areas, since such obstacles could always be circumvented by an enemy.[163] The focus should be on the deployment of light infantry rather than 'four-and-twenty-pounders', as proposed by Howe, who had become 'quite mad about fortifications'.[164] Cornwallis was thus relieved when York followed his advice about avoiding fixed batteries in favour of concentrating resources, so that they could be deployed where needed, should an invasion begin.[165]

The continued demands on the Royal Artillery Regiment and lack of any ending to the war led Cornwallis in the spring of 1798 to propose a plan for increasing the number of cadets at the Royal Military Academy. Like all good administrators he wanted to avoid unnecessary costs. To achieve this his scheme had two elements. The first was to increase the total number of students from ninety to a hundred, allocating sixty places for the king's forces and forty for the East India Company. Simultaneously, an extra corps of students would start their studies in schools around Woolwich. After making sufficient progress, the recruits would be called into the academy proper as vacancies occurred, allowing yet more to start their training in the schools. This would ensure a faster supply of trained personnel, while facilitating a future merger of the crown's forces with those of the East India Company. However, before he could deliver his paper to the board, a serious rebellion broke out in Ireland. Once again Cornwallis appeared to be the only person with the necessary military and political skills to deal with this dangerous situation. Since his presence was immediately required in Ireland, it was his secretary Apsley who presented his paper on 14 June 1798 to the Ordnance Board for expanding the Royal Military Academy.[166]

FOURTEEN

Bringing Peace to Ireland

The British government had been concerned about Ireland since the War of American Independence, during which the Irish Parliament demanded release from the constraint of having to submit its legislation to the Privy Council in London for approval. A weakened British government of necessity had to agree. From 1782 Ireland was once again a sovereign country, joined to Britain only by a common sovereign.[1] In practice, British control was not entirely eliminated: the king still appointed the Irish executive and retained command of the army there.

The immediate crisis passed, but not the disquiet in Britain about the weakened links between the two kingdoms. Another cause for unease was that the settlement of 1782 had not changed the exclusive composition of the Irish Parliament, representing as it did only the 10 per cent of the population that belonged to the Anglican Church of Ireland. Only those who took the prescribed oaths of conformity to its doctrines could vote or hold office. The result was to exclude both the three-quarters of the population who were Roman Catholic and the 15 per cent who were Presbyterian. This was at a time when enlightened opinion was advocating greater toleration, rejecting political systems based on religious exclusion.

Soon there were other causes for disquiet. In 1785 Pitt proposed a free trade agreement to stimulate commerce between the two kingdoms and strengthen their ties. The Irish Parliament, anxious to protect its nascent cotton and linen industries, rejected the plan. Then in 1788 the regency crisis (see above, pp. 189–90) produced fears that the Irish Parliament might support the prince of Wales, to the horror of George III and his ministers.[2] But it was the ideological challenges of the French

Map 7. Ireland.

Revolution that threw the most searching light on the 1782 constitutional settlement. The emphasis on liberty, equality, and the rights of man inevitably found support among those sections of the Irish population currently excluded from the political system. Although the Catholic and Presbyterian hierarchies rejected the secular and republican nature of Jacobinism, the same was not true for much of the population, for whom the eviction of oppressive landlords and the abolition of Church tithes were key issues. And while many abhorred the Reign of Terror in Revolutionary France, a significant minority led by the Society of United Irishmen welcomed the resultant war as an opportunity to free Ireland from British control. Formed in 1791 on republican principles, the Society sought to create a country in which Protestants and Catholics could live in peace and harmony under the banner of liberty and the rights of man.[3]

The need to broaden support for the crown among the population led the Pitt ministry to press the Irish legislature to pass a Catholic Relief Act in 1793, removing some of the legal restrictions imposed on that church. Among the concessions was the right to vote for those Catholics who possessed a 40 shilling freehold. Then in 1795 William Wentworth, Earl Fitzwilliam, was appointed lord lieutenant, seemingly with a mandate to implement further reform. However, the idea of emancipation for other religious groups was anathema to the Anglo-Irish elite, who swiftly persuaded Pitt that such a measure would destabilise the kingdom and burden the British taxpayer. Fitzwilliam was summarily recalled and replaced by the earl Camden.[4]

These events merely confirmed to the United Irishmen that more drastic methods were necessary, if Ireland was to be freed from the grip of its repressive neighbour. Approaches were accordingly made for help from the French Directorate, which had seized power from Robespierre and the Jacobins in July 1794. The French were more than ready to oblige, seeing this as a golden opportunity to weaken Britain and impose a humiliating peace. The result was the dispatch of General Hoche's expeditionary force, which successfully eluded the British fleet before arriving on 21 December 1796 in Bantry Bay. However, a violent gale subsequently scattered the French armada, necessitating a return to France.[5]

The incident led Camden to make his request for the dispatch of a more senior officer as commander-in-chief. When Cornwallis declined the offer, Ralph Abercromby was sent instead. The appointment proved a fractious one, since

Abercromby disapproved of the Irish government's repressive measures for controlling the countryside. Although no further invasion was attempted in 1797, the country was awash with rumours in early 1798 about the impending arrival of the French and an internal rising by the United Irishmen. This time Camden asked to be released from his post, not least because of his disagreements with Abercromby, and belief that the civil and military authority should be placed into the hands of one person, preferably those of Cornwallis.[6] However, Pitt wanted to avoid further political upheavals, having enough problems in Britain. He was also conscious that Cornwallis's sympathy for the Catholics was likely to antagonise the ruling Anglo-Irish elite. As he informed Camden on 31 March 1798, he had 'great doubts whether his temper of mind and prejudices on Irish subjects make him qualified for the task'. For the moment Camden should stay and rely on Lieutenant-General Gerard Lake, the next most senior officer, to command the army.[7]

Camden was not pleased by this response, in part because he doubted Lake's 'capacity' to manage 'the complicated nature of the service in Ireland'. However he promised to do his best.[8] Most importantly he instructed Lake to continue Dublin Castle's policy of repression, using the 1796 Insurrection Act to place the country under martial law. News then arrived that the French were preparing another naval armament at Toulon, which Bonaparte was to command, prompting frenzied rumours of an impending invasion. In this situation the Dublin branch of the United Irishmen determined in late May to launch a pre-emptive uprising, not only in the capital but throughout Ireland. The plot in Dublin was foiled before it could be implemented, after an informer had betrayed the details.[9] Nevertheless, large numbers of poorer Catholics rose in the south and west to rid themselves of their landlords and British oppressors. This was despite the Catholic hierarchy's plea to its communicants to have nothing to do with 'the irreligious and wicked agitators' who were attempting 'to overturn and destroy the constitution' of the country.[10] The uprising was particularly formidable in the county of Wexford.

These events immediately unnerved Camden. When the ministry was slow to answer his pleas for reinforcements, he renewed his clamour about his being 'perfectly inadequate' for the task. Cornwallis was the obvious candidate to deal with the worsening situation and 'his inclination to the Catholic cause ought not to weigh against' his appointment.[11] The ministry responded by dispatching 2,000 Guardsmen and a number of other units. But when London heard of a serious uprising in Ulster, Pitt bowed to Camden's pleas. After conversing with Cornwallis on the morning of 11 June, he informed George III that the master-general's 'zeal for the public service' had induced 'him without hesitation to accept the arduous situation of lord lieutenant and to repair to Ireland without delay'.[12] However, Cornwallis's mission was not simply one of repression. Recent events had only emphasised to Pitt and his colleagues the inadequacies of Ireland's system of government. What was required, he told Camden on 11 June, was 'some permanent settlement which may provide for the internal peace of the country and secure its connection with Great Britain'. This objective he was 'convinced [could] be attained only by a Union' of the two kingdoms.[13]

Cornwallis left no personal thoughts about his new assignment, though within ten days of arriving, he confided to Ross: 'If I can accomplish the great object of consolidating the British Empire, I shall be sufficiently repaid.'[14] Unquestionably, his perennial sense of duty played an important part in his decision. He was also not without knowledge of Ireland, having served there for a time as colonel of his regiment (see above, pp. 18–19). It was difficult not to agree with Adam Smith that, apart from any economic benefit, a union would deliver Ireland from an 'oppressive aristocracy' which governed on the 'most odious of all distinctions, those of religious and political prejudices'.[15] Correcting such abuses offered a more constructive role than mere military pacification, though holding both the lord lieutenancy and command of the army meant placing himself in the middle of a political, social, and religious maelstrom, something he had refused to consider twelve months earlier. Yet he knew from his experience in India that possessing both civil and military authority would make it easier to effect the changes that were clearly necessary.

Despite his earlier insistence, Cornwallis did not make Catholic emancipation a precondition for accepting the assignment. One reason was undoubtedly his knowledge that George III was opposed to such an idea. Indeed, the king on first hearing of the ministerial plans, told Pitt firmly: 'Lord Cornwallis must clearly understand that no indulgence can be granted to Catholics further than has been I am afraid inadvisably done.' He should instead focus on achieving a union of the two kingdoms.[16] George III passionately believed that 'no country can be governed where there is more than one established religion'. The granting of further rights to Catholics must inevitably undermine the Church of Ireland and of England too, if the principle was extended.[17] For the moment Pitt said nothing, while Cornwallis decided that the restoration of order must be his first priority. But the potential for trouble was clearly there.

Unlike his journey to India, Cornwallis was able to depart immediately, since no special arrangements were necessary concerning his estate, Brome now being of an age to manage these responsibilities. A rapid departure also relieved Cornwallis from the solicitations of countless office-seekers, as had happened in 1786. He left London on 16 June, reaching Parkgate in Cheshire three days later, where he boarded one of the packet boats that regularly crossed the Irish sea. The journey proved a speedy one, since he arrived in Dublin Harbour at around 5 a.m. on 20 June.[18] Here he was greeted by two lords of the Irish Privy Council, who escorted him to Dublin Castle along streets lined with troops. At the castle he was received by Camden who conducted him to the council chamber, where the letters patent appointing him were read and the oaths of office taken.[19]

Cornwallis's first task was to be briefed about Lake's plan of campaign. This seemed so well designed, he told Portland, as to render it unnecessary for him 'to think of proceeding immediately to join the army'.[20] His confidence was boosted by the news that the Guards brigade had arrived at Waterford and that several militia regiments from Britain had volunteered to serve during the uprising.[21] Even better news arrived the next day: Lake had defeated the main rebel army in the south at Vinegar Hill, a few miles north of Wexford near Enniscorthy. Good progress had also been made in Ulster, where General George Nugent had earlier routed the United Irishmen at the town of Antrim. At the beginning of July 1798 Cornwallis was able to inform Ross that the rebels had been dispersed everywhere except for some 'vagabonds' in the Wicklow Mountains.[22]

Despite these successes Cornwallis was not entirely satisfied about the progress of the campaign, since he knew that what happened after an engagement was often as important as the battle itself. Indiscriminate violence would only make subsequent reconciliation more difficult. Currently, 'any man in a brown coat' (without uniform) and found within several miles of the battlefield 'is butchered without discrimination', he told Portland a week after arriving.[23] Sadly, 'The violence of our friends, and their folly in endeavouring to make it a religious war, added to the ferocity of our troops, who delight in murder, most powerfully counteract all plans of conciliation.' That included a union.[24]

The first objective, therefore, was to stop the indiscriminate killing. He proposed to achieve this by authorising the senior officers to allow the 'deluded wretches', with certain exceptions, to return home quietly after 'delivering up their arms and taking the oath of allegiance'. He simultaneously tried to change the language of government, avoiding the use of '*Catholicism* instead of Jacobinism, as the foundation of the present rebellion'. Finally, courts-martial were to be held in place of summary executions, and no sentences were to be carried out before the proceedings had been submitted for Cornwallis's approval. Proclamations to this effect were issued on 3 July in the *Dublin Gazette*.[25]

The need for such measures was underlined by Cornwallis's next report on 8 July to Portland, in which he acknowledged that the military situation was not as encouraging as he initially thought. Large rebel bands still roamed some areas, while the rest of Ireland was in a state of passivity, rather than showing 'any friendly or even peaceable intentions' towards the authorities. Nevertheless, intelligence indicated that the rebels were tiring of the contest and ready to surrender if their lives were spared. Their readiness to do so was confirmed by the response to his proclamations, leading Cornwallis to propose to Portland a more general pardon, subject to certain exclusions. Only those found guilty of 'deliberate murder' should suffer death. Those who planned the uprising would be banished, either for life or a specified period according to the gravity of their offences. Lastly, bills of attainder should be limited to three or four of the most dangerous activists who were currently out of the country.[26] Among them was Wolfe Tone, the most prominent United Irishman. Portland duly agreed.

However justified these measures, the bishop of Dromore predicted that Cornwallis, though very civil, 'will not be a favourite here, for he is very sober himself and does not push the bottle'. He was also 'too merciful to the rebels'.[27] The observations were apposite, since Cornwallis was already politically at odds with the chief officers of state, who were all members of the Anglo-Irish elite. This placed him ironically in a position similar to that on his arrival in India, when he had also faced an entrenched clique under Macpherson (see above, pp. 142–3, 148–9). Camden subsequently accused Cornwallis of coming to Ireland 'with a settled bad opinion of all the old adherers of government and a determination to estrange himself from them' in favour of the Catholics.[28] Whatever the truth of this, Camden was certainly right that Cornwallis was determined to avoid the example of his predecessors, who had allowed their authority to be manipulated for the benefit of the ruling elite. He had resisted such challenges to his authority in India and would do so again in Ireland.

Nevertheless, the danger remained that he might succumb like Fitzwilliam to the machinations of a cabal, for as he admitted to Pitt, in the 'direction of parliamentary and legal proceedings, I cannot feel very confident in my own judgement'.[29] Fortunately, he had found in the young acting Irish secretary, Robert Stewart, Viscount Castlereagh, someone in whom he could confide and who was sympathetic to the aims of the British ministry. As he later acknowledged to Ross, Castlereagh 'had pointed out all the characters' with whom he had to deal and shown him where Camden had failed in allowing 'dangerous persons to gain an ascendency over him'.[30] Nevertheless, it was a gamble to rely solely on a man of just twenty-nine years of age, both for running the Dublin Castle bureaucracy and managing the Irish House of Commons.

Although the rebellion had subsided, the country continued in a dangerous condition, as he confided to Ross on 24 July. Apart from six state trials of the leaders in Dublin, there was no law other than that dispensed by the military. Ross well knew 'the horrors' of courts-martial, even when well administered. He could judge then how they must 'be conducted by Irishmen heated with passion and revenge'. Sadly, Cornwallis could not see any future amelioration of the situation, since 'the conversation of the principal persons . . . all tend to encourage this system of blood'. The talk 'even at my table, where you will suppose I do all I can to prevent it, always turns on hanging, shooting, burning'. 'If a priest has been put to death, the greatest joy is expressed by the whole company . . . So much for Ireland and my wretched situation.'[31]

It was such attitudes that made the fate of the state prisoners in Dublin so troublesome. These were the middle- and upper-class rebel leaders who had been arrested in Dublin before they could act on their planned uprising. At the end of July, a number of them offered to make a full confession in return for banishment to any country with which Britain was at peace. A principal motive for the offer was to save two of their number, Oliver Bond and William Byrne, who had been tried and sentenced to death.[32] Cornwallis was ready to accept the proposal, thinking the departure of the state prisoners was preferable to further trials, which could only raise the political temperature. He also thought that more knowledge about the conspiracy would be useful. The legal establishment, however, remained utterly opposed to such clemency.[33] Several executions accordingly went ahead, including that of Byrne.[34]

Despite this setback, Cornwallis determined to persevere with a policy of clemency that was consistent with public safety. A powerful ally suddenly came to his assistance in the form of the lord chancellor, John FitzGibbon, earl of Clare, who had been ill during the initial discussions about the prisoners. Now he threw his considerable authority into supporting acceptance of their proposal, thus removing one element from the inflammatory cocktail of tribal bitterness.[35] The return to normality was also assisted by the ending of hostilities in the Wicklow Mountains, where Cornwallis's policy of encouraging people to return home under the protection of their written passes was having a beneficial effect.[36] But it was still unclear to Cornwallis how the Anglo-Irish political establishment could be brought to accept a union on 'which the safety of Great Britain and Ireland so much depends'.[37] It was difficult even to broach the topic.

By now Cornwallis had a settled routine and manner for conducting business, as Brigadier-General Sir John Moore observed when he called at Dublin Castle in mid-July to receive some orders. Cornwallis 'received me very kindly, and kept me nearly three quarters of an hour conversing on the state of the country, that of the troops, [and] the service' in general. He then explained that he wanted Moore to command an elite corps, 'ready to be detached to any quarter in which danger or commotion was threatened'. That evening Moore dined at the castle, observing that 'the style was very different from that of the other Lord-Lieutenants'. Everybody was 'in boots and uniforms, without forms or ceremony'.[38] Moore noted the same informal routine later in the year. 'Lord Cornwallis lives without ceremony with his aides-de-camp', as though on a campaign. 'He breakfasts at nine and immediately afterwards retires with his secretary. The adjutant-general is shown in to him first, and then the different officers, civil and military in succession; and he continues to do business and to write till two or three o'clock, when he gets on horseback and rides till six.' Dinner was usually served at half past six or seven for ten or twelve persons. Moore noted that though Cornwallis had held many great offices, he had done so without altering 'in any degree the simplicity of his character or manners'.[39]

Any complacency that the crisis was over was quickly shattered with the news on 23 August 1798 that a French force had landed in Killala Bay, west of Sligo. The enemy were known to have been assembling forces at Brest for some time, though their destination remained uncertain. The 1,100 men now landed under General Jean Joseph Amable Humbert were in fact the advance guard of a second larger force of 3,000 men. Humbert's instructions were to establish a base, raise support in the countryside, and await the planned reinforcement.[40]

Cornwallis's scheme for an elite force under Moore hence proved opportune. When Moore called at the castle the following morning, he found Cornwallis studying 'the great map of Ireland', having already formulated his plan for meeting the crisis. Lake was to proceed to Galway and take command of 3,000 militia west of the River Shannon currently with General Francis Hutchinson. Simultaneously, General Nugent in Ulster was to form a corps east of Sligo to prevent an enemy irruption into that province. Cornwallis himself, after gathering as many troops as possible from the Dublin garrison, would advance westwards with Moore to Athlone or Carrick-on-Shannon, depending on the latest intelligence. All the officers had strict orders not to risk an action until Cornwallis could assist them and the strength of the enemy had become clear.[41]

Cornwallis set off late on 25 August, travelling by boat along the Grand Canal to Tullamore, before advancing to Kilbeggan, which the army reached on 27 August.[42] The journey from Tullamore was personally painful for Cornwallis, suffering as he did from a swollen foot, which forced him to travel by carriage.[43] That night he learnt that Humbert had defeated Lake and Hutchinson at the town of Castlebar. Despite Cornwallis's admonition, Hutchinson had left Galway for Castlebar, where he heard that the French were advancing to attack. Hutchinson, confident of stopping his foe, persuaded Lake that the troops should stand their ground. Both men failed to realise that Humbert was approaching on a little-used mountain road, which forced them to redeploy their men at the last minute. After a brief artillery exchange the French charged with fixed bayonets, causing the Longford and Kilkenny militias to flee.[44] The fighting was over within minutes.

The news from Castlebar confirmed Cornwallis in the wisdom of his previous orders not to engage precipitously before the nature of the emergency was fully understood. He was sufficiently alarmed to ask Portland on 28 August for an immediate reinforcement from Britain.[45] Nevertheless, the campaign still had to proceed. The army accordingly set off for Athlone where it arrived on the afternoon of 29 August. After establishing a strong encampment, Cornwallis resumed his advance on 31 August for Tuam, only to halt again at Ballinamore Bridge for the 2nd and 29th Foot Regiments, which were marching from Wexford to join him, along with the Guards from Waterford.[46] Here he was joined by Lake and Hutchinson with the remnants of their command.

Cornwallis's plan at this point was based on the supposition that Humbert would remain where he was to await reinforcements from France. Since his own army now numbered some 10,000 men, Cornwallis decided on 2 September to send Lake to the upper reaches of the Shannon, while the main army marched through Tuam towards Hollymount in readiness for an assault on Castlebar. However, late on 4 September he heard that the French had suddenly left that town in the direction of Sligo, although their precise destination was unknown. He immediately ordered Moore with his elite corps to reinforce Lake, while he made a forced march towards Carrick-on-Shannon to prevent a French advance on Dublin. He was now confident that both he and Lake had sufficient strength to deal with Humbert, should an action be necessary before they united their forces. But as a further precaution he ordered the Guards, then at Birr, to march to Kilbeggan, whence they could join either division of the army, or fall back to defend the capital.[47]

Cornwallis reached Carrick-on-Shannon on 7 September, where he learnt that Humbert had crossed the river higher up. Reassuringly, Lake was in close pursuit, having prevented the French from destroying a key bridge. Despite the want of support from the countryside, Humbert continued his march towards Granard, hoping to elude Lake in his rear and Cornwallis to his right. However by the morning of 8 September he found himself facing overwhelming odds. After a brief exchange of fire with Lake at Ballinamuck, he indicated a readiness to surrender.[48] Terms were soon agreed whereby the French became prisoners of war with the usual honours according to European practice, serving their captivity in Britain. Cornwallis ended the campaign by applauding the army for its extraordinary marches in pursuit of a very resourceful enemy. The yeomanry in particular deserved praise for not tarnishing their courage and loyalty by wanton acts of cruelty against their fellow subjects.[49]

Despite the successful conclusion to the campaign, rumours soon circulated in Dublin that Cornwallis had been outsmarted by the French commander.[50] Only the yeomanry had saved the city. The source for this story seems to have been Buckingham, who had arrived with his county militia only to be left behind to garrison the capital.[51] As a former lord lieutenant he believed that he should have been at the centre of the crisis and vented his frustration to his brother, Lord Grenville, the foreign secretary, and others ready to listen. Cornwallis admitted to Moore that he might have been overly cautious. However, in 'the present state of Ireland', it would have been 'unpardonable for the chance of a little personal glory, to run the smallest unnecessary risk'. Many of Cornwallis's troops were so 'bad and undisciplined' that 'if I had met with the least check, the country was gone'. Moore himself was in no doubt about his commander-in-chief's performance: 'Lord Cornwallis was the only person in the army who always suspected the Shannon and Dublin to be the objects' of the enemy. Throughout the campaign he had shown 'much prudence and judgement'.[52]

If Cornwallis thought he would be allowed to complete a leisurely pacification of Ireland, he was quickly disabused of the notion. The news of his success had no sooner reached Britain than the ministry began recalling the reinforcements recently sent to him. Bonaparte's mysterious destination had proved to be Egypt, not Ireland, raising the spectre that he might threaten India via the Gulf of Arabia. The ministers consequently believed more troops were needed for the Mediterranean. Cornwallis was not convinced by these arguments. The security of Ireland should surely take precedence, since the second, more powerful flotilla was believed to have sailed from Brest and might be expected shortly off the Irish coast. The best estimate was that it comprised two ships of the line and seven frigates, carrying 3,000 troops. Apart from the Guards, Ireland had few regulars. The eight British regiments officially on the Irish establishment were mere skeleton units used for recruiting other corps. The other four regiments which had come to Ireland in June were also short of numbers and were essential for strengthening the local militia and fencible units.[53]

However, the black clouds overhanging Ireland miraculously lifted. First news arrived in early October that Admiral Nelson had destroyed the French Mediterranean fleet at the Battle of the Nile in Aboukir Bay, thus imprisoning Bonaparte's army in Egypt. Then Cornwallis learnt that the French armament for Ireland had been intercepted off Lough Swilly in the north of the country by a British squadron under

Commodore Sir John Warren, resulting in the capture of seven frigates with 2,500 men on board.[54] Among the captives was Wolfe Tone. Perhaps the last embers of rebellion could now be finally extinguished, allowing a grim chapter in Ireland's history to be closed.

The ending of hostilities meant that Cornwallis could address the conundrum of how and when to broach the idea of a union. Discreet enquiries suggested that some members of the elite were receptive to the plan because of the need for British protection. But whatever their fears, they were still adamantly opposed to admitting Catholics to any future united Parliament. Even Clare, the lord chancellor, whom Cornwallis considered 'the most right-headed politician in this country', subscribed to this view.[55]

This brought Cornwallis to the heart of the matter. How could the aversion of the existing political class to even modest concessions for the Catholics be overcome? As he explained to Portland in a long letter dated 16 September 1798, 'The principal personages here, who have long been in the habit of directing the councils of the Lord Lieutenant, are perfectly well intentioned . . . but they are blinded by their passions and prejudices'. They 'talk of nothing but strong measures, and arrogate to themselves the exclusive knowledge of a country, of which, from their mode of governing it, they have, in my opinion, proved themselves totally ignorant'.[56] Cornwallis had 'shown all civility and kindness' to them, 'but I am afraid they are not satisfied with me, because I have not thrown myself blindly into their hands'. Nevertheless, he could only repeat his view that 'some mode must be adopted to soften the hatred of the Catholics to our government'. Whether this could be done by hopes of future advantages from a union with Britain, meaning emancipation, or by some provision for their clergy and modification of the tithe, he would not say, except that the first was the most desirable. For, without such accommodation, Ireland would for ever remain an 'intolerable burden to Great Britain'.[57]

Knowing that Clare was about to depart for England for discussions with the ministry, Cornwallis thought it advisable to warn Pitt in early October about the lord chancellor's attitude to the Catholics. Clare would certainly be fair minded on the subject of union and be sincere in his wishes for the future welfare of both Kingdoms. However, like the rest of the governing class, he was irrevocably hostile to the admission of Catholics to Parliament. Such attitudes only reinforced Cornwallis's view that Britain must 'make a union with the Irish nation' rather than 'with a party in Ireland'. He accepted that a union would not immediately convert the Catholics into good subjects, but believed that should the 'most popular of their grievances' be removed 'we should get time to breathe', thereby checking 'the rapid progress of discontent and disaffection'.[58] Otherwise, an agreement limited to 'Great Britain and the Protestants in Ireland' might prove 'an insuperable bar, instead of being a step towards the admission of Catholics, which is the only measure that can give permanent tranquillity to this wretched country'.[59] Prophetic words indeed.

Concerned that Clare's views might prove overly persuasive, Cornwallis resolved to send the Irish under-secretary, William Elliot, to London to ensure that his own opinions were listened to effectively, as he informed Pitt on 17 October. Elliot had been 'much in my confidence', and there were 'few persons who can give a more dispassionate opinion on the state of this wretched country'. Timing was critical, for should the ministers decide to extend 'the privileges of the union to the Roman Catholics, the present appears the only opportunity which the British ministry can have of obtaining any credit' for such an initiative, 'which must otherwise in a short time be extorted from them'.[60]

It was at this point that Cornwallis's relations with Portland suddenly deteriorated. Portland was angry because Cornwallis had written only three official letters since his departure for Ireland, leaving Castlereagh and his military secretary, Captain Herbert Taylor, to keep the Home Office informed. Summoning all his ducal authority, Portland pontificated that Taylor was 'a person unknown to the state and occupying a position unknown in the lord lieutenant's establishment'. What would the country think should Parliament demand to see the official correspondence? In future 'all matters of state' should be 'treated as hereto before in dispatches addressed to me and under Your Excellency's own signature'.[61] In issuing this rebuke he was warmly applauded by Grenville.[62]

Cornwallis's lack of correspondence may have reflected his previous practice in America and India where letter writing was necessarily limited to a few dispatches each year. He forgot that Ireland was just forty-eight hours away by special courier.

Elliot, now in London, did his best to calm the troubled waters. He explained that writing was difficult for Cornwallis whilst he was so engrossed in both civil and military affairs.[63] The danger was that if Dublin Castle failed to brief the British ministers adequately, they would obtain their information through other, less friendly channels. A coterie of self-promoted pundits had already formed around Pitt, composed of former lord lieutenants like Buckingham and Camden and their acolytes, William Eden and his son-in-law, Robert Hobart, Buckingham's former chief secretary. Cornwallis was aware of these mischievous 'half-ministers [and] deputy ministers', but not seemingly of the threat they posed to his administration.[64] Fortunately, Dundas retained his '*enthusiastic* confidence' in Cornwallis, since he too favoured 'a union on the broadest basis'.[65] In the event Pitt stepped in to counsel caution, fearing a rift in his Cabinet. He suggested that any neglect on Cornwallis's part in writing to Portland was unintentional and should be accepted as such.[66]

Meanwhile, the case for union still had to be made, whatever was decided about the Catholics. The British might try to influence the debate, but the issue could only be settled constitutionally by the Irish Parliament. This made the speaker of the Irish House of Commons, John Foster, a key figure in any battle for a legislative union. Ominously, he was known to be a strong supporter of the 1782 constitutional settlement.[67] Foster was not someone with whom Cornwallis readily empathised, being in Cornwallis's eyes part of the clique that had so badly failed the Irish people. Despite an initial friendly discussion in early November, Foster soon reciprocated the lord lieutenant's lack of esteem, prompting him to follow the lord chancellor to London, though with the contrary aim of bolstering the arguments for the retention of separate legislatures.[68]

With the topic of union being openly discussed at dinner tables on both sides of the Irish Channel, Cornwallis recognised that it was time to address the issue more publicly. But first he needed the details of the ministerial plans so that he could 'communicate them to our friends'.[69] Portland duly obliged on 12 November 1798, outlining nine main heads for discussion. First, Irish members of the new legislature would take the same oaths as presently in the British Parliament, subject to 'such alterations as may be enacted by the United Parliament', hinting at the future admission of Catholics. However, the Church of Ireland would remain the established church as a fundamental article of the union. Tariffs and trade would be synchronised, and the national debt of the two countries adjusted proportionately. The courts of justice in Ireland would continue as currently, though the House of Lords rather than the Privy Council would be the final court of appeal. Lastly, the post of lord lieutenant would remain for administrative purposes. Portland foresaw few difficulties for Dublin Castle, given that the interests of Ireland were 'so fully and impartially attended to'.[70] Westminster's myopia about the country was yet another obstacle for Cornwallis to overcome during the next eighteen months.

In a second letter Portland addressed the issue of Irish representation. 'Two great outlines' must be observed. One was that Ireland should have no more than 100 seats in the new imperial lower house, since anything higher would be unacceptable to the existing membership. The second principle was that there should be no change in the methods of election. The government did not want innovations to the electoral system, for fear of opening the demand for similar reform in Britain.[71] The Irish Commons currently comprised 300 seats. On a population basis, Ireland, with 4 million inhabitants, should have 223 seats to equal the 558 currently representing 10 million Britons. However, representation in both countries was not based on numbers, but mainly on land and wealth. Scotland with 1.5 million inhabitants had received just forty-five seats in 1707. Ireland, therefore, must expect a similar reduction, given its much lower commercial and landed income.[72] The means for reducing the number of MPs was left to Dublin Castle to decide.

Pitt simultaneously sent a separate letter, explaining why the issue of Catholic emancipation was being shelved. Although Elliot had presented Cornwallis's arguments very strongly for bringing them into Parliament, Pitt had not been persuaded of their practicality. He thought that once the union had been established, some provision might be made for the Catholic clergy together with an adjustment of the tithe, believing that these offered the 'best chance of gradually putting an end to the evils most felt in Ireland'.[73] All that Pitt would offer for the moment was an assurance that there would be 'no clause in the Act of Union which shall prevent the Catholic question from being taken up hereafter'.[74]

Cornwallis was disappointed at this outcome, believing that it 'would not have been much more difficult to have included the Catholics'. Passing the union itself he did not think would be onerous, though it would involve distasteful bargaining with the Anglo-Irish establishment. He once again expressed his disgust to Ross: 'Those who are called principal persons here, are men who have been raised into consequence, only by having the entire disposal of the patronage of the crown in return for their undertaking the management of the country.' This was 'because the lord lieutenants were too idle or too incapable to manage' the business themselves. The local grandees 'are detested by everybody but their immediate followers, and have no influence but what is founded on the grossest corruption'.[75]

Yet however distasteful he found it, Cornwallis promised Portland that he would make the 'utmost efforts to further the great work, so important to preserving this kingdom in connection with Great Britain'.[76] He accordingly began talks with the Anglo-Irish leaders in an effort to secure their support in the forthcoming session of the Irish Parliament, though as he ruefully reflected to Ross, 'when you send for a man on such business, he must stay with you and talk to you as long as he likes'.[77] Castlereagh similarly contacted leading merchants, lawyers, and lesser gentry for their views. Everything suggested that opposition to a union was greatest in Dublin, where fears were widespread about a loss of influence, should the legislature be transferred to Westminster.[78]

Although Catholics were excluded from public office, many of their middle class had been enfranchised by the Catholic Relief Act of 1793. Their support, therefore, might prove crucial, should elections be held, as Cornwallis warned Portland. Much depended on the Catholic hierarchy and principal laity, for should they oppose a union, it would deprive government of its 'principal strength in the south and west' and very likely 'prove fatal to the measure'.[79] Fortunately, Castlereagh had found most of the hierarchy supportive of the scheme, seeing 'any transfer of power from their opponents as a boon'. The same was true of most Catholic merchants, believing a union would be good for their trade. As for the northern Presbyterians, they had yet to express a firm opinion. However, Castlereagh believed their traditional opposition to the Anglo-Irish elite meant that they were likely to soften their stance, provided some support was given to their clergy and a reduction made in their tithes.[80]

The intention at Westminster was that the issue of union should be introduced simultaneously into the legislatures of both kingdoms immediately after Christmas. Yet despite the recent efforts of Cornwallis and Castlereagh to win converts, the evidence was clear that many Irish MPs remained opposed to the proposal.[81] It was for this reason that Castlereagh wanted the British Parliament to broach the subject first, giving a strong signal of the ministerial commitment to a union, but Portland refused to do this on procedural grounds.[82] His decision coincided with the return of Foster from England, seemingly ready to oppose Dublin Castle. Equally alarming was that two leading Irish peers, Lord Downshire and Lord Ely, were likely to support him. Between them they controlled eighteen seats in the Irish Parliament. Clearly their help would be vital in securing a favourable outcome.[83]

This uncertainty led Cornwallis to ponder the expediency of removing from office those who were openly against the measure, or who used language equally inconsistent with their position in government. On the other hand, he was still hopeful that a steadfast British ministry and the natural authority of government would counteract any tendency to opposition. He accordingly suggested to Portland that dismissals for the moment should be limited to the chancellor of the Exchequer, Sir John Parnell, whose opposition to a union was too blatant to be overlooked.[84] But Portland could be assured that Cornwallis would 'pursue the same line of conduct without favour or partiality, whenever I may think it will tend to promote the success of the measure'.[85]

The Irish Parliament assembled on 22 January 1799 to hear Cornwallis deliver the king's speech. Union was not expressly mentioned other than the desirability of 'some permanent adjustment . . . for consolidating the British Empire'.[86] A debate then followed in both houses. In the Lords there appeared to be a solid majority for some such adjustment. However, in the Commons the opposition defiantly moved an amendment that the house was ready to adopt 'any measure, short of surrendering their free, resident and independent legislature as established in 1782'. This was only defeated by one vote. An equally close contest ensured over the speech itself. Castlereagh, recognising that more preparation was required, immediately announced that he was withdrawing the intended plan of union.[87] But despite this concession, the opposition launched another attack two days later, proposing an amendment to the loyal address that deleted all reference to a union. They carried this by 109 to 104 votes, amid scenes that put Castlereagh in mind of a fox hunt rather than a debate.[88]

Who was to blame for this debacle? Under-secretary Edward Cooke blamed Cornwallis: he had failed to consult the country gentlemen and had angered the Protestant interest by his earlier criticism of the yeomanry.[89] But Castlereagh's lack of experience was also a factor. As late as 21 January he calculated that the government would secure between 160 and 170 votes, a mistake which he subsequently acknowledged to Portland.[90] Inevitably, Buckingham was quick to demand Cornwallis's recall. Grenville too lamented that he had supported Cornwallis's original appointment. Nevertheless, he counselled patience to his brother. Finding someone who possessed the necessary political and military talents would be difficult. Even the great duke of Marlborough would scarcely have been equipped to deal with the current situation.[91]

This left Dublin Castle licking its wounds, contemplating whether to use the carrot or the stick. The weapon of further dismissals was certainly available, though Cornwallis still preferred to delay such action.[92] Nevertheless, it was irksome that the proposed union was opposed principally by the 'borough-mongers, lawyers and persons who from local circumstances thought they should be losers'. This was in stark contrast to the interests of the mass of the population. But the fluidity of the situation was emphasised by reports that elements in the anti-union party were offering emancipation to the Catholics, if they petitioned their support for the Irish legislature. This only reinforced Cornwallis's conviction that Catholic relief must be included as part of the government's overall scheme, in order to pre-empt any such move.[93] His arguments were to no avail. Portland, backed by his Cabinet colleagues, merely reiterated that Catholic emancipation could only be granted 'through the medium of a union and by the means of a united parliament'.[94]

Castlereagh, meanwhile, had begun a more detailed post-mortem into the administration's defeat, starting with an investigation into the personal interests of the opposition. He noted that those most likely to be affected by the proposed reduction in Irish representation were the eighty-four members who were returned for closed boroughs, where the vote was so restricted as to make them a kind of private property. Whatever scheme of representation was adopted, their owners were certain to see their influence and investment diminished. So far, the government had made no mention of compensation in their plans for redistributing the seats. Castlereagh now set to work to remedy this deficiency, calculating that the owners might be bought out at a cost of between £600,000 and £800,000. But he simultaneously recognised the need to mend fences with the county gentry. Many of the latter had been angered at reports that their representation would be reduced to one seat. He accordingly proposed to restore two seats to each county, giving them sixty-four of the hundred Irish seats in the new Imperial Parliament. This left the remaining thirty-six seats to be distributed among the larger towns, with one seat for Trinity College.[95] Cornwallis readily agreed to Castlereagh's proposals, having previously stated his preference for rewarding the counties and 'great commercial towns' over the claims of the closed boroughs.[96]

One problem for Dublin Castle was a lack of money for funding pro-union literature, including the printing of 10,000 copies of Pitt's recent speeches on the subject of union to the British House of Commons. Securing the provincial press was also costing money. The Irish government had a Secret Service fund but an act of 1793 reserved this strictly for the detection and prevention of 'treasonable and other dangerous conspiracies'.[97] The revelation that Irish parliamentary funds were being used to abolish the Irish Parliament was certain to create a storm of unimaginable fury. Pitt had already dispatched £5,000 to meet the castle's needs, yet more would clearly be needed.[98] This was one aspect of political management that Cornwallis was happy to leave to Castlereagh and the under-secretaries.

Nevertheless, much of the country remained in a disturbed state, ready to rise should the French arrive. In Antrim Loyalists had been assaulted in their homes, mail coaches stopped, and travellers everywhere robbed, while in Cork the tithe collectors had been cruelly mistreated. The maiming of cattle continued in many western counties. Cornwallis admitted to Portland his disappointment that the policy of leniency had not been more successful.[99] However, one reason for the renewed disturbances was a shortage of grain. Cornwallis, with his experience of famine in India, immediately urged the Irish Parliament to allow the importation of foreign corn, and received for once the unqualified thanks of both houses of the Irish Parliament.[100]

Predictably, Portland took a different view of the renewed disturbances, suggesting that Cornwallis had been too lenient. He should instead have made a wider seizure of disaffected persons and the deportation of the state prisoners his priority.[101] Cornwallis quickly responded that the home secretary had misconstrued his meaning. Although he had spoken of leniency, this did not mean that the resources of government had not been fully used, whatever his opponents might assert. The yeomanry, militia, and even the regulars had been widely deployed to protect Loyalist lives and property. But he could never allow those forces, as previously, 'to pursue their private quarrels and gratify their personal resentments' by robbing and murdering anyone they branded 'with the name of rebels'.[102] To show that he had not been unduly lenient, his new military secretary, Colonel Edward Littlehales, had drawn up detailed lists of those who had faced public justice. These revealed that 400 cases had been submitted to Cornwallis for review as lord lieutenant: 131 men had been condemned to death, of whom eighty-one were executed. Yet many more had been executed by the army in the immediate aftermath of the uprising, whose cases never came before Cornwallis. Another 418 had been banished or transported by these same military tribunals. Lastly, great numbers had been convicted at the autumn assizes.[103] There had been no undue leniency.

Although the Irish Parliament had adjourned for the summer, this did not mean that the battle to secure the union was suspended. The rhetoric of parliamentary debate now had to give way to the skills of political management, if the necessary legislation was to be secured. This was something for which Cornwallis admitted he was very ill qualified. He told Ross: 'It has ever been the wish of my life to avoid all this dirty business, and I am now involved in it beyond all bearing . . . How I long to kick those whom my public duty obliges me to court!'[104] He was reminded of Swift's poem about Irish politics in the age of Walpole:

So to effect his monarch's ends.

From hell a viceroy devil ascends,

His budget with corruption cramm'd,

The contributions of the damn'd.

Which with unsparing hand he strews,

Through courts and senates as he goes,

And then at Beelzebub's black hall,

Complains his budget was too small.

The one solace was that Brome and Lady Louisa had arrived for a stay in Phoenix Park lodge, the lord lieutenant's summer residence outside Dublin.[105]

Cornwallis's distaste for the opponents of union at least made the forthcoming dismissals less tiresome. Further leniency now would be taken for weakness. Among those removed was the speaker's son from his post at the Revenue Board.[106] Earlier, Cornwallis had feared that dismissals might consolidate the ranks of the opposition, but this did not happen. Indeed, the administration appeared to be gaining ground everywhere, in part because opponents now recognised that they could no longer expect to keep their offices. Opinion had also been helped by the publication of several pro-union tracts and the efforts of the government's friends to mobilise support in the counties.[107] The improving state of the economy was also helpful, as was the ending of the famine. A good harvest was in prospect and the trade in linens was buoyant.[108]

These factors persuaded Cornwallis to make a tour of the southern counties to consolidate support for the proposed union. Such a visit would also allow him to speak more authoritatively about Ireland, since his opinions so far had been formed almost entirely from a Dublin perspective.[109] He invited Brome to accompany him, leaving Louisa in Phoenix Park with Castlereagh's wife Emily for company. The first stop was Kilkenny, where two loyal addresses were made to Cornwallis, expressing an 'earnest desire for an union' and 'the warmest approbation of the measures of my administration'.[110] Similar marks were forthcoming at Waterford, Cork, and Limerick.[111] He mused: 'Were the Commons of Ireland as naturally connected with the people as they are in England . . . I should feel that the question was in a great degree carried'.[112] The only thing to mar his optimism was an incident that took place after his return to Dublin, when a sentry fired on him as he sought entry to the castle while alone. Cornwallis neglected to give the countersign, probably because he did not hear the sentry's challenge. Others suspected that the soldier was a United Irishman. Cornwallis himself made light of the episode, though his staff insisted hereafter that he was always accompanied by an aide when outside the safety of the castle or Phoenix Park lodge.[113]

Despite the success of his tour, the security of the country remained a constant preoccupation, following news of a union of the French and Spanish fleets at Cádiz. Cornwallis remained confident of dealing with any insurrection in Ireland, but less so when it came to external threats, given that '10,000 infantry of the best quality' had recently been withdrawn in preparation for a new continental venture.[114] Cornwallis admitted to Ross that he was totally in the dark about the ministry's plan: 'No man in Britain or Ireland enjoys less of this kind of confidence than myself.'

Dundas had attempted to explain the matter, but no one else in the Cabinet had given him 'the most distant hint' of what was happening.[115]

The ministry's latest venture was the dispatch in late August 1799 of an expeditionary force to Holland under the duke of York to liberate that country from French occupation. Cornwallis was inevitably sceptical about the plan and was not surprised to learn subsequently that the ministry had recalled the expedition, after failing to make any progress beyond an initial landing. This was despite the assistance of a large corps of Russian troops. Hopefully some of the returnees might be sent to strengthen the Irish defences in case the French made another landing. Violence had broken out again in Waterford and Tipperary, forcing Cornwallis to justify his policies once more to the home secretary.[116] The problem was that until the country was truly quiet, the Loyalists would not abate their activities, being intent on turning martial law 'into a more violent and intolerable tyranny than that of Robespierre'. 'The vilest informers' were being used 'to attack by the most barefaced perjury, the lives of all who are suspected of being, or of having been, disaffected.' Even eminent Catholics were in peril. Cornwallis constantly attempted to prevent these excesses, before they drove the country once more into open rebellion.[117]

One cheering piece of news was that the British forces in India had completed the conquest of Mysore, in which Wellesley had played a prominent part with the 33rd Foot Regiment. In the course of the campaign Seringapatam had been stormed and Tipu Sultan killed. The details were scanty, making Cornwallis eager for more information, though the fate of the two princes, who had previously been in his custody, was not one of his concerns. In the changed environment of the French Revolutionary Wars, Cornwallis could only reflect that 'this is indeed a great event, and perfectly secures us in that part of the world'.[118] Tipu had always appeared to be a usurper and cruel tyrant, so it was easy to believe that he had met his just deserts. Later, Cornwallis learnt that the Indian army were forwarding Tipu's sword and turban to him in a 'flattering token of remembrance and regard'.[119] It was a welcome break from the 'wretched business of courts-martial' with their 'dismal scenes of wives, sisters, fathers, kneeling and crying' for sentences to be reprieved.[120]

Having already visited the south in search of support for the union, Cornwallis decided in October 1799 to make a similar tour of the north, before the next session of the Irish Parliament, when another attempt would be made to pass the bill. Cornwallis's first stop was Dundalk. Here he not only received an address from the corporation in favour of the union, but also one from the local priests and principal Catholic inhabitants. Armagh was similarly receptive. The first potential difficulty occurred at Belfast, where support for the United Irishmen was strong. In the event a public dinner and ball was arranged by the town corporation, on the understanding that only those favourable to union be present. One hundred and fifty subsequently attended. He then proceeded to Antrim, Coleraine, Londonderry, and Strabane, where the principal inhabitants all offered their support. However, he decided to avoid the counties of Down, Monaghan, Cavan, and Fermanagh, where the plan for union had powerful enemies. For most of the tour he was accompanied by Henry Alexander, the MP for Londonderry, who ensured that the arrangements proceeded smoothly.[121]

With the meeting of Parliament approaching, Cornwallis suggested to Portland, as a minor concession, that the six surviving Irish Catholic peers might be allowed to participate in the choice of the twenty-eight temporal lords, who were to represent the Irish peerage in the new Imperial Parliament.[122] Currently, these peers were excluded from the Irish upper chamber. However, as he reported to Ross, the ministers had rejected the idea, influenced by 'the narrow-minded prejudices of the Protestant party'. It was further confirmation of his lack of influence in London, despite his still being master-general of the Ordnance and notionally a member of the Cabinet.[123] As he told Ross, with some bitterness: 'My opinions have no weight on your side of the water, and yet I am kept here to manage matters of a most disgusting nature to my feelings, merely I believe, to prevent my interfering with others in military commands.' But the ministry need not fear on the latter score, as his only wish was 'for a peaceable retirement'.[124]

The year thus ended on a sour note for Cornwallis, not least because the battle to secure the union was by no means won. The conundrum remained that 'we have a lukewarm, and in some instances an unwilling majority', while 'the enemy have a bold and deeply interested minority'. The contest therefore was likely to be much closer than people imagined.[125] Another £10,000 tranche of Secret Service money would clearly be necessary.[126]

The new session of Parliament opened on 16 January 1800, with Cornwallis giving a robust account of recent allied successes against the French and their traitorous allies, conveniently overlooking the abortive landing in Holland.[127] The opposition again attempted to amend the loyal address in reply to the king's speech, deprecating any discussion of a union. They were buoyed by the appearance of Henry Grattan, whose oratory and leadership had helped secure the settlement of 1782. Nevertheless, after a debate lasting eighteen hours, the vote went in favour of the administration by 138 to 96 votes.[128] The opposition then attempted to rouse popular feeling on the streets of Dublin. An inflammatory handbill asked whether 60,000 armed Irishmen, meaning the militia and yeomanry, would tamely stand by and see the constitution of their country destroyed. Cornwallis was sufficiently alarmed to urge the immediate dispatch of reinforcements from Britain.[129]

The main parliamentary battle finally began on 6 February 1800 with a debate in the Commons over whether to consider the plan of legislative union. A motion in favour was eventually carried by 158 votes to 115, a majority of 43, though a few defections from the government occurred, aided by opposition offers of £2,000 to £5,000 to those owners of closed boroughs who wished to sell up.[130] These initiatives were more than offset by Castlereagh's revised plans to compensate owners with sums of up to £15,000. A similar division in the Lords passed more decisively, where the lord chancellor ironically made a four-hour speech condemning the opposition's corrupt attempts to purchase a majority. Equally important, as Castlereagh commented to Portland, was 'the firmness with which Lord Cornwallis conducted himself, and the steps taken both within and without the House, to repress mob interference'. This had 'given our friends better confidence'.[131]

Since passage of the Union Bill now looked secure, Cornwallis decided it was time to punish the more extreme members of the opposition for their disloyalty. At the top of his list was the marquess of Downshire, who as colonel of the County Down militia had invited his men to sign a petition against the union. This breached the convention that the military did not engage in politics. Cornwallis immediately sent a senior officer to investigate.[132] His report gave Cornwallis all the evidence he needed to secure Downshire's dismissal from the militia and removal from the Privy Council. As he subsequently informed Portland, Downshire's actions constituted not only a serious 'breach of military duty' but a threat to 'the authority of government'. Permitting 'any private soldier' in uniform 'with a musket on his shoulder to give an opinion on a political question' was inadmissible.[133] Downshire, realising he had gone too far, then visited Cornwallis to remonstrate about his treatment. He found the lord lieutenant in no mood to compromise. 'I told him my mind in strong language and he went away as meek as a lamb.'[134]

Slowly but steadily, Castlereagh and Clare steered the actual Union Bill through the two Houses of Parliament. The principle itself was passed in the Commons by a vote of 161 to 115 on 18 February 1800, after another eighteen-hour debate.[135] As the certainty of the measure became clearer the country became measurably calmer, though the opposition used every possible stratagem to delay if not defeat the measure in the Commons, including a call for new elections.[136] By 22 March all the articles in the bill had been passed by the house and forwarded without major amendment to the Lords.[137] Six days later the Lords followed suit.

In response to this news Portland wrote a fulsome letter conveying the ministers' approbation of what Cornwallis had achieved.[138] Cornwallis himself preferred to acknowledge the role played by others, especially 'the extraordinary talents and good services of Lord Castlereagh, to whom the success of this great and most difficult undertaking ought in justice to be principally attributed'.[139] Most remarkable had been Castlereagh's improvement as a speaker, which had made him master of the Irish Commons, despite 'the unpopularity which his cold and distant manners' created in 'private society'.[140]

Although Cornwallis had attained the great objective of union, he still had to fulfil the promises made to the politicians and their allies for supporting the government. The prospect of further jobbing led him to ponder how quickly he could leave 'this wretched country'. He would certainly 'retire as soon as I can reconcile it to the duty which I owe to my country'.[141] His mood was not improved by the ministerial ignorance about Ireland, which constantly led them to mistake 'an interested, violent, and prejudiced party, who call themselves friends to England and to the Protestant interest, for the people of Ireland'. The problem, as in India, was finding a suitable successor. How damaging it would be if Cornwallis was succeeded by a member of the Anglo-Irish elite, since all the advantages of the union would be lost. What was needed was someone who could command the confidence and good will of both factions, which Cornwallis believed he had attained. It reinforced his determination not to leave the Catholics 'as I found them'.[142]

The anti-unionists made one final attempt to derail the plan of union by moving an address to George III, asking him to refuse his consent to the measure. This was comfortably defeated by 135 votes to 77, after which the bill had its third reading with an equally sizeable majority of 65.[143] It was time to start rewarding the supporters of the administration. Various inducements had been offered by Cornwallis, including the creation of sixteen new Irish peers and the promotion of six existing peers to a seat in the new united House of Lords. Cornwallis believed that he had been as economical as possible in making these commitments, confident in his assumption that he had authority to do whatever was necessary to secure a favourable vote.[144] He was accordingly shocked when Portland, in the king's name, queried several of his proposed creations.[145]

His anger was for once palpable, as his reply to Portland reveals. Even 'in the most severe trials I have hitherto been able to conduct myself with a firmness becoming a man of honour and integrity'. Now Portland was forcing him to tell those he was about to disappoint either that 'I will not keep my word with them, or acknowledge that I have pretended to have powers which I did not possess'. Whether any of his agreements were advantageous or not, Cornwallis was bound as a man of honour to stand by them. The creation of sixteen new Irish peers was hardly extravagant, given that a similar number were created in the British peerage following the 1796 election. At least one of the promotions had originated with Pitt himself. Thus, if the king could not approve of his recommendations, he must allow Cornwallis to retire from a station he 'could no longer hold with honour . . . or with a prospect of advantage to his service'.[146]

Castlereagh immediately supported his chief, telling Camden that Portland's dispatch was 'peculiarly ungracious' to Cornwallis, conveying an apparent disapprobation of most of his engagements. The position was clear: 'If the Irish government' was unable 'to keep faith with the various individuals who have acted upon a principle of confidence in their honour, it is morally impossible . . . that either Cornwallis or I can remain in our present situations'.[147]

In the event the episode proved a storm in a teacup. As Castlereagh accurately predicted to Cooke, Pitt was unlikely to abandon Cornwallis 'on a point of patronage, after what he has accomplished'.[148] Portland quickly recognised his error, writing a suitably apologetic letter, though still asserting that he had been misconstrued. It had never been his intention that Cornwallis should break any of his promises.[149] Cornwallis attributed the fracas to the Cabinet's usual lack of interest in Irish matters.

'Dundas knew nothing of the business while Pitt never saw the [duke] of Portland's letter of 13 June, the style of which was certainly that of a severe reprimand.' This was inexcusable, 'for he well knows the sort of letters' which Portland was 'apt to write'. Ironically Pitt now agreed to the creation of eighteen Irish peers and promised more if necessary.[150] The final tally included twenty-eight new creations, a further twenty promotions within the Irish peerage, and the six elevations to the British House of Lords.[151] In addition, twenty-seven members of the Irish Parliament received sinecures or pensions.[152]

The exercise had not been cheap. The proprietors of the eighty-four boroughs ultimately disenfranchised were compensated to the sum of £1,260,000, double what Castlereagh had originally forecast.[153] The Secret Service expenditures were also substantial. Between £20,000 and £30,000 had been borrowed from British sources, and another £18,000 found from savings on the Irish civil list. The money had secured the purchase of two borough seats, helped win the election of several supporters, and met the cost of printing pamphlets and other promotional materials. Historians are divided on how far the union had been secured by corruption. Yet even by eighteenth-century political norms, the union had only been achieved by bending the spirit if not the letter of what was acceptable.[154] Cornwallis himself had no doubts about the methods used.

However, money alone had not secured the acceptance of union. In attributing the credit for this remarkable achievement, Castlereagh was quick to acknowledge where it belonged. It was 'the wisdom and ability' of Cornwallis that had secured this great measure. Castlereagh himself had merely 'to follow his instructions, and to take care that no inadvertence on my part should counteract the effects which his talents and the authority of his high character were calculated to produce'.[155] Clare was equally complimentary, telling Camden that Cornwallis had rightly been given 'much of the merit which attaches to our success in the measure'. He had stooped much 'against his nature to the political traffic imposed upon him . . . without committing himself in any manner to our Irish chiefs'. 'I am now quite satisfied that he has on the whole been the man of all others best selected for the crisis.'[156] Differences over the Catholic issue had seemingly been forgotten.

This outburst of admiration, however, could not lift Cornwallis's gloom about the wider state of world affairs. Earlier in the year the powers of northern Europe had formed an Armed Neutrality League to resist the Royal Navy's enforcement of British restrictions on trade with France. Now the Austrians had been routed in Italy and faced the likelihood of a dictated peace from Bonaparte. In such circumstances, Grenville's haughty rejection of recent French peace overtures was inexcusable. The foreign secretary's argument that Britain should continue fighting until the French monarchy was restored was pure folly. What hope, Cornwallis asked, was there 'that the British navy can restore the French monarchy?' It reaffirmed his view that Grenville was 'a most dangerous minister'. Leaving 'a Cabinet in which [Grenville] had too much sway' was his firm intention.[157]

Nevertheless, he affected to remain optimistic about Ireland. Writing to William Cornwallis in June 1800, he commented: 'This important event has totally changed the relative situation of this country, and if the English government act wisely, those evils which have brought not only Ireland but the whole British Empire to the brink of destruction, may, in the course of a few years, be entirely removed.' As for himself, he was ready to come home. After being 'employed so long in situations of labour and anxiety', he felt old at the age of sixty-one and looked 'with impatience for the hour of quiet and retirement'.[158]

The continued threat to Ireland from outside forces prompted Cornwallis to consider another tour of the western counties, to assess potential invasion routes. The country itself was gratifyingly quiet, though many of the gentry continued to call for help on the slightest rumour, which Cornwallis tried to downplay to prevent an excuse for yet more violence. Dublin itself was peaceful, as evidenced by his procession through an immense crowd to St Patrick's Cathedral for the installation of a new archbishop. During the procession, many in the crowd called out 'there he is; that's he; God bless him'. This was a compliment indeed for someone who had 'governed the country above two years by martial law'.[159]

Cornwallis eventually set off on his western tour on 16 August 1800, an 'auspicious day', he reminded Ross, being the twentieth anniversary of the Battle of Camden. His first call was Slane Castle after which he proceeded to Dundalk, Newry, Enniskillen, Sligo, Galway, and Limerick, before eventually returning to Dublin via

Athlone. The country everywhere seemed quiet, though this did not diminish his desire for reinforcements, since widespread disaffection could be expected should an invasion occur. He believed that eventually 'the mass of the people of Ireland may be reclaimed, but it must take time to effect this'. Until then the government would be 'under the melancholy necessity of considering the majority of the Irish people as enemies', requiring the army 'to keep our own countrymen in subjection'.[160]

Reinforcements, however, were not forthcoming because the ministry were again considering operations in the Mediterranean as a way of changing the strategic outlook. Cornwallis was not impressed, thinking that Bonaparte, now first consul of France, would not be troubled by such diversions. He told Ross: 'Would to God that we had peace almost on any terms, for it is evident that we cannot make war.'[161] In a paper written for Dundas on the advisability of attacking Cuba or the River Plate region of South America, Cornwallis acknowledged that 'whilst we are at war, and have the means of acting, we should not remain entirely on the defensive'. But the regiments raised with such difficulty in 1799 should not be squandered on capricious adventures under officers without experience. 'The expense likewise of expeditions is enormous, and the disgrace attending' any failure was unlikely 'to promote that most desirable object, a good peace'. Of course, if there was 'a reasonable prospect of success', an attempt might be justified. Nevertheless, he could not disguise his belief that the best thing at present was to conserve the nation's resources until an object of real importance emerged.[162]

He was momentarily relieved, therefore, when he heard on 8 October 1800 that the Mediterranean expedition had been laid aside and that 5,000 of the 20,000 men assembled at Gibraltar would be sent to Ireland.[163] Yet the project was no sooner cancelled than it was activated again, this time with the Spanish ports of Cádiz or Ferrol as targets.[164] Cornwallis was not pleased, knowing the impossibility of protecting Ireland with 'our fleets at all seasons of the year'.[165] His recent tour had revealed there were few points for stopping an enemy, should they land between Bantry Bay and Lough Swilly. The problem was that with 'so long an extent of coast' it would be 'very difficult to assemble a sufficient force to make any opposition to the progress of a capable and active enemy'. In lieu of reinforcements, the construction of 'two or three tolerably good fortresses' would be helpful, 'to cover the assembling of the army'. But the failure of Richmond's previous proposals for large military projects made Cornwallis hesitant about forwarding his ideas, until Castlereagh informed him that Pitt was now favourable to such expenditure. Cornwallis duly forwarded his proposals to Portland.[166]

One Ordnance matter that could now proceed was a merging of the British and Irish boards. Earlier he had despaired of effecting anything at the Ordnance, reflecting that 'at my time of life and with the sentiments I feel towards some of my late [Cabinet] colleagues, it is not likely that I should establish any important reform'. Too many people were strutting around in the style of Bonaparte, wearing 'a heavy hat and feather, a buttoned waistcoat, and a cursed sash' around the waist. Such parading was unlikely to produce victory.[167] Cornwallis eventually submitted his ideas for merging the two departments to Portland in early February 1801. Among his proposals was the creation of a seventh artillery battalion.[168]

Cornwallis was also asked about a plan of York to create a battalion of riflemen. He had, of course, long been opposed to what he called 'the nonsense of a rifle corps'.[169] Although rifles were excellent for snipers, the slow rate of reloading made any such unit useless in close combat, as the American war had demonstrated, where one Hessian regiment had exchanged its rifles for muskets.[170] However, York ignored Cornwallis this time, opting to equip every regiment with a rifle platoon.[171] To Cornwallis, it seemed that York had placed himself 'entirely in the hands of the Guards' with 'all their prejudices'. What 'a melancholy thing' it was to see such 'destruction merely to gratify the caprice of Princes'. It was a lament of someone unhappy about a changing world.[172]

An underlying reason for his discontent was the lack of news about further initiatives respecting Ireland. Portland had written in September 1800 that the ministry were considering provision for the Catholic and Dissenting clergy together with an amelioration of the tithes.[173] But he remained apprehensive that the Cabinet lacked the firmness to seize the opportunity of rendering the union advantageous to the empire. Echoing his earlier advice to Pitt, he told Ross: 'Those things which, if now liberally granted, might make the Irish a loyal people, will be of little avail when they are extorted on a future day.' Nevertheless, he did not despair of achieving some good.[174] To improve the odds, he decided in late October 1800 to send Castlereagh to London once more to urge the ministers to adopt 'the only measure which can ever make the mass of the people in Ireland good subjects'. To facilitate that objective, he would stay in Ireland until the summer of 1801.[175]

Yet even guarded optimism was difficult regarding the latest ministerial attempts to salvage the country's military fortunes. The fleet at Gibraltar had first gone to Cádiz, only to find a siege impractical, whereupon it had sailed to the Spanish naval base at Ferrol. Here too nothing was accomplished, leading Cornwallis to cry out in frustration to Ross: 'What a disgraceful and what an expensive campaign we have made!' The sight of 'twenty-two thousand men . . . floating round the greater part of Europe' had made Britain the 'laughing stock of friends and foes' alike.[176] Ireland in consequence remained dangerously weakened for want of troops.[177]

With the first meeting of the new united Parliament fast approaching, Cornwallis formally requested Portland to take the next step regarding reform in Ireland. Although the union provided the means for remedying Ireland's problems, 'no permanent or radical cure has hitherto been applied; and I feel it to be my duty . . . to lay before Your Grace such opinions' as he had formed during his lord-lieutenancy. 'Although other causes' had contributed to the dissentions in the country, 'no man who is acquainted with Ireland can deny that the violence of religious animosities has been, and still continues to be, the principal source of all its miseries'. Anyone doubting this had only to read Castlereagh's recent tract on the 'Catholic question'. The danger was that if nothing was done, the issue would be taken up by the Whig opposition with mischievous consequences. Surely it would be better if Portland took 'every means in your power . . . to secure to the government the management and the ultimate credit of the measure'.[178]

Meanwhile, the newspapers, ignorant of these divisions, were predicting that Cornwallis was to be made a duke. This was a most unlikely outcome, he told Ross. Except for Dundas, he had never met with kindness or civility from the rest of the ministry. He did not think in any case that his finances were equal to such an exalted rank, especially if Brome continued to dissipate his fortune: not only was his son extravagant, he also lived 'in a state of apathy'. Such was his indolence that he would 'not look at an account', nor 'give himself the trouble of inquiring what balance he has at Hoare's' bank. However, Ross was not to say anything as 'it would only make him dislike me', and that would be 'the supreme of evils'.[179] Cornwallis's relationship with his son had clearly undergone a significant change: now that he was approaching old age he was fearful of losing Brome's goodwill.

The day of legislative union, 1 January 1801, passed without incident in Dublin. 'We fired our guns', Cornwallis informed Castlereagh, and 'hoisted our new flags and standard'. A number of people gathered in the yard of Dublin Castle and the adjacent streets, seemingly out of curiosity, for there were no 'expressions of ill humour or disapprobation'.[180] However, any personal euphoria was quickly dispersed by the news that Portland had circulated a paper to the Cabinet, refuting the principle of emancipation espoused in Castlereagh's recent tract. Castlereagh, in response, quickly reminded Pitt that the Cabinet had previously indicated its support for the measure while he was in London in October 1799. It was on this foundation that Cornwallis had persuaded the Catholic hierarchy not to oppose the plan for a union, hinting that emancipation would likely follow its adoption. Their support had proved crucial in mobilising the southern and western counties in favour of union. Now the imputation would be made that both Cornwallis and the ministry had deceived the Catholics in seeking their help.[181]

This intervention by the Irish secretary seemingly turned the scales. However, because the Cabinet was divided, Pitt allowed the ministers to vote as they pleased. A slight majority favoured emancipation, though several formidable opponents, notably the lord Chancellor, Lord Thurlow, did not.[182] Nevertheless, Castlereagh's lobbying in London was sufficient for Cornwallis to believe that a substantial measure of emancipation would shortly be enacted, providing Pitt stood firm.[183] To ensure success, Cornwallis requested the Catholic hierarchy not to petition the new Parliament about their grievances.[184] Parliamentarians preferred to dispense rights rather than concede them. But to Castlereagh he confidently commented: 'Nobody would have believed, three years ago, that union, Catholic emancipation, and the restoration of perfect tranquillity, could have taken place in so short a time.'[185] He was in for a rude awakening.

Like many others, Cornwallis had reckoned without George III, forgetting the king's warning at the start of his Irish mission that there must be no further concessions to the Catholics. George III now reaffirmed to Pitt that 'when he consented to a union of the two kingdoms, it was always grounded on a trust that the uniting of the established churches of the two kingdoms would forever shut the door to any further measures with respect to the Roman Catholics'. He had not adopted these opinions on the spur of the moment: they were the principles on which he had acted for the last forty years, and from which he could never depart. To abandon them now would be a violation of his coronation oath to protect the established Church.[186]

What followed was equally unexpected, even by George III. Pitt submitted his resignation as first lord of the Treasury, a post he had held for seventeen years. Historians have spent much time ascertaining the reasons for his sudden departure. In reality the causes were mundane rather than conspiratorial. Although Pitt accepted the idea of emancipation, he had other weighty matters to deal with, not least the conduct of the war and the need to keep a divided administration together. He had not been in good health, and the divisive issue of emancipation seems to have been a step too far for a man drained of energy and political purpose. Others must now deal with the issue.[187]

For Cornwallis the news was deeply upsetting: 'It is too mortifying a reflection, when all the difficulties were surmounted . . . that the fatal blow should be struck from the quarter' that had the most to gain from the measure. The melancholy outcome meant 'that Ireland is again to become a millstone about the neck of Britain, and to be plunged into all its former horrors and miseries'.[188] Although Pitt urged his colleagues not to follow his example, several members of the Cabinet determined to do so on principle. However, enough support remained for an administration to be formed under Henry Addington, the speaker of the Commons and a close ally of Pitt. Indeed, the new ministry was essentially a revamping of the existing one. The main difference was that it would now be dominated by the opponents of Catholic emancipation.[189]

This outcome made Cornwallis's own course clear. As he told Ross on 15 February: 'No consideration could induce me to take a responsible part with any administration' that intended 'to persevere in the old system of proscription and exclusion in Ireland'. But he would not quit in a petulant manner. While awaiting a successor he would counsel the Catholics to be patient, assuring them that their cause would eventually succeed. He would then resign his office as master-general on returning to London, which he was happy to do, having originally accepted it 'unwillingly . . . as a Cabinet Office'.[190] After this he would 'retire altogether from public life, but without resentment', since he detested the factional politics associated with opposition and wished the government no ill. His remaining days would be spent quietly at Culford Park, as he had so often promised himself, providing Bonaparte allowed him to do so.[191]

Pitt, ever the politician, recognised that an explanation ought to be given to the Catholics about what had happened, though without specifically blaming the king.

The line should be that the ministers had resigned because of an insurmountable obstacle. However, they remained attached to the principle of emancipation, even though they were no longer in office.[192] Cornwallis undertook to do this in two memoranda, thinking written testimony would be less open to uncertainty of meaning. He handed these to Lord Fingall, the leading Irish Catholic peer, and John Troy, the Roman Catholic archbishop of Dublin, for circulation among their co-religionists.[193] The first paper, drafted by Pitt, attempted to explain the reasons for the ministerial resignations. The other conveyed Cornwallis's private sentiments. The tone of both papers was that the Catholic hierarchy should realise that 'their future hopes must depend upon strengthening their cause by good conduct'.[194] However, in the second document Cornwallis attempted to reinforce this message by pointing out the advantage of 'having so many characters of eminence pledged not to embark in the service of government, except on the terms of the Catholic privileges being obtained'.[195] He was to regret using the word 'pledged'.

Any lingering hopes that emancipation might still be possible were extinguished with the news that George III had suffered a relapse of his mental illness.[196] Though he soon recovered, he attributed the return of his condition to the ministerial attempt to force emancipation on him in breach of his coronation oath. The immediate response of Pitt and his colleagues was that no further consideration of the measure would be possible during the lifetime of the king. Cornwallis immediately agreed.[197] Nevertheless, such an outcome, he told Ross, had 'so overcome my spirits, that for some days I have not been able to write'. In prospect was a weak administration, which could neither make war nor peace and which 'very soon will drive Ireland into the desperate state' from which it had just been rescued.[198]

Cornwallis's attention now focused his successor. Although the legislative branch of government had moved to Westminster, he still believed someone of 'very superior qualities' should be appointed, who could 'make himself independent of the influences' to which his predecessors had been subject.[199] His wish seemed to have been granted when he received a private letter from Philip Yorke, earl of Hardwicke, stating that he was to be the new lord lieutenant and that he intended to pursue the same system of conciliation as Cornwallis.[200] He himself only learnt officially of the appointment when it was published three weeks later in the *London Gazette*. Once again Portland had gratuitously snubbed Cornwallis in not formally advising him of his impending replacement, as was customary.[201] The home secretary had truly shown himself to be 'a weak and puny statesman' in his handling of Irish affairs.[202]

Nevertheless, Cornwallis was quick to welcome his successor, though another matter had yet to be settled before he could go. Lake, the most senior officer after Cornwallis in Ireland, had recently been appointed commander-in-chief in India and was about to leave, raising the question of a successor who could work harmoniously with Hardwicke. Momentarily Cornwallis feared that he might have to remain himself.[203] Disturbances had occurred in County Limerick, though he believed low wages rather than Jacobin ideology were the cause.[204] Rumours were also circulating in Britain that he was remaining in Dublin in expectation of receiving some mark of gratitude for his services. He affected to be unmoved by such gossip, telling an old family friend, the Reverend Benjamin Grisdale, that the 'ungracious circumstances' of his retirement were nothing compared to the misery of the population that he was leaving behind.[205] At least affairs overseas had brightened. In March 1801 Abercromby had defeated the French army in Egypt, while the following month Nelson had destroyed the Danish navy at Copenhagen. Equally promising was the accession of Alexander I to the Russian throne on the assassination of Paul I; the new tsar was less favourable to France. Quite unexpectedly, Britain had a 'fair opportunity of treating' for peace, especially as Grenville was no longer foreign secretary, having like Cornwallis resigned his office on the issue of emancipation. Any negotiations now with France would hopefully be conducted with 'prudent firmness', rather than blustering 'arrogance!'[206]

The final step in the changing of the guard came with the news in mid-May that a replacement commander-in-chief had been found. To Cornwallis's surprise, the nominee was none other than Medows, his former deputy in India, prompting him to joke that 'the king's confidential servants' must surely 'want the assistance of Willis', who had treated George III while he was mentally incapacitated.[207] The appointment made him especially anxious that everything was ready for his successor, since another French armament was preparing at Brest. The senior officers, accordingly, had their orders and every corps appropriate instructions, wherever the enemy appeared. The aim was to have 20,000 men assembled at various key locations within six days of a landing.[208]

Hardwicke eventually arrived on 25 May and was received in the same manner as Cornwallis three years earlier.[209] Once the ceremonies were concluded Cornwallis retired to the lodge in Phoenix Park to prepare for his own departure. This occurred two days later in the early evening, when he left Dublin with Hardwicke in the state coach, accompanied by 'a great number of the nobility and persons of distinction'. Along the route the streets were lined with people 'who testified their respect by repeated wishes for his welfare and safe return to Britain'.[210] At the harbour he boarded the yacht *Dorset* for his journey back to Parkgate. The demonstrations of public goodwill as he departed seemed a fitting testimony to his attempts at bringing peace to Ireland.

FIFTEEN

Attempting Peace with France

Adverse winds eventually carried Cornwallis's ship to Holyhead, where he disembarked on the evening of 28 May 1801. His plan was to travel to London, after an overnight stay in Shrewsbury with Sir Charles Oakley, the former governor of Madras. However, the roads and weather were so bad that he only reached his ultimate destination on the morning of 2 June 1801, where Brome had reserved an apartment for him at the York Hotel in Albemarle Street until his own house was ready.[1]

As always business came before pleasure. His first engagement, therefore, was to resign his position as master-general of the Ordnance. After this, he told Lichfield, he was determined 'to retire absolutely from all public and political life, and to pass the remainder of my days in Suffolk'.[2] The partridge shooting season was approaching, promising some well-earned relaxation and pleasure. He would also be able to enjoy reunions with his family and friends in a convivial environment. The first few weeks were hence spent at Culford Park with Brome and Louisa and their two daughters, together with Mary and Mark Singleton.[3]

But though out of office, Cornwallis still had residual matters to deal with concerning Ireland and the Ordnance. 'I am beyond measure persecuted by letters from Ireland, claiming promises and recommendations to Lord Hardwicke', he confided to Ross in early July.[4] However, he was pleased to learn that the new lord lieutenant was relying on the Dublin Castle bureaucracy for advice rather than the former elite.[5] Less pleasing was Sir Richard Musgrave's dedication to him of his recently completed *History of the Rebellions in Ireland*. The book was virulently anti-Catholic, and Cornwallis quickly refused to endorse a 'violent work' which was 'calculated to revive old feuds'.[6]

The prospect of quiet retirement in any case quickly lost its attraction, with the renewal of French invasion plans. In early July he accordingly wrote to the duke of York offering his services should they be needed. York quickly accepted the offer, putting Cornwallis in charge once more of the eastern district covering the area between the River Thames and the Wash.[7] Such a posting should have pleased Cornwallis, since his headquarters at Colchester were no more than a day's ride from Culford Park. However, the suddenness of the appointment left him complaining that he had no suitable mount or military staff. 'Fortune could not have persecuted me more severely', he told Ross. Egypt would have been a preferable posting.[8] He was no happier on arrival. The tedium of life in a garrison town did not worry him, not having been spoilt 'by the constant enjoyment of the pleasurable gratifications of the world'. However, the prospect of certain disgrace, should the enemy effect a landing, was deeply disturbing. 'What could I hope for with eight weak regiments of militia . . . and two regiments of dragoons?'[9] The offer of the king's sons, Prince Edward and Prince William, to serve under him was little consolation.

Although he approved of the ministry's attempts to improve the country's defences, he remained convinced that the navy would necessarily remain the nation's principal bulwark, as 'we should make a sad business of it on shore'. But he knew that he was out of step with current military opinion, especially about the use of artillery. He suspected that he had only been put in charge of the eastern district because of 'the popular estimation which I am supposed to possess, and not to any respect for my military talents'. If it really was intended to entrust the defence of Kent and Sussex to the incompetent Sir Samuel Hulse of the Foot Guards, 'it is of very little consequence what army you place under his command'.[10] Like many other leaders approaching retirement, he found his lack of influence hard to bear.

As summer turned to autumn, he remained 'out of sorts, low spirited and tired of everything', not least because of the situation abroad. The French still had an army in Egypt, while at home the defences left much to be desired, should the naval shield be breached.[11] But his irritation at being marginalised was about to end, for in late September he received a request to travel to London on 'business of considerable importance'. Perhaps his talents as a military commander were again to be recognised.[12] However, on arriving he found that the business on which he was 'to be employed was not that of making war'.[13] Instead, he was to go to France as the British minister plenipotentiary to sign a treaty of peace, which the Addington ministry had been secretly negotiating. The financial burden of the war, the disruption of commerce, and increasing social unrest due to the high price of corn had all been strong inducements to consider a cessation of arms. The improved military and naval situation in Europe was another factor. With war weariness similarly affecting France, even Bonaparte recognised that it was time to think of peace.

A channel for talks had been provided by the presence in London of Louis-Guillaume Otto, the agent for French prisoners. The first meeting had occurred within days of the ministry being formed, conducted on the British side by Robert Jenkinson, Lord Hawkesbury, Addington's foreign secretary. Progress had been slow, and the discussions frequently came close to collapse. However, by the end of September a preliminary draft treaty had been agreed. Britain was to return its various overseas conquests, except Ceylon and Trinidad, which had been taken from Holland and Spain.[14] Egypt was to be restored to the Ottoman Empire, and Malta returned to the Order of Knights of the Hospital of St John, under the protection of an as yet unnamed third power. France on her side would evacuate the kingdom of Naples and the Papal States in Italy. The integrity of Portugal's frontiers in Europe and South America were also to be assured.[15] To close any loopholes, Spain, the Dutch Batavian Republic, Portugal, Naples, and Turkey were to be invited to the proceedings.

Since a congress in Paris might appear to favour the French, it was agreed that the definitive version of the treaty should be decided in the city of Amiens in north-eastern France. This would assist communication with London, though the odds heavily favoured the French, since their messengers could complete a round trip in twenty-four hours, whereas the route to London via Calais and Dover would require a minimum of three days.

Cornwallis was an obvious choice to head the British mission. He was known to favour peace, and spoke French. He also had a considerable reputation as a soldier and administrator, ensuring Napoleon's respect. As Hawkesbury informed the king: 'The military reputation and character of Marquess Cornwallis will give him advantages in treating with the French government, which no other person would possess in an equal degree.'[16] Although Cornwallis had little knowledge of European diplomacy, he would be assisted by an experienced diplomat, Anthony Merry, who had participated in the preliminary discussions and was already in Paris preparing the way. The ministerial assumption was that only a few small details remained to be settled. The French minister plenipotentiary at Amiens was to be Napoleon Bonaparte's elder brother Joseph. Like Cornwallis, he was not a professional diplomat.

Nevertheless, Cornwallis was initially disappointed that the mission was not a military one. However, he had a number of positive reasons for accepting it. He would not have to deal with Grenville, working instead with the more congenial Hawkesbury. Second, he had long favoured a negotiated peace, believing that Britain could do little on the Continent without effective allies. Although the French monarchy had not been restored, the new regime of Bonaparte at least promised internal stability and an end to the gruesome bloodshed of Marat and Robespierre. Hopefully, France was ready to re-enter the traditional European order. Finally, the terms drafted by Hawkesbury and Otto were neither discreditable to Britain nor to the interests of her remaining allies, Portugal, Naples, and Turkey. As he explained to William Cornwallis: 'I have long considered peace to be necessary for the preservation of our country.' He had not therefore felt 'at liberty to refuse the mission when it was pressed upon me, although nothing could be more disagreeable'.[17]

One other factor was the desire of the British public for peace. Nine years of desultory warfare had produced negligible results. Admittedly, several of his old Cabinet colleagues were opposed to the project, believing Britain was surrendering far more than she would gain. Grenville in particular was excoriating, describing the terms as 'miserably defective' and 'an act of weakness and humiliation'.[18] Pitt, however, was in favour and his support guaranteed that any such peace was likely to be accepted by Parliament.[19] The *Morning Chronicle* certainly welcomed Cornwallis's appointment: here was a man who would conduct the negotiations in 'perfect good faith', having 'long considered the contest with France as an idle waste of blood and treasure'.[20]

By the second week of October the details began falling into place. Cornwallis was to proceed to his destination via Paris, 'at the particular invitation of Bonaparte', so that he could witness the festive illuminations on 9 November to celebrate the peace. After that Cornwallis would travel to Amiens where the definitive text was to be agreed and signed. Accompanying him would be his son Brome, his private secretary Littlehales, Colonel Miles Nightingall, and another seasoned diplomat, Francis Moore.[21] Cornwallis's limited role in the mission meant that he had to decline an offer of assistance from his old colleague in India, Sir John Kennaway: 'As the winding up of the present business is to be left principally in the hands of those who have hitherto conducted it, I could not avail myself of your talents on the present occasion.'[22] The mission would be suitably equipped with three messengers and sixteen servants, plus an array of horses and coaches, the latter luxuriously fitted out, with the Garter arms emblazoned on each door.[23]

Before setting out, Cornwallis visited Hawkesbury to receive his official instructions. These stated that he was to repair to France to meet the ministers plenipotentiary of France, Spain, and the Dutch Batavian Republic. In the negotiations he was to be guided by the preliminary draft treaty, except for articles 4, 10, and 13 concerning Malta, the cost of maintaining prisoners, and the Newfoundland fisheries, where certain points remained to be adjusted. On these Cornwallis would receive fresh instructions as necessary.[24] Hawkesbury then presented three additional issues which Cornwallis was to raise privately with Napoleon. The first concerned the restoration of George III to the electorship of Hanover; the second sought compensation for the former ruling family of Holland; and the third was to secure the return to Sardinia of its Piedmontese territories.[25]

Hanover had become a collateral issue after its occupation by Prussia during Britain's confrontation with the League of Armed Neutrality. Although the league had been dissolved on the assassination of Tsar Paul I in 1801, the Prussians had continued to occupy the electorate, much to George III's concern. The ministry hoped that the French might support its return, to prevent Prussia becoming the predominant power in Germany. Regarding Holland, the ministers were anxious that compensation should be paid to the former ruling House of Orange for the loss of its property with the creation of the Batavian Republic. The matter had been discussed during the preliminary articles but not included, because of French assurances that suitable arrangements were being made elsewhere. But one thing was clear: the ministry would not 'abandon the interests of that illustrious House'. Ties of family, trade, and strategic interest were of too long standing to ignore. Finally, the ministers were anxious that Sardinia should recover its lands in northern Italy to redress the balance of power there. However, this issue was not to compromise the other dynastic objectives, or jeopardise the articles already settled in the preliminary agreement.[26]

Cornwallis eventually set off for France via Dover on 3 November. The journey was prolonged by bad weather on both sides of the Channel. However, his reception at Calais and along the route to Paris was everywhere cordial; Napoleon had even ordered the roads to be repaired for his comfort. Nevertheless, on entering Paris he experienced only 'the most melancholy reflections', prompted by the bloody events that had been perpetrated there during the Revolution.[27] The next morning, 8 November, he called on Charles Maurice de Talleyrand-Périgord, the French foreign minister, who was personally civil. Talleyrand began by saying that Napoleon was eager to see him, though his reception would be delayed for twenty-four hours because of the festive illuminations. Talleyrand then suggested that most of the outstanding points could be decided in Paris before his departure for Amiens. Cornwallis replied that he must first obtain permission from London, since other parties were concerned in the negotiations.[28] Diplomatic protocol was clearly not something that Talleyrand valued.

The initial audience with Napoleon took place on the morning of 10 November at the Tuileries Palace, with Talleyrand in attendance. Despite the magnificent setting, Napoleon received Cornwallis in the simple uniform of a cavalryman.[29] Throughout he was 'gracious to the highest degree', enquiring after George III's health and affirming, that while Britain and France remained friends, there would be no interruption to the peace of Europe. Cornwallis responded by complimenting Napoleon on bringing order and tranquillity to France after the horrors of the Revolution, which 'made us respect him as a statesman and legislator'. These latter achievements had in consequence removed British apprehensions concerning future relations with France. Cornwallis spoke with conviction, since the previous night he had been 'astonished to find such a multitude so perfectly quiet' and equally civil to the British party while enjoying the festive illuminations. An aide then informed Cornwallis that the first consul would grant him a private audience before he left for Amiens, though this had become less important following intelligence from Hawkesbury that the Prussians intended to evacuate Hanover without any preconditions.[30] It was one less issue to resolve.

Nevertheless, elsewhere alarm bells were already ringing. In the aftermath of Cornwallis's departure, the ministry had learnt that the French were preparing an expedition to Saint-Domingue, where the slave population under Toussaint

Louverture had seized control. The size of the armada was such as to threaten Britain's position in the Caribbean, compelling the ministry to take expensive precautionary measures. The ministry naturally wished to avoid such costs. Cornwallis was accordingly to make the British concerns known, especially regarding the plan to transport the French troops on ships of the line, which were superfluous to the expedition's professed objective, the suppression of the slave rebellion.[31]

Cornwallis raised the Saint-Domingue issue at his next meeting with Talleyrand on 12 November. The minister replied that the expedition had been planned before the signing of the preliminaries and that it was urgently required to prevent a massacre of the white population at Cape François. Ships of the line were being used to facilitate a speedy passage to the Caribbean and had been stripped of their guns to accommodate the troops. They constituted therefore no threat to the other powers, especially as the French now abhorred the principles of Jacobinism. He then insinuated once more that everything might be settled before Cornwallis left for Amiens, to which Cornwallis merely replied that he was still awaiting authorisation from London.[32] This was duly granted, since the ministers believed that a private interview with Napoleon would allow Cornwallis to settle the remaining points more quickly. However, he was to be circumspect in what he said, since Talleyrand was known to take advantage of unguarded utterances.[33]

With Hanover no longer an issue, attention turned to the subject of Malta and its strategic position in the Mediterranean. The island was currently in British hands, following its capture from the French, who had in turn wrested it from the Knights Hospitaller during Napoleon's passage to Egypt. The Knights had governed the island since 1530, though sovereignty technically lay with Ferdinand IV, king of Naples. All sides affected to believe that the Knights should be restored to their rightful position. The problem was that few thought they could do so with their own resources, thus necessitating a third power to guarantee their independence. The Russian ambassador in London had previously indicated that Tsar Alexander might provide a garrison, which the British ministry believed was the best available option. A number of the Knights had sought sanctuary in Russia following its seizure by Napoleon and had in gratitude elected Tsar Paul as their grand master. Although the new tsar was less enthusiastic about the Knights, the Russians were still interested in the island's status. However, by the time Cornwallis reached Paris it had become clear that the Russian ambassador had exceeded his brief. The tsar would not provide a garrison, though he might still act as guarantor.[34]

In the light of these developments, Hawkesbury wrote to Cornwallis on 16 November with the ministry's latest proposals regarding Malta. The Knights were to be restored to the civil administration of the island, and their ranks opened to Maltese inhabitants of noble rank to reduce foreign membership. The suzerainty of the king of Naples was to be reaffirmed, making him responsible for the provision of a garrison. The cost of this should be partially met by Britain and France, and the whole settlement guaranteed by the Russian tsar.[35]

By now the British hope of resolving the outstanding issues through a private interview with Napoleon had receded. Since the initial introduction, the first consul had shown no disposition for any such meeting. Cornwallis had not even been able to present his staff, as was customary. A move to Amiens began to appear more attractive, since Cornwallis would only be dealing with Joseph Bonaparte, who appeared to be 'well-meaning although not very able'. Such a location might also help check the 'chicanery and intrigue' of Talleyrand, who was clearly trying to keep the negotiations in Paris without the participation of the Spanish or Dutch ministers plenipotentiary. Cornwallis consequently informed Hawkesbury in his next dispatch of 20 November that he would depart for Amiens on 27 November, though he would be available for private discussions until then. He would also reiterate to Talleyrand the importance of having the ministers of Spain and Holland present at Amiens to confirm the cession of Trinidad and Ceylon. In the meantime, he asked Hawkesbury whether he should recognise the Helvetic, Cisalpine, and Ligurian republics, which the French had created in Switzerland and Northern Italy. So far he had ignored them.[36]

Life in Paris was not without attraction for the British party, as Littlehales noted for Ross's benefit. Cornwallis was in good health and had received marked attention from every class of people, the first consul excepted. He had dined with most of the French ministers and made a visit to the opera, where 'he was greeted with loud and general acclamation'.[37] Three of Napoleon's leading generals, Louis-Alexandre Berthier, André Masséna, and Jean Victor Marie Moreau had also offered him hospitality amidst great conviviality.[38] The British party had in addition visited the Corps législatif, or Parliament, where Littlehales noted that sentries were stationed at every doorway, giving the proceedings the appearance of a puppet show. Although Napoleon had re-established law and order in France, the despotic nature of his regime was clear for all to see. The Whig opposition in Britain should take note when making their claims about French liberty.[39]

Cornwallis's proposal to leave for Amiens resulted in a first formal session with Joseph Bonaparte, who began by declaring that he was a stranger to the diplomatic arts and would not attempt to gain points by cunning or chicanery. He imagined that Cornwallis would act similarly, given his reputation as an officer and a gentleman. He next surveyed the various articles, starting with the fourth, concerning the suzerainty of the king of Naples as guarantor of Malta, which he seemed to support. When Cornwallis queried whether Naples had sufficient weight for so onerous a task, Joseph mentioned giving Russia this responsibility. However, the French were anxious to avoid a Russian garrison on the island, since this would open the Mediterranean to their fleets. The result might be 'the speedy dissolution of the Ottoman Empire' and peace in Europe.[40] Cornwallis said nothing in response, knowing that the tsar had already rejected the idea of sending Russian troops.

Joseph Bonaparte then raised two further issues. The first, Article 10, concerned the British demand for compensation for subsisting the prisoners of both nations, since the French had refused to accept any responsibility for them in defiance of international law. Joseph countered that no such charges were customarily levied by the continental powers. Cornwallis in turn suggested that the matter might be settled if the French ceded the island of Tobago. The inhabitants were English speaking, and its return would be a gesture that would be well received in Britain. To this Joseph made no reply. He turned instead to Article 13, regarding access to the Newfoundland fisheries, which the French wished to adjust. Cornwallis quickly replied that any concessions here were unlikely, since popular clamour on this issue had nearly destroyed the ministry of Lord Bute during the negotiations of the 1763 Peace of Paris.[41]

Cornwallis's determination to leave for Amiens on 27 November finally produced a private half-hour audience with the first consul. Both men began by assuring the other of their peaceful intentions. Bonaparte in particular alluded to the economic distress caused by the war. After a digression about Saint-Domingue, Cornwallis raised the British hope that provision would be made for the prince of Orange, to which Bonaparte readily assented. He was, however, less accommodating about restoring Sardinia's lost Piedmontese territories, and was equally opposed to making Russia the guarantor of Malta's independence. He proposed instead that the island's fortifications should be levelled so that it ceased to have any strategic value. He next mentioned the British demands regarding the upkeep of the prisoners, but dismissed the idea of conceding Tobago in lieu. However, he would exchange Tobago for one of the former French islands in the West Indies, or alternatively for Pondicherry, subject to an agreement with the local nawab. Cornwallis immediately countered that there was no ruler there with whom he could negotiate, nor would the British government countenance any such acquisition, to which Napoleon commented '*vous êtes bien dur*' ('you are very hard'). The first consul ended the interview with a tentative proposal that the two nations agree a protocol for removing disaffected persons from their respective territories, perhaps motivated by recent attempts on his life and that of George III. On this point Cornwallis judged it prudent to make no reply.[42] The interview revealed that several important points still had to be settled, and that the chances of an early accord at Amiens were slim, since the first consul had made it clear that he would only make concessions for larger gains elsewhere.[43] Napoleon was famed for his personal charm, but it had won him no favours on this occasion.

The British party accordingly left Paris for Amiens on 29 November, though not before Cornwallis had been assured that his conduct had the king's approval.[44] Joseph Bonaparte followed four days later. At the opening session on 4 December the two representatives first exchanged their credentials showing that they had plenipotentiary powers to negotiate. The discussion then turned to the British requirement that the representatives of Spain and the Batavian Republic were present and empowered to cede Trinidad and Ceylon to Britain. Joseph replied that the Dutch representative, Rutger Jan Schimmelpenninck, was expected any day, though the Spanish minister would be delayed. However, he saw no reason why the main business between France and Britain should not proceed. Joseph then invited Cornwallis to start the process by presenting a protocol with his thoughts on the final version of the treaty. Cornwallis acknowledged the sense of this, but insisted that he must first have Hawkesbury's permission before deviating from the preliminary articles concerning the presence of Spain and Holland. He also emphasised that the final treaty must be written in both languages and not, as Joseph thought, in French alone.[45]

While awaiting a response from Hawkesbury, Cornwallis informed Ross about his recent meeting with Napoleon and the prospect of a winter in Amiens. The first consul was 'quick, animated', and spoke like a king concerning public affairs. Yet Cornwallis was in no doubt that his government was essentially a military dictatorship, 'in most respects wisely, but not mildly administered'. Nevertheless, the quiet acquiescence of the population indicated that Napoleon's power would not be easily shaken. As for Amiens, Cornwallis was not enamoured. He was too much of a 'John Bull' to delight in foreign society, especially among the present inhabitants, who had 'all the disagreeable qualities of the old French', without their accomplishments. He ended with the familiar refrain of wanting to be back at Culford Park, from where he would not be easily removed.[46] Ross knew better than to believe that. The call of duty and desire to be active would always supersede any scheme of retirement, whatever his doubts about undertaking new challenges and protests to the contrary.

Hawkesbury duly responded to Cornwallis's request for latitude regarding the presence of Spain and the Batavian Republic, by drafting a list of six points in the articles which still needed clarification. First, the government of Malta must be truly independent, though more detail was needed before the defence of the island could be entrusted to the king of Naples. In any case every attempt should be made to reinvigorate the Knights themselves. On the cost of subsisting the prisoners, Cornwallis already had the details of what France's share ought to be. As to extending French access to the Newfoundland fisheries, Hawkesbury confirmed that this was totally inadmissible. He then turned to the issue of compensation for the prince of Orange and the restoration of the king of Sardinia's Piedmontese territories. If France agreed to these, Britain would recognise the satellite Cisalpine and Ligurian republics, and the kingdom of Etruria. But there should be a single treaty signed by all the parties, rather than several bilateral ones, as the French seemed to favour. The eventual presence of Spain and Holland, therefore, could not be dispensed with.[47]

When the talks resumed on 11 December the two ministers plenipotentiary accordingly focused on Hawkesbury's list of points, starting with Malta. Cornwallis suggested that if the Order of the Knights Hospitaller was to be revived, British and French membership of it must be equal. Joseph Bonaparte agreed, but pointed out that the citizens of both powers were no longer eligible for membership, which required proof of nobility and adherence to the Catholic faith. The French had abolished hereditary nobility, while the British had in the main long ago ceased to be Catholics. The safest thing regarding Malta was to destroy the fortifications. Cornwallis responded by reaffirming the British preference for a garrison from a third power, until the Knights could look after themselves. He also reminded Joseph that Britain expected all the remaining combatants – Spain, the Batavian Republic, Turkey, and Portugal – to be included in one general treaty. To this the Frenchman made no objection.[48]

Cornwallis was hence surprised on 16 December to receive a note from Joseph Bonaparte stating that the French government could not admit a minister from Portugal. He offered two reasons for this. First, the interests of Portugal were already represented by the British delegation. Second, the presence of so many ministers plenipotentiary must necessarily slow down the completion of the negotiations. Joseph admitted with some embarrassment that he should have voiced his government's objections earlier. Cornwallis in response said that he must refer the matter to London.[49] Until this point, he had believed his French counterpart to be 'a very sensible, modest, gentlemanlike man, totally free from diplomatic chicanery'.[50] The events of the last twenty-four hours now suggested that the Frenchman lacked the authority of a true minister plenipotentiary, being a mere puppet of his masters in Paris.

Cornwallis was right to be suspicious, though wrong in believing that Joseph Bonaparte was inconsequential, since the constant shifting of the French position was largely a deliberate negotiating tactic on his part. As he subsequently reminded his brother, the British could only be beaten in negotiation by using their own weapons of 'imperturbability and inertia'. It was these tactics which had allowed them to triumph in the peace negotiations of 1763 and 1783. This time France would prevail, using 'patience and firmness' until her objectives were secured.[51] Joseph was far from being the honest gentleman, devoid of diplomatic cunning and chicanery.

By now Christmas had arrived, though it brought Cornwallis little cheer: Brome was now returning home with Littlehales, having 'contributed much to keep up our spirits'. This left only Moore, Nightingall, and Merry for company. Although Merry had proved a competent diplomat, 'he does not conduce much to our amusement'. Cornwallis's mood was not improved by his suffering 'one of those attacks in my legs and feet to which I am subject'. Another dispiriting factor was that Bonaparte and Talleyrand were about to visit Lyon on state business, which was likely to prolong the

Congress. Cornwallis was also conscious that the new French government was not as stable as he had imagined. He could only hope that the regime survived until the definitive treaty was signed. As it was, 'I dare not guess when I shall be so happy as to leave this dismal town and the wretched society which it affords.'[52]

Cornwallis's fears were soon realised: on 26 December Joseph Bonaparte presented the French version of what they believed the definitive treaty should comprise. To Cornwallis's dismay, the protocol included points different from what he thought had been agreed during his interview with the first consul. The British wish to compensate the House of Orange had seemingly opened the door to 'new matter of every species'. Cornwallis's immediate response, as he told Addington the following day, was to insist on 'a strict adherence to the preliminaries', thereby precluding further discussion about the East Indies, Portugal, and the Newfoundland fisheries. This was surely the 'only mode . . . for extricating ourselves from our present difficulties'.[53] Merry agreed, observing that the French counter-project took away 'all the advantages given us by the preliminaries', while giving nothing 'in return for the sacrifices we have made'.[54]

The result was another series of discussions though, as Cornwallis reported to Hawkesbury on 30 December, little progress had been made. The problem was that after securing Joseph Bonaparte's consent to something, there was no guarantee that he would 'not recede from it in our next conversation'. Malta was a case in point. After excluding the king of Naples as guarantor of the island, Joseph suddenly revived the idea of that power underwriting Malta's independence. Cornwallis had immediately repeated that Naples alone did not have the resources for that role. Joseph seemed to accept this, and assured his counterpart that he would seek a fresh mandate from Paris, substituting the tsar of Russia instead. However, Cornwallis doubted much good would come from such request, given that the matter would be handled by 'a man so devoid of honour and principle as Talleyrand'. It was very provoking, given British willingness to accommodate the French expedition to Saint-Domingue. Nevertheless, Cornwallis would continue 'to unite firmness with as much moderation as circumstances will admit'.[55]

He had no sooner penned these thoughts than the mood of the French delegation suddenly changed on New Year's Eve, Cornwallis's sixty-third birthday, raising the hope that the remaining difficulties might be overcome, though the cause of these 'fluctuating' attitudes was unknown.[56] The discussions accordingly continued into the first week of January 1802. One remaining obstacle was the apparent French determination to exclude the Dutch representative from the Congress, perhaps to strengthen the Batavian Republic in some undisclosed way. However, Cornwallis refused to be deterred and in another long session on the night of 9 January he reiterated the necessity for the Dutch delegate, Schimmelpenninck, to be present so that he could confirm the cession of Ceylon. The Dutchman had been in Amiens for some time waiting to be admitted. To this demand Joseph eventually acceded. But the Frenchman flatly refused to make any concession on France's liability for sharing the cost of the upkeep of prisoners. His stance seemed so firm that Cornwallis could only request Hawkesbury's final determination whether to accept the inevitable or to abort the entire proceedings and return home.[57]

Next day the Dutch minister was finally inducted into the negotiations, where he reluctantly confirmed his government's acceptance of the preliminary articles, including the ceding of Ceylon.[58] It meant one less hurdle to overcome. Cornwallis also believed he had made progress on the key issue of Malta, leaving just the prisoner matter and compensation for the House of Orange to complete the agenda. Yet he could not help noticing that the French were once again keeping 'strictly to the letter of the preliminaries' regarding Britain's claims, while denying their own obligations, despite the liberal forbearance of the British negotiators. Cornwallis rightly lamented that the prince of Orange's circumstances had not been settled in the preliminary articles, though he still doubted that the first consul would ignore everything that had passed during their private interview in Paris.[59]

Life outside the Congress was equally disagreeable, as Nightingall recorded for Ross. Some evenings the British were able to dine privately in their own lodgings. However, protocol required that they attend various dinners or receptions hosted each week by Joseph Bonaparte, Schimmelpenninck, Cornwallis himself, and the mayor and prefect of Amiens. Most of the French attendees appeared to be persons of easy virtue, Nightingall observed. Even Joseph Bonaparte lacked the manners of a gentleman, though he tried to be civil. Certainly, it was not 'the sort of society Lord Cornwallis would mix with by choice'. Cornwallis's only recreation was a gentle ride on horseback when the weather permitted. But even this was frequently denied him, since he was again 'much troubled with the old complaint in one of his feet'.[60]

Writing to Ross a few days later, Cornwallis admitted that he 'suffered much uneasiness and anxiety' over whether the French sincerely wanted peace or were merely temporising in order to achieve as yet undisclosed objectives. Although the negotiations had recently taken a turn for the better, a final treaty was still far from certain. Even if one were concluded it was unlikely to enhance the credit of those involved. Nevertheless, Cornwallis remained certain about the ruinous consequences of 'persevering in a hopeless war'. He would 'be satisfied', therefore, with any peace that was not dishonourable and which afforded Britain 'as reasonable a prospect of future safety as the present very extraordinary circumstances of Europe will admit'.[61]

The talks, consequently, continued in their customary fitful manner. In mid-January the British ministry dropped its demand regarding the presence of a Portuguese or Turkish minister plenipotentiary at the Congress. The hope was that the French would reciprocate by ensuring the arrival of the long-delayed Spanish envoy. Until he appeared a peace could not be concluded, making it difficult for the ministry to calculate whether its next budget should be for war or peace.[62] But fresh meetings only brought further difficulties. After the British ministers in London had grudgingly agreed to make Naples the guarantor of Malta's independence, Joseph Bonaparte reversed his position, conceding that the scheme was impracticable.[63] The result was yet another French protocol on 21 January, in which Joseph affirmed that the Knights' own forces and a guarantee from the major powers was all that was needed to secure Malta's independence.[64] Clearly, this did not meet British requirements, though as Cornwallis pointed out in a second private letter to Hawkesbury, the alternative of a Neapolitan garrison, given the weakness of Naples as a military power, would hardly prevent the French from seizing Malta whenever it suited them. Cornwallis was fighting 'the best battle in my power' to effect a satisfactory outcome.[65] The problem was the disproportionate resources of the two sides. As he observed to Ross: 'What can be expected from a nation naturally overbearing and insolent, when all the powers of Europe are prostrating themselves at its feet.' What could 'one little island' do, which was limited by land 'to a strict and at best a very inconvenient defensive?'[66] Only British forbearance had kept the discussions alive.

That forbearance was still copiously needed, since two days later Joseph Bonaparte again raised French claims respecting the Newfoundland fisheries and commercial access to India, despite Cornwallis's repeated rejection of both. The discussion then moved to the matter of compensation for the prince of Orange. Now it was the turn of the French minister plenipotentiary to be negative, affirming that Cornwallis had read too much into his private meeting with the first consul in Paris. However, Napoleon was disposed to find the House of Orange suitable territory in Germany to mollify George III. But this seeming concession was followed by a demand that Britain recognise the Ligurian and Cisalpine republics, which Cornwallis countered by demanding territorial compensation for the king of Sardinia.[67]

Although Cornwallis's prospects of leaving Amiens appeared negligible, he was heartened in early February by the arrival of the Spanish plenipotentiary, Don José Nicolás de Azara.[68] Even so, this did nothing to ameliorate the apparently flippant attitude of the French to the talks, as was demonstrated four days later on 4 February, when Joseph Bonaparte affirmed that his government now totally rejected the idea of even a temporary Neapolitan garrison in Malta: the Knights could manage on their own. As Cornwallis confided to Hawkesbury: 'In no instance have they appeared to feel themselves bound by any thing that has passed at private interviews, when it has suited their convenience to set it aside.' He now faced the difficult choice of either breaking off the negotiations or pursuing a different plan which did not place Malta at the mercy of the French. Perhaps the first consul's earlier suggestion of demolishing the fortifications might be the answer.[69]

While combating the French negotiators, Cornwallis had his first taste of dealing with the Spanish. Azara began by criticising the ambitions of the first consul, suggesting that Britain and Spain should arrange their affairs without French interference. Clearly the alliance between France and Spain was not one made in heaven.[70] Azara then made several demands: the first that the Portuguese border be the one settled in the recent Treaty of Badajoz; the second that Britain recognise the king of Tuscany; the third that Spain have right of access to the Cape of Good Hope; and the fourth that his country be allowed to trade with the British East Indies. Since these matters had not been previously discussed by the ministry, Cornwallis could only refer them to Hawkesbury, though he ventured the opinion that a useful commerce might be opened for the East India Company between Manila and Calcutta.[71]

Meanwhile, Cornwallis still had to answer the latest 'extraordinary protocol' presented by Joseph Bonaparte on 4 February concerning Malta. In the hope of expediting matters, he suggested a private meeting without the professional diplomats being present, so that they could express their thoughts more freely, to which Joseph agreed. The meeting duly took place on 8 February. Cornwallis began by noting the harsh tone of the last French protocol, which suggested a change of view. Joseph responded that his government was still committed to an amicable outcome to the negotiations. The tone of his last proposal was prompted by some unwarranted assumptions by the king of Napes. The discussion then turned to the composition of the Malta garrison, which Bonaparte thought might be recruited, either from the countries with membership of the Knights Hospitaller, or 'some prince in Germany'. The principal powers of Europe would remain as guarantors. To this Cornwallis responded that the present state of Germany meant that any such arrangement would give the French undue influence. Cornwallis wearily observed to Hawkesbury that Malta offered the French 'an unlimited field for cavil and chicane'.[72]

Fortunately, the Spanish envoy seemed more accommodating at a second meeting, admitting that his list of outstanding matters could be negotiated in a separate convention.[73] Nevertheless Cornwallis acknowledged to Ross his 'apprehension that an unguarded expression or an error in judgement on my part might be the cause of renewing a bloody, and . . . hopeless war, or, what would be still more dreadful, might dishonour and degrade my country'. He would rather be 'in the backwoods of America', 200 miles from his supplies, or 'on the banks of the Kaveri without' heavy artillery. Hopefully, the 'temperance and firmness' he had displayed on those occasions would carry him through his current dangers.[74]

These twists and turns were sufficiently disturbing by the end of February for Hawkesbury to consider an ultimatum: unless the French government resolved matters satisfactorily, Cornwallis was to leave Amiens and end the negotiation.[75] But just when affairs appeared at their bleakest, Cornwallis noted a sudden French earnestness 'to bring the treaty to a speedy conclusion'.[76] The result was the presentation on 6 March of two new protocols, showing some accommodation on the part of the Paris government. The French would now accept a Neapolitan garrison of 2,000 men and were ready to indemnify the prince of Orange. The French desire for a peaceful outcome was reaffirmed the next day when Joseph

Bonaparte stated that his government would accept all of Britain's demands regarding Malta, provided the British were flexible about the cost of maintaining the prisoners. Although the French still desired a separate accord with Turkey, they would allow them to accede to the definitive treaty.[77]

The removal of these obstacles renewed Cornwallis's confidence that a peace would be agreed, as he informed Addington in a short letter dated 10 March 1801. It was very gratifying for him at this stage of his life 'to have been the instrument in bringing the negotiation to a successful and honourable issue'. He could only thank the prime minister for entrusting him with an undertaking that was so essential to the well-being of the nation.[78]

One remaining task was the drafting of the English version of the treaty. This was a task that Cornwallis naturally assigned to Merry, 'whose talents and assiduity merit every degree of praise'.[79] The final texts were then dispatched to Hawkesbury on 13 March for approval.[80] However, if Cornwallis thought that everything was concluded he was mistaken, since the Cabinet still noted some details of wording that were unacceptable to them. The first emendation was that a new grand master of the Knights Hospitaller must be elected before the treaty was signed, to pre-empt the restoration of Baron Hompesch, a former holder of the office, who was considered pro-French. Second, the Batavian Republic must be responsible for compensating the prince of Orange. Finally, the continued presence of French troops at Otranto in the kingdom of Naples must end, since it was contrary to the recent treaty between those two states. Should the other powers at the Congress refuse to accede to these points, Cornwallis was to inform them that the British government had gone as far as it could and that its minister plenipotentiary would leave Amiens in eight days' time. The ministers were fearful that, if these points were not addressed, the British public would accuse them of making too many concessions.[81]

While agreeing with Hawkesbury's sentiments, Cornwallis decided that the tone of these latest instructions was too harsh, and decided to use more conciliatory language. He prepared instead a paper on the alterations which the British Cabinet thought essential. Joseph in turn expressed a willingness to find an accommodation. His main reservation concerned the wording of the article about the settlement of the prisoner issue, though he readily accepted the exclusion of Baron Hompesch as grand master of the Knights. The other points he considered mere linguistic technicalities, designed to avoid embarrassment to one party or the other. Nevertheless, he would send Cornwallis's paper to Paris for a final resolution.[82]

Joseph received his reply three days later, confirming that he had been given some latitude regarding the latest British requirements. It now became obvious why the French had so often changed their position concerning the prince of Orange and the inclusion of Turkey in the final draft: the first consul had committed himself to contrary provisions in previous treaties with those powers.[83] Nevertheless, the changed French tone prompted Cornwallis to assume responsibility for suspending the order for his immediate departure. Hawkesbury quickly approved, though he emphasised that Cornwallis was still to return home if Britain's final points were not immediately accepted.[84] The government was having difficulty raising money to fund its proposed budget because of uncertainty surrounding the negotiations. Cornwallis was therefore to send his most expeditious messenger to London, 'the moment our fate is determined'.[85]

Cornwallis accordingly met Joseph Bonaparte at 10 p.m. on 24 March for one final attempt at an accommodation, when, after five hours of discussion, the remaining differences were resolved.[86] In effecting this outcome, Cornwallis once again complimented Merry on his 'diplomatic skill and experience' in 'a line that was perfectly new' to him.[87] Two days were then required for writing fair copies of the treaty for ratification in London and Paris. At last Cornwallis could think of going home, comforted by the thought that his days of foreign travel were over.

Despite constant attempts by the French to alter its terms, the final version of the treaty, comprising twenty-two articles, was close to what had been originally agreed in the preliminaries. Britain returned all her conquests except Trinidad and Ceylon, while France evacuated the Papal States and Naples. The Knights Hospitaller were restored to Malta and allowed to elect a new grand master without interference from other powers. Furthermore, Britain would only have to evacuate the island once the Maltese and Neapolitan forces were in place. The island's neutrality would thereafter be guaranteed by the great powers of Europe. All prisoners were to be repatriated, and a commission established to adjudicate the cost of subsisting them. No changes were to be made respecting the Newfoundland fisheries or access to India. Although Turkey and Portugal were not included as contracting parties, they were invited to accede to the terms and their territorial integrity was recognised with only minor adjustment. Finally, compensation was to be paid to the House of Orange for the loss of the family's personal property.[88] The only significant omission from a British perspective was the failure to restore to Sardinia her Piedmontese territories.

Although the preliminaries in October 1801 had been received with general acclaim by a war-weary British nation, the mood in April 1802 was more sombre. The first consul's ambition appeared to have no limits following the annexation of the Cisalpine Republic and acquisition of Louisiana from Spain.[89] However, the main criticism of the treaty centred on the return of Malta to the Knights Hospitaller, with little more than a paper guarantee from the major powers regarding the island's independence once the British garrison was withdrawn. Another concern was that Britain was returning most of its conquests, including the sugar islands of Martinique and Saint Lucia. To many this seemed a shameful surrender of the costly gains made in the pursuit of Pitt's maritime strategy. Finally, the issue of prisoner maintenance had clearly been surrendered, while there was no provision made for the recovery of British property sequestrated during the French Revolution, other than through France's ordinary law courts.[90]

However, attempts to make Cornwallis responsible for these failings were misplaced, since his brief had been the implementation of the government's instructions. These he had carried out with meticulous care. In reality, critics of the treaty like Grenville and some later historians have too readily overlooked the weakness of Britain's position during the Amiens negotiations. Austria had been defeated, Spain had become a client state of France, while Prussia and Russia had opted for neutrality. At home, the country was threatened with social turmoil, financial stress, and the threat of invasion. The return of Malta and the other overseas conquests were the necessary price for ending almost nine years of bloody and inconclusive warfare. The difficulty for Cornwallis and the ministry was that they were negotiating with Napoleon Bonaparte, who, like most dictators, trampled on any agreement whenever it suited his purpose. Despite these obstacles, Cornwallis had kept the negotiations strictly conformable to the preliminary articles, so that none of the ministry's objectives were lost. At the very least, the treaty provided a breathing space, which allowed Britain to resume the war in 1803 in a stronger position than she might otherwise have enjoyed.[91]

SIXTEEN

Last Call

There were no cheering crowds as Cornwallis returned home. Six months of wearisome negotiation had dampened public enthusiasm, especially in Britain, where the terms had not lived up to expectation. Cornwallis was not unduly worried, consoling himself that he had done his duty and achieved a settlement in accordance with his instructions. He still believed that the peace would benefit the country and hopefully prove enduring.

After reporting to the king and the leading ministers, Cornwallis was free to deal with his personal affairs, telling Kennaway that he was glad to be home and hoped that his travels were over.[1] But the call of public business was not entirely ended, for York quickly asked him to review some proposals regarding the defence of Ireland. This reminded him that he had previously suggested to Portland the construction of several fortresses in central and western Ireland, though without response. He agreed with the present analysis that the area most exposed to an invasion was that between Bantry Bay and Lough Swilly. However, the need for an army of 60,000 regulars was surely excessive. Cornwallis himself had often had barely 5,000 regulars, managing most of the time with part-time fencibles and militia.[2]

The Treaty of Amiens also required attention, since it still had to be approved by Parliament, where he knew there would be considerable opposition, not least from Grenville, his old bête noir. Cornwallis's dislike of public speaking led the ministry to entrust the defence of the treaty in the Lords to Thomas Pelham, earl of Chichester. During the debates on the 5 and 13 May 1802, Grenville recited a long catalogue of the treaty's failings, sarcastically prefacing his remarks with how grieved he was to see the name of 'so noble a character as Lord Cornwallis' affixed to the document. Apart from the inadequacy of the arrangements for Malta, Grenville also stressed the want of proper safeguards for the Cape of Good Hope. The ministry had abjectly failed to achieve either the status quo before the war or the right of Britain to retain her conquests during it.[3] But when Grenville described the provisions for the Dutch royal family as shameful, Cornwallis broke his customary reserve by rising 'up with honest warmth', to ask 'if any man could for a moment believe the House of Orange . . . would not be amply indemnified for the losses which it had sustained'.[4] His honour had been impugned, and his anger was palpable.

Despite Grenville's attack, the treaty passed the Lords by 122 votes to 16 and the majority in the lower house was equally impressive. The size of the vote emboldened Addington to seek a mandate from the country by calling a general election. For Cornwallis this meant another trying contest in Eye, since reports were circulating that two city merchants, Mr Cobb and Mr Stratton, intended to mount a challenge.[5] He momentarily considered hiring lawyers to validate each voter's credentials, but was deterred by the cost. Indeed, he told Ross, 'I have resolved neither to bribe or open any house except Brome Hall, where I can take care that nothing shall be charged that is not properly expended.'[6] He was as good as his word. After entertaining the freemen for two days, Cornwallis suspended further treating until the votes had been cast.[7] His decision proved fully justified, as he subsequently told Ross: 'After all the alarms and disquietude, the opposition proved truly contemptible.' Cornwallis's two candidates, his brother William and Lichfield's eldest son, James, each polled 114 votes while Cobb and Stratton received just 15 apiece.[8]

Although Cornwallis recognised that Catholic emancipation was shelved for the rest of George III's reign, he was still hopeful that other conciliatory measures might be forthcoming, notably the abolition of tithes and the payment of the Catholic clergy. Cornwallis spoke several times to Addington on the subject, who seemed receptive to the idea and promised to talk to the king. But, as Cornwallis confessed to Alexander Marsden, the Irish secretary, George III was 'too much elated by having obtained his own emancipation' to listen to any 'unpleasant suggestions' from his ministers. Nevertheless, he remained certain that if the government failed to act, all hope 'of any permanent tranquillity in Ireland' would be lost.[9] At least his successor was conducting himself 'with good sense, moderation and propriety'.[10]

Despite his repeatedly expressed wish to retire, Cornwallis now found that the reality of retirement was far from providing the happiness and contentment that he craved. After a life of constant activity, it proved difficult to sit quietly while the world passed him by. In truth, he had never been able to fill the void left by Jemima's death. This personal emptiness, as much as a desire to service his king and country, explains his continued wish to engage in public affairs, however much he might protest that this was not the case.

One area where Cornwallis's opinion was still valued was India. In July 1802 Castlereagh replaced Dundas as president of the Board of Control, and within weeks of taking office proposed to visit Culford Park. He was preceded in September by a large number of 'India papers', to enable the pair to go 'deeply into that business'. At issue was the conduct of Marquess Wellesley, now governor-general of Bengal. He and the Court of Directors had become deeply disenchanted with each other: the Directors because of Wellesley's readiness to involve the Company in military adventures; Wellesley because the Directors refused to accept his appointments. Cornwallis agreed that Wellesley's views 'were rather too lofty', but thought he should remain governor-general for another year, provided he modified his more objectionable ideas.[11]

As winter approached, Cornwallis realised that his endeavours at Amiens had been in vain: Bonaparte was clearly preparing for further military adventures. Yet it did not change his opinion that only the great powers acting together could produce results. The defeat of France 'will never be effected by our fleet, or the capture of some French islands in the West Indies'.[12] He returned to this theme two weeks later: 'I am much afraid that our golden dreams of peace have entirely vanished, which I lament as sincerely as any man in this kingdom.' In contrast to popular opinion, he could not see 'any advantage that this country can derive from a naval war with France'. The only certainty would be a massive increase in the nation's debt.[13] Only dependable continental allies would allow Britain 'to play the game against Bonaparte that our ancestors did against Louis XIV'. The logic of the situation was clear: 'unless we are ourselves assaulted' or the European powers agreed on effective action, 'we ought . . . to remain quiet and restore our finances'.[14]

His disenchantment was not eased by the increasing lack of ministerial contact. This in turn induced a sense of uncertainty over whether to accept that his active life was over, or to engage once more in public affairs by attending the forthcoming opening of Parliament. He still felt mentally alert and physically 'equal to a pretty good day's' shooting, though his marksmanship had deteriorated. 'The sport however amuses me, and is an inducement to take exercise.' His two granddaughters also brought him pleasure, as did the possibility of a male heir, since Louisa was pregnant again and planning to have her child at Culford Park.[15]

By mid-November 1802 his mind was set, as he informed Ross. He would attend the opening of Parliament to repay the trust that Addington had previously placed in him as the British minister plenipotentiary at Amiens.[16] But he had another reason too, which was to ask the ministry to make some provision for his family, for 'I feel very sensibly that Brome must be ruined unless something is secured to him at the expiration of the annuity of the East India Company'. Cornwallis believed that recompense was due for his services in India and Ireland. But he was aware that it would be difficult to speak to the minister at such a busy time in the political calendar. In the event his doubts about undertaking such a mission proved well founded. After a short stay in London, he returned empty-handed.[17]

As Christmas approached, Cornwallis urged Ross to bring his family to Culford Park for the entertainment of the younger generation, since a recent outbreak of whooping cough was over.[18] He also wanted to discuss Castlereagh's plan to move Jonathan Duncan from the governorship of Bombay, to which he had been appointed in 1795, so that the ministry could place an experienced soldier there.[19] This reflected the deteriorating situation in Europe, where Bonaparte continued to rearrange the smaller states as though pieces on a chess board. In the event Duncan kept his governorship. But a long discussion with Merry in February 1803 did nothing to remove Cornwallis's apprehensions that war was unavoidable.[20] His fears were confirmed a few weeks later with William Cornwallis's appointment to command the Channel Fleet. His task was the blockade of France's Atlantic ports.[21] The Treaty of Amiens was dead.

Cornwallis accepted these events philosophically, focusing instead on the possibility that his services might be required again. It was with this in mind that he visited London in June 1803 to attend one of the king's levees.[22] Though he had often talked of a peaceful retirement, now that Britain was again at war he was anxious to serve his king and country. The ministry had recently passed an act creating a

French-style mass levy in the form of a greatly expanded volunteer militia.[23] Cornwallis quickly entered into the spirit of the measure by inviting the young men of Tower Hamlets to answer the nation's call.[24]

The need for troops was enhanced by an attempted uprising in Ireland. The affair was quickly suppressed, but it still left Cornwallis gloomily reflecting that 'any little services that I have rendered' there were unravelling like the Treaty of Amiens. However, he refused to accept defeat, wondering if he should offer to serve once more, though it would be 'a melancholy thing, at my time of life, to go for an indefinite period to Ireland', unless it was 'advantageous to my family'.[25] He might in any case be required closer to home, should the French land 'a respectable body' of troops, though the prospects of repulsing them were poor with David Dundas once more in charge of the army's deployment. It was all very irksome, especially as he was plagued by applications to use 'my *great power* and *unbounded influence*' for appointments of various kinds, including that of aide-de-camp to himself.[26]

Cornwallis had for some time been concerned about his domestic arrangements. Brome was so 'lost in indolence and apathy' as to be 'incapable of any management' in financial matters. Lady Louisa was of equal concern. Though she was 'attentive to the housekeeping account', she was regardless of 'expense in others of a more serious nature'. He told Ross: 'I am sorry to say that neither of them feel the horror that I have, of being indebted to tradesmen.' He continued: 'When I was last in Ireland, they spent every farthing of my income, including the Tower, regiment and Ordnance.' Inevitably, 'these matters prey upon my mind and get the better of my spirits entirely'.[27] It made a position on the civil list even more imperative for Brome and his family. Perhaps he should seek a new opening himself to ease the family's situation.

Suddenly, Cornwallis's desire to be employed appeared about to be realised when in late August 1803 he received a summons to call on Addington in London. In the offing was the possibility of replacing General Henry Fox as commander-in-chief in Ireland. However, nothing came of the discussion, after the Cabinet decided that 'it would not be advisable that I should be sent to that country'.[28] This was despite his giving assurances that he would not meddle in Irish politics and would obey the lord lieutenant in every respect. Inevitably, he suspected that his old adversaries, led by Portland, had conspired to prevent his appointment.[29] He was right to think so, as both Lichfield and Castlereagh confirmed. In the immediate aftermath of the latest rising, the king had repeatedly said that 'Cornwallis must go to Ireland'. What prevented the appointment was 'the violent Protestant feeling in the Cabinet'.[30]

His disappointment was keenly felt, as he confided to Ross, and was made all the greater because of 'the solitary life' he now led at Culford Park, which gave him 'considerable time for meditation'. He found it hard 'to sit down quietly by myself, without occupation or object, to contemplate the dangers of my country', and yet unable to do anything should the enemy land.[31] However, he did not brood for long, writing the same day to York that in the event of an invasion, he was ready 'to serve in any part of the world' where the king might think it proper to employ him. 'I can truly assure you that you will find no general officer more zealous for your honour or more anxious to execute your commands.'[32]

York replied politely that he would transmit Cornwallis's sentiments to the king.[33] But as the days turned into weeks it became clear that the French were not about to invade, and that he must accept being 'laid quietly on the shelf'.[34] Yet he still resisted that fate, speculating to Ross as to whether he should go to London 'to put myself in the way of being noticed'.[35] Illness then intervened, with the return of his old complaint of swollen feet, though by late October he had convinced himself that although he had not yet taken 'the field against the partridges, I am perfectly well able to do it against the French'. Everything seemingly depended on the wishes of York.[36]

Like many public figures fading from view, he increasingly affected to find fault in every direction. Duncan would have only had himself to blame had he been removed from Bombay. Wellesley was foolish in not limiting the boundaries of British India through an alliance with the Maratha Confederacy. Castlereagh clearly had ambitions that went far beyond the Board of Control, making it unlikely that he would 'apply himself' to 'a permanent system' for 'our Asiatic empire'. One thing Cornwallis did commend was Addington's plan for expanding the militia. Despite their limitations, Cornwallis was convinced that they would 'add very materially to the confidence' and 'security of this country'.[37]

This was just as well, since at the start of 1804 the country entered a period of political instability. In late January the king suffered another short episode of derangement. Then the Addington ministry collapsed, after Pitt withdrew his support, leaving the country for several weeks without an effective government. Cornwallis was scathing about these developments, comparing them to the formation of the Fox–North ministry in 1783. Pitt had pulled down an admittedly weak administration, but opened up the appalling prospect of a government headed by Fox and Grenville, two men who throughout their political lives had agreed on nothing. Pitt's conduct was both 'very injudicious, and highly discreditable'.[38]

Eventually, a new ministry was formed by Pitt, without Fox or Grenville. Nevertheless, the political world continued to forget Cornwallis, as he admitted to his brother William. In prospect was a summer spent 'dozing quietly upon the shelf at home'.[39] This proved the case: he spent August caring for his four grandchildren, 'a very proper occupation for an old general that is laid by'.[40] But peace and quiet did nothing to reduce Cornwallis's simmering resentment about the lack of recognition for his part in carrying the Act of Union and conducting the negotiations at Amiens. He had clearly been discarded as a soldier, while nothing had been done for Brome. In early August 1804 his anger boiled over in another outburst against David Dundas. Surely Pitt and his colleagues did not think that someone 'who can neither write nor talk intelligibly' could be 'a good general?'[41] He was forgetting that his negative views about the war were ill calculated to endear him to those responsible for its conduct.

Cornwallis had never been an effective courtier and was clearly paying the price for his reserve. Nevertheless, he decided to break his habit of dignified detachment by stating his case to Pitt, despite his diffidence in matters 'where self is concerned'. Would Ross inspect what he had written?[42] But however well drafted, no response was forthcoming. He was hurt by this. 'I thought as an old friend and colleague, I might have had two or three civil lines.' Cornwallis could only deduce that he had offended Pitt by 'voting to the end' for Addington's administration, even though six of the present Cabinet had done the same.[43]

The approach of autumn 1804 found Cornwallis once more at Culford Park. His main focus now was necessarily on the family, since Louisa was expecting her fifth child. Cornwallis was anxious for her to give birth at Culford Park, which would be more restful than a garrison town like Ipswich, where Brome's militia was quartered. Yet he dreaded the arrival of another girl. Four granddaughters were more than enough, much as he delighted in their company. A boy was needed to sustain the Cornwallis lineage.[44] Perhaps he had forgotten that his own parents had had five daughters before producing four sons. He was pleased, therefore, that Louise decided to have the child at Culford Park, but was disappointed when on 17 November 1804 she delivered him a fifth granddaughter.[45]

Writing to the Reverend Grisdale on 6 October Cornwallis confessed: 'I know nothing of public affairs, and, with the exception of Lord Melville [Dundas] . . . I have not been in the most distant manner noticed by the present administration'. He was surprised consequently to learn a few days later that Castlereagh proposed to visit him at Culford Park to discuss the state of India. Instead of ending the Company's disputes with the Maratha Confederacy, Wellesley had begun new hostilities against Yashwant Rao Holkar, another prince of that nation. In the words of Charles Grant, now chairman of the Company, their governor-general had 'criminally involved himself in all the difficulties of another war against an able and powerful chief'.[46] Clearly, he would have to be recalled.

At the last moment, Castlereagh had to visit Pitt instead at his country retreat of Walmer Castle, much to Cornwallis's disappointment, 'as I should have liked to have had some conversation with him'. But he was excited by the possibility of even 'a temporary appointment' in India, until George Barlow assumed the governorship there.[47] Ross sensibly advised his friend to be cautious and not to rush off to London on some whimsical notion, only to be rebuffed and humiliated. Cornwallis meekly agreed, adding that nothing would induce him to return to India, except 'the firm persuasion that it was the earnest wish of government and of the respectable part of the Directors'. He acknowledged that it would be 'a desperate act to embark for India at the age of sixty-six', but, 'prepared as I am to forego all further comforts and gratifications in this world for the sake of my family, I cannot sacrifice my character and my honour' by declining to go.[48] The ingrained lure of active service was once again proving too strong for Cornwallis to resist.

Towards the end of November 1804, Castlereagh dispatched two large packets of India papers to Culford Park, which he asked Cornwallis to inspect prior to his visit.[49] At their subsequent meeting on 5 December, Castlereagh confirmed that Pitt had 'entered thoroughly into the business', and was 'decidedly of opinion' that

Wellesley 'could not be suffered to remain in the government'. That being the case, Pitt, Melville, and Castlereagh believed that it 'would be to the utmost advantage to this country' that Cornwallis 'should succeed him', since the appointment of a Company employee like Barlow was 'at present out of the question'.[50]

In reply, Cornwallis affirmed that however challenging the assignment for someone of his age, he believed he was in good health and, feeling 'awkwardly circumstanced by being totally set aside', would not refuse any situation in which he might be useful. Apart from making peace with Holkar, his main task would be to undo Wellesley's expensive subsidiary treaties, which had reduced many native princes to the status of Company vassals.[51] But he was genuinely disappointed that Barlow could not succeed him, being someone he respected, not least for completing the Cornwallis Code.[52]

For the moment the appointment was to remain secret, until the Company was ready to publish the details.[53] He could, however, choose his staff. As always Cornwallis wanted to keep the arrangements simple. The main consideration was to have a secretary with whom he felt at ease. George Robinson, the former Bengal military auditor-general, seemed a natural choice, though he now had a family. Cornwallis was relieved, accordingly, to learn after Christmas that Robinson would accompany him after all. He would also have a personal physician, Dr John Fleming, who would travel incognito to prevent unwelcome attention to his master's age and physical condition. Finally, Captain John Gore had offered him passage on the 50-gun warship *Medusa*, which Cornwallis quickly accepted, as 'I should feel so much at my ease on board his ship'.[54]

None of the family was to accompany Cornwallis. Brome had his young family to attend to. Singleton was occupied at the Ordnance. Mary, however, was 'very melancholy' about the appointment. Unlike her brother, she had no children to enrich her life, and was about to lose a father to whom she had always been close and might not see again.[55]

The invitation to Cornwallis to become once more the governor-general of Bengal and commander-in-chief in India was formally issued by Grant on 4 January 1805. Cornwallis's mission was to rectify the 'extraordinary situation of their affairs' that had 'recently occurred in Hindustan'. Grant then listed the reasons for appointing him, the first being his previously demonstrated regard for the system which

Parliament had 'established for the management of British India'. Equally important had been his earlier 'wise moderation and good faith toward the native powers, whose confidence and attachment' were thereby strengthened. Finally, they acknowledged his 'supreme attention to improvements in the internal state of the Company's territories, and in their finances', which constituted 'the true sources of their prosperity'. All these attributes seemed best calculated to restore the Company's fortunes on a 'firm and equitable basis', relieving the Directors 'from the enormous load of debt by which they are oppressed'.[56]

The appointment was officially announced by the Court of Directors on Wednesday 9 January, though rumours were already circulating in the press about its likelihood.[57] Cornwallis himself went to London on 15 January to start his preparations. Inevitably, as in 1786, the news of his appointment was the signal for a deluge of applications for positions in India. He told Kennaway that even if the Company hired forty large vessels they still could not carry half the people who had asked to go to India.[58] However, it was not until 21 March that Cornwallis took the oath of office in East India House, which was followed by a sumptuous banquet at the London Tavern, attended by York, Melville, Castlereagh, and the governor of the Bank of England.[59] He admitted to William Cornwallis, that life had become frantic, he being 'plagued to death from morning till night' by ministers and other official business. To add to his 'misfortunes, poor Robinson, my secretary is not well and can afford me no assistance'. For all these reasons, he wished 'very much to be off' on his journey.[60]

One unexpected irritant was a letter from the historian Francis Plowden, who was revising his three-volume *History of Ireland*. Plowden wanted to clarify the circumstances of Cornwallis's 'pledge' not to take office again without assurances that Catholic emancipation would be enacted (see above, pp. 306–7). In view of his new appointment as governor-general and the return to office of his former colleagues, it was difficult not to conclude that a gross breach of faith to Ireland's Catholics had been committed. However, many of Cornwallis's 'supposed' friends were asserting that he had never given 'such pledge to Dr Troy'. Plowden was accordingly offering Cornwallis a chance to explain himself, since he was anxious 'to hand down to posterity' a truthful account of what had happened.[61] Cornwallis replied that he no longer had a copy of the paper, nor a distinct recollection of the words used in it. But he was certain that any 'pledge' was not intended as an irrevocable refusal to take office again until Catholic emancipation was granted. What he and his colleagues meant was that they remained supportive of the measure, should an opportunity allow its implementation.[62]

Another task requiring Cornwallis's attention was the making of a new will. Mary was to receive, as sole beneficiary, the income from £10,000-worth of stock, which was to be held in trust for her by Lichfield and Sydney. This was to ensure that neither the capital nor the income could be used to pay Singleton's debts or those of any future spouse, should she be widowed and remarry. The rest of his real and personal estate he bequeathed to Brome. Here too his lands in Suffolk, Norfolk, and Middlesex were placed under the stewardship of Lichfield and Sydney.[63] These were sensible precautions, given that neither of his children had shown much judgement in financial matters.

Before leaving, Cornwallis attended the king's levee on 5 April 1805, for a short audience with George III.[64] Soon afterwards, he set off for Portsmouth, accompanied by Castlereagh, Brome, Robinson, and Nightingall, where they arrived on Saturday 13 April. Here they found Captain Gore awaiting them. With a favourable easterly wind, the ship sailed the following morning, pushing past the Needles into the Channel.[65]

The *Medusa* made good speed, reaching the Cape Verde Islands just north of the equator on 5 May. As Cornwallis wrote to Ross: 'We are in a good ship and well accommodated, and as pleasantly circumstanced in every respect, as landsmen can be in a long voyage.'[66] Nevertheless, Gore observed that 'the sudden transition from cold to excessive heat, and from systematic exercise to a sedentary life' was affecting Cornwallis's health.[67] Also noticeable was his loss of appetite. This was despite the provision of Bristol spring water and fresh protein in the form of 'fowls'.[68] The ship proceeded with equal felicity after rounding the Cape, reaching Madras on 19 July 1805 in just three months. Here the inhabitants presented a loyal address, extolling 'the justice, wisdom and moderation' of Cornwallis's earlier administration.[69] But in a short letter to Brome, he admitted his apprehension at having 'undertaken a task too arduous for a man of my age'. The one consolation was that should he be fortunate enough 'to render any real service to my country and to my family, I shall close my eyes without repining'.[70]

A week later, on the evening of 29 July, he had reached Calcutta, though he opted to land early the next day. Before disembarking, he urged Wellesley not to deploy any European troops, it being the height of summer. Wellesley, however, with his love of parade, dispatched his carriages, servants, and staff to receive his successor at the waterside. According to William Hickey, who witnessed the event, Cornwallis was both surprised and vexed by the ceremony, growling to his secretary: 'what! what! what is all this, Robinson, hey?', speaking in the staccato manner to which he had become prone during official engagements. When Robinson explained that the cavalcade had been sent as a mark of respect, Cornwallis replied: 'Too civil, too civil by half. Too many people. I don't want them, don't want one of them, I have not yet lost the use of my legs, Robinson, hey? Thank God, I can walk.' The whole procession then proceeded slowly on foot to the new Government House, where Wellesley was waiting to receive them. Despite this attempt to prove his physical fitness, Hickey noted that everyone was 'greatly shocked to see how ill His Lordship looked and what a wreck' compared to what he 'had been when formerly in Bengal'.[71]

After embracing Wellesley at the foot of the stairs, the two men entered Government House, where breakfast had been prepared. A tour of the building then followed. Everywhere Cornwallis was dismayed by the munificence of the structure, especially the suite of rooms reserved for himself. It was all on a scale quite foreign to his style of living. He also disliked the presence of sentries everywhere, even outside his bedroom, and one of his first directives was to order them back to the guardroom. The dignitaries then gathered in the council chamber for the formal handing over of office. Wellesley sat in the president's chair, his hat on his head, while Cornwallis's credentials were read and the necessary oaths taken. Wellesley then rose from his seat, took off his hat, bowed to Cornwallis, and left the chamber. The next day Hickey observed Wellesley taking his evening drive in a coach and six escorted by dragoons and outriders. Ten minutes later Cornwallis appeared, driving himself in a phaeton, drawn by 'a pair of steady old jog-trot horses', accompanied only by Robinson.[72] The contrast between the two regimes could not have been starker.

The official ceremonies in any case were quickly overtaken by the demands of Cornwallis's mission. As he shortly informed the Court of Directors, 'an inquiry into the state of our finances' was among the first tasks to be undertaken. One early economy was the suspension of work on a new country residence for the governor-general at Barrackpore, 15 miles north of Calcutta. Another was a reduction in the personnel of the college that Wellesley had established. Cornwallis agreed that 'the young gentlemen' should receive instruction 'to qualify themselves for the important and responsible stations they were destined to fill'. However, the main requirement for an effective bureaucracy was 'knowledge of the country's languages'. The college curriculum, therefore, 'should be confined to that object'. Except for 'the appointment of able professors' and interpreters, other posts like those of provost and vice-provost could be dispensed with, especially as Wellesley had re-imposed the oppressive sayer duties (see above, pp. 201, 228) to pay their salaries.[73]

However, Cornwallis's most pressing task in the first days of his administration was the dispatch of orders to Lake, informing him of the Company's intention to end 'this most unprofitable and ruinous warfare' against Holkar. The rainy season would shortly interrupt 'material military operations', providing an opportunity for negotiations, which Cornwallis would conduct in person. Lake was accordingly to refrain from 'any act of aggression' unless his army was in danger.[74] Peace was all the more necessary because of the Company's precarious finances, which was reflected in the heavy discount on its certificates.[75] Hence, the news that Mahadji Scindia and Holkar were sending ambassadors to Lake's headquarters was hugely encouraging.[76]

Cornwallis's plan was to leave Calcutta on 8 August, just ten days after arriving, though he admitted to Ross that he had been unwell on the voyage to India and 'was greatly reduced in flesh'. Since landing, he had also been afflicted with 'those swellings' with which he had been so often troubled in his feet and knees. His hope was that the journey up the Ganges would bring relief.[77] As to his recent loss of weight and accompanying abdominal discomfort, he ascribed this to 'an irritation of the stomach and bowels'.[78] He may have been correct in this diagnosis, since his condition was symptomatic of either bowel or stomach cancer. Nevertheless, he was so focused on the task in hand that he was seemingly unaware of how perilous his state of health actually was.[79]

Although Scindia and Holkar appeared ready to talk, Cornwallis still had to be prepared to fight. Before setting out, he had another look at the Company's finances.

The most burdensome and least useful part of the military establishment were the numerous bodies of irregulars that Wellesley had hired. Many of these corps had contracts which made their dismissal difficult, but others were not so protected, allowing their prompt disbandment. Such reductions were essential, since the pay of the British regulars was five months in arrears. The same was true of the civil departments, making Cornwallis doubtful whether the Company could mobilise effectively to fight another war. The only means of even temporarily meeting the shortfall was by using the £200,000 of bullion that had been sent from Britain for the Company's Chinese investment.[80]

The second area for urgent retrenchment was Wellesley's subsidiary treaties, which had effectively made the courts of Pune and Hyderabad dependencies of the Company. How this process could be reversed, without incurring further entanglements or acquisition of unprofitable territories, was not clear.[81] A start, however, could be made by instructing the Company's residents at Pune and Hyderabad to avoid all 'intrigues, oppression, and chicanery' in the government of those 'distracted and desolated provinces'.[82] The cost of administering such entities was the last thing the Company needed.

Nevertheless, Wellesley's policy of expanding British India had widespread support in Bengal, in contrast to attitudes fifteen years before. The maxim now was 'that a system of power was preferable to one of conciliation'.[83] To Cornwallis such views were the opposite of what was desirable. Clearly, they needed correcting, not least among the military. While journeying upstream towards Benares, he accordingly wrote to Colonel John Malcolm, one of the senior commanders on the frontier, deprecating 'the effects of the almost universal frenzy . . . for conquest and victory'. Such sentiments were 'as opposite to the interests' of Britain as they were 'to the laws of our country'.[84] He wrote similarly to Lake on 30 August. It was the opinion 'of all reflecting men of every description, that it is physically impracticable for Great Britain, in addition to all other embarrassments, to maintain so vast and so unwieldy an empire in India'. The 'brilliant gazettes' about martial prowess were poor reward for the constant 'calls for reinforcements of men and for remittances of money'. The reality was that 'our finances are at the lowest ebb and that we literally have not the means of carrying on the ordinary business of government'. He concluded by apologising for not writing the letter himself, being unable to hold a pen except when signing documents.[85]

Lake's response was predictably hostile, he seeing Cornwallis's dispatch of 30 August as an implied censure. He resented Cornwallis's arrival, both as governor-general and commander-in-chief, which effectively meant his own demotion. He would in consequence return to Europe at the first opportunity. In his next letter of 23 September 1805, Cornwallis attempted to mollify his disgruntled colleague, whom he had known since the American war. Lake should understand that Cornwallis had never 'yet accepted a civil government to which the military authority was not also annexed'. Cornwallis's appointment, therefore, was not an indication that Lake was unfit for the position of commander-in-chief. Surely the two of them could find an arrangement that suited both.[86]

It was to be Cornwallis's last letter to Lake or anybody else. Within forty-eight hours, Robinson reported to Castlereagh from the city of Buxar that, since Cornwallis's arrival in India, his constitution had proved unequal to the rigours of the Indian climate: 'From that time to the present, without suffering from the influence of any specific complaint, a gradual state of increasing weakness and debility has reduced him at length to a condition that affords no hope of recovery.' Although he 'continued till within these few days to give his attention' to business, 'I am persuaded he can no longer conduct it to any efficient purpose, without a change so great and rapid as to amount almost to a miracle'. Barlow had consequently been asked to join them at Benares.[87]

To Ross, Robinson gave more intimate details. 'It is not only the loss of bodily strength we have to deplore: the powers of his mind are unfortunately failing him fast; he dozes away the remnant of life that is left to him and wakes but to a perfect unconsciousness of what is passing around him.' Death would now be a blessing for 'this great and good man'. He suggested that Ross should inform Brome of his father's condition, but spare him the details 'of his imbecility'. Then, in a postscript, he added that Cornwallis had suddenly asked about Scindia and other details that Robinson had related to him that morning. The old soldier was still trying to do his duty.[88]

To aid Cornwallis's recovery, Dr Fleming proposed they proceed upstream in hopes of finding cooler weather. A six-month voyage to England in any case must prove fatal. The journey continued accordingly, yet by early October, on Barlow's arrival, the end was clearly approaching. The flotilla had now reached the town of Ghazipur, not far from Benares. Here Cornwallis spent his last four days in a residence overlooking the Ganges, attended by his faithful aides, Robinson, and his military secretary, Miles Nightingall. Both men made a point of sleeping in an adjacent room 'to administer every possible comfort to him in his last moments'.[89] Their devotions ceased on 5 October 1805 when Cornwallis drew his last breath, seemingly without pain in these final hours and days of his life.[90]

The climate and distance meant that Cornwallis's body could not be returned to Calcutta or forwarded to Britain. Instead Barlow, Nightingall, and Robinson supervised the erection of a temporary mausoleum by the Ganges. This would have to do until a more suitable structure could be built. Here Cornwallis was interred according to the rites of the Church of England, surrounded by his aides and military escort. In death, at least, Cornwallis received a simple ceremony devoid of pomp and circumstance.[91]

The news of Cornwallis's demise at the age of sixty-six reached Calcutta on 12 October and was immediately announced in the local *Gazette*. The paper noted that as a 'patriot, a statesman, a warrior and a man, the character of the Marquess Cornwallis shines with distinguished lustre'. British India would forever proudly associate 'its happiness, its prosperity and renown' with 'the grateful remembrance of its venerated benefactor'. The flag was to be flown at half-mast on the ramparts of Fort William until sunset, and a salute of sixty-six guns fired, one every minute to mark his years. Similar tokens of respect were to be observed at all the principal stations in Bengal, Madras, and Bombay. The inhabitants of Calcutta also agreed to raise money for a permanent memorial to replace the temporary structure at Ghazipore.[92]

The task of carrying the doleful news to Europe was entrusted to Gore aboard the *Medusa*. Travelling with him was Robinson. The return journey was almost as quick as the outward passage, taking just three and a half months. However, the messengers arrived to find a nation already in mourning. A week before, Pitt, the country's long-serving prime minister, had died from exhaustion and prolonged ill health at the age of forty-six. His death followed the earlier loss of Nelson at Trafalgar on 21 October 1805, which had just been commemorated at a public funeral in St Paul's Cathedral. Three of the country's most illustrious leaders had been taken within four months of one another. Nevertheless, Castlereagh immediately tabled a motion in the Commons on Saturday 1 February 1806, for a monument to be erected to the memory of Cornwallis in St Paul's. In the debate the following Monday,

Castlereagh acknowledged that only individuals of 'splendid and signal services' to the nation were honoured in this fashion. The noble marquess was a man whose character and conduct 'disarmed all party feeling'. Although no orator, he combined 'the professional knowledge of a soldier' with a 'degree of political judgement, which made him equally serviceable to his country in the civil and military capacity'. He had demonstrated these abilities most conspicuously in India, adopting 'those two grand principles to which the good government and prosperity of those countries must be principally attributed. The first was giving the native inhabitants a fixed and certain property in the lands they cultivated, and the second was the introduction of a stable administration of justice.' Another eminent achievement had been the principal 'management of the union in Ireland', which Cornwallis rightly considered 'one of the most essential services' he had rendered to his country. As to Amiens, the peace had been overwhelmingly approved by Parliament, giving the government time 'to meet the difficulties in which this country was now placed'. Nothing could be more fitting, hence, than a memorial to Cornwallis's 'high and unblemished character, his long and eminent services, and his unwearied zeal and devotion, to the last moments of his life, in the cause of his country'.[93]

Castlereagh was supported by Grant, Philip Francis, William Wilberforce, and Charles James Fox. However, a couple of dissenting voices were raised. Windham questioned Cornwallis's achievement concerning the ill-fated Treaty of Amiens, while one of the new Irish representatives condemned Cornwallis's role in securing the Act of Union: this had only been accomplished by the most shameful corruption, which would ultimately ruin Ireland.[94] Despite this, Castlereagh's resolution passed unanimously.

The East India Company was similarly respectful of their late governor-general. On the arrival of the *Medusa* the Directors resolved to wear mourning for one month in his honour.[95] They also proposed to make an ex-gratia payment of £40,000 to Cornwallis's family for their loss.[96] In its formal resolution the Court of Directors began by expressing its 'gratitude to the late Marquess Cornwallis, who, after a long series of eminent services to his country and the East India Company', had again answered the call of the nation 'to undertake in a most critical situation . . . the arduous employment of governor-general'. There he immediately began 'the great work of restoring tranquillity upon a just and solid basis', while starting the equally necessary 'retrenchment in the vast expenditures of the Company'. Sadly, 'his incessant labours' had been terminated by death, 'to the unspeakable loss of the Company and the nation'. Since the Company could no longer reward Cornwallis himself, they owed it to his family to make proper compensation. The Directors accordingly agreed unanimously to pay his salary as governor-general to Brome for the remainder of the year and for one year thereafter.[97] Cornwallis had succeeded at least in his desire to make one further provision for his family.

Elsewhere commemorative gestures were made, placing Cornwallis in the pantheon of British statesmen. In India, statues were commissioned at Fort William and Fort St George. Nor was he forgotten in Suffolk, where the corporation and inhabitants of Eye paid tribute at a special service, which ended stirringly with Handel's aria: 'The trumpet shall sound and the dead be raised.'[98] But first Cornwallis had to receive his final resting place overlooking the Ganges. In 1814 Cornwallis's old colleague Lord Rawdon, now the governor-general, was appalled to find the structure still unfinished. The government in Calcutta, suitably ashamed, quickly allotted money to end 'this disgraceful state'.[99] The 70-foot-high stone and brick mausoleum was finally completed in 1823.[100]

Cornwallis died a national hero. What of his subsequent reputation? Nineteenth-century historians, like most of his contemporaries, continued to exonerate him for losing America, preferring to blame George III and his 'wicked' ministers.[101] As for India, his reputation remained high because of his judicial and administrative reforms, which set the stage for the high-water mark of the Victorian imperial mission. If the union of Britain and Ireland appeared increasingly fraught, the blame was directed at later politicians rather than Cornwallis. As the distinguished Irish historian William Edward Hartpole Lecky commented: 'If a wise and liberal statesmanship had followed the union, it might perhaps have been rendered permanent.'[102] That his tenure at the Ordnance remained unnoticed was largely because no critical shortages occurred in military supplies and equipment under his watch. Finally, the aborted Treaty of Amiens became a mere footnote to the subsequent triumph of British arms on the Iberian Peninsula and at Waterloo. Consequently, Cornwallis remained a respected proconsul, a man who had helped shape Britain's second empire. If he lacked the intellectual brilliance of his peers, he compensated for this by his outstanding competence.[103]

Since 1945, interpretations have changed radically. 'Empire' has become a pejorative word, descriptive of an era when Britain selfishly exploited the wealth of three continents under the self-serving banners of the rule of law, free trade, and the white man's burden. In this climate Cornwallis has been largely ignored, because he does not fit the image of a cruelly exploitative imperialist. If his American campaigns are remembered, it is as a foil to the brilliance of Washington and Greene. Otherwise, his part in helping Britain survive the French Revolutionary Wars has been overlooked, as has his role in carrying the union, where Castlereagh and Pitt are given such credit as remains. Paradoxically, Cornwallis's reputation perhaps remains brightest in India, where his administrative reforms continue to be acknowledged, even by nationalist historians, meriting a volume in the *Encyclopaedic History of the Indian Freedom Movement*.[104]

Whatever his reputation, the study of Cornwallis remains important because of his pivotal role at critical moments in the history of Britain, Ireland, India, and America. In America, he did his best for king and country, proving himself a dynamic commander, popular with his men, though failing, like the rest of the British establishment, to understand why the Americans had rejected what he and his contemporaries considered a model of constitutional government. The struggle, however, did teach him that there were limits to British power. Without passive acceptance by the governed, no government could maintain its authority. America also saw the start of Cornwallis's long commitment to rooting out corruption and waste in government.

He carried these lessons to India. Here, his reforms, as Castlereagh noted, were aimed as much at improving the lives of Hindus and Muslims as they were designed to make the Company profitable, since for Cornwallis the two objectives were compatible. Few of his initiatives were original to him, which were the result of changing attitudes in Britain. But he implemented the new ideas with sensible firmness, making British rule an apparent model of humanity and efficiency, when compared to the feudal states of India or the kingdoms of the absolute monarchs of Europe. He also demonstrated that Britain's presence in India did not necessarily require the subjugation of the entire continent: the war with Tipu Sultan was genuinely unwelcome to him and he remained committed to the view that Indians should be left to rule themselves in areas not already under the Company's control.

That his vision for a balance of power in India was subverted by Wellesley and his successors was hardly Cornwallis's fault. Similarly, the failure of many of his initiatives in Bengal to operate as intended should not detract from his efforts to make British governance more humane and acceptable.

Regarding Cornwallis's achievements in Britain, his plans for reforming the Ordnance were overtaken by events. Nevertheless, there were no critical shortage of weapons and no technologies were overlooked for want of support. As to Ireland, Cornwallis has rarely been given sufficient acknowledgement, both for trying to end the 1798 rebellion humanely and for seeking an inclusive union. Had his enlightened views been implemented, the history of nineteenth-century Britain and Ireland might have been very different. It would certainly have been less fractious. At Amiens, meanwhile, Cornwallis proved a tenacious negotiator, despite the attempts of Talleyrand and Joseph Bonaparte to alter the previously agreed terms. He did so in the conviction that peace would benefit Britain, believing that nothing could be achieved on the Continent without the support of the other major powers. Pitt, Grenville, and Dundas were simply misguided in thinking that a maritime strategy could succeed, as subsequent events proved.

Finally, Cornwallis's career provides an example of a public servant who put his country before personal gratification. Throughout his public life he showed a sense of decency and humanity in regard to all, regardless of race, creed, rank, or wealth. These qualities were allied to a deep sense of responsibility for those under him, showing in many respects the best side of human nature. This empathy resulted in a surprisingly liberal attitude to the world in which he lived. This did not make him a democrat, or an advocate of equality (hardly surprising for someone born into the aristocracy), though it does not excuse his prejudice against Indians. Nevertheless, after the American war he usually exhibited progressive attitudes, as shown by his reluctance to embrace war; his dislike of slavery; his condemnation of gratuitous cruelty; his attempts to alleviate famine; his support for ability over hereditary entitlement; his desire to eliminate corruption from public office; and his detestation of religious bigotry. Lastly, he demonstrated throughout his life an ingrained honesty and integrity, in both his public and private dealings, qualities often lacking today. If, in his final years, he did not quite live up to the family motto, 'Virtue conquers envy', he certainly made a commendable attempt to do so.

Appendix: Organisation of the British Army, *c.* 1760–1800

OFFICER RANKS BY SENIORITY

Field-Marshal

General

Lieutenant-General

Major-General

Brigadier-General: temporary brevet rank

Colonel: commanding officer of a regiment

Lieutenant-Colonel: second-in-command of a regiment or commanding officer of a battalion

Major: senior officer after lieutenant-colonel in a regiment or battalion

Captain: commander of an infantry company or cavalry troop

Lieutenant: commander of an infantry platoon or second officer in a cavalry troop

Ensign: lowest commissioned infantry officer, equivalent to a modern second lieutenant

UNIT ORGANISATION

Infantry

Regiment: a corps with a wartime establishment of 800–1,000 men, often recruited territorially; rarely up to strength, frequently having no more than 250–400 men in the field

Battalion: usually the second corps of a foot regiment with a similar establishment of 800–1,000 men

APPENDIX

Company: unit of 80–100 men, normally with eight companies to each regiment or battalion

Platoon: unit of 20–30 men, three to each company

Cavalry (excluding the Life and Horse Guards)

Regiment: normally 360–450 men and horses, divided into squadrons and troops; often under strength

Squadron: unit of 120–150 men

Troop: unit of 30 men

OTHER CATEGORIES OR TERMS

Brigade: a temporary grouping of two or more infantry regiments or battalions, usually supported by artillery and cavalry

Grenadiers: an elite company of the physically largest men in each foot regiment or battalion, used for spearheading attacks; often grouped together for operational purposes

Guards: the three regiments of Foot Guards, often acting as a brigade

Light Infantry: an elite company in each foot regiment, used for reconnaissance and other dangerous missions; such companies were frequently amalgamated into a single corps for field service

Endnotes

ABBREVIATIONS

Davies   K.G. Davies (ed.), *Documents of the American Revolution, 1770–1783*, 21 vols (Dublin, 1972–81)

FO   Foreign Office Papers, National Archives, Kew

HMC   Historical Manuscripts Commission

HO   Home Office Papers, National Archives, Kew

IOR   India Office Records, British Library, London

KRO   Kent Record Office, Maidstone

NAM   National Army Museum, London

NLI   National Library of Ireland, Dublin

NLS   National Library of Scotland, Edinburgh

NRS   National Records of Scotland, Edinburgh

PGW   W.W. Abbott, et al. (eds), *The Papers of George Washington: Revolutionary War Series*, 28 vols (Charlottesville, 1985–ongoing)

PHC   Papers of Sir Henry Clinton, William L. Clements Library, Ann Arbor, Michigan

PRO/30   Public Record Office Papers, Non-Government Collections, National Archives, Kew

PRONI   Public Record Office of Northern Ireland, Belfast

Ross   Charles Ross (ed.), *Correspondence of Charles, First Marquis Cornwallis*, 3 vols (London, 1858)

Saberton   Ian Saberton (ed.), *The Cornwallis Papers: The Campaigns of 1780 and 1781 in the Southern Theatre of the American Revolutionary War*, 6 vols (Uckfield, 2010)

WLCL   William L. Clements Library, Ann Arbor, Michigan

WO   War Office Papers, National Archives, Kew

PREFACE

1. The earliest source for this story about Cornwallis's council of war is the American officer, General James Wilkinson, *Memoirs of My own Times*, 3 vols (Philadelphia, 1816), I, 139, though he makes no reference to the foxhunting anecdote. However, most historians have accepted it as something that a member of the British upper class might have said.

CHAPTER 1: AN IRRESISTIBLE IMPULSE

1. Franklin Wickwire and Mary Wickwire, *Cornwallis and the War of Independence* (London, 1971), 10–11.

2. Ross/I, 1.

3. Ann Weikel, 'Cornwallis, Sir Thomas (1518/19–1604), administrator', *Oxford Dictionary of National Biography*, vol. 13 (2004).

4. Wickwire and Wickwire, *War of Independence*, 10–13; Ross/I, 2.

5. Wickwire and Wickwire, *War of Independence*, 14–15.

6. John Debrett, *The Peerage of the United Kingdom of Great Britain and Ireland* (London, 1820), 102–3.

7. Ross/I, 3; *London Evening Post*, 25–27 January 1739.

8. Debrett, *Peerage*, 102–3.

9. Wickwire and Wickwire, *War of Independence*, 18–24.

10. Lewis Namier and John Brooke, *The House of Commons, 1754–1790*, 3 vols (London, 1964), II, 256. The college later commissioned a copy of John Singleton Copley's portrait of Cornwallis: see pp. 246–7.

11. Cornwallis to Brome, 8 September 1791: Ross/II, 116–17.

12. Ross/I, 3.

13. Wickwire and Wickwire, *War of Independence*, 24–5.

14. Cumberland to Cornwallis, 1 July 1757: Ross/I, 4.

15. Cornwallis to James Cornwallis, 23 May 1792: PRO/30/11/183.

16. Cornwallis to Lichfield, 23 May 1792, KRO/U/24/C/1.

17. Roguin to Earl Cornwallis, 23 January 1758: Ross/I, 4–6.

18. Brome to Thomas Townshend, 2 September 1758, Ross/I, 7.

19. Richard Middleton, *The Bells of Victory: The Pitt–Newcastle Ministry and the Conduct of the Seven Years' War, 1757–1762* (Cambridge, 1985), 13–18.

20. Brome to Thomas Townshend, 2 September 1758: Ross/I, 7; Wickwire and Wickwire, *War of Independence*, 27–8.

21. Ross/I, 8.

22. Earl Cornwallis to William Cornwallis, 1 September 1761: HMC, *Report on Manuscripts in Various Collections, Volume 6: The Manuscripts of Cornwallis Wykeham-Martin Esq.* (London, 1909), 299. Also quoted in George Cornwallis-West, *Life and Letters of Admiral Cornwallis* (London, 1927), 24.

23. Namier and Brooke, *House of Commons*, II, 256.

24. Earl Cornwallis to William Cornwallis, 3 May 1761: HMC, *Report on Various Collections*, VI, 297–8.

25. Ross/I, 8–9; Daniel Baugh, *The Global Seven Years War, 1754–1763* (Harlow, 2011), 533–4.

26. Elizabeth Cornwallis to William Cornwallis, 13 July 1762: HMC, *Report on Various Collections*, VI, 300.

27. Namier and Brooke, *House of Commons*, I, 379.

28. *Journal of the House of Lords*, XXX, 293: 25 November 1762.

29. Ibid., 300–17: 9 December 1762.

30. He later turned down the Home Office for this reason: see p. 247.

31. *Journal of the House of Lords*, XXX, 340–51: 10 March 1763; ibid., 351–61: 14 March 1763.

32. John Almon, *The History of the Late Minority, Exhibiting the Conduct, Principles and Views of that Party* (London, 1765), 91.

33. *Journal of the House of Lords*, XXX, 381: 28 March 1763; ibid., 387: 30 March 1763.

34. William Cobbett, *The Parliamentary History of England from the Earliest Period to the Year 1803*, 36 vols (London, 1806–20), XV, 1, 315–16.

35. *London Evening Post*, 10–12 May 1763.

36. *Journal of the House of Lords*, XXX, 426–9: 29 November 1763.

37. William James Smith (ed.), *The Grenville Papers*, 4 vols (London, 1852–53), II, 159.

38. Cornwallis-West, *Admiral Cornwallis*, 27–8.

39. Debrett, *Peerage*, 102–3.

40. Quoted in Cornwallis-West, *Admiral Cornwallis*, 21–2.

41. Dowager countess to William Cornwallis, 7 August 1763: HMC, *Report on Various Collections*, VI, 302–3.

42. Wickwire and Wickwire, *War of Independence*, 12–13, 31–2.

43. Dowager countess to William Cornwallis, 19 October 1764: HMC, *Report on Various Collections*, VI, 308–9.
44. Wickwire and Wickwire, *War of Independence*, 395, footnote 1.
45. Robert Beatson, *A Political Index to the Histories of Great Britain and Ireland*, 2 vols (London, 2nd edn, 1788), I, 290.
46. *Journal of the House of Lords*, XXXI, 227–8: 17 December 1765.
47. Rockingham to George III, 3 February 1766: Sir John Fortescue (ed.), *The Correspondence of George the Third, from 1760 to December 1783*, 6 vols (London 1927–28), II, 253.
48. *Journal of the House of Lords*, XXXI, 303–5: 11 March 1766.
49. *St James's Chronicle*, 18–20 March 1766; *London Chronicle*, 1–3 May 1766.
50. *London Evening Post*, 23–25 December 1766.
51. *St James's Chronicle*, 20–22 March 1766.
52. J.M. Brereton and A.C.S. Savory, *The History of the Duke of Wellington's Regiment (West Riding), 1702–1992* (Halifax, 1993), 74–5.
53. Ibid., 55.
54. *Public Advertiser*, 22 July 1766.
55. *London Evening Post*, 12–14 February 1767.
56. *Journal of the House of Lords*, XXXII, 3–10: 24 November 1767.
57. Sale of property belonging to Captain James Jones, 23 January 1758: PRO/30/11/281, fols 44–6.
58. *St James's Chronicle*, 15–19 July 1768.
59. The lack of further children may have been due to Jemima's poor health: see p. 42.
60. Beatson, *Political Index*, II, 217.
61. Ross/I, 11–12. For the full text and provenance of Junius's authorship, see John Cannon (ed.), *The Letters of Junius* (Oxford, 1978), 463, 468–71.
62. Cannon (ed.), *Letters of Junius*, 470–1.
63. At the Court of St James, 21 November 1770: PRO/30/11/272.
64. Ross/I, 12–3; At the Court of St James, 23 January 1771: PRO/30/11/272.
65. John Alden, *Stephen Sayre: American Revolutionary Adventurer* (Baton Rouge, 1983), 67–86.
66. General return of the 33rd Foot Regiment, 22 June 1769: WO/27/16.
67. *General Evening Post*, 25–27 June 1771.
68. Ibid., 27–29 June 1771.
69. *Morning Chronicle*, 5 April 1774.
70. Review of the 33rd Foot Regiment by Sir William Howe, 31 March 1774, Plymouth: WO/27/30.
71. Roger Lamb, *Memoir of His own Life* (Dublin, 1811), 89–90; David Smith, '*Whispers across the Atlantick*': *General William Howe and the American Revolution* (London, 2017), 13.
72. War Office to Cornwallis, 5 April 1774: WO/4/92.
73. Lamb, *Memoir*, 90.
74. Brereton and Savory, *History of the Duke of Wellington's Regiment*, 106–7.
75. *Journal of the House of Lords*, XXXIV, 267–70: 30 November 1774.
76. Ibid., 363–7: 21 March 1775.
77. Inspection return, 17 July 1775: WO/27/35.
78. Brereton and Savory, *History of the Duke of Wellington's Regiment*, 57.

CHAPTER 2: THE CALL OF DUTY

1. Cornwallis to dowager countess, 2 September 1776: HMC, *Report on Various Collections*, VI, 315.
2. This attitude was true of most Britons: see Ira D. Gruber, 'The American Revolution as a Conspiracy: The British View', *William and Mary Quarterly* 26 (July 1969), 360–72.
3. *London Gazette*, 17–21 October 1775.
4. North to George III, 26 November 1775: Fortescue (ed.), *Correspondence of George the Third*, III, 294–5.
5. Germain to Cornwallis, 26 November 1775: HMC, *Report on the Manuscripts of Mrs Stopford-Sackville . . .*, 2 vols (London, 1904–10), II, 19.
6. *London Evening Post*, 28–30 November 1775.

7. Ross/I, 13; Wickwire and Wickwire, *War of Independence*, 407, endnote 1.
8. *Morning Post*, 16 January 1776.
9. Germain to Cornwallis, 6 December 1775: WLCL/PHC/12.
10. Philips to Clinton, December 1775: ibid. Philips repeated his concerns a month later: January 1776: ibid.
11. *London Chronicle*, 7–9 December 1775; *Middlesex Journal*, 14–16 December 1775.
12. David Syrett, *The Royal Navy in American Waters, 1775–1783* (Aldershot, 1989), 35–6.
13. Cornwallis to Germain, 7 March 1776: Ross/I, 21.
14. Narrative of proceedings of the Loyalists in North Carolina, 25 April 1776: Davies/XII, 112–17.
15. Germain to Clinton, 6 December 1775: Davies/XI, 203–5.
16. William B. Willcox (ed.), *The American Rebellion: Sir Henry Clinton's Narrative of his Campaigns, 1775–1782* (New Haven, 1954), 26–7.
17. Memorandum relating to the expedition, 28 June 1776: WLCL/PHC/13; Clinton to Germain, 8 July 1776: Davies/XII, 162–4.
18. Howe to Germain, 10 August 1776: HMC, *Mrs Stopford-Sackville*, II, 37–8; Richard Middleton, *The War of American Independence, 1775–1783* (Harlow, 2012), 51.
19. Lord Rawdon to earl of Huntingdon, 3 September 1776: HMC, *Report on the Manuscripts of the Late Reginald Rawdon Hastings, Esq., of the Manor House, Ashby de la Zouche*, 4 vols (London, 1928–47), III, 181.
20. Howe to Germain, 3 September 1776: Davies/XII, 216–18.
21. Stirling to Washington, 29 August 1776: *PGW*/6, 159–60. Stirling's title was not recognised in Britain.
22. Cornwallis to dowager countess, 2 September 1776: HMC, *Report on Various Collections*, VI, 315; Ira D. Gruber, *The Howe Brothers and the American Revolution* (New York, 1972), 115.
23. Howe to Germain, 30 November 1776: Davies/XII, 263.
24. 'Journal of Deputy-Adjutant-General Major Stephen Kemble': *The Kemble Papers*, Collections of the New-York Historical Society for 1883, 2 vols (New York, 1884), I, 411.
25. Howe to Germain, 30 November 1776: Davies/XII, 262–3.
26. Joseph P. Tustin (ed.), *Diary of the American War: A Hessian Journal: Captain Johann Ewald, Field Jaegers Corps* (New Haven, 1979), 18. Many attempts have been made to explain Howe's leisurely conduct during the 1776 campaign. The usual explanation is that he was reluctant to lose men, following the bloody engagement at Bunker Hill. The contrary argument, that he wanted to avoid inflicting unnecessary casualties in aid of reconciliation, is developed most fully by Gruber, *Howe Brothers*.
27. 'Journal of Kemble': *Kemble Papers*, I, 101.
28. Tustin (ed.), *Ewald Diary*, 22–4.
29. Howe to Germain, 20 December 1776: Davies/XII; Tustin (ed.), *Ewald Diary*, 24.
30. Ibid., 30.
31. Friedrich Ernst von Muenchhausen, *At General Howe's Side, 1776–1778: The Diary of General William Howe's Aide-de-Camp, Captain Friedrich von Muenchhausen*, trans. Ernst Kipping (Monmouth Beach, 1974), 6.
32. Washington to Lund Washington, 10 December 1776: *PGW*/7, 289.
33. Charles Stedman, *The History of the Origin, Progress, and Termination of the American War*, 2 vols (London, 1794), I, 219–20. See pp. 44–5 for the 1779 parliamentary enquiry.
34. Howe to Germain, 20 December 1776: Davies/XII, 266–7.
35. Ibid., 267.
36. *Examination of Lieutenant-General the Earl Cornwallis before a Committee of the House of Commons upon Sir William Howe's papers, 6 May 1779*, John Almon (ed.), *The Parliamentary Register, or History of the Proceedings and Debates of the House of Commons, First Series: 1774–1780*, 17 vols (London, 1775–80), XIII, 4–5. (Henceforth the First Series is cited unless otherwise specified.)
37. David Hackett Fischer, *Washington's Crossing* (New York, 2004), 189–90.
38. Muenchhausen, *At General Howe's Side*, 8.
39. Fischer, *Washington's Crossing*, 290–1.

40. Brereton and Savory, *History of the Duke of Wellington's Regiment*, 67.
41. Fischer, *Washington's Crossing*, 299–307.
42. Ibid., 317–19.
43. Washington to Hancock, 5 January 1777: *PGW*/7, 519–23.
44. According to Ewald, *Diary*, 50–1, the army left behind its stores, sick and wounded, and most of its baggage. For secondary accounts see John Ferling, *Almost a Miracle: The American Victory in the War of Independence* (New York, 2007), 182–6.
45. Cornwallis to Germain, 8 January 1777: WLCL, Lord George Germain Papers, V.
46. Howe to Germain, 5 January 1777: Davies/XIV, 27–8.
47. Muenchhausen, *At General Howe's Side*, 8.
48. Howe to Germain, 20 December 1776: Davies/XII, 268–9.
49. Howe to Germain, 20 January 1777: Davies/XIV, 33.
50. *Narrative of Lieutenant-General Sir William Howe in a Committee of the House of Commons, 29 April 1779*, Almon (ed.), *Parliamentary Register*, XII, 319–50.
51. *Examination of Lieutenant-General the Earl Cornwallis*: ibid., XIII, 5.
52. R. Arthur Bowler, *Logistics and the Failure of the British Army in America, 1775–1783* (Princeton, 1975), 69.
53. Tustin (ed.), *Ewald Diary*, 53–4.
54. Howe to Germain, 24 April 1777: Davies/XIV, 72; Washington to Owen Biddle, 14 April 1777: *PGW*/9, 157–8.
55. Howe to Germain, 2 April 1777: Davies/XIV, 64–5.
56. Howe to Carleton, 5 April 1777: ibid., 66–7.
57. Howe to Germain, 20 January 1777: ibid., 33.
58. Howe to Germain, 5 July 1777: ibid., 127–9; Gruber, *Howe Brothers*, 227–9.
59. William Abbatt (ed.), *Major Andre's Journal, Operations of the British Army under Lieutenant-Generals Sir William Howe and Sir Henry Clinton* (Tarrytown, 1930), 25–8.
60. Howe to Germain, 5 July 1777: Davies/XIV, 127–9; Abbatt (ed.), *Major Andre's Journal*, 31–3; Muenchhausen, *At General Howe's Side*, 20.
61. Willcox (ed.), *American Rebellion*, 65, endnote 15.
62. Ibid., 65.
63. Abbatt (ed.), *Major Andre's Journal*, 34.
64. Muenchhausen, *At General Howe's Side*, 21.
65. Muenchhausen noted headquarters' concern that the rebels were said to have fifty-two cannon on an island in the river: ibid., 23.
66. Syrett, *Royal Navy in American Waters*, 78–80.
67. Tustin (ed.), *Ewald Diary*, 74; Ira D. Gruber (ed.), *John Peebles' American War: The Diary of a Scottish Grenadier, 1776–1782* (Mechanicsville, 1998), 131.
68. Abbatt (ed.), *Major Andre's Journal*, 36; Syrett, *Royal Navy in American Waters*, 78–9.
69. Gruber (ed.), *John Peebles' American War*, 119.
70. Abbatt (ed.), *Major Andre's Journal*, 38–42.
71. Tustin (ed.), *Ewald Diary*, 83–4.
72. Quoted in Matthew H. Spring, *With Zeal and with Bayonets only: The British Army on Campaign in North America, 1775–1783* (Norman, 2008), 73–4.
73. Howe to Germain, 10 October 1777: Davies/XIV, 202–4; Abbatt (ed.), *Major Andre's Journal*, 45–7. For Washington's account, see his letter to Hancock, 11 September 1777: *PGW*/11, 200–1.
74. Abbatt (ed.), *Major Andre's Journal*, 47.
75. Howe to Germain, 10 October 1777: Davies/XIV, 206.
76. Gruber (ed.), *John Peebles' American War*, 138.
77. Howe to Germain, 10 October 1777: Davies/XIV, 206–8; Abbatt (ed.), *Major Andre's Journal*, 54–7.
78. Washington to Hancock, 10 August 1777: *PGW*/10, 569–74.
79. Stedman, *American War*, I, 296–7.
80. Gruber (ed.), *John Peebles' American War*, 149.

81. Lord Howe to Philip Steven, 25 October 1777: Davies/XIV, 243–6. Syrett, *Royal Navy in American Waters*, 81–4.
82. Howe to Germain, 28 November 1777: Davies/XIV, 263–4.
83. Cornwallis to dowager countess, 29 November 1777: HMC, *Report on Various Collections*, VI, 315–16.
84. Abbatt (ed.), *Major Andre's Journal*, 66.
85. Howe to Germain, 13 December 1777: Davies/XIV, 272–3.
86. Ibid., 272.
87. Stedman, *American War*, I, 308–9.
88. Howe to Germain, 13 December 1777: Ross/I, 30–1.
89. Cornwallis-West, *Admiral Cornwallis*, 82.
90. Tustin (ed.), *Ewald Diary*, 110.
91. *Daily Advertiser*, 20 January 1778.
92. *General Evening Post*, 17–20 January 1778.
93. Howe to Germain, 16 January 1778: Davies/XV, 29.
94. Wickwire and Wickwire, *War of Independence*, 105.
95. *St James's Chronicle*, 26 February 1778; *Morning Chronicle*, 10 March 1778.
96. *St James's Chronicle*, 17–19 March 1778.
97. Ross/I, 32.
98. *Journal of the House of Lords*, XXXV, 375–7: 17 March 1778; ibid., 388: 23 March 1778.
99. Ross/I, 32; *Journal of the House of Lords*, XXXV, 420–5: 7 April 1778.
100. George III to Cornwallis, 10 March 1778: PRO/30/11/60.
101. Germain to Cornwallis, 12 April 1778: Ross/I, 33.
102. Germain to Clinton, 12 April 1778: WLCL/PHC/33.
103. Cornwallis to Clinton, 12 March 1778: WLCL/PHC/32.
104. Tustin (ed.), *Ewald Diary*, 123.
105. *St James's Chronicle*, 11–14 April 1778.
106. Ross/I, 13, footnote 5.
107. Carlyle to Germain, 11 April 1778: HMC, *Mrs Stopford-Sackville*, II, 106.
108. Gruber (ed.), *John Peebles' American War*, 186.
109. Germain to Clinton, 21 March 1778: Davies/XV, 74–6.
110. Cornwallis to Germain, 17 June 1778: Ross/I, 33.
111. Piers Mackesy, *The War for America, 1775–1783* (Cambridge, MA, 1964), 189.
112. Abbatt (ed.), *Major Andre's Journal*, 77. The mistreatment of the inhabitants by British troops is discussed in Stephen Conway, '"The Great Mischief Complain'd of": Reflections on the Misconduct of British Soldiers in the Revolutionary War', *William and Mary Quarterly* 47 (July 1990), 370–90.
113. Clinton to Germain, 5 July 1778: Davies/XV, 159–61.
114. Quoted in Spring, *With Zeal and with Bayonets*, 239.
115. Clinton to Germain, 5 July 1778: Davies/XV, 161–3; William B. Willcox, *Portrait of a General: Sir Henry Clinton in the War of American Independence* (New York, 1964), 231–6. For Washington's account of the battle, see his letter to Henry Laurens, 1 July 1778: *PGW*/16, 2–6.
116. Clinton to Germain, 5 July 1778: Davies/XV, 163.
117. Germain to Clinton, 8 March 1778: ibid., 58–62.
118. Cornwallis to Clinton, 20 August 1778: WLCL/PHC/39. Ross's appointment as aide had been announced on Cornwallis's return to Philadelphia: Headquarters, 10 June 1778: *Kemble Papers*, I, 592.
119. Clinton to Germain, 8 October 1778: Davies/XV, 210–11.
120. Cornwallis to Clinton, 28 September 1778: Ross/I, 35; Abbatt (ed.), *Major Andre's Journal*, 97–8.
121. Baylor to Washington, 19 October 1778: *PGW*/17, 456–7.
122. Clinton to Germain, 8 October 1778: Davies/XV, 210–11.
123. Cornwallis-West, *Admiral Cornwallis*, 86.
124. Clinton to Germain, 8 October 1778: Davies/XV, 209–10.

125. Clinton to Germain, 24 November 1778: Ross/I, 37–8.
126. Gruber (ed.), *John Peebles' American War*, 233.
127. Cornwallis to William Cornwallis, 22 December 1777: HMC, *Report on Various Collections*, VI, 319.
128. Cornwallis to Clinton, 22 January 1779: WLCL/PHC/51.
129. Memorandum on Clinton's successor, 26 December 1778: KRO/U/1350/O/74/22; *Public Ledger*, 23 December 1778.
130. Cornwallis to Clinton, 22 January 1779: WLCL/PHC/51.
131. Wickwire and Wickwire, *War of Independence*, 114.
132. Cornwallis to William Cornwallis, 21 October 1779: HMC, *Report on Various Collections*, VI, 321–2.
133. Cornwallis to Clinton, 4 April 1779: WLCL/PHC/55.
134. Cornwallis to William Cornwallis, 5 May 1779: HMC. *Report on Various Collections*, VI, 319.
135. Amherst to Germain, 9 April 1779: WO/34/229; Amherst to George III, 10 April 1779: KRO/U/1350/O/74/31.
136. Germain to Clinton, 11 April 1779: Ross/I, 38–9.
137. Amherst to Cornwallis, 15 April 1779: WO/34/229.
138. Cornwallis to William Cornwallis, 5 May 1779: HMC, *Report on Various Collections*, VI, 319.
139. Gruber, *Howe Brothers*, 340–1.
140. Cornwallis to Clinton, 4 April 1799: WLCL/PHC/55.
141. *Examination of Lieutenant-General Earl Cornwallis*, Almon (ed.), *Parliamentary Register*, XIII, 1–16.
142. Gruber (ed.), *John Peebles' American War*, 280–1.
143. *Examination of Lieutenant-General Earl Cornwallis*: Almon (ed.), *Parliamentary Register*, XIII, 17–32.
144. Directions for Lord Cornwallis's health, undated (*c.* April 1779): PRO/30/11/277; prescription from Robert Knox, 15 May 1779: ibid.
145. *St James's Chronicle*, 3–5 June 1779.

CHAPTER 3: IMPLEMENTING BRITAIN'S SOUTHERN STRATEGY

1. Clinton to Germain, 20 August 1779: Davies/XVII, 188–9.
2. Quoted in Willcox (ed.), *American Rebellion*, xxxii.
3. Gruber (ed.), *John Peebles' American War*, 284.
4. Clinton to Cornwallis, 23 September 1779: PRO/30/11/61; Clinton to Germain, 26 September 1779: Davies/XVII, 221–2.
5. Arbuthnot to Sandwich, 19 September 1779: G.R. Barnes and J.H. Owen (eds), *The Private Papers of John, Earl of Sandwich, 1771–1782*, 4 vols (London, 1933–38), III, 134–5.
6. Clinton to Germain, 30 September 1779: Davies/XVII, 229–30.
7. Germain to Clinton, 7 March 1778: Davies/XV, 60–1.
8. Clinton to Germain, 25 October 1778: ibid., 232.
9. Middleton, *War of American Independence*, 127–32.
10. Mackesy, *War for America*, 277–8.
11. Memorandum, 11 December 1779: WLCL/PHC/80.
12. Clinton to Newcastle, 12 December 1779: ibid.
13. Clinton to Smith, 5 March 1780: WLCL/PHC/88.
14. Clinton memorandum, undated (*c.* 31 March–2 April 1780): WLCL/PHC/90.
15. Cornwallis to William Cornwallis, 21 October 1779: HMC, *Report on Various Collections*, VI, 321–2.
16. Cornwallis to dowager countess, 11 November 1779: ibid., 323.
17. Gruber (ed.), *John Peebles' American War*, 318–19.
18. Clinton to Germain, 9 March 1780: Davies/XVIII, 54.
19. Gruber (ed.), *John Peebles' American War*, 342; Carl P. Borick, *A Gallant Defense: The Siege of Charleston, 1780* (Columbia, 2003), 62–3.

20. Tustin (ed.), *Ewald Diary*, 205–6.
21. Clinton to Germain, 9 March 1780: Davies/XVIII, 54.
22. Clinton to Smith, 5 March 1780: WLCL/PHC/88.
23. Germain to Clinton, 4 November 1779: Davies/XVII, 250.
24. Clinton to William Eden, 20 March 1780: WLCL/PHC/89.
25. Clinton memorandum, undated (*c.* 2 April 1780): WLCL/PHC/90.
26. William T. Bulger (ed.), 'Sir Henry Clinton's "Journal of the Siege of Charleston"', *South Carolina Historical Magazine* 66 (July 1965), 147–74; 149.
27. Clinton memorandum, undated (*c.* 2 April 1780): WLCL/PHC/90.
28. Ibid.
29. Ibid.
30. Memorandum of a conversation with Cornwallis, 3 April 1780: WLCL/PHC/91.
31. Germain to Clinton, 4 November 1779: Davies/XVII, 251–2.
32. Willcox, *Portrait of a General*, 316–18.
33. Bulger (ed.), 'Sir Henry Clinton's "Journal"', undated (*c.* 2 April 1780), 150; ibid., 5 April 1780, 153–4; Clinton to Cornwallis, 6 April 1780: WLCL/PHC/91.
34. Bulger (ed.), 'Sir Henry Clinton's "Journal"', 5 April 1780, 154.
35. Ibid., 4 April 1780, 153–4.
36. Philips to Clinton, December 1775: WLCL/PHC/12.
37. Bulger (ed.), 'Sir Henry Clinton's "Journal"', 10 April 1780, 158.
38. Ibid., 2 April 1780, 150.
39. Stedman, *American War*, II, 179–80; Borick, *Gallant Defense*, 133–5.
40. Clinton to Arbuthnot, 8 April 1780: WLCL/PHC/92.
41. Arbuthnot to Clinton, 22 April 1780: WLCL/PHC/94; Stedman, *American War*, II, 179–80.
42. Clinton to Cornwallis, 23 April 1780: WLCL/PHC/94.
43. Robert D. Bass, *The Green Dragoon: The Lives of Banastre Tarleton and Mary Robinson* (Orangeburg, SC, 1973), 47–8.
44. Cornwallis to Tarleton, 25 April 1780: Saberton/I, 24–5.
45. Cornwallis to Clinton, 26 April 1780: WLCL/PHC/95; Arbuthnot to Clinton, 27 April 1780: ibid.
46. Arbuthnot to Germain, 15 May 1780: HMC, *Mrs Stopford-Sackville*, II, 164.
47. Bulger (ed.), 'Sir Henry Clinton's "Journal"', 26 April 1780, 166; Willcox, *Portrait of a General*, 318–19.
48. Cornwallis to Clinton, 7 May 1780: Saberton/I, 20–1.
49. Clinton to Germain, 13 May 1780: Davies/XVIII, 86–9; Borick, *Gallant Defense*, 217–22.
50. Stedman, *American War*, II, 185–6.
51. For Clinton's relationship with Arbuthnot, see Willcox, *Portrait of a General*, 283 *passim*.
52. Clinton to Germain, 13 May 1780: Davies/XVIII, 89.
53. Borick, *Gallant Defense*, 219–20.
54. Cornwallis to Amherst, 13 May 1780: WO/34/163.
55. Clinton to Germain, 14 May 1780: Davies/XVIII, 90–1; Willcox (ed.), *American Rebellion*, 177.
56. Cornwallis to Leslie, 12 November 1780: Ross/I, 68–9.
57. Clinton to Eden, 30 May 1780: WLCL/PHC/102.
58. Ordered by Sir Henry Clinton, 12 May 1780: Willcox (ed.), *American Rebellion*, 440–1; Banastre Tarleton, *A History of the Campaigns of 1780 and 1781, in the Southern Provinces of North America* (London, 1787), 68–70.
59. Clinton to Ferguson, 22 May 1780: Willcox (ed.), *American Rebellion*, 441; Clinton to Cornwallis, 28 May 1780: Saberton/I, 53.
60. Clinton to Eden, 30 May 1780: WLCL/PHC/102.
61. Cornwallis to Clinton, 18 May 1780: Saberton/I, 43–4.
62. Cornwallis to Clinton, 30 May 1780: WLCL/PHC/102.
63. Tarleton to Cornwallis, 29 May 1780: ibid.
64. Tarleton to Cornwallis, 30 May 1780: Davies/XVIII, 99–100; Tarleton, *History of the Campaigns*, 28–31; Bass, *Green Dragoon*, 78–83.

65. Cornwallis to Clinton, 2 June 1780: Saberton/I, 54–5.
66. Draft plan, 4 June 1780: ibid., 123–4. The islands chosen were James, Johns, Edisto, Saint Helena, and Port Royal.
67. Stedman, *American War*, II, 195–6.
68. Clinton to Cornwallis, 1 June 1780: Saberton/I, 56–9.
69. Rankin to Clinton, 20 May 1780: WLCL/PHC/99.
70. Clinton to Cornwallis, 1 June 1780: Saberton/I, 60–2.
71. A proclamation, 1 June 1780: Tarleton, *History of the Campaigns*, 74–6.
72. Willcox (ed.), *American Rebellion*, 181.
73. Proclamation of His Excellency, 3 June 1780: WLCL/PHC/103; Stedman, *American War*, II, 194–5.
74. Cornwallis to Clinton, 30 June 1780: Saberton/I, 161.
75. Cornwallis to Patterson, 10 June 1780: Ross/I, 46; Cornwallis to Balfour, 11 June 1780: ibid., 46–7.
76. Cornwallis to Arbuthnot, 29 June 1780: Saberton/I, 159.
77. Stedman, *American War*, II, 198–9.
78. Rawdon to Cornwallis, 7 July 1780: Saberton/I, 193–4.
79. Stedman, *American War*, II, 198–9, 213–4.
80. Franklin Benjamin Hough, *The Siege of Charleston under the Command of Admiral Marriott Arbuthnot and Sir Henry Clinton* (Albany, 1862), 202.
81. Cornwallis to Balfour, 17 July 1780: Saberton/I, 250.
82. Cornwallis to Clinton, 30 June 1780: ibid., 160–1.
83. Cornwallis to William Cornwallis, 4 July 1780: HMC, *Report on Various Collections*, VI, 325.
84. Cornwallis to Clinton, 14 July 1780: Saberton/I, 168–9.
85. Colonel George Turnbull to Rawdon, 12 July 1780: ibid., 201; Bass, *Green Dragoon*, 89.
86. Rawdon to Cornwallis, 2 July 1780: Saberton/I, 190.
87. Cornwallis to Rawdon, 6 July 1780: ibid., 191.
88. Cornwallis to Clinton, 15 July 1780: ibid., 170.
89. Ferguson to Cornwallis, 20 July 1780: ibid., 293.
90. Balfour to Cornwallis, 20 July 1780: ibid., 253.
91. Cornwallis to Brown, 17 July 1780: ibid., 274–5.
92. A proclamation, by the Right Honourable Charles Earl Cornwallis, 18 July 1780: Tarleton, *History of the Campaigns*, 121–2.
93. Ibid., 122–6.
94. Stedman, *American War*, II, 197–8.
95. John S. Pancake, *This Destructive War: The British Campaign in the Carolinas, 1780–1782* (Tuscaloosa, 1985), 67.
96. Cornwallis to Clinton, 6 August 1780: Saberton/I, 175–9.
97. Martin to Germain: Davies/XVIII, 140.
98. Cornwallis to Clinton, 23 August 1780; Saberton/II, 15–16.
99. Return of troops at Camden, 13 August 1780: Saberton/II, 233–4.
100. Cornwallis to Germain, 21 August 1780: Saberton/II, 12. The American numbers were closer to 1,000 Continentals and 3,000 militia.
101. Cornwallis to Germain, 21 August 1780: Davies/XVIII, 149.
102. Ibid., 149–50.
103. Pancake, *This Destructive War*, 104–5.
104. Stedman, *American War*, II, 209; Tarleton, *History of the Campaigns*, 106–7.
105. Quoted in Spring, *With Zeal and with Bayonets*, 113–14.
106. Gates to the president of Congress, 20 August 1780: Tarleton, *History of the Campaigns*, 145–7.
107. Cornwallis to Germain, 21 August 1780: Saberton/II, 14.
108. Cornwallis to Clinton, 23 August 1780: ibid., 16–17.
109. Ibid., 16.
110. Clinton to Germain, 20 September 1780: Davies/XVIII, 171.

111. Cornwallis to Amherst, 21 August 1780: Saberton/II, 21.
112. Amherst to Germain, 6 November 1780: Saberton/III, 46.
113. Cornwallis to Germain, 21 August 1780: Saberton/II, 14.
114. Cornwallis to Cruger, 18 August 1780: ibid., 19.
115. Cornwallis to Clinton, 3 September 1780: ibid., 43.
116. Ibid., 43–4.
117. Cornwallis to Wemyss, 28 August 1780: Saberton/II, 208–9.
118. Cornwallis to Wemyss, 31 August 1780: ibid., 210.
119. Cornwallis to Balfour, 3–6 September 1780: ibid., 71.
120. Cornwallis to Balfour, 10 November 1780: Saberton/III, 69.
121. Cornwallis to Balfour, 3 September 1780: Saberton/II, 71–3.
122. Cornwallis to Balfour, 12 September 1780: ibid., 79–80.
123. Cornwallis to Balfour, 18 September 1780: ibid., 86.

CHAPTER 4: TAKING THE WAR TO THE ENEMY

1. Cornwallis to Clinton, 22 September 1780: Saberton/II, 44–6.
2. Ibid., 46.
3. Cornwallis to Balfour, 27 September 1780: Saberton/II, 100.
4. Ibid., 99; Stedman, *American War*, II, 216.
5. A proclamation, 27 September 1780: Saberton/II, 332.
6. Cornwallis to Balfour, 3 July 1780: Saberton/I, 245.
7. Cornwallis to Clinton, 29 August 1780: Saberton/II, 42; Cornwallis to Balfour, 29 August 1780: ibid., 64–5.
8. A declaration, 9 September 1780: ibid., 150–1.
9. Ferguson to Cornwallis, 28 September 1780: ibid., 159.
10. Cornwallis to Ferguson, 5 October 1780: ibid., 161; Cornwallis to Balfour, 5 October 1780: ibid., 109.
11. Ferguson to Cornwallis, 6 October 1780: ibid., 165.
12. Captain DePeyster to Cornwallis, 11 October 1780: ibid., 166–7.
13. Ferling, *Almost a Miracle*, 462–3.
14. Cornwallis to Clinton, 3 December 1780: Ross/I, 497–500.
15. Rawdon to Clinton, 29 October 1780: ibid., 62–3.
16. Ibid., 62.
17. Balfour to Rawdon, 26 October 1780: Saberton/II, 131; Elizabeth Fenn, *Pox Americana: The Great Smallpox Epidemic of 1775–1782* (New York, 2002), 118–24, notes that yellow fever and malaria were widespread at this time in the Carolinas.
18. Stedman, *American War*, II, 224–5.
19. Clinton to Leslie, 10 October 1780: Saberton/II, 50.
20. Rawdon to Leslie, 24 October 1780: Davies/XVIII, 56–7.
21. Rawdon to Clinton, 28 October 1780: Saberton/II, 57–9.
22. Cornwallis to Balfour, 1 November 1780: Saberton/III, 59.
23. Cornwallis to Balfour, 10 November 1780: ibid., 68–9.
24. Tarleton to Turnbull, 5 November 1780: ibid., 333–4.
25. Cornwallis to Tarleton, 9 November 1780: ibid., 335.
26. Tarleton to Cornwallis, 11 November 1780: ibid., 336–7.
27. A proclamation, 11 November 1780: ibid., 338.
28. Cornwallis to Tarleton, 9 November 1780: ibid., 335.
29. Tarleton to Cornwallis, 24 November 1780: ibid., 341; Cornwallis to Clinton, 3 December 1780: ibid., 25–6.
30. Balfour to Cornwallis, 17 November 1780: ibid., 85; Bass, *Green Dragoon*, 113.
31. Washington to Clinton, 6 October 1780: Saberton/III, 15–16.
32. Clinton to Washington, 6 October 1780: ibid., 16.
33. Washington to Clinton, 16 October 1780: ibid., 17.

34. Cornwallis to Clinton, 4 December 1780: ibid., 27–8.
35. Cornwallis to Clinton, 3 December 1780: ibid., 27.
36. Clinton to Cornwallis, 13 December 1780: ibid., 32.
37. Cornwallis to Clinton, 29 December 1780: Ross/I, 76.
38. Cornwallis to Balfour, 1 January 1781: Saberton/III, 119; Cornwallis to Rawdon, 31 December 1780: ibid., 234–5.
39. Cornwallis to Balfour, 5 January 1781: ibid., 123–4.
40. Cornwallis to Hayes, 5 December 1780: ibid., 461.
41. Isaac Allen to Cornwallis, 31 December 1780, ibid., 290.
42. Cornwallis to Tarleton, 2 January 1781: Tarleton, *History of the Campaigns*, 244–5.
43. Tarleton to Cornwallis, 4 January 1781: ibid., 245–6.
44. Cornwallis to Tarleton, 5 January 1780: ibid., 246–7.
45. Cornwallis to Tarleton, 11 January 1781: ibid., 248; Cornwallis to Balfour, 12 January 1781: Saberton/III, 133.
46. Cornwallis to Tarleton, 7 January 1781: ibid., 362–3.
47. Tarleton to Cornwallis, 16 January 1781: ibid., 365–6.
48. Tarleton, *History of the Campaigns*, 214–18; Morgan to Greene, 19 January 1781: Richard K. Showman, et al. (eds), *The Papers of General Nathanael Greene*, 13 vols (Chapel Hill, 1976–2005), VII, 152–5; Don Higginbotham, *Daniel Morgan: Revolutionary Rifleman* (Chapel Hill, 1961), 135–55.
49. Stedman, *American War*, II, 325.
50. Cornwallis's report to Clinton appears to have relied on Tarleton's verbal account only, 18 January 1781: Saberton/III, 35–6.
51. Cornwallis to Tarleton, 30 January 1781: Tarleton, *History of the Campaigns*, 252.
52. Cornwallis to Germain, 18 January 1781: Saberton/III, 47.
53. Tarleton, *History of the Campaigns*, 218–22.
54. Roderick Mackenzie, *Strictures on Lt Col. Tarleton's 'History of the Campaigns of 1780 and 1781 in the Southern Provinces of North America'* (London, 1787), 107–10. Similar charges were made by Stedman, *American War*, II, 324–5.
55. Cornwallis to Rawdon, 21 January 1781: Saberton/III, 251.
56. Cornwallis to Clinton, 18 January 1781: Davies/XX, 32–3.
57. Cornwallis to Germain, 17 March 1781: ibid., 86.
58. O'Hara to Grafton, 20 April 1781: George C. Rogers, Jr (ed.), 'Letters of Charles O'Hara to the Duke of Grafton', *South Carolina Historical Magazine* 65 (July 1964), 158–80; 173–4.
59. Cornwallis to Rawdon, 21 January 1781: Saberton/III, 251.
60. Cornwallis to Howard, 22 January 1781, ibid., 375.
61. Cornwallis to Rawdon, 25 January 1781: ibid., 252.
62. Cornwallis to Greene, 4 February 1781: Saberton/IV, 74–5. An agreement was eventually reached on 3 May 1781: ibid., 88.
63. Cornwallis to Rawdon, 25 January 1781: Saberton/III, 252.
64. O'Hara to Grafton, 20 April 1781: Rogers (ed.), 'Letters of Charles O'Hara', 174.
65. Stedman, *American War*, II, 326.
66. O'Hara to Grafton, 20 April 1781: Rogers (ed.), 'Letters of Charles O'Hara', 174.
67. Roger Lamb, *An Original and Authentic Journal of Occurrences during the Late American War: From Its Commencement to the Year 1783* (Dublin, 1809), 343–4.
68. Cornwallis to Germain, 7 March 1781: Davies/XX, 86–9.
69. Greene to Washington, 15 February 1781: Showman, et al. (eds), *Papers of General Nathanael Greene*, VII, 293.
70. Greene to Steuben, 15 February 1781: Willcox (ed.), *American Rebellion*, 487.
71. Cornwallis to Craig, 21 February 1781: Saberton/IV, 25.
72. Cornwallis to Rawdon, 30 February 1781: Ross/I, 84.
73. Headquarters, 16–17 February 1781: WLCL, Cornwallis Orderly Book.
74. A proclamation, 20 February 1781: Saberton/IV, 55.

75. Lee to Greene, 23 February 1781: Showman, et al. (eds), *Papers of General Nathanael Greene*, VII, 336.
76. Greene to Washington, 28 February 1781: ibid., 369.
77. Cornwallis to Germain, 17 March 1781: Davies/XX, 88–9; Lee to Greene, 25 February 1781: Showman, et al. (eds), *Papers of General Nathanael Greene*, VII, 347–8.
78. Stedman, *American War*, II, 334–5.
79. Cornwallis to Craig, 5 March 1781: Saberton/IV, 26.
80. Cornwallis to Germain, 17 March 1781: ibid., 17. Greene's actual numbers were around 4,500.
81. Cornwallis to Germain, 17 March 1781: ibid., 17–18.
82. Lamb, *Original and Authentic Journal*, 362.
83. Lawrence E. Babits and Joshua B. Howard, *Long, Obstinate and Bloody: The Battle of Guilford Court House* (Chapel Hill, 2009), 161–2, traces the origins of this story to Henry Lee's *Memoirs*, who at this point was on the American left dealing with the Hessian Regiment von Bose and not in a position to observe the incident. There is also no mention of the incident in Cornwallis's correspondence or that of O'Hara to Grafton.
84. Cornwallis to Germain, 17 March 1781: Saberton/IV, 18–19.
85. Greene to president of Congress, 16 March 1781: Showman, et al. (eds), *Papers of General Nathanael Greene*, VII, 433–5.
86. Casualties at the Battle of Guilford, 15 March 1781: Ross/I, 85–6. The total deployed were 1,638 rank and file and 286 officers and non-commissioned officers, making a total of 1,924.
87. O'Hara to Grafton, 20 April 1781: Rogers (ed.), 'Letters of Charles O'Hara', 177–8. An equally grim picture was painted by Stedman, *American War*, II, 346.
88. Greene to the president of Congress, 16 March 1781: Showman, et al. (eds), *Papers of General Nathanael Greene*, VII, 435; ibid., 440–1, endnote 16.
89. 16 March 1781: WLCL, Cornwallis Orderly Book.
90. Cornwallis to Germain, 17 March 1781: Saberton/IV, 19.
91. Cornwallis to Philips, 10 April 1781: ibid., 114.
92. Stedman, *American War*, II, 347.
93. Ibid., 346.
94. Cornwallis to Balfour, 21 February 1781: Saberton/IV, 41–2.
95. Cornwallis to Greene, 16 March 1781: Showman, et al. (eds), *Papers of General Nathanael Greene*, VII, 443.
96. Greene to Cornwallis, 17 March 1781: ibid., 444.
97. 21 March 1781: WLCL, Cornwallis Orderly Book.
98. Highlanders to Cornwallis, undated (*c.* March 1781): Saberton/IV, 59–60.
99. Cornwallis to Balfour, 5 April 1781: ibid., 42–3.
100. Draft summons to arms, undated (*c.* late March 1781): ibid., 59.
101. O'Hara to Grafton, 20 April 1781: Rogers (ed.), 'Letters of Charles O'Hara', 177.
102. State of the troops fit for duty, 15 January to 1 April 1781: Saberton/IV, 61–2.
103. O'Hara to Grafton, 20 April 1781: Rogers (ed.), 'Letters of Charles O'Hara', 173–4.
104. Cornwallis to Balfour, 5 April 1781: Saberton/IV, 42–3.
105. Cornwallis to Balfour, 6 April 1781: ibid., 43–4.
106. Cornwallis to Germain, 18 April 1781: Davies/XX, 112.
107. Cornwallis to Dr Webster, 23 April 1781: Ross/I, 92.
108. Gruber (ed.), *John Peebles' American War*, 440.
109. Rawdon to Cornwallis, 7 March 1781: Saberton/IV, 47–9.
110. Cornwallis to Philips, 10 April 1781: Ross/I, 87.
111. Cornwallis to Clinton, 10 April 1781: Davies/XX, 108.
112. McAlester to Cornwallis, undated (*c.* March 1781): Saberton/IV, 138–9.
113. Greene to Washington, 29 March 1781: Showman, et al. (eds), *Papers of General Nathanael Greene*, VII, 481–2.
114. Cornwallis to Rawdon, 15 April 1781: Saberton/IV, 121; Cornwallis to Balfour, 21 April 1781: ibid., 121–2.

115. Cornwallis to Balfour, 22 April 1781: ibid., 122.
116. Cornwallis to Germain, 23 April 1781: ibid., 107.
117. Ibid.
118. Cornwallis to Clinton, 23 April 1781: ibid., 112–13.
119. Cornwallis to Balfour, 24 April 1781: ibid., 122.
120. State of the troops at Wilmington, 15 April 1781: ibid., 142–4; Wickwire and Wickwire, *War of Independence*, 454–5.
121. Cornwallis to Balfour, 30 April 1781: Saberton/IV, 175–6.
122. Cornwallis to Tarleton, 5 May 1781: ibid., 157.
123. Cornwallis to Tarleton, 8 May 1781: ibid., 162.
124. Cornwallis to Craig, 12 May 1781: ibid., 168; 14 May 1781: WLCL, Cornwallis Orderly Book.
125. Cornwallis to Tarleton, 14 May 1781: Saberton/IV 153; John Graves Simcoe, *A Journal of the Queen's Rangers* (Philadelphia, 1844), 209.

CHAPTER 5: RECKONING AT YORKTOWN

1. Cornwallis to Rawdon, 20 May 1781: Ross/I, 98.
2. Clinton to Philips, 30 April 1781: Saberton/V, 59–61.
3. Cornwallis to Clinton, 20 May 1781: Ross/I, 99.
4. Clinton to Philips, 10 March 1781: Saberton/V, 7–9.
5. Clinton to Philips, 30 April to 3 May 1781: ibid., 59–61; William Rankin's proposals (undated enclosure): ibid., 61–2.
6. Lieutenant George Robertson to Cornwallis, 22 May 1781: ibid., 206.
7. Cornwallis to Clinton, 26 May 1781: ibid., 89–90.
8. Ibid.
9. Ibid., 91.
10. Cornwallis to Clinton, 30 June 1781: Saberton/V, 104.
11. 3 June 1781: WLCL, Cornwallis Orderly Book; Simcoe, *Journal*, 212.
12. Lafayette to Greene, 18 June 1781: Showman, et al. (eds), *Papers of General Nathanael Greene*, VIII, 411; Simcoe, *Journal*, 213–18.
13. Michael Kranish, *Flight from Monticello: Thomas Jefferson at War* (New York, 2010), 291–3.
14. Tustin (ed.), *Ewald Diary*, 305–6.
15. Clinton to Cornwallis, 29 May 1781: Saberton/V, 118–20.
16. Clinton to Cornwallis, 11 June 1781: ibid., 95–6.
17. Cornwallis to Clinton, 30 June 1781: ibid., 104–5.
18. Ibid., 106–7.
19. Cornwallis to Clinton, 8 July 1781: Saberton/V, 116–17; Paul David Nelson, *Anthony Wayne: Soldier of the Early Republic* (Bloomington, 1985), 135–7.
20. Clinton to Cornwallis, 19 June 1781: Saberton/V, 135–6.
21. Clinton to Cornwallis, 8 July 1781: ibid., 140–2.
22. Clinton to Philips, 10 March 1781: ibid., 8.
23. Patterson to Germain, 22 February 1780: Davies/XVIII, 50.
24. Clinton to Cornwallis, 11 July 1781: Saberton/V, 142–3; Graves to Cornwallis, 12 July 1781: ibid., 145–6.
25. Cornwallis to Clinton, 26 July 1781: Saberton/VI, 14–15.
26. Cornwallis to Rawdon, 23 July 1781: ibid., 62–3.
27. Cornwallis to O'Hara, 2 August 1781: ibid., 43–4.
28. Hudson to Cornwallis, 9 August 1781: ibid., 56–7.
29. Cornwallis to Clinton, 12 August 1781: ibid., 19.
30. Cornwallis to Clinton, 16 August 1781: ibid., 24–5.
31. Cornwallis to O'Hara, 4 August 1781: ibid., 44.
32. O'Hara to Cornwallis, 5 August 1781: ibid., 44–5; O'Hara to Cornwallis, 9 August 1781: ibid., 47–8.
33. Cornwallis to O'Hara, 7 August 1781: ibid., 46.

34. Cornwallis to Clinton, 22 August 1781: ibid., 27–8.
35. Cornwallis to Clinton, 20 August 1781: ibid., 26–7.
36. O'Hara to Cornwallis, 11 August 1781: ibid., 49.
37. Germain to Clinton, 4 April 1781: Davies/XX, 99; Clinton to Cornwallis, 19 June 1781: Saberton/V, 135–6.
38. Larrie D. Ferreiro, *Brothers at Arms: American Independence and the Men of France and Spain who Saved It* (New York, 2016), 256–8; Jonathan Dull, *The French Navy and American Independence: A Study of Arms and Diplomacy, 1774–1787* (Princeton, 1975), 243–4; Thomas E. Chavez, *Spain and the Independence of the United States: An Intrinsic Gift* (Albuquerque, 2002), 200–2.
39. Richard Middleton, 'Naval Resources and the British Defeat at Yorktown, 1781', *Mariner's Mirror* 100 (February 2014), 29–43.
40. Hood to Clinton, 25 August 1781: Willcox (ed.), *American Rebellion*, 561–2.
41. Cornwallis to Clinton, 31 August 1781: Saberton/VI, 29.
42. Cornwallis to Clinton, 2 September 1781: ibid., 30.
43. Cornwallis to Clinton, 4 September 1781: ibid., 30.
44. Cornwallis to Clinton, 8 September 1781: ibid., 31.
45. Syrett, *Royal Navy in American Waters*, 192–204.
46. Cornwallis to Clinton, 8 September 1781: Saberton/VI, 31.
47. Tarleton, *History of the Campaigns*, 366–8.
48. Clinton to Cornwallis, 27 August 1781: Willcox (ed.), *American Rebellion*, 562.
49. Clinton to Cornwallis, 2 September 1781: Saberton/VI, 32–3.
50. Clinton to Cornwallis, 6 September 1781: ibid., 33–4.
51. Cornwallis to Clinton, 16 September 1781: ibid., 34–5.
52. Tarleton, *History of the Campaigns*, 367–8.
53. Ibid., 369–70.
54. Charles Cornwallis, first Marquess Cornwallis, *An Answer to that Part of the Narrative of Lieutenant-General Sir Henry Clinton, KB, which Relates to the Conduct of Lieutenant-General Earl Cornwallis . . .* (London, 1783), xi–xii.
55. Cornwallis to Clinton, 29 September 1781: Saberton/VI, 36–7.
56. Clinton to Cornwallis, 24 September 1781: ibid., 35–6.
57. Cornwallis to Clinton, 29 September 1781: ibid., 36–7.
58. Clinton to Cornwallis, 25 September 1781: ibid., 37.
59. Washington to president of Congress, 1 October 1781: John C. Fitzpatrick, (ed.), *The Writings of George Washington from the Original Manuscript Sources, 1745–1799*, 39 vols (Washington, DC, 1931–44), XXIII, 158–9.
60. Cornwallis to Clinton, 3 October 1781: Saberton/VI, 38.
61. General orders, 29 September 1781: Fitzpatrick (ed.), *Writings of George Washington*, XXIII, 152.
62. Cornwallis to Clinton, 11 October 1781: Saberton/VI, 39–40.
63. Clinton to Cornwallis, 30 September 1781: ibid., 38–9.
64. Cornwallis to Clinton, 12 October 1781: ibid., 40.
65. Journal of the operations of the French corps under comte de Rochambeau: Tarleton, *History of the Campaigns*, 444.
66. Cornwallis to Clinton, 15 October 1781: Saberton/VI, 40–1.
67. Washington's diary for 9 October 1781: Donald Jackson and Dorothy Twohig (eds.), *The Diaries of George Washington*, 6 vols (Charlottesville, 1976–79), III, 426.
68. Washington's diary for 16 October 1781: Jackson and Twohig (eds), *Diaries*, III, 429.
69. Cornwallis to Clinton, 20 October 1781: Davies/XX, 246.
70. Cornwallis to Clinton, 20 October 1781: Saberton/VI, 128. According to the return sent to Clinton, the army suffered 133 killed, 285 wounded, with 63 missing: WLCL/PHC/262.l.
71. Cornwallis to Washington, 17 October 1781: Saberton/VI, 112.
72. Washington to Cornwallis, 17 October 1781: ibid., 113.
73. Cornwallis to Washington, 17 October 1781: ibid., 113–14.
74. Washington to Cornwallis, 18 October 1781: ibid., 114–15.

75. Cornwallis to Washington, 18 October 1781: ibid., 115.
76. Articles of capitulation, 19 October 1781: ibid., 117–21.
77. State of the army, 18 October 1781: ibid., 116–17.
78. James Thacher, *A Military Journal during the American Revolutionary War from 1775–1783* (Boston, 1827), 289.
79. Washington's diary for 19 October 1781: Jackson and Twohig (eds), *Diaries*, III, 433; Douglas Southall Freeman, *George Washington: A Biography*, 7 vols (New York, 1948–57), V, 391.
80. Cornwallis to Clinton, 20 October 1781: Saberton/VI, 125–9.
81. Ibid.
82. William Franklin to Clinton, 19 December 1781: Davies/XX, 279–82.
83. Cornwallis parole, 28 October 1781: Saberton/VI, 131.
84. Cornwallis to Washington, 27 October 1781: ibid., 129–30; Washington to Cornwallis, 27 October 1781: ibid., 130.
85. There was a notional scale for the exchange of officers: see Proposed tariff, March 1780: PRO/30/11/6; Washington to president of Congress, 3 December 1781: Fitzpatrick (ed.), *Writings of George Washington*, XXIII, 369.
86. Freeman, *George Washington*, VI, 399.
87. Arnold Whitridge, *Rochambeau: America's Neglected Founding Father* (New York, 1965), 227–8.
88. Thacher, *Military Journal*, 302.
89. Ibid., 288–9.
90. Laurens to Cornwallis, 5 November 1781: Saberton/VI, 182.
91. Cornwallis to Rochambeau, 25 November 1781: ibid., 165; Whitridge, *Rochambeau*, 228–9.
92. Allen French (ed.), *The Diary of Frederick Mackenzie, Giving a Daily Narrative of His Military Service as an Officer of the Regiment of Royal Welch Fusiliers during the Years 1775–1781 . . .*, 2 vols (Cambridge, MA, 1930), II, 698.
93. Clinton to Germain, 29 October 1781: Davies/XX, 252–3. For an analysis of this viewpoint and other matters relating to the naval campaign, see Middleton, 'Naval Resources'.
94. Interview with Cornwallis, undated (*c.* 20 November 1781): WLCL/PHC/184.
95. French (ed.), *Diary of Frederick Mackenzie*, II, 682–3.
96. Clinton to Cornwallis, 30 November 1781: Saberton/VI, 152.
97. Cornwallis to Clinton, 2 December 1781: Davies/XX, 269.
98. Franklin to Clinton, 14 November 1781: WLCL/PHC/183.
99. Franklin to Clinton, 19 December 1781: Davies/XX, 280–1; Mary Beth Norton, *The British Americans: The Loyalist Exiles in England, 1774–1789* (London, 1974), 171.
100. French (ed.), *Diary of Frederick Mackenzie*, II, 704–5.
101. Charles Grey to Clinton, 31 January 1781: WLCL/PHC/191.
102. Deposition of the master and passengers of the Greyhound, 17 January 1782: Saberton/VI, 188–9; Franklin Wickwire and Mary Wickwire, *Cornwallis: The Imperial Years* (Chapel Hill, 1980), 3–5.
103. Charles Stevenson to Clinton, 7 February 1782: WLCL/PHC/191.
104. *General Evening Post*, 24–26 January 1782.
105. *London Courant*, 24 January 1782.
106. Norton, *British Americans*, 170.
107. Middleton, 'Naval Resources', 40–2.

CHAPTER 6: THE SEARCH FOR A NEW ROLE

1. George III to Germain, 22 January 1782: Fortescue (ed.), *Correspondence of George the Third*, V, 339.
2. Quoted in Willcox, *Portrait of a General*, 459.
3. Dowager countess to William Cornwallis, 2 April 1782: HMC, *Report on Various Collections*, VI, 330.
4. *Journal of the House of Lords*, XXXVI, 376–83: 7 February 1782; Cobbett, *Parliamentary History*, XXII, 985–9.

5. Charles Townshend to William Cornwallis, 6 February 1782: HMC, *Report on Various Collections*, VI, 327–8.
6. *Journal of the House of Lords*, XXXVI, 383–94: 11 February 1782.
7. Charles Stevenson to Clinton, 7 February 1782: WLCL/PHC/191.
8. Jervis to Clinton, 7 February 1782: ibid.
9. Charles Mellish to Clinton, 4/5 December 1781: WLCL/PHC/185; Charles Grey to Clinton, 31 January 1782: WLCL/PHC/191; Willcox, *Portrait of a General*, 456–7.
10. Charles Townshend to William Cornwallis, 6 February 1782: HMC, *Report on Various Collections*, VI, 327–8.
11. Earl A. Reitan, *Politics, Finance, and the People: Economical Reform in England in the Age of the American Revolution, 1770–1792* (Basingstoke, 2007), 64–6.
12. 'Examination of the Right Honourable Lieutenant-General Earl Cornwallis, 27 February, 1 March 1782', *The Seventh Report of the Commissioners Appointed to Examine, Take, and State, the Public Accounts of the Kingdom* (London, 1782), 32–3.
13. Clinton's response to these charges can be found in his memorandum, 'Evidence given by Cornwallis in the 7th Report of the Commissioners', June 1782: WLCL/PHC/195. For further discussion of this issue see R. Arthur Bowler, 'Sir Henry Clinton and Army Profiteering: A Neglected Aspect of the Clinton–Cornwallis Controversy', *William and Mary Quarterly* 31 (January 1974), 111–22.
14. Middleton, *War of American Independence*, 299–300.
15. Cornwallis to George III, 19 March 1782: Ross/I, 136.
16. George III to Cornwallis, 28 March 1782: ibid., 136–7.
17. Dowager countess to William Cornwallis, 3 April 1782: HMC, *Report on Various Collections*, VI, 331
18. Cornwallis to William Cornwallis, 27 May 1782: ibid., 334–5.
19. Cornwallis to William Cornwallis, 1 May 1782: ibid., 333.
20. Cornwallis to Shelburne, 31 May 1782: Ross/I, 137.
21. George III to Shelburne, 17 June 1782: Fortescue (ed.), *Correspondence of George the Third*, VI, 61.
22. Willcox, *Portrait of a General*, 471–2.
23. John Heyrick (town clerk) to Cornwallis, 11 December 1782: PRO/30/11/272.
24. Washington to Carleton, 30 July 1782: Saberton/VI, 184.
25. Cornwallis to Carleton, 4 August 1782: Ross/I, 139.
26. Cornwallis to Ross, 23 December 1782: ibid., 142–3; Cornwallis to Ross, 4 January 1783: NAM/1997/04/115/1.
27. [Clinton] to the editor of the *Morning Chronicle*, June 1782: WLCL/PHC/195.
28. Henry Clinton, *Narrative of Lieutenant-General Clinton, KB, Relative to His Conduct during Part of His Command of the King's Troops in North America . . .* (London, 1783).
29. Cornwallis to Ross, 15 January 1783: Ross/I, 144.
30. Benjamin F. Stevens (ed.), *The Campaign in Virginia, 1781: An Exact Reprint of Six Rare Pamphlets on the Clinton–Cornwallis Controversy . . .*, 2 vols (London, 1888), I, x.
31. Cornwallis to Ross, 15 January 1783: Ross/I, 144.
32. Cornwallis, *Answer to that Part of the Narrative*.
33. Richard Middleton, 'The Clinton–Cornwallis Controversy and Responsibility for the British Surrender at Yorktown', *History* 98 (2013), 370–89.
34. Stevens (ed.), *Campaign in Virginia*, I, xii–xiii.
35. Henry Clinton, *Observations on Some Parts of the Answer of Earl Cornwallis to Sir Henry Clinton's Narrative* (London, 1783).
36. Gibbon to Clinton, undated (*c.* early March 1783): WLCL/PHC/196.
37. Cornwallis to Ross, 13 August 1783: NAM/1997/04/115/1.
38. Cornwallis to Ross, 8 October 1783: ibid.
39. Cornwallis to Ross, 26 October 1783: Ross/I, 147–8.
40. Cornwallis to Ross, 5 September 1783: ibid., 146–7.
41. John Brooke, *King George III* (London, 1972), 244–5; Alfred H. Burne, *The Noble Duke of York* (London, 1949), 19.

42. Grenville to Cornwallis, 22 August 1783: Ross/I, 145–6.
43. Cornwallis to Ross, 5 September 1783: ibid., 146.
44. Cornwallis to Ross, 13 November 1783: ibid., 149.
45. Cornwallis to Ross, 23 February 1784: ibid., 160.
46. Cornwallis to Ross, 26 October 1783: ibid., 147–8.
47. Cornwallis to Ross, 13 November 1783: ibid., 149.
48. Brooke, *King George III*, 253.
49. For the political and constitutional issues, see John Ehrman, *The Younger Pitt*, 3 vols (London, 1969–96), I, 118–56.
50. Cornwallis to Ross, 16 December 1783: Ross/I, 152.
51. Cornwallis to Ross, 19 December 1783: ibid., 153.
52. Cornwallis to Ross, 2 January 1784: ibid., 154–5.
53. Cornwallis to Sydney, 8 January 1784: ibid., 155.
54. Cornwallis to William Cornwallis, 1 May 1782: HMC, *Report on Various Collections*, VI, 333.
55. Cornwallis to Ross, 2 January 1784: Ross/I, 154–5.
56. Cornwallis to Ross, 24 January 1784: ibid., 156; Norton, *British Americans*, 190–2.
57. Cornwallis to Ross, 22 January 1784: NAM/1997/04/115/1; Cornwallis to Ross, 4 March 1784: ibid.
58. Cornwallis to Ross, 7 February 1784: Ross/I, 158–9
59. Cornwallis to Ross, 17 February 1784: ibid., 160; Cornwallis to Ross, 23 February 1784: ibid., 160–1.
60. Namier and Brooke, *House of Commons*, II, 67; III, 165–6.
61. Cornwallis to Ross, 8 May 1784: Ross/I, 166–7.
62. Cornwallis to Ross, 9 May 1784: ibid., 167.
63. Cornwallis to Ross, 23 November 1783: ibid., 151.
64. Cornwallis to Ross, 9 May 1784: NAM/1997/04/115/1.
65. Cornwallis to Ross, 25 May 1784: Ross/I, 168–9.
66. Ibid.
67. Sydney to Cornwallis, 3 August 1784: Ross/I, 172–3.
68. Pitt's India Act (An Act for the Better Regulation and Management of the Affairs of the East India Company . . .), 24 Geo. 3 sess. 2 c. 25.
69. Cornwallis to Ross, 4 August 1784: Ross/I, 172.
70. Cornwallis to Sydney, 4 August 1784: ibid., 173.
71. Cornwallis to Ross, 3 September 1784: ibid., 174.
72. Cornwallis to Ross, 19 September 1784: ibid., 174.
73. Cornwallis to Ross, 4 August 1784: NAM/1997/04/115/1.
74. Cornwallis to Ross, 13 June 1784: Ross/I, 169.
75. Cornwallis to Sydney, 3 November 1784: ibid., 175–7.
76. Cornwallis to Ross, 3 November 1784: ibid., 176–7.
77. Cornwallis to Ross, 6 November 1784: ibid., 177–8.
78. Cornwallis to Pitt, 8 November 1784: ibid., 179–80.
79. Cornwallis to Ross, 10 November 1784: ibid., 181; Cornwallis to Pitt, 19 November 1781: ibid., 161.
80. The king's Most Excellent Majesty in council, 1 December 1784: PRO/30/11/272.
81. Pitt to Cornwallis, 8 February 1785: PRO/30/11/270.
82. Cornwallis to Ross, 23 February 1785: Ross/I, 184–5.
83. Cornwallis to Ross, 7 March 1785: ibid., 185.
84. Frederick II to Cornwallis, 9 August 1785: ibid., 193.
85. Carmarthen to Cornwallis, 2 September 1785: ibid., 195–7.
86. Cornwallis to Ross, 9 September 1785: ibid., 194–5.
87. Cornwallis to Ross, 5 October 1785: ibid., 204–5.
88. Cornwallis to Ross, 9 September 1785: ibid., 194–5.
89. Joseph Ewart to Carmarthen, 10 September 1785: ibid., 197–9; Cornwallis to Ross, 5 October 1785: ibid., 205.

90. Summary of what the king of Prussia said to Lord Cornwallis, 17 September 1785: ibid., 201–4.
91. Frederick II to Cornwallis, 24 September 1785: ibid., 204.
92. Cornwallis to Ross, 5 October 1785: ibid., 204–5.
93. Carmarthen to Ewart, 7 October 1785: ibid., 206.
94. Cornwallis to Ross, 5 October 1785: ibid., 204–5.
95. Cornwallis to Ross, 5 October 1785: ibid., 204–5.
96. Cornwallis to Ross, 26 November 1785: NAM/1997/04/115/1.
97. Cornwallis to Ross, 3 December 1785: ibid.
98. *The Times*, 12 December 1785; *Morning Herald and Daily Advertiser*, 19 December 1785.
99. Cornwallis to Ross, 3 December 1785: NAM/1997/04/115/1.
100. Cornwallis to Ross, 14 December 1785: ibid.
101. Ibid.
102. Cornwallis to Ross, 25 December 1785: NAM/1997/04/115/1.
103. Cornwallis to Ross, 7 January 1786: ibid.
104. Cornwallis to Ross, 30 January 1786: ibid.
105. Cornwallis to Ross, 13 February 1786: ibid. Frederick Cornwallis, archbishop of Canterbury, had died in March 1783.
106. Cornwallis to Ross, 23 February 1786: Ross/I, 208.

CHAPTER 7: GOVERNOR-GENERAL OF BENGAL

1. H.V. Bowen, *The Business of Empire: The East India Company and Imperial Britain, 1756–1833* (Cambridge, 2006), 1–18.
2. Regulating Act of 1773 (An Act for Establishing Certain Regulations for the Better Management of the Affairs of the East India Company, as well in India as in Europe), 13 Geo. 3 c. 64; G.S. Chhabra, *Advanced Study in the History of Modern India, Volume 1: 1707–1813* (New Delhi, 2011), 241–2.
3. Jeremy Bernstein, *Dawning of the Raj: The Life and Trials of Warren Hastings* (Chicago, 2000), 82–177.
4. Ehrman, *Younger Pitt*, I, 451–3.
5. Reitan, *Politics, Finance, and the People*, 62–94, 163–225.
6. Cost of making the settlement between Mr Singleton and Lady Mary, 21 April 1786: PRO/30/11/280.
7. Cornwallis to Pitt, 30 April 1786: KRO/U/24/C/5.
8. The applications can be found in PRO/30/11/137.
9. Bass, *Green Dragoon*, 250–1.
10. *The Times*, 8 April 1786.
11. Cornwallis to Wakeham, 25 February 1786: PRO/30/11/292.
12. George III to Cornwallis, 13 April 1786: PRO/30/11/195.
13. East India Company to Charles, Earl Cornwallis, 21 April 1786: ibid.
14. East India Company to Charles, Earl Cornwallis, 21 April 1786: IOR/H/24.
15. East India Company Act 1786 (An Act to Explain and Amend Certain Provisions of an Act Made in the Twenty-fourth Year of the Reign of His Present Majesty . . .), 26 Geo. 3 c. 16.
16. *Morning Chronicle*, 2 January 1786.
17. *The Times*, 23 March 1786; Almon, *Parliamentary Register, Second Series*, XIX, 412–40.
18. *The Times*, 6 April 1786.
19. Cornwallis to John Michie, 22 April 1786: IOR/H/379; Ross/I, 208–9 and endnote 1; General abstract of the private receipts and disbursements of Marquis Cornwallis whilst governor-general, 1 May 1786 to 4 July 1793: PRO/30/11/54.
20. Directors to the governor-general and council at Fort William, 12 April 1786: IOR/H/379, articles 13–29.
21. Ibid., articles 31–54.
22. Pitt's India Act, 24 Geo. 3 sess. 2 c. 25.
23. Directors to the governor-general and council at Fort William, 12 April 1786: IOR/H/379, articles 78–87.

24. William Devayne and Nathaniel Smith to Cornwallis, 12 April 1786: PRO/30/11/8.
25. Hastings to Cornwallis, (dated) March 1786: PRO/30/11/197.
26. Hastings to Cornwallis, 21 May 1786: PRO/30/11/137.
27. Minute of the Court of Directors, 11 April 1786: IOR/B/104.
28. John Shore, Baron Teignmouth, *Memoir of the Life and Correspondence of John, Lord Teignmouth*, 2 vols (London 1843), I, 118–24.
29. Cornwallis to Lichfield, 6 May 1786: Ross/I, 210.
30. Cornwallis to the Directors, 24 August 1786: PRO/30/11/9.
31. Lady Amelia Campbell to Cornwallis, 21 February 1787: PRO/30/11/14.
32. Macpherson to Cornwallis, 1 September 1786: PRO/30/11/9.
33. Minute from Earl Cornwallis on taking charge of the government, 18 September 1786: IOR/H/379.
34. Shore to Hastings, 16 February 1787: Teignmouth, *Memoir*, I, 129.
35. Macpherson to Cornwallis, 22 July 1786: PRO/30/11/8; Macpherson to Cornwallis, 1 September 1787: PRO/30/11/9.
36. Cornwallis to Secret Committee, 16 November 1786: PRO/30/11/156.
37. Macpherson to Cornwallis, 24 September 1786: PRO/30/11/9.
38. Cornwallis to Malet, 27 September 1786: Ross/I, 222–3.
39. Cornwallis to Sydney, 17 September 1786: ibid., 219–20.
40. Grant to Cornwallis, 16 April 1787: ibid., 286–7.
41. Shore to H.J. Chandler, 13 November 1786: Teignmouth, *Memoir*, I, 127–8.
42. Review of the Company investments since 1774: PRO/30/11/11. A lakh was 100,000 rupees, equivalent to £10,000 sterling at an exchange rate of 2 shillings to the rupee.
43. Cornwallis to Campbell, 14 November 1786: PRO/30/11/159.
44. Review of the Company investments since 1774: PRO/30/11/11.
45. Cornwallis to Grant, 20 October 1786: PRO/30/11/184.
46. Paper on the Company's investments, by Charles Grant, 31 October 1786: PRO/30/11/10; Ainslie Thomas Embree, *Charles Grant and British Rule in India* (London, 1962), 96–7.
47. Taylor to Cornwallis, 12 November 1786: PRO/30/11/11.
48. Cornwallis to the Directors, 16 November 1786: PRO/30/11/153.
49. Ibid.
50. Propositions for the General Bank of India, 9 December 1786: PRO/30/11/12.
51. McCall to Cornwallis, 1 November 1786: PRO/30/11/11.
52. Hay to Cornwallis, 25 November 1786: ibid..
53. Cornwallis to Hay, 25 November 1786: PRO/30/11/188.
54. Cornwallis kept a notebook with the names, dates, and ships on which he sent his letters: PRO/30/11/57.
55. Cornwallis to Brome, 17 September 1786: Ross/I, 218.
56. Cornwallis to Brome, 28 December 1786: ibid., 236.
57. Cornwallis to Lichfield, 18 September 1786: ibid., 220.
58. Cornwallis to Lichfield, 13 November 1786: KRO/U/24/C/1.
59. Alfred Spencer (ed.), *Memoirs of William Hickey, 1749–1809*, 4 vols (London, 1923–5), III, 307.
60. Cornwallis to Dundas, 15 November 1786: PRO/30/11/150.
61. Cornwallis to Dundas, 15 November 1786: Ross/I, 227.
62. Cornwallis to Secret Committee, 28 December 1786: PRO/30/11/156.
63. Cornwallis to Messrs Bateman, Rider and Henchman, 15 January 1787: Ross/I, 242.
64. Cornwallis to Dundas, 23 January 1787: PRO/30/11/150.
65. Grant to Cornwallis, 19 September 1787: PRO/30/11/19; Embree, *Charles Grant*, 49.
66. Cornwallis to the Directors, 16 December 1787: PRO/30/11/153.
67. Cornwallis to Secret Committee, 23 January 1787: PRO/30/11/156.
68. Shore to Dundas, 15 March 1787: Arthur Aspinall, *Cornwallis in Bengal: The Administrative and Judicial Reforms of Lord Cornwallis, 1786–1793* (Manchester, 1931), 21.
69. Cornwallis to Dundas, 28 December 1786: Ross/I, 237–8.
70. Cornwallis to Dundas, 16 February 1787: ibid., 247–8.
71. Macpherson to Cornwallis, 28 February 1787: PRO/30/11/14.

72. Cornwallis to Dundas, 23 January 1787: PRO/30/11/150.
73. Ibid.
74. Cornwallis to Dundas, 30 November 1786: Ross/I, 233.
75. Cornwallis to Dundas, 28 December 1786: ibid., 238.
76. Cornwallis to Dundas, 15 November 1786: ibid., 227.
77. Teignmouth, *Memoir*, I, 121.
78. Statement by Mr Stuart, 22 January 1787: PRO/30/11/13.
79. Stuart to Cornwallis, 25 January 1787: ibid.

CHAPTER 8: SETTING THE AGENDA

1. Shore to H.J. Chandler, 13 November 1786: Teignmouth, *Memoir*, I, 127–8.
2. Spencer (ed.), *Hickey Memoirs*, III, 294.
3. Cornwallis to Brome, 11 January 1789: Ross/I, 388.
4. William Armstrong to Cornwallis, 22 September 1786: PRO/30/11/9.
5. Haldane to William Watts, 20 February 1789: PRO/30/11/28.
6. Shore to Chandler, 14 October 1793: Teignmouth, *Memoir*, I, 258–9.
7. Cornwallis to John Kennaway, 24 January 1787: PRO/30/11/188.
8. Reverend Thomas Blanchard to Cornwallis, 30 September 1786: PRO/30/11/9; Cornwallis to Blanchard, 30 September 1786: ibid.
9. Haldane to Murray, 17 October 1786: PRO/30/11/10.
10. Shore to Mrs Shore, 21 January 1787: Teignmouth, *Memoir*, I, 133.
11. William Townshend to Cornwallis, 7 July 1788: PRO/30/11/139.
12. Spencer (ed.), *Hickey Memoirs*, III, 292–4.
13. Ibid., 294.
14. Ibid., 306.
15. Soumyendra N. Mukherjee, *Sir William Jones: A Study in Eighteenth-Century British Attitudes to India* (Cambridge, 1968), 80.
16. Lynn Zastoupil and Martin Moir (eds), *The Great Indian Education Debate: Documents Relating to the Orientalist–Anglicist Controversy, 1781–1843* (Richmond, England, 1999), 77–9.
17. Cornwallis to Campbell, 7 January 1787: PRO/30/11/159.
18. Directors to the governor-general and council, 12 April 1786: IOR/H/379.
19. Cornwallis to the Directors, 17 February 1787: Ross/I, 249.
20. Bathurst to Revenue Board, March 1787: PRO/30/11/15.
21. Cornwallis to Dundas, 17 May 1787: PRO/30/11/150.
22. Aspinall, *Cornwallis in Bengal*, 22.
23. Cornwallis to Dundas, 5 March 1787: PRO/30/11/150; they were required to do so by Article 41 of the 1784 Act.
24. Pott to Cornwallis, 5 March 1787: PRO/30/11/15.
25. Seton to Cornwallis, (dated) March 1787: ibid.
26. Shore to Hastings, 16 February 1787: Teignmouth, *Memoir*, II, 125.
27. Pitt's India Act, 24 Geo. 3 sess. 2 c. 25.
28. Cornwallis to Sydney, 15 August 1787: Ross/I, 273.
29. Cornwallis to Sydney, 7 January 1788: ibid., 309–10.
30. Cornwallis to Burton, 14 July 1787: PRO/30/11/182.
31. Cornwallis to anon., 23 August 1787: Ross/I, 277.
32. Stuart to Cornwallis, 18 August 1787: PRO/30/11/18.
33. Kennaway to Cornwallis, 20 July 1787: ibid.
34. Cornwallis to Grant, 6 November 1787: PRO/30/11/184.
35. Grant to Cornwallis, 19 September 1787: PRO/30/11/19.
36. Governor-general and council to the Directors, 31 July 1787: Ross/I, 268.
37. Cornwallis to the Directors, 2 August 1789: ibid., 548; Cornwallis to the Directors, 18 August 1787: ibid., 273–4; Cornwallis to Dundas, 26 August 1787: ibid., 278.
38. Cornwallis to Dundas, 14 August 1787: ibid., 271.

39. Cornwallis to the Directors, 1 November 1788: PRO/30/11/153.
40. Yonge to Cornwallis, July 1787: PRO/30/11/127.
41. Penderel Moon, *The British Conquest and Dominion of India* (London, 1989), 243.
42. Raymond Callahan, *The East India Company and Army Reform, 1783–1798* (Cambridge, MA, 1972), 53–4.
43. Cornwallis to York, 10 November 1786: Ross/I, 225–6.
44. Cornwallis to Dundas, 30 November 1786: ibid., 233.
45. Cornwallis to Dundas, 16 February 1787: ibid., 247.
46. Cornwallis to Campbell, 19 March 1787: PRO/30/11/159.
47. Cornwallis to Dundas, 5 March 1787: PRO/30/11/150.
48. Cornwallis to the Directors, 18 August 1787: Ross/I, 523–4.
49. Cornwallis to Fawcett, 12 August 1787: PRO/30/11/184.
50. Cornwallis to Fawcett, 8 November 1789: ibid.
51. Cornwallis to McCall, 31 October 1787: PRO/30/11/20.
52. Cornwallis to Boddam, 20 January 1788: PRO/30/11/182.
53. Cornwallis to Campbell, 2 February 1787: PRO/30/11/159.
54. Banks to Yonge, 12 January 1787: PRO/30/11/13.
55. Yonge to Cornwallis, 21 January 1787: ibid.
56. Kydd to Haldane, 15 September 1787: PRO/30/11/19.
57. Cornwallis to Campbell, 2 February 1787: PRO/30/11/159.
58. Cornwallis to the Directors, 4 March 1787: PRO/30/11/153.
59. Cornwallis to Secret Committee, 4 March 1787: PRO/30/11/157.
60. Cornwallis to Lichfield, 5 March 1787: KRO/U/24/C/1.
61. Malet to Cornwallis, 24 March 1787: PRO/30/11/15; Cornwallis to Dundas, 14 August 1787: PRO/30/11/150.
62. Cornwallis to Lichfield, 17 August 1787: KRO/U/24/C/1.
63. Cornwallis to Dundas, 5 March 1787: Ross/I, 253.
64. Cornwallis to the Directors, 18 August 1787: PRO/30/11/153.
65. Stuart to Cornwallis, 30 August 1787: PRO/30/11/18.
66. Cornwallis to Grant, 4 September 1787: PRO/30/11/184.
67. Cornwallis to the Directors, 18 August 1787: PRO/30/11/153; see also Cornwallis to Dundas, 14 August 1787: Ross/I, 270–1.
68. Campbell to Cornwallis, 2 August 1787: PRO/30/11/118.
69. Cornwallis to Secret Committee, 7 September 1787: PRO/30/11/157.
70. Cornwallis to Stuart, 31 October 1787: PRO/30/11/171.
71. Hastings to Cornwallis, March 1786: PRO/30/11/197; Cornwallis to the nawab wazir, 15 April 1787: PRO/30/11/16.
72. Cornwallis to the Directors, 4 March 1787: PRO/30/153.
73. Barlow to Cornwallis, 4 June 1787: PRO/30/11/17.
74. Cornwallis to Dundas, 16 November 1787: NLS, Ms 3385.
75. Cornwallis to the nawab wazir, 15 April 1787: PRO/30/11/16.
76. Cornwallis to the nawab wazir, 5 October 1787: PRO/30/11/20; Cornwallis to Otto Ives, 2 October 1787: ibid., fols 116–20.
77. Cornwallis to the Directors, 16 November 1787: Ross/I, 300–1.
78. Cornwallis to Dundas, 16 February 1787: PRO/30/11/150.
79. Memorandum for the commanding officers, 28 October 1787: PRO/30/11/194.
80. Cornwallis to Dundas, 16 November 1787: Ross/I, 299. Cornwallis wrote similarly to the duke of York, 10 December 1787: ibid., 304–5.
81. Cornwallis to the Directors, 18 August 1787: PRO/30/11/153. The Directors duly agreed, 8 April 1789: PRO/30/11/123.
82. Blair to Cornwallis, 25 October 1787: PRO/30/11/20.
83. Cornwallis to Lichfield, 7 November 1787: KRO/U/24/C/1.
84. Cornwallis to Lichfield, 12 December 1787: ibid.; Cornwallis to Lichfield, 22 December 1787: ibid.
85. Cornwallis to Lichfield, 7 November 1787: ibid.

86. Cornwallis to Motteux, 10 December 1787: PRO/30/11/185.
87. Cornwallis to Brunswick, undated (*c.* December 1787: PRO/30/11/182). However, Cornwallis was misinformed about the identity of the Prussian commander, who was Ferdinand's cousin, Duke Charles William Ferdinand, the former hereditary prince, who had also played a prominent role during the Seven Years' War.
88. Cornwallis to Lichfield, 12 December 1787: Ross/I, 303–4; Bass, *Green Dragoon*, 250–1.
89. Fawcett to Cornwallis, 30 December 1787: PRO/30/11/138; Mackenzie, *Strictures*.
90. Grant to Cornwallis, 6 April 1787: Ross/I, 362–3.

CHAPTER 9: THE PROGRAMME GATHERS PACE

1. Grant to Cornwallis, 6 April 1788: ibid., 360.
2. Cornwallis to Dundas, 11 February 1788: PRO/30/11/150.
3. Cornwallis to the Directors, 3 March 1788: PRO/30/11/153.
4. Cornwallis to the Directors, 3 November 1788: Ross/I, 533–4. The full details of these reforms can be found in the National Archives of India (ed.), *Fort William – India House Correspondence*, Indian Records Series, 21 vols (Delhi, 1949–85), XVI, 203–37.
5. Cornwallis to the Directors, 6 January 1789: PRO/30/11/154.
6. Prince of Wales to Cornwallis, 12 March 1788: Ross/I, 350–1.
7. Cornwallis to prince of Wales, 1 November 1788: Arthur Aspinall (ed.), *Correspondence of George, Prince of Wales, 1770–1812*, 8 vols (London, 1963–70), I, 362.
8. Cornwallis to the Directors, 10 January 1788: PRO/30/11/153.
9. Cornwallis to the Directors, 1 November 1788: ibid.
10. Ibid.
11. Adam Smith, *An Enquiry into the Nature and Causes of the Wealth of Nations* (London, reprint 1884), 465–524.
12. Mrs Henry Baring (ed.), *The Diary of the Right Honourable William Windham, 1784–1810* (London, reprint 1886), 13 September 1785, 64.
13. Cornwallis to the Directors, 1 November 1788: PRO/30/11/27.
14. Amherst to Cornwallis, 15 April 1788: PRO/30/11/23.
15. Amherst to Cornwallis, 2 February 1789: PRO/30/11/28.
16. Minutes of the Secret Court of Directors, 16 March 1791: IOR/L/PS/1/1, fols 134–5; Ehrman, *Younger Pitt*, I, 419–22.
17. Cornwallis to Secret Committee, 8 March 1789: PRO/30/11/157.
18. Cornwallis to the Directors, 2 August 1789: Ross/I, 546–7.
19. Cornwallis to Dundas, 14 August 1787: PRO/30/11/150.
20. Benjamin Whitehead to Cornwallis, October 1788: PRO/30/11/26.
21. Cornwallis to the Directors, 10 February 1790: Ross/II, 477–8; Ranajit Guha, *A Rule of Property for Bengal: An Essay on the Idea of Permanent Settlement* (Durham, NC, 3rd edn, 1996), 137–9.
22. Extracts of proceedings of the governor-general and council regarding the coinage, April–December 1788: PRO/30/11/30; Whitehead to Cornwallis, 4 November 1788: PRO/30/11/27.
23. C.A. Bayly, *Rulers, Townsmen and Bazaars: North Indian Society in the Age of British Expansion, 1770–1870* (Cambridge, 1983), 211.
24. Cornwallis to the Directors, 2 August 1789: Ross/I, 546.
25. Cornwallis to the Directors, 2 November 1789: ibid., 443–4.
26. Cornwallis to the Directors, 7 March 1789: PRO/30/11/154.
27. Reflections upon measures to be taken for the reduction of interest, by William Larkins, 6 October 1789: PRO/30/11/32.
28. Cornwallis to Dundas, 7 November 1789; NLS, Ms 3385; Cornwallis to the Directors, 7 December 1789: PRO/30/11/154; Cornwallis to Dundas, 5 December 1789: PRO/30/11/150.
29. Cornwallis to the Directors, 1 August 1789: PRO/30/11/154.
30. Debate in the Commons on the East India Company budget for 1786 to 1787, 23 May 1788: Cobbett, *Parliamentary History*, XXVII, 557–73; East India Budget for 1787 to 1788, 1 July 1789: ibid., XXVIII, 184–208.

31. East India Budget for 1788 to 1789, 31 March 1790: ibid., 600–25.
32. Dundas to Cornwallis, 4 June 1790: PRO/30/11/116.
33. Cornwallis to the Directors, 6 November 1788: Ross/I, 541.
34. Brooke to Revenue Board, 10 January 1788: PRO/30/11/22.
35. Cunningham to Cornwallis, 16 September 1788: PRO/30/11/26.
36. Cornwallis to the Directors, 3 November 1788: Ross/I, 535–6.
37. Narendra Krishna Sinha, *The Economic History of Bengal from Plassey to the Permanent Settlement*, 2 vols (Calcutta, 1956–62), II, 119–26.
38. Shore to W.B. Rous, 22 February 1789: Teignmouth, *Memoir*, II, 169.
39. Cornwallis to the Directors, 8 March 1789: PRO/30/11/150; Guha, *Rule of Property*, 195–7.
40. Directors to the governor-general, 12 April 1786: IOR/H/379.
41. Brooke to Revenue Board, 8 May 1789: PRO/30/11/30.
42. Cornwallis to the Directors, 2 August 1789: Ross/I, 544–6.
43. Minute of the governor-general, 13 September 1789: ibid., 552–4.
44. Cornwallis to Smith, 8 December 1789: PRO/30/11/187.
45. Cornwallis to Dundas, 5 December 1789: Ross/I, 453.
46. Minute of the governor-general, 10 February 1790: Ross/II, 463–78.
47. Pitt's India Act, 24 Geo. 3 sess. 2 c. 25, Article 39.
48. Bernstein, *Dawning of the Raj*, 89–90, 144.
49. Aspinall, *Cornwallis in Bengal*, 125–7.
50. Jones to Cornwallis, 19 March 1788: Garland Cannon (ed.), *The Letters of Sir William Jones*, 2 vols (Oxford, 1970), II, 794–800.
51. Jones to Cornwallis, 13 April 1788: ibid., 801.
52. Mukherjee, *Sir William Jones*, 50–2.
53. Cornwallis to Dundas, 8 March 1789: PRO/30/11/150.
54. Jorg Fisch, *Cheap Lives and Dear Limbs: The British Transformation of the Bengal Criminal Law, 1769–1817* (Wiesbaden, 1983), 14–15.
55. Cornwallis to Dundas, 8 March 1789: PRO/30/11/150.
56. Cornwallis to the Directors, 2 August 1789: Ross/I, 547–8.
57. Replies of W. Lodge, et al., 5 January 1790: NLS, Ms 3386.
58. Jeremiah Church to Cornwallis, 20 January 1787: PRO/30/11/13.
59. Anon. to Haldane, 7 November 1788: PRO/30/11/27.
60. Cornwallis to the Directors, 2 August 1789: Ross/I, 547.
61. Ibid.; Wickwire and Wickwire, *Imperial Years*, 95–6.
62. Cornwallis to Dundas, 1 November 1788: Ross/I, 370–3.
63. Ibid.
64. Ibid.
65. Dundas to Cornwallis, 7 April 1789: PRO/30/11/114.
66. Dundas to Cornwallis, 3 April 1789: ibid.
67. Dundas to Cornwallis, 7 April 1789: ibid.
68. Phillipson to Cornwallis, 1 April 1788: PRO/30/11/138; Grisdale to Cornwallis, 4 April 1788: ibid.
69. Cornwallis to Dundas, 1 November 1789: Ross/I, 440–2.
70. Spencer (ed.), *Hickey Memoirs*, III, 344.
71. Cornwallis to Dundas, 21 December 1788: PRO/30/11/150.
72. Cornwallis to Pitt, 9 August 1789: PRO/30/8/125.
73. Cornwallis to Dundas, 8 August 1789: Ross/I, 414.
74. Cornwallis to Dundas, 18 February 1789: PRO/30/11/150.
75. Cornwallis to Pitt, 6 November 1788: Ross/I, 380.
76. Cornwallis to Medows, 23 October 1788: PRO/30/11/174.
77. Cornwallis to Pitt, 6 November 1788: Ross/I, 379–80.
78. Stuart to Cornwallis, 18 December 1789: PRO/30/11/33.
79. Dundas to Cornwallis, 23 May 1790: PRO/30/11/116.

80. Sir George Yonge's report to George III, 20 July 1787: PRO/30/11/112; memorandum by Mr Dundas, undated (*c*. July 1787): Ross/I, 330–2.
81. Ibid.
82. Cornwallis to Yonge, 7 March 1788: PRO/30/8/125.
83. Sydney to Cornwallis, 28 March 1788: PRO/30/11/23; Yonge to Cornwallis, 28 March 1788: ibid.
84. Dundas to Cornwallis, 26 March 1788: Ross/I, 355; Callahan, *East India Company and Army Reform*, 85–95.
85. 'A Bill for Removing any Doubt Respecting the Power of the Commissioners for the Affairs of India', March 1788: PRO/30/11/113.
86. A meeting of the officers at Chunar, 23 February 1789: PRO/30/11/29.
87. White to Cornwallis, 10 March 1789: ibid.
88. Cornwallis to the Directors, 6 March 1789: Ross/I, 542.
89. Ibid.
90. Ibid., 543.
91. Callahan, *East India Company and Army Reform*, 3–4; Seema Alavi, *The Sepoys and the Company: Tradition and Transition in Northern India, 1770–1830* (New Delhi, 1995), 46–9.
92. Cornwallis to Barrington, 27 December 1788: Ross/I, 384–5.
93. Ibid.
94. Zastoupil and Moir (eds), *Great Indian Education Debate*, 1–22
95. Campbell to Cornwallis, 5 August 1787: PRO/30/11/118; Campbell to Cornwallis, 25 November 1787: ibid.
96. Bengal Council to Campbell, 8 October 1788: PRO/30/11/28.
97. Cornwallis to Dundas, 24 January 1789: NLS, Ms 3385.
98. Cornwallis to Horne, 20 June 1789: Ross/I, 402.
99. Horne to Cornwallis, 17 July 1789: PRO/30/11/134.
100. Cornwallis to Musgrave, 5 October 1789: Ross/I, 438.
101. Cornwallis to Holland, 5 October 1789: PRO/30/11/184.
102. Anon. to Cornwallis, 9 November 1789: PRO/30/11/33. The author Benjamin Roebuck was a Madras merchant: see Roebuck to Cornwallis, 21 January 1790: PRO/30/11/35.
103. Edward Townshend to Cornwallis, 7 April 1789: PRO/30/11/139.
104. Cornwallis to Brome, 14 August 1789: Ross/I, 422–3.
105. Spencer (ed.), *Hickey Memoirs*, III, 349. It is not clear whether the 'whole settlement' meant only Europeans.
106. Cornwallis to Brome, 14 August 1789: Ross/I, 422–3.
107. Cornwallis to Rawdon, August 1789: PRO/30/11/186.
108. Cornwallis to Grenville, 9 November 1789: Aspinall (ed.), *Correspondence of George, Prince of Wales*, I, 44–5.
109. Wickwire and Wickwire, *War of Independence*, 12–13.
110. Cornwallis to Lichfield, 7 December 1789: KRO/U/24/C/1.
111. Caroline Cornwallis to Cornwallis, 23 February 1789: PRO/30/11/139
112. Cornwallis to Lichfield, 9 November 1789: KRO/U/24/C/1.
113. Spencer (ed.), *Hickey Memoirs*, III, 361
114. Cornwallis to Brome, 11 January 1790: PRO/30/11/276.

CHAPTER 10: AN UNWELCOME WAR

1. An account of Tipu Sultan by Alexander Dixon, deputy adjutant-general at Madras, 14 December 1789: PRO/30/11/33.
2. Address by Tipu Sultan to Musselmen in the nizam's camp, December 1786: PRO/30/11/12.
3. Moon, *British Conquest and Dominion*, 290–1.
4. Minute of the governor-general, 2 April 1790: Ross/II, 10–11.
5. Richard Johnson to Cornwallis, 3 February 1790: PRO/30/11/34.
6. Cornwallis to Secret Committee, 12 April 1790: PRO/30/11/157.

7. Cornwallis to Dundas, 8 August 1789: PRO/30/11/150.
8. Cornwallis to Pitt, 15 April 1790: PRO/30/11/175.
9. Pitt's India Act, 24 Geo. 3 sess. 2 c. 25.
10. Minute of the governor-general, 5 February 1790: Ross/I, 472–4.
11. Cornwallis to Dundas, 7 February 1790: ibid., 474–5.
12. Cornwallis to Lichfield, 13 February 1790: ibid., 480–1.
13. Cornwallis to Kennaway, 28 January 1790: ibid., 470–2; Cornwallis to Malet, 28 February 1790: ibid., 482–4.
14. Cornwallis to Kennaway and Malet, 28 January 1790: ibid., 472–4.
15. Cornwallis to Dundas, 7 February 1790: ibid., 474–5.
16. Cornwallis to Dundas, 3 March 1790: PRO/30/11/151.
17. Minute of the governor-general, 2 April 1790: Ross/II, 12.
18. Cornwallis to Dundas, 10 April 1790: NLS, Ms 3385.
19. Minute of the governor-general, 2 April 1790: Ross/II, 13.
20. Cornwallis to Medows, 11 February 1790: PRO/30/11/174.
21. Draft articles, 22 March 1790: PRO/30/11/35; Kennaway to Cornwallis, 22 March 1790: ibid.
22. Treaty of Offensive and Defensive Alliance, 1 June 1790: PRO/30/11/36.
23. Cornwallis to Dundas, 1 April 1790: Ross/II, 8.
24. Cornwallis to Medows, 30 March 1790: PRO/30/11/174.
25. Cornwallis to Medows, 11 July 1790: PRO/30/11/174.
26. Cornwallis to the Directors, 10 August 1790: PRO/30/11/154.
27. Charles Townshend to Cornwallis, 23 July 1789: Ross/II, 4–6.
28. Cornwallis to York, April 1790: ibid., 9.
29. Cornwallis to Medows, 1 May 1790: PRO/30/11/174.
30. Malet to Cornwallis, 25 May 1790: PRO/30/11/36; Kennaway to Medows, 26 May 1790: ibid.
31. Malet to Cornwallis, 7 June 1790: ibid.
32. Cornwallis to Medows, 11 June 1790: ibid.
33. Cornwallis to Medows, 27 June 1790: PRO/30/11/174.
34. Cornwallis to Dundas, 9 August 1790: PRO/30/11/151.
35. Dundas to Cornwallis, 8 August 1789: PRO/30/11/115, fols 163–6.
36. Cornwallis to Dundas, 4 April 1790: Ross/II, 13–20.
37. Ibid.
38. Dundas to Cornwallis, 13 November 1790: PRO/30/11/116.
39. Cornwallis to the Directors, 10 April 1790: PRO/30/11/154.
40. Stuart to Cornwallis, 19 June 1790: PRO/30/11/36.
41. Mercer to Cornwallis, 11 August 1790: PRO/30/11/37.
42. Mercer to Cornwallis, 4 September 1790: PRO/30/11/38; Cornwallis to Mercer, 3 October 1790: ibid.
43. Stuart to Cornwallis, 12 July 1790: PRO/30/11/37.
44. Cornwallis to Stuart, 13 July 1790: PRO/30/11/171. Cornwallis clearly suspected Peter Speke as the agent provocateur.
45. Stuart to Cornwallis, 14 July 1790: PRO/30/11/37.
46. Guha, *Rule of Property*, 196–7.
47. Governor-general and council to the Directors, 16 August 1790: Ross/II, 496–7.
48. Replies of W. Lodge, et al., 5 January 1790: NLS, Ms 3386.
49. Cornwallis to the Directors, 10 April 1790: Ross/II, 487.
50. Jones to Cornwallis, 20 November 1790: ibid., 57.
51. Minute of the governor-general for regulating the criminal courts of justice, enclosed in his letter to Mr Dundas, 23 November 1790: NLS, Ms 3386, paragraphs 18–19.
52. Ibid., paragraphs 22–3; Thomas Brooke to Cornwallis, 27 March 1790: NLS, Ms 3386.
53. Minute of the governor-general, 23 November 1790: ibid.; B.B. Misra, *The Central Administration of the East India Company, 1773–1834* (Manchester, 1959), 324–5.
54. Minute of the governor-general, 23 November 1790: NLS, Ms 3386, paragraphs 22, 39, and 49.

55. Ibid., paragraphs 24–44.
56. Ibid., paragraph 20; Om Prakash (ed.), *Lord Cornwallis: Administrative Reforms and British Policy (Encyclopaedic History of Indian Freedom Movement Series)* (New Delhi, 2002), 164–5.
57. Minute of the governor-general, 23 November 1790: NLS, Ms 3386.
58. Jones to Lee, 1 October 1786: Cannon (ed.), *Letters of Sir William Jones*, II, 712–13.
59. Cornwallis to Medows, 5 August 1790: PRO/30/11/174.
60. Cornwallis to Medows, 25 August 1790: ibid.
61. Cornwallis to Medows, 17 September 1790: ibid.
62. Cornwallis to Medows, 3 October 1790: ibid.
63. Ibid.
64. Cornwallis to Medows, 12 October 1790: PRO/30/11/174.
65. Cornwallis to Medows, 20 October 1790: ibid.
66. Cornwallis to the Directors, 1 November 1790: PRO/30/11/154.
67. Cornwallis to Lichfield, 16 November 1790: Ross/II, 52–3.
68. Cornwallis to prince of Wales, 18 November 1790: Aspinall (ed.), *Correspondence of George, Prince of Wales*, II, 111–12.
69. Cornwallis to Malet, 31 October 1790: PRO/30/11/38.
70. Minute of the governor-general, 6 November 1790: Ross/II, 49–50.
71. Cornwallis to Dundas, 12 November 1790: PRO/30/11/151.
72. Spencer (ed.), *Hickey Memoirs*, IV, 7–8.
73. Cornwallis to Brome, 16 November 1790: Ross/II, 53.
74. Minute of the governor-general, 3 December 1790: ibid., 57–8; Spencer (ed.), *Hickey Memoirs*, IV, 5.
75. Cornwallis to Lichfield, 5 December 1790: Ross/I, 58–9.

CHAPTER 11: CLIPPING TIPU'S WINGS

1. Cornwallis to Medows, 15 December 1790: PRO/30/11/174.
2. Ibid.
3. Cornwallis to Abercromby, 17 December 1790: PRO/30/11/181.
4. Cornwallis to Kyd, 9 November 1790: Ross/II, 500.
5. Cornwallis to Robinson, 9 November 1790: ibid., 500–1.
6. Spencer (ed.), *Hickey Memoirs*, IV, 14.
7. Cornwallis to Abercromby, 7 January 1791: PRO/30/11/181.
8. Cornwallis to Dundas, 27 January 1791: Ross/II, 80–1.
9. Cornwallis to Murray, 13 February 1791: PRO/30/11/185.
10. Kennaway to Cornwallis, 11 January 1791: PRO/30/11/40.
11. Cornwallis to Kennaway, 18 January 1791: ibid.
12. Malet to Cornwallis, 18 February 1791: PRO/30/11/41.
13. Cornwallis to the Directors, 20 April 1791: PRO/30/11/155; John Fortescue, *A History of the British Army*, vol. 3, *1763–1793* (London, 1911), 571–2.
14. Cornwallis to Lichfield, 23 February 1791: Ross/II, 86.
15. Cornwallis to Deen Rezza Khan, 17 January 1791: ibid., 78–9.
16. General orders, 25 February 1791: ibid., 87.
17. Cornwallis to the Directors, 20 April 1791: PRO/30/11/155; Fortescue, *British Army*, III, 572–8.
18. Cornwallis to Floyd, 6 April 1791: Ross/II, 88–9.
19. Abercromby to Cornwallis, 26 January 1791: PRO/30/11/128; Abercromby to Cornwallis, 26 February: ibid.
20. Abercromby to Cornwallis, 6 April 1791: ibid.
21. Cornwallis to Kennaway, 2 April 1791: Ross/II, 87–8.
22. Cornwallis to the Directors, 20 April 1791: PRO/30/11/155.
23. Cornwallis to Wunt, 8 May 1791: Ross/II, 506–7.
24. Cornwallis to Wunt, 10 May 1791: ibid., 91.

25. Cornwallis to Abercromby, 16 May 1791: PRO/30/11/181. A fuller account can be found in Cornwallis to the Directors, 7 September 1791: Ross/II, 516–18; Fortescue, *British Army*, III, 582–4.
26. Cornwallis to Abercromby, 16 May 1791: PRO/30/11/181; Cornwallis to Oakley, 16 May 1791: Ross/II, 92.
27. Cornwallis to Malet, 17 May 1791: ibid., 92.
28. Cornwallis to Tipu Sultan, 19 May 1791: ibid., 93–5.
29. Persian translator to Syed Ahmed Ali, 27 May 1791: ibid., 95.
30. Kennaway to Cornwallis, 25 May 1791: PRO/30/11/43.
31. Abercromby to Cornwallis, 20 May 1791: PRO/30/11/128.
32. Cornwallis to Abercromby, 21 May 1791: PRO/30/11/181; Cornwallis to Abercromby, 22 May 1791: PRO/30/11/181.
33. Cornwallis to Abercromby, 3 June 1791: ibid.
34. Shore to Caldecott, 31 December 1791: Teignmouth, *Memoir*, I, 211–13.
35. Cornwallis to Dundas, 21 April 1791: PRO/30/11/151.
36. Cornwallis to Oakley, 2 July 1791: Ross/II, 95–6.
37. Cornwallis to Kennaway, 10 July 1791: ibid., 510–12.
38. Recapitulation of the arguments previously urged . . . to Behroo Punt, 9 July 1791: PRO/30/11/44.
39. Kennaway to Cornwallis, 14 August 1791: ibid.
40. Cornwallis to the Directors, 24 October 1791: PRO/30/11/155; Cornwallis to Kennaway, 9 November 1791: PRO/30/11/46.
41. Cornwallis to Abercromby, 20 July 1791: PRO/30/11/181.
42. Murray to Hay, 23 May 1791: PRO/30/11/44; Murray to Hay, 23 June 1791: ibid.
43. Cornwallis to Murray, 6 August 1791: PRO/30/11/185.
44. Cornwallis to Lichfield, 13 July 1791: Ross/II, 97–9.
45. Cornwallis to Lichfield, 20 August 1791: ibid., 104; Namier and Brooke, *House of Commons*, I, 22–7.
46. Charles Townshend to Cornwallis, 10 February 1790: PRO/30/11/34.
47. Palgrave to Cornwallis, 15 November 1791: PRO/30/11/140.
48. Debate in the Commons on the war with Tipu Sultan, 28 February 1791: Cobbett, *Parliamentary History*, XXVIII, 1278–90.
49. Cornwallis to Lichfield, 20 August 1791: Ross/II, 106; Cornwallis to Dundas, 3 September 1791: ibid., 113–14.
50. Major-General Grenville to Cornwallis, 4 May 1791: ibid., 124.
51. Cornwallis to Dundas, 3 September 1791: PRO/30/11/151.
52. Cornwallis to the Directors, 8 September 1791: PRO/30/11/155.
53. Cubbage to Abercromby, 18 August 1791: PRO/30/11/128.
54. Cornwallis to Stuart, 7 August 1791: PRO/30/11/172.
55. Translation of a letter from Tipu Sultan, 26 August 1791: PRO/30/11/44.
56. Cornwallis to Oakley, 26 August 1791: Ross/II, 108.
57. Cornwallis to Abercromby, 13 September 1791: PRO/30/11/181.
58. Cornwallis to the Directors, 24 October 1791: PRO/30/11/155; Alexander Dirom, *A Narrative of the Campaign in India which Terminated the War with Tippoo Sultan in 1792* (London, 1794), 42–9.
59. Cuppage to Cornwallis, 6 November 1791: PRO/30/11/46; Cornwallis to Cuppage, 11 November 1791: Ross/II, 130–1.
60. Cornwallis to Pitt, 3 December 1791: PRO/30/11/175.
61. Cornwallis to Abercromby, 22 November 1791: PRO/30/11/181.
62. Colonel Patrick Ross to Cornwallis, 2 December 1791: PRO/30/11/46; Dirom, *Narrative*, 66–77.
63. Cornwallis to the Directors, 26 December 1791: PRO/30/11/155.
64. Cornwallis to Lichfield, 29 December 1791: Ross/II, 132–3.
65. Dirom, *Narrative*, 84.
66. Cornwallis to Kennaway, 2 January 1792: PRO/30/11/47.
67. Cornwallis to Abercromby, 8 January 1792: PRO/30/11/181; Dirom, *Narrative*, 101–6.
68. Malet to Cornwallis, 16 January 1792: PRO/30/11/46.

69. Cornwallis to Dundas, 13 January 1792: Ross/II, 140–1; Cornwallis to the Directors, 4 March 1792: ibid., 528–30.
70. Cornwallis to Abercromby, 27 January 1792: PRO/30/11/181; Cornwallis to Abercromby, 28 January 1792: ibid.; Cornwallis to Abercromby, 5 February 1792: ibid.
71. Dirom, *Narrative*, 113–14, 122–4.
72. Ibid., 130–2.
73. Cornwallis to the Directors, 4 March 1792: Ross/II, 530.
74. Orders for the attack on Seringapatam, 1792: PRO/30/11/194; Cornwallis to the Directors, 4 March 1792: Ross/II, 530–2.
75. Dirom, *Narrative*, 140–1.
76. Ibid., 161, 166; Spencer (ed.), *Hickey Memoirs*, IV, 71.
77. Cornwallis to Oakley, 8 February 1792: Ross/II, 147–8; Fortescue, *British Army*, III, 596–608.
78. Cornwallis to the Directors, 4 March 1792: Ross/II, 533–4.
79. Dundas to Cornwallis, 10 November 1790: PRO/30/11/116.
80. Dundas to Cornwallis, 21 May 1791: PRO/30/11/117.
81. Secret Committee to Cornwallis, 21 September 1791: Ross/II, 159.
82. Cornwallis to Pitt, 23 January 1792: ibid., 145.
83. Cornwallis to the Directors, 4 March 1792: ibid., 535.
84. Cornwallis to Oakley, 28 February 1792: ibid., 527–8; Cornwallis to the Directors, 4 March 1792: Ross/II, 534–5; Dirom, *Narrative*, 214–16.
85. Copy of the preliminary articles, 22 February 1792: Ross/II, 151–2.
86. Cornwallis to Oakley, 20 February 1792: ibid., 150–1.
87. Cornwallis to prince of Wales, 5 April 1792: Aspinall (ed.), *Correspondence of George, Prince of Wales*, II, 662.
88. The painting is in the National Army Museum, London.
89. Cornwallis to Oakley, 26 February 1792: Ross/II, 152.
90. Cornwallis to the Directors, 4 March 1792: ibid., 535.
91. Cornwallis to Oakley, 11 March 1792: ibid., 157; Cornwallis to Oakley, 13 March 1792: ibid., 157–8.
92. Cornwallis to the Directors, 4 April 1792: ibid., 537; Dirom, *Narrative*, 245–7.
93. Cornwallis to the Directors, 4 March 1792: Ross/II, 536–7.
94. Cornwallis to Fawcett, 8 March 1792: PRO/30/11/184.
95. Cornwallis to Stuart, 29 February 1792: PRO/30/11/172.
96. Cornwallis to York, 6 April 1792: Ross/II, 160–1.
97. Cornwallis to Lichfield, 4 May 1792: ibid., 166; Cornwallis to the Directors, 4 March 1792: ibid., 536.
98. Cornwallis to Dundas, 9 April 1792: ibid., 161–2.
99. Cornwallis to the Directors, 5 April 1792: ibid., 539–40.
100. Cornwallis to the Directors, 2 May 1792: PRO/30/11/155.
101. Cornwallis to Dundas, 4 March 1792: Ross/II, 155–6. Hickey agreed with this assessment of Graham: Spencer (ed.), *Hickey Memoirs*, IV, 77. The appointment was ultimately rescinded.
102. Cornwallis to Dundas, 18 June 1792: Ross/II, 171–2.
103. Cornwallis to Dundas, 28 April 1792: PRO/30/11/151.
104. Cornwallis to Medows, 27 April 1792: PRO/30/11/174.
105. Cornwallis to Stuart, 1 May 1792: PRO/30/11/172.
106. Cornwallis to Stuart, 11 June 1792: ibid.
107. Dundas to Cornwallis, 17 September 1792: Ross/II, 216.
108. Cornwallis to Pitt, 23 January 1792: ibid., 144–5.
109. Cornwallis to Medows, 25 March 1790: PRO/30/11/174.
110. Cornwallis to the Directors, 10 August 1790: PRO/30/11/154.
111. Governor-general and council, 21 June 1790: Ross/II, 492–3.
112. Cornwallis to the Directors, 16 August 1790: ibid., 495–6.
113. Cornwallis to the Directors, 9 July 1792: PRO/30/11/155.

114. The insidious effect of freedom of contract, alienable property tenures and ownership in fee simple which replaced communitarian values is discussed by C.A. Bayly, *Imperial Meridian: The British Empire and the World, 1780–1830* (Harlow, 1989), 6, 159.

CHAPTER 12: COMPLETING THE MISSION

1. Spencer (ed.), *Hickey Memoirs*, IV, 71.
2. Address of the inhabitants of Calcutta, 30 July 1792: PRO/30/11/214.
3. Address of the inhabitants of Calcutta [partially in Sanskrit], 31 July 1792: ibid.
4. Cornwallis to Stuart, 7 April 1792: PRO/30/11/172.
5. John Bristow, chairman of the meeting, 25 April 1792: PRO/30/11/213.
6. Cornwallis to the Directors, 26 August 1792: PRO/30/11/155.
7. Propositions for reducing the native corps, 18 April 1792: PRO/30/11/48.
8. Cornwallis to the Directors, 7 July 1792: PRO/30/11/155.
9. Graham to Cornwallis, 31 January 1792: PRO/30/11/48.
10. Cornwallis to Dundas, 30 August 1792: PRO/30/11/151.
11. Governor-general and council, 25 August 1792: Ross/II, 546–9.
12. Cornwallis to Lichfield, 19 January 1793: KRO/U/24/C/1.
13. Cornwallis to Dundas, 15 October 1792: Ross/II, 183.
14. Minute of the governor-general, 3 December 1792, enclosed in a letter to Mr Dundas, 10 December 1792: NLS, Ms 3386; Harald Fischer-Tiné and Michael Mann, *Colonialism as Civilizing Mission: Cultural Ideology in British India* (Wimbledon, 2004), 47.
15. Minute of the governor-general, 3 December 1792: NLS, Ms 3386.
16. Jones to Lee, 28 September 1788: Cannon (ed.), *Letters of Sir William Jones*, II, 820.
17. Minute of the governor-general, 3 December 1792: NLS, Ms 3386.
18. Christopher Hawes, *Poor Relations: The Making of a Eurasian Community in British India, 1773–1833* (Richmond, 1996), 55–6.
19. Minute of the governor-general, 3 December 1792: NLS, Ms 3386.
20. Ibid.
21. Ibid.
22. Governor-general and council to the Directors, 6 March 1793: Ross/II, 562.
23. Cornwallis to the Directors, 7 March 1793: ibid., 217–18.
24. Cornwallis to Dundas, 7 March 1793: ibid., 219.
25. Shore to Cornwallis, 23 March 1793: Teignmouth, *Memoir*, II, 237.
26. Aspinall, *Cornwallis in Bengal*, 94–5.
27. A summary of the regulations can be found in Aspinall, *Cornwallis in Bengal*, 95–9; see also Index for the Regulations of 1793: PRO/30/11/205.
28. Barlow to Cornwallis, 25 August 1794: PRO/30/11/54.
29. Barlow to Cornwallis, 30 December 1794: ibid.
30. Barlow to Cornwallis, 30 December 1794: ibid; Aspinall, *Cornwallis in Bengal*, 95. However it was decided in 1797 that an Act of Parliament was required to authenticate the codes: Misra, *Central Administration*, 38.
31. Dundas to Cornwallis, 17 September 1792: Ross/II, 214–15.
32. Ibid.
33. Cornwallis to the Directors, 7 March 1793: Ross/II, 218.
34. Cornwallis to Dundas, 7 March 1793: ibid., 219.
35. The extensiveness of the problem is challenged by Rajat Datta, *Society, Economy and the Market: Commercialization in Rural Bengal, c. 1760–1800* (New Delhi, 2000), 264.
36. Governor-general and council to the Directors, 6 March 1793: Ross/II, 558–9.
37. Governor-general and council to the Directors, 6 March 1793: ibid., 560.
38. Governor-general and council to the Directors, 6 March 1793: ibid., 560–1.
39. Shore to Dundas, 23 March 1793: Teignmouth, *Memoir*, II, 237.
40. Cornwallis to Dundas, 24 March 1793: Ross/II, 220–1.
41. Misra, *Central Administration*, 191.

42. Cornwallis to Lichfield, 11 March 1793: KRO/U/24/C/1.
43. Cornwallis to the Directors, 7 July 1792: PRO/30/11/155.
44. Cornwallis to Dundas, 7 March 1793: Ross/II, 219.
45. Cornwallis to Dundas, 24 March 1793: ibid., 221.
46. Cornwallis to Abercromby, 7 May 1793: PRO/30/11/181.
47. Cornwallis to Braithwaite, 19 May 1793: PRO/30/11/182.
48. Callahan, *East India Company and Army Reform*, 119–21.
49. Cornwallis to Dundas, 10 December 1792: Ross/II, 186–7.
50. Cockerell to Cornwallis, 16 September 1792: PRO/30/11/53.
51. Cornwallis to Tipu Sultan, 29 May 1793: Ross/II, 223.
52. Cornwallis to Oakley, 20 June 1793: ibid., 224–5.
53. Governor-general and council to the Directors, 1 August 1793: ibid., 225–6.
54. Braithwaite to Cornwallis, 10 June 1793: PRO/30/11/52.
55. Cornwallis to Braithwaite, 26 June 1793: PRO/30/11/182.
56. Cornwallis to Braithwaite, 13 July 1793: ibid.
57. Cornwallis to the Directors, 1 August 1793: Ross/II, 225–6.
58. Cornwallis to the Directors, 18 September 1793: ibid., 226–7.
59. Cornwallis to William Cornwallis, 13 July 1793: HMC, *Report on Various Collections*, VI, 386.
60. Cornwallis to William Cornwallis, 15 September 1793: ibid., 387.
61. Cornwallis to the Directors, 18 September 1793: Ross/II, 226–7.
62. Cornwallis to William Cornwallis, 17 December 1793: HMC, *Various Collections*, VI, 387–8.
63. Shore to Chandler, 14 October 1793: Teignmouth, *Memoir*, II, 258–9.
64. Shore to Cornwallis, 10 November 1793: PRO/30/11/122.
65. Cornwallis to Shore, 9 October 1793: Ross/II, 228.
66. Shore to Cornwallis, 10 November 1793: PRO/30/11/122.
67. Shore to Chandler, 14 October 1793: Teignmouth, *Memoir*, 258–9.
68. Address to Charles, Marquess Cornwallis, 5 November 1793: PRO/30/11/214; John Bristow to Shore, 3 March 1794: PRO/30/11/213.
69. Wickwire and Wickwire, *Imperial Years*, 179.
70. Cornwallis to Dundas, 3 February 1794: Ross/II, 235.
71. Speech by Henry Dundas on the finances of the East India Company, 20 December 1796: PRO/30/11/207.
72. Barbara D. Metcalf and Thomas R. Metcalf, *A Concise History of Modern India* (Cambridge, 3rd edn, 2012), 78–9.
73. Guha, *Rule of Property*, 137–41. The argument that Bengal remained in decline has been challenged by Datta, *Society, Economy and the Market*, 1–17, passim.
74. Crispin Bates, *Subalterns and Raj: South Asia since 1600* (London, 2007), 45–6.
75. Misra, *Central Administration*, 251–2; Fischer-Tiné and Mann, *Colonialism*, 43.
76. Misra, *Central Administration*, 260–2.
77. Sinha, *Economic History*, II, 232; Misra, *Central Administration*, 192–3, 252–3.
78. Aspinall, *Cornwallis in Bengal*, 174–5; Prakash (ed.), *Lord Cornwallis*, 347–8.
79. See, for example, ibid.
80. Misra, *Central Administration*, 378, 384–5; Moon, *British Conquest*, 260–1.

CHAPTER 13: MINISTER OF THE CROWN

1. At a general court of the United Company, 26 June 1793: PRO/30/11/215.
2. At a general Court of Directors, 30 January 1793: ibid.
3. Brome was enrolled at St John's College, Cambridge.
4. Charlotte to Cornwallis, 5 February 1794: PRO/30/11/270.
5. Wellesley to Cornwallis, 1 April 1794: PRO/30/11/234; Cornwallis to Shore, 10 June 1796: Ross/II, 307.
6. Cornwallis to Shore, 12 March 1794: ibid., 237–8.
7. *The Times*, 10 April 1794.

8. Bernstein, *Dawning of the Raj*, 256.
9. John Almon, *The Parliamentary Register or History of the Proceedings and Debates of the House of Commons, Second Series: 1780–1796*, 45 vols (London, 1784–96), XXXIX, 168–9.
10. *The Times*, 7 April 1794; Wickwire and Wickwire, *Imperial Years*, 183.
11. There is a copy of this portrait in Dublin Castle.
12. Cornwallis to Shore, 12 March 1794: Ross/II, 237.
13. Pitt to George III, 29 April 1791: Arthur Aspinall (ed.), *The Later Correspondence of George III*, 5 vols (Cambridge, 1962–68), I, 529.
14. Cornwallis to Pitt, 23 January 1792: Ross/II, 145.
15. Ehrman, *Younger Pitt*, II, 287–90.
16. Pitt to Cornwallis, 19 April 1794: PRO/30/11/216.
17. Dundas to Cornwallis, 29 May 1794: Ross/II, 239–41; Ehrman, *Younger Pitt*, II, 333–7.
18. Grenville to George III, 27 May 1794: Aspinall (ed.), *Later Correspondence*, II, 212–13.
19. Dundas to Cornwallis, 29 May 1794: Ross/II, 239–41.
20. Amherst to Cornwallis, 25 May 1794: PRO/30/11/216; Amherst to Cornwallis, 28 May 1794: ibid.
21. York to Cornwallis, 22 April 1794: PRO/30/11/277.
22. York to Dundas, 6 June 1794: Ross/II, 245–6. Concern about events in Poland may also have been a factor in the emperor's decision: see Burne, *Noble Duke of York*, 154.
23. York to Dundas, 6 June 1794: Ross/II, 243–4.
24. Cornwallis to Dundas, 8 June 1794: ibid., 247
25. Cornwallis to Pitt, 11 June 1794: PRO/30/11/217.
26. Cornwallis to York, 18 June 1794: Ross/II, 250.
27. Cornwallis to York, 21 June 1794: PRO/30/11/217; Malmesbury to Grenville, 21 June 1794: James Howard Harris, earl of Malmesbury (ed.), *Diaries and Correspondence of James Harris, First Earl of Malmesbury*, 4 vols (London, 1844), III, 103–4.
28. Malmesbury's diary for 22 June 1794: ibid. 116.
29. Cornwallis to Dundas, 21 June 1794: PRO/30/11/217.
30. Cornwallis to York, 30 June 1794: ibid.
31. Cornwallis to Pitt, 2 July 1794: ibid.
32. Ibid.
33. Cornwallis to Lord St Helens, 7 July 1794: PRO/30/11/217.
34. Cornwallis to Lichfield, 26 July 1794: Ross/II, 256.
35. Spencer and Thomas Grenville to Lord Grenville, 12 August 1794: ibid., 257–8.
36. Cornwallis to Ross, 15 August 1794: ibid., 258.
37. Pitt to Cornwallis, 24 August 1794: ibid., 259–60.
38. Cornwallis to Pitt, 25 August 1794: ibid., 261–2; see also Cornwallis to Ross, 28 August 1794: ibid., 263–4.
39. Spencer to Cornwallis, 15 September 1794: ibid., 270–1.
40. Cornwallis to Dundas, 14 September 1794: ibid., 268–9.
41. Ibid.
42. Cornwallis to Shore, 7 September 1794: Ross/II, 265–6.
43. Cornwallis to Lichfield, 25 September 1794: KRO/U/24/C/2.
44. Cornwallis to York, 8 November 1794: Ross/II, 272–5.
45. York to Cornwallis, 24 November 1794: ibid., 278–9.
46. Anon. to Cornwallis, 11 November 1794: ibid., 276.
47. H. Verney (ed.), *The Journals and Correspondence of General Sir Harry Calvert* (London, 1853), 367.
48. Cornwallis to Ross, 21 November 1794: Ross/II, 275.
49. Quoted in Burne, *Noble Duke of York*, 201.
50. Dundas to York, 27 November 1794: Ross/II, 277; Dundas to Cornwallis, 27 November 1794: ibid., 276–7.
51. J.C. Long, *Lord Jeffery Amherst: A Soldier of the King* (New York, 1933), 319.
52. Ehrman, *Younger Pitt*, II, 492.
53. Ibid., 287–95.

54. Dundas to Pitt, undated (*c.* September 1794): PRO/30/8/157; Burne, *Noble Duke of York*, 184–6.
55. Pitt to George III, 28 January 1795: Aspinall (ed.), *Later Correspondence*, II, 298.
56. Cornwallis to Ross, 30 December 1795: Ross/II, 281.
57. Cornwallis to Ross, 26 January 1795: ibid., 283–4.
58. Cornwallis to Ross, 3 February 1795: NAM/1997/04/115/2.
59. George III to Pitt, 10 February 1795: PRO/30/8/103.
60. Cornwallis to Dundas, 2 February 1795: Ross/II, 286–7.
61. Cornwallis to Pitt, 21 May 1795: PRO/30/8/125. Ross had been promoted to Major General in February 1795.
62. Beatson, *Political Index*, I, 390; commission to be master-general of the Ordnance, 23 February 1795: PRO/30/11/219.
63. A. Forbes, *A History of the Army Ordnance Services*, 3 vols (London, 1929), I, 94–6.
64. Cornwallis to Ross, 18 February 1795: NAM/1997/04/115/2.
65. Grant to Cornwallis, 21 February 1795: PRO/30/11/231.
66. *The Times*, 18 March 1795.
67. Cornwallis to Ross, 3 February 1795: NAM/1997/04/115/2.
68. Ehrman, *Younger Pitt*, II, 547–8.
69. Cornwallis to Dundas, 10 February 1795: PRO/30/11/236.
70. Cornwallis to Dundas, 10 February 1795: NRS/GD/51/1/608/3.
71. Cornwallis to Dundas, 10 February 1795: PRO/30/11/236.
72. Cornwallis to Dundas, 21 March 1795: ibid.
73. Cornwallis to CO Danbury Camp, 29 June 1795: ibid.
74. F. Duncan, *History of the Royal Regiment of Artillery,* 2 vols (London, 1879), II, 74.
75. Apsley to Colonel Farrington, 23 February 1795: PRO/30/11/236.
76. Green to Cornwallis, 18 February 1795: PRO/30/11/224.
77. List of surveys and plans taken from HM Drawing Room, 24 February 1795: ibid.
78. Apsley to Captain C. Holloway, 9 March 1795: PRO/30/11/236.
79. Instructions to Captain L. Hay, 9 March 1795: ibid.
80. Apsley to Napier, 25 April 1795: ibid.
81. Cornwallis to Prince Edward, 23 May 1795: ibid.
82. Apsley to Cartwright, 12 May 1795: ibid.
83. Cornwallis to Ross, 25 May 1795: Ross/II, 290–1.
84. Cornwallis to Grafton, 16 April 1797: PRO/30/11/59.
85. Cornwallis to Pitt, 17 May 1795: PRO/30/8/125.
86. Crew to Ordnance inspectors at Birmingham, 6 May 1795: WO/46/24.
87. Crew to Trotter, 17 July 1795: ibid.; Crew to Miller, 27 July 1795: ibid.
88. Crew to Trotter, 21 December 1795: ibid.
89. Forbes, *History of the Ordnance*, I, 107–8.
90. Apsley to Colonel Brownrigg, 6 June 1795: PRO/30/11/236. Brownrigg was York's military secretary.
91. Apsley to Brownrigg, 18 June 1795: ibid.
92. Ordnance Board minute, 28 May 1795: WO/47/2366.
93. Fawcett to Cornwallis, 23 April 1795: PRO/30/11/270.
94. Cornwallis to Ross, 4 June 1795: NAM/1997/04/115/2.
95. Cornwallis to Ross, 20 September 1795: Ross/II, 296.
96. Cornwallis to Brome, 27 June 1797: PRO/30/11/276.
97. Cornwallis to Ross, 28 June 1795: Ross/II, 293.
98. Abercromby to Cornwallis, 18 December 1794 (received 21 August 1795): ibid., 293–4.
99. Cornwallis to Ross, 4 June 1795: NAM/1997/04/115/2.
100. Ehrman, *Younger Pitt*, II, 567–77.
101. Dundas to Cornwallis, 28 July 1795: PRO/30/11/230.
102. Ehrman, *Younger Pitt*, II, 566–7.
103. Crew to Cornwallis, 26 October 1795: WO/46/24.

104. Almon, *Parliamentary Register, Second Series*, XLIII, 581.
105. Michael Duffy, *Soldiers, Sugar and Seapower: The British Expeditions to the West Indies and the War against Revolutionary France* (Oxford, 1987), 188–97.
106. Cornwallis to Ross, 28 January 1796: Ross/II, 299.
107. Ehrman, *Younger Pitt*, II, 287.
108. Ibid., 530–3.
109. Abercromby to Cornwallis, 1 June 1796: PRO/30/11/229.
110. Cornwallis-West, *Admiral Cornwallis*, 314.
111. Cornwallis to Ross, 18 March 1796: Ross/II, 299.
112. Cornwallis to Ross, 22 March 1796: ibid., 303.
113. Spencer to Cornwallis, undated (*c.* April 1796): Julian Corbett (ed.), *Private Papers of George, Second Earl Spencer, First Lord of the Admiralty, 1794–1801*, 4 vols (London, 1913–24), I, 229.
114. Cornwallis to York, 20 June 1796: PRO/30/11/59.
115. Ordnance Board minute, 8 April 1796: WO/47/2560.
116. Crew to Trotter, 25 April 1796: WO/46/24.
117. Ordnance Board minute, 17 June 1796: WO/47/2561.
118. Crew to Ross, 30 July 1796: WO/46/24; Crew to the chevalier d'Almeida, 5 August 1796: ibid.
119. Memorandum respecting Mr Raby, 4 August 1796: PRO/30/11/59.
120. Cornwallis to Ross, 15 April 1796: Ross/II, 304.
121. Ordnance Board minute, 7 January 1796: WO/47/2560.
122. Dundas to Cornwallis, 19 August 1796: Ross/II, 310–11.
123. Cornwallis to Twiss, 10 August 1796: PRO/30/11/59.
124. Cornwallis to Francis Schutz, 12 October 1796: ibid.
125. Cornwallis to Fawcett, 4 November 1796: ibid.
126. Duncan, *History of the Royal Artillery*, II, 31.
127. Cornwallis to York, 25 November 1796: PRO/30/11/59. For a critical view of Cornwallis's ideas on the artillery, see Richard Glover, *Peninsula Preparation: The Reform of the British Army, 1795–1809* (Cambridge, 1988), 38–9.
128. Gordon to York, 1 February 1797: WO/46/25.
129. Cornwallis to York, 22 February 1797: PRO/30/11/59.
130. York to Cornwallis, 19 February 1797: WO/46/25.
131. Cornwallis to York, 22 February 1797: ibid.
132. York to Cornwallis, 22 February 1797: PRO/30/11/221.
133. Memorandum to Mr Dundas, February 1797: WO/46/25.
134. Abercromby to Cornwallis, 10 March 1796: Ross/II, 311; Major William Scott to Cornwallis, 24 February 1796: PRO/30/11/56.
135. Cornwallis to Ross, 26 January 1795: Ross/II, 284. Cornwallis's plan to reform the Company's army can be found in his letter to Dundas, 7 November 1794: ibid., 572–82.
136. Robinson to Cornwallis, 3 September 1796: ibid., 323–4.
137. Dundas to Cornwallis, 18 January 1797: ibid., 319–20.
138. Cornwallis to Dundas, 19 January 1797: ibid., 320–1.
139. Cornwallis to Ross, 23 January 1797: NAM/1997/04/115/2.
140. George III to Pitt, 20 January 1797: Aspinall (ed.), *Later Correspondence*, II, 545.
141. Cornwallis to Ross, 24 January 1797: Ross/II, 322.
142. Abercromby to Cornwallis, 5 July 1796: ibid., 322; Shore to Cornwallis, 6 July 1796, Teignmouth, *Memoir*, I, 379–80.
143. Robinson to Cornwallis, 3 September 1796: Ross/II, 323–4.
144. Cornwallis to Ross, 9 May 1797: ibid., 326–7.
145. Cabinet minute, 26 February 1797: ibid., 325–6.
146. Baring (ed.), *Windham Diary*, 11 May 1797, 383.
147. Duncan, *History of the Royal Artillery*, II, 71.
148. Ehrman, *Younger Pitt*, III, 30–1.

149. Baring (ed.), *Windham Diary*, 31 May 1797, 367; Peter Jupp, *Lord Grenville, 1759–1834* (Oxford, 1985), 203–4.
150. Camden to Portland, 28 April 1797: HO/100/69.
151. Portland to Camden, 19 May 1797: ibid.
152. Baring (ed.), *Windham Diary*, 3 May 1797, 361–2.
153. Camden to Cornwallis, 23 May 1797: Ross/II, 327–8.
154. Portland to Cornwallis, 28 May 1797: ibid., 328–9.
155. Portland to Camden, 11 June 1797: HO/100/69.
156. *General Evening Post*, 15–18 April 1797.
157. Ehrman, *Younger Pitt*, III, 50–4.
158. Cornwallis to Ross, 20 August 1797: Ross/II, 329.
159. Cornwallis to Ross, 15 December 1797: ibid., 329–30.
160. Cornwallis to Wellesley, 23 February 1798: ibid., 333; Glover, *Peninsula Preparation*, 122–6, suggests that Cornwallis exaggerated the lack of light infantry.
161. Cornwallis to Ross, 20 March 1798: Ross/II, 334.
162. Cornwallis to Ross, 31 March 1798: ibid., 336.
163. Cornwallis to Ross, 14 April 1798: ibid., 336.
164. Cornwallis to Ross, 20 April 1798: NAM/1997/04/115/2.
165. Cornwallis to Ross, 24 April 1798: Ross/II, 336–7.
166. Ordnance Board minute, 14 June 1798: WO/47/2565; Glover, *Peninsula Preparation*, 191–2.

CHAPTER 14: BRINGING PEACE TO IRELAND

1. S.J. Connolly, *Divided Kingdom: Ireland, 1630–1800* (Oxford, 2008), 416–20.
2. Ehrman, *Younger Pitt*, I, 195–216, 663–4.
3. Ibid., 438–71; Marianne Elliott, *Partners in Revolution: The United Irishmen and France* (London, 1982).
4. Ehrman, *Younger Pitt*, III, 430–40.
5. Marianne Elliott, *Wolfe Tone: Prophet of Irish Independence* (New Haven, 1989), 320–8.
6. Camden to Pitt, 26 March 1798: PRO/30/8/326; Camden to Pitt, 7 April 1798: ibid.
7. Pitt to Camden, 31 March 1798: KRO/U/840/O/190A.
8. Camden to Pitt, 26 March 1798: PRO/30/8/326; Camden to Pitt, 10 April 1798: ibid.
9. Camden to Portland, 24 May 1798: HO/100/76; Thomas Packenham, *The Year of Liberty: The Great Irish Rebellion of 1798* (London, 1997), 88–103.
10. Address of Dr Troy, archbishop of Dublin, to the clergy: Charles Vane, marquess of Londonderry (ed.), *Memoirs and Correspondence of Viscount Castlereagh, Second Marquess of Londonderry*, 12 vols (London, 1848–53), I, 209–11.
11. Camden to Pitt, 6 June 1798: PRO/30/8/326.
12. Pitt to George III, 11 June 1798: Aspinall (ed.), *Later Correspondence*, III, 77–8.
13. Pitt to Camden, 11 June 1798: KRO/U/840/O/190A.
14. Cornwallis to Ross, 1 July 1798: Ross/II, 357–8.
15. Smith, *Wealth of Nations*, 757–8.
16. George III to Pitt, 11 June 1798: PRO/30/8/104; Packenham, *Year of Liberty*, 242.
17. George III to Pitt, 13 June 1798: PRO/30/8/104; Ehrman, *Younger Pitt*, III, 176.
18. Castlereagh to Wickham, 20 June 1798: HO/100/81.
19. Form for receiving Marquess Cornwallis: NLI, Genealogical Office, Ms 96.
20. Cornwallis to Portland, 21 June 1798: Ross/II, 354.
21. Portland to Cornwallis, 21 June 1798: HO/122/5.
22. Cornwallis to Ross, 1 July 1798: Ross/II, 357–8.
23. Cornwallis to Portland, 28 June 1798: ibid., 356–7.
24. Cornwallis to Ross, 1 July 1798: ibid., 357–8.
25. Cornwallis to Portland, 28 June 1798: ibid., 356–7. A bill was subsequently passed giving legislative authority for the proclamation: 38 Geo. 3 c. 55.
26. Cornwallis to Portland, 8 July 1798: Ross/II, 358–60.

27. William Edward Hartpole Lecky, *A History of Ireland in the Eighteenth Century*, 6 vols (London, 1913), V, 103–4.
28. Camden to Castlereagh, undated (*c.* 8 March 1799): PRONI/D/3030/692.
29. Cornwallis to Pitt, 20 July 1798: Ross/II, 366–7.
30. Cornwallis to Ross, 8 December 1798: Ross/III, 8–9.
31. Cornwallis to Ross, 24 July 1798: Ross/II, 370–1.
32. Elliot to Thomas Pelham, 28 July 1798: John Thomas Gilbert (ed.), *Documents Relating to Ireland, 1795–1804* (Dublin, 1893), 143–4.
33. Cornwallis to Portland, 26 July 1798: Ross/II, 372–4.
34. Lecky, *History of Ireland*, V, 28–9.
35. Ann C. Kavanaugh, *John FitzGibbon, Earl of Clare: Protestant Reaction and English Authority in Late Eighteenth-Century Ireland* (Dublin, 1997), 346–7.
36. Memorandum on the state of affairs in the county of Wicklow, 20 August 1798: Ross/II, 387–9.
37. Cornwallis to Ross, 10 August 1798: ibid., 383.
38. F.J. Maurice (ed.), *The Diary of Sir John Moore*, 2 vols (London, 1904), I, 308.
39. Ibid., 327–8.
40. Packenham, *Year of Liberty*, 298–9.
41. Maurice (ed.), *Diary of Sir John Moore*, I, 312–13.
42. Castlereagh to Wickham, 26 August 1798: Ross/II, 394.
43. Maurice (ed.), *Diary of Sir John Moore*, I, 315.
44. Lake to Taylor, 27 August 1798: HO/100/78; Statement of Major-General Hutchinson, 21 September 1798: Ross/II, 411–13; Packenham, *Year of Liberty*, 309–11.
45. Cornwallis to Portland, 28 August 1798: Ross/II, 394.
46. Taylor to Castlereagh, 31 August 1798: ibid., 396.
47. Cornwallis to Portland, 5 September 1798: ibid., 400.
48. Cornwallis to Portland, 8 September 1798: ibid., 402–3.
49. General orders, 8 September 1798: ibid., 403–4.
50. G.C. Bolton, *The Passing of the Irish Act of Union: A Study in Parliamentary Politics* (Oxford, 1966), 64.
51. Cornwallis to Ross, 23 November 1798: Ross/II, 445–6.
52. Maurice (ed.), *Diary of Sir John Moore*, I, 324.
53. Cornwallis to Pitt, 25 September 1798: Ross/II, 414–16; see also Cornwallis to Ross, 30 September 1798: ibid., 416.
54. Packenham, *Year of Liberty*, 336–8; Elliott, *Wolfe Tone*, 386–7.
55. Cornwallis to Pitt, 25 September 1798: Ross/II, 416; Kavanaugh, *FitzGibbon*, 344.
56. Cornwallis to Portland, 16 September 1798: Ross/II, 406–7.
57. Ibid.
58. Cornwallis to Pitt, 8 October 1798: Ross/II, 417–18.
59. Cornwallis to Thomas Pelham, 15 October 1798: Gilbert (ed.), *Documents Relating to Ireland*, 192–3.
60. Cornwallis to Pitt, 17 October 1798: Ross/II, 420–1.
61. Portland to Cornwallis, 4 November 1798: HO/100/79.
62. Richard Temple-Nugent-Brydges-Chandos-Grenville, second duke of Buckingham and Chandos (ed.), *Memoirs of the Courts and Cabinets of George III*, 4 vols (London, 1853–55), II, 407.
63. Elliot to Castlereagh, 24 October 1798: Londonderry (ed.), *Memoirs and Correspondence*, I, 404–5.
64. Cornwallis to Dundas, 15 November 1798, NRS/GD/51/1/331.
65. Elliot to Castlereagh, 9 November 1798: Londonderry (ed.), *Memoirs and Correspondence*, I, 430–1.
66. Memorandum from Mr Pitt, 3 November 1798: Ross/II, 433.
67. A.P.W. Malcomson, *John Foster: The Politics of the Anglo-Irish Ascendancy* (Oxford, 1978), 81–2.
68. Cornwallis to Castlereagh, 7 November 1798: Londonderry (ed.), *Memoirs and Correspondence*, I, 428.
69. Cornwallis to Pitt, 1 November 1798: Ross/II, 429; Bolton, *Act of Union*, 70–1.
70. Portland to Cornwallis, 12 November 1798: Ross/II, 436–7.

71. Portland to Cornwallis, 25 November 1798: ibid., 456–7.

72. Points to be considered in an Act of Union, undated (*c.* 1798): NLI, Ms 887; Bolton, *Act of Union*, 85–7.

73. Pitt to Cornwallis, 17 November 1798: Ross/II, 441–3.

74. Cornwallis to Ross, 15 November 1798: NAM/1997/04/115/3.

75. Cornwallis to Ross, 23 November 1798: Ross/II, 445–6.

76. Cornwallis to Portland, 27 November 1798: HO/100/79.

77. Cornwallis to Ross, 23 November 1798: Ross/II, 445.

78. Castlereagh to Wickham, 23 November 1798: ibid., 446–8.

79. Cornwallis to Portland, 2 January 1799: Ross/III, 28–9.

80. Castlereagh to Wickham, 23 November 1798: Ross/II, 446–8.

81. Castlereagh to Portland, 5 January 1799: Ross/III, 30–2.

82. Memorandum, 15 January 1799: HO/100/85; Portland to Cornwallis, 17 January 1799: ibid.

83. Cornwallis to Portland, 11 January 1799: Ross/III, 34–5; Bolton, *Act of Union*, 98.

84. Cornwallis to Portland, 11 January 1799: ibid., 34–6.

85. Cornwallis to Portland, 16 January 1798: ibid., 38.

86. Lecky, *History of Ireland*, V, 219–20.

87. Cornwallis to Portland, 23 January 1799: Ross/III, 40–4.

88. Cornwallis to Portland, 25 January 1799: ibid., 48–50; Castlereagh to Portland, 28 January 1799: HO/100/85.

89. Lecky, *History of Ireland*, V, 229.

90. Castlereagh to Portland, 21 January 1799: Londonderry (ed.), *Memoirs and Correspondence*, II, 126–7; Castlereagh to Portland, 28 January 1798: ibid., 142–5.

91. Grenville to Buckingham, 28 January 1799: Buckingham and Chandos (ed.), *Memoirs of the Courts and Cabinets*, II, 429–31.

92. Cornwallis to Portland, 23 January 1799: Ross/III, 45.

93. Cornwallis to Portland, 26 January 1799: ibid., 52.

94. Portland to Castlereagh, 29 January 1799: Londonderry (ed.), *Memoirs and Correspondence*, II, 148.

95. Memorandum relative to opposition to the Union from personal interests, 1 February 1799: Londonderry (ed.), ibid., III, 68–9.

96. Suggestions of the lord lieutenant as to the representation of Ireland, 7 December 1798: Ross/III, 6–7.

97. Gilbert (ed.), *Documents Relating to Ireland*, v–vi, 3–88.

98. Castlereagh to Wickham, 2 January 1799: Ross/III, 27; David Wilkinson, ' "How Did They Pass the Union?": Secret Service Expenditure in Ireland, 1799–1804', *History* 82 (April 1997), 223–51.

99. Cornwallis to Portland, 14 February 1799: Ross/III, 60–2.

100. Patrick M. Geoghegan, *The Irish Act of Union: A Study in High Politics, 1798–1801* (Dublin, 1999), 81–2.

101. Portland to Cornwallis, 3 March 1799: Ross/III, 72.

102. Cornwallis to Portland, 11 March 1799: ibid., 73–4.

103. Castlereagh to Wickham, 6 March 1799: HO/100/86.

104. Cornwallis to Ross, 20 May 1799: Ross/III, 100–1.

105. Cornwallis to Ross, 8 June 1799: ibid., 102.

106. Cornwallis to Portland, 26 June 1799: ibid., 106–8.

107. Cornwallis to Portland, 22 June 1799: ibid., 104–6.

108. Cornwallis to Portland, 20 July 1799: Londonderry (ed.), *Memoirs and Correspondence*, II, 351–2.

109. Ibid.

110. Cornwallis to Ross, 24 July 1799: Ross/III, 119.

111. Cornwallis to Portland, 14 August 1799: ibid., 124–5.

112. Cornwallis to Portland, 13 August 1799: ibid., 121–2.

113. Ibid., 121.

114. Cornwallis to Dundas, 19 July 1799: ibid., 116–18; Cornwallis to Ross, 14 August 1799: ibid., 123; Piers Mackesy, *War without Victory: The Downfall of Pitt, 1799–1802* (Oxford, 1984), 55–8.
115. Cornwallis to Ross, 16 September 1799: Ross/III, 130–1.
116. Cornwallis to Portland, 17 September 1799: ibid., 131–2.
117. Cornwallis to Ross, 16 November 1799: ibid., 144–5.
118. Cornwallis to Ross, 16 September 1799: ibid., 130.
119. Cornwallis to Ross, 24 December 1799: ibid., 151–2.
120. Cornwallis to Castlereagh, 26 September 1799: ibid., 135.
121. Cornwallis to Portland, 22 October 1799: ibid., 138–40.
122. Cornwallis to Portland, 22 November 1799: ibid., 145–6.
123. Cornwallis to Ross, 29 November 1799: ibid., 147–8.
124. Cornwallis to Ross, 26 December 1799: ibid., 153.
125. Cornwallis to Ross, 28 December 1799: ibid., 153.
126. Castlereagh to John King, 2 January 1800: ibid., 156; Geoghegan, *Irish Act of Union*, 97.
127. Speech to the two houses, 16 January 1800: HO/100/95.
128. Cornwallis to Ross, 16 January 1800: Ross/III, 163.
129. Cornwallis to Portland, 21 January 1800: ibid., 168–9.
130. Castlereagh to Portland, 7 February 1800: ibid., 182–3.
131. Castlereagh to Portland, 11 February 1800: ibid., 186.
132. Cornwallis to Portland, 4 February 1800: ibid., 178–9.
133. Cornwallis to Portland, 14 February 1800: HO/100/93.
134. Cornwallis to Lichfield, 5 February 1800: Ross/III, 183–4.
135. Cornwallis to Portland, 18 February 1800: ibid., 194–6.
136. Cornwallis to Portland, 14 March 1800: ibid., 212–13.
137. Cornwallis to Portland, 22 March 1800: ibid., 214–17.
138. Portland to Cornwallis, 7 April 1800: ibid., 226–8.
139. Cornwallis to Portland, 29 March 1800: ibid., 220–2.
140. Cornwallis to Ross, 18 May 1800: ibid., 235.
141. Cornwallis to Grisdale, 21 April 1800: ibid., 228–9.
142. Cornwallis to Ross, 21 May 1800: ibid., 237–8.
143. Cornwallis to Portland, 7 June 1800: ibid., 247–9.
144. Cornwallis to Portland, 9 June 1800: ibid., 251–3; List of persons recommended to His Majesty for the Peerage of Ireland, undated (*c.* 9 June 1800): ibid., 253–6; see also Cornwallis to Portland, 3 June 1800: ibid., 244–7.
145. Portland to Cornwallis, 13 June 1800: ibid., 257–62.
146. Cornwallis to Portland, 17 June 1800: ibid., 262–6.
147. Castlereagh to Camden, 18 June 1800: Londonderry (ed.), *Memoirs and Correspondence*, III, 326–9.
148. Castlereagh to Cooke, 21 June 1800: ibid., 330–1.
149. Portland to Cornwallis, 27 June 1800: Ross/III, 271–4.
150. Cornwallis to Ross, 11 July 1800: ibid., 276–8.
151. List of creations: ibid., 318–19. Several creations here were not connected with the issue of union.
152. Geoghegan, *Irish Act of Union*, 128.
153. List of boroughs disfranchised: Ross/III, 321–4.
154. Ehrman, *Younger Pitt*, III, 187–8; Wilkinson, ' "How Did They Pass the Union?" ', 223–51; Geoghegan, *Irish Act of Union*, 120–9, 205–6.
155. Castlereagh to Portland, 6 July 1800: Londonderry (ed.), *Memoirs and Correspondence*, III, 357.
156. Quoted in Wickwire and Wickwire, *The Imperial Years*, 247–8.
157. Cornwallis to Ross, 3 July 1800: Ross/III, 269–70.
158. Cornwallis to William Cornwallis, 13 June 1800: HMC, *Report on Various Collections*, VI, 393.
159. Cornwallis to Ross, 16 August 1800: Ross/III, 288.
160. Cornwallis to Portland, 2 September 1800: Londonderry (ed.), *Memoirs and Correspondence*, III, 374–5.
161. Cornwallis to Ross, 17 September 1800: Ross/III, 292.

162. Draft extract, 7 September 1800: ibid., 292–3; Mackesy, *War without Victory*, 144.
163. Cornwallis to Ross, 8 October 1800: Ross/III, 294.
164. Cornwallis to Ross, 24 October 1800: ibid., 296.
165. Cornwallis to Portland, 1 November 1800: ibid., 296–7.
166. Cornwallis to Ross, 6 November 1800: ibid., 300–1.
167. Cornwallis to Ross, 22 April 1800: ibid., 229.
168. Cornwallis to Portland, 3 February 1801: HO/100/105.
169. Cornwallis to Ross, 23 December 1799: NAM/1997/04/115/3.
170. Cornwallis to Ross, 4 February 1800: Ross/III, 177.
171. Glover, *Peninsular Preparation*, 130–1.
172. Cornwallis to Ross, 21 June 1800: NAM/1997/04/115/3.
173. Portland to Cornwallis, 25 September 1800: Ross/III, 293–4,
174. Cornwallis to Ross, 8 October 1800: ibid., 294.
175. Cornwallis to Ross, 24 October 1800: ibid., 296.
176. Cornwallis to Ross, 6 November 1800: ibid., 300–1; Fortescue, *British Army*, IV, 789–96.
177. Cornwallis to Portland, 1 November 1800: Ross/III, 299–300; Cornwallis to Portland, 18 November 1800: ibid., 305.
178. Cornwallis to Portland, 1 December 1800: Ross/III: ibid., 306–7.
179. Cornwallis to Ross, 14 December 1800: NAM/1997/04/115/3.
180. Cornwallis to Castlereagh, 2 January 1801: Londonderry (ed.), *Memoirs and Correspondence*, IV, 13.
181. Castlereagh to Pitt, 1 January 1801: Ross/III, 326–30.
182. Ehrman, *Younger Pitt*, III, 496–504.
183. Cornwallis to Castlereagh, 14 January 1801: Ross/III, 331–2.
184. Cornwallis to Castlereagh, 22 January 1801: Londonderry (ed.), *Memoirs and Correspondence*, IV, 21.
185. Cornwallis to Castlereagh, 2 February 1801: ibid., 24–5.
186. George III to Pitt, 1 February 1801: PRO/30/8/104.
187. Ehrman, *Younger Pitt*, III, 504–23.
188. Cornwallis to Ross, 26 February 1801: NAM/1997/04/115/3.
189. Charles John Fedorak, *Henry Addington, Prime Minister, 1801–1804: Peace, War and Parliamentary Politics* (Akron, 2002), 26–46.
190. Cornwallis to Ross, 15 February 1801: Ross/III, 337.
191. Cornwallis to Lichfield, 17 February 1801: ibid., 338–9.
192. Castlereagh to Cornwallis, 9 February 1801: ibid., 335.
193. Statement about the two papers, March 1801: PRO/30/8/327.
194. Memorandum 1: Mr Pitt's Sentiments, March 1801: Ross/III, 347–8.
195. Memorandum II: Sentiments of a Sincere Friend to the Catholic Cause, March 1801: ibid., 349.
196. Portland to Cornwallis, 23 February 1801: ibid., 341–2.
197. Cornwallis to Castlereagh, 7 March 1801: Londonderry (ed.), *Memoirs and Correspondence*, IV, 76–7.
198. Cornwallis to Ross, 9 March 1801: Ross/III, 346–7.
199. Cornwallis to Ross, 26 February 1801: ibid., 340–1.
200. Cooke to Castlereagh, 27 February 1801: Londonderry (ed.), *Memoirs and Correspondence*, IV, 63.
201. Portland to Cornwallis, 19 March 1801: Ross/III, 351.
202. Cornwallis to Ross, 24 June 1801: NAM/1997/04/115/4.
203. Cornwallis to Ross, 1 May 1801: Ross/III, 357–8.
204. Cornwallis to Portland, 4 May 1801: ibid., 358.
205. Cornwallis to Grisdale, 15 May 1801: ibid., 362.
206. Cornwallis to Ross, 18 April 1801: ibid., 356.
207. Cornwallis to Grisdale, 9 May 1801: ibid., 359.
208. Cornwallis to Ross, 12 May 1801: ibid., 361
209. Form for receiving Earl Hardwicke: NLI, Genealogical Office, Ms 96.
210. Report from Dublin Castle, 27 May 1801: HO/100/105.

CHAPTER 15: ATTEMPTING PEACE WITH FRANCE

1. Cornwallis to Ross, 28 May 1801: Ross/III, 364; Cornwallis to Ross, 30 May 1801: ibid., 365.
2. Cornwallis to Lichfield, 12 March 1801: ibid., 349–50.
3. Cornwallis to Ross, 19 July 1801: ibid., 377–8.
4. Cornwallis to Ross, 2 July 1801: ibid., 377.
5. Cornwallis to Ross, 19 July 1801: ibid., 377–8.
6. *Morning Chronicle*, 6 August 1801.
7. York to Cornwallis, 2 July 1801: PRO/30/11/268.
8. Cornwallis to Ross, 23 July 1801: Ross/III, 378–9.
9. Ibid., 379.
10. Cornwallis to Ross, 4 August 1801: Ross/III, 380.
11. Cornwallis to Ross, 17 September 1801: ibid., 382.
12. Cornwallis to Ross, 22 September 1801: ibid., 382–3.
13. Cornwallis to Ross, 30 September 1801: ibid., 383.
14. The conquests returned by Britain included Martinique, Tobago, and Saint Lucia in the West Indies and Pondicherry in India. Minorca was also returned to Spain and the Cape to Holland.
15. Preliminary articles of peace, 1 October 1801: KRO/U/269/O/1999/1; Fedorak, *Henry Addington*, 597–68.
16. Hawkesbury to George III, 5 October 1801: Aspinall (ed.), *Later Correspondence*, III, 614–15.
17. Cornwallis to William Cornwallis, 10 November 1801: Cornwallis-West, *Admiral Cornwallis*, 372.
18. Ehrman, *Younger Pitt*, III, 558–9.
19. Cornwallis to Ross, 9 October 1801: Ross/III, 383; Ehrman, *Younger Pitt*, 559–63.
20. *Morning Chronicle*, 17 October 1801.
21. Cornwallis to Ross, 16 October 1801: Ross/III, 383–4.
22. Cornwallis to Kennaway, 19 October 1801: ibid., 384.
23. *The Times*, 22 October 1801; ibid., 26 October 1801.
24. George III to Cornwallis, instructions, 1 November 1801: KRO/U/269/O/199/1.
25. Hawkesbury to Cornwallis, 1 November 1801: Ross/III, 388–9.
26. Ibid.
27. Cornwallis to Ross, 8 November 1801: Ross/III, 390; *The Times*, 2 November 1801.
28. Cornwallis to Hawkesbury, 8 November 1801: PRO/30/11/264.
29. Steven Englund, *Napoleon: A Political Life* (New York, 2004), 201.
30. Cornwallis to Hawkesbury, 10 November 1801: Ross/III, 390–1.
31. Memorandum, 7 November 1801: ibid., 391; Hawkesbury to Cornwallis, 7 November 1801: KRO/U/269/O/199/1.
32. Cornwallis to Hawkesbury, 12 November 1801: PRO/30/11/264.
33. Hawkesbury to Cornwallis, 14 November 1801: Ross/III, 392–3.
34. Ibid.
35. Hawkesbury to Cornwallis, 16 November 1801: Ross/III, 393–4.
36. Cornwallis to Hawkesbury, 20 November 1801: ibid., 394–6.
37. Littlehales to Ross, 21 November 1801: ibid., 397.
38. *Morning Chronicle*, 19 November 1801.
39. Littlehales to Ross, 21 November 1801: Ross/III, 397.
40. Heads of conversation, 24 November 1801: ibid., 397–8.
41. Ibid., 398–9.
42. Cornwallis to Hawkesbury, 3 December 1801: Ross/III, 399–404.
43. John D. Grainger, *The Amiens Truce: Britain and Bonaparte, 1801–1803* (Woodbridge, 2004), 58–9.
44. Hawkesbury to Cornwallis, 27 November 1801: FO/27/59.
45. Cornwallis to Hawkesbury, 6 December 1801: Ross/III, 404–6.
46. Cornwallis to Ross, 7 December 1801: ibid., 406.
47. Hawkesbury to Cornwallis, 5 December 1801: ibid., 406–7.
48. Cornwallis to Hawkesbury, 13 December 1801: ibid., 411–13.

49. Cornwallis to Hawkesbury, 19 December 1801: ibid., 415–16.
50. Cornwallis to Ross, 15 December 1801: ibid., 413–14.
51. Michael Broers, *Napoleon, Volume 1: Soldier of Destiny, 1769–1805* (London, 2014), 262–3.
52. Cornwallis to Ross, 25 December 1801: Ross/III, 418.
53. Cornwallis to Addington, 27 December 1801: ibid., 418–19.
54. Fedorak, *Henry Addington*, 81.
55. Cornwallis to Hawkesbury, 30 December 1801: Ross/III, 420–1.
56. Cornwallis to Hawkesbury, 31 December 1801: ibid., 424.
57. Cornwallis to Hawkesbury, 10 January 1802: ibid., 432–3.
58. Cornwallis to Hawkesbury, 11 January 1802: KRO/U/269/O/199/3.
59. Cornwallis to Hawkesbury, 10 January 1802: Ross/III, 434–5.
60. Nightingall to Ross, 10 January 1802: ibid., 435–7.
61. Cornwallis to Ross, 16 January 1802: ibid., 437.
62. Hawkesbury to Cornwallis, 16 January 1802: Ross/III, 438.
63. Cornwallis to Hawkesbury, 17 January 1802: PRO/30/11/264.
64. Cornwallis to Hawkesbury, 21 January 1802: ibid.
65. Cornwallis to Hawkesbury (private), 21 January 1802: Ross/III, 440.
66. Cornwallis to Ross, 21 January 1802: ibid., 439.
67. Cornwallis to Hawkesbury, 23 January 1802: ibid., 441–3.
68. Cornwallis to Hawkesbury, 1 February 1802: PRO/30/11/265.
69. Cornwallis to Hawkesbury, 5 February 1802: Ross/III, 446–7.
70. The Spanish were aggrieved at having to give up Louisiana to France and Trinidad to Britain: Grainger, *Amiens Truce*, 64–5.
71. Cornwallis to Hawkesbury, 5 February 1802: Ross/III, 448–9.
72. Cornwallis to Hawkesbury, 9 February 1802: ibid., 450–1.
73. Cornwallis to Hawkesbury, 22 February 1802: ibid., 458–9.
74. Cornwallis to Ross, 26 February 1802: ibid., 460.
75. Hawkesbury to Cornwallis, 2 March 1802: KRO/U/269/O/199/1.
76. Cornwallis to Hawkesbury, 26 February 1802: Ross/III, 460–1.
77. Cornwallis to Hawkesbury, 10 March 1802: ibid., 463–7.
78. Cornwallis to Addington, 10 March 1802: ibid., 468.
79. Cornwallis to Hawkesbury, 10 March 1802: ibid., 468–9.
80. Cornwallis to Hawkesbury, 13 March 1802: ibid., 469–72; draft final version, 14 March 1802: FO/27/60.
81. Hawkesbury to Cornwallis, 14 March 1802: Ross/III, 472–7.
82. Cornwallis to Hawkesbury, 17 March 1802: ibid., 477–80.
83. Cornwallis to Hawkesbury, 20 March 1802: ibid., 480–1.
84. Hawkesbury to Cornwallis, 22 March 1802: ibid., 481–2.
85. Ibid., 482.
86. The final adjustments are described in Cornwallis's letter of 28 March 1802: Ross/III, 485–7.
87. Cornwallis to Hawkesbury, 27 March 1802: ibid., 484.
88. There is a copy in Cobbett, *Parliamentary History*, XXXVI, 557–64.
89. Ehrman, *Younger Pitt*, III, 566–8.
90. *Morning Chronicle*, 31 March 1802.
91. Fedorak, *Henry Addington*, 89–111.

CHAPTER 16: LAST CALL

1. Cornwallis to Kennaway, 10 April 1802: Ross/III, 488.
2. Cornwallis to York, May 1802: ibid., 488–91.
3. *Morning Chronicle*, 5 May 1802. Debate in the Lords on the Definitive Peace, 13 May 1802: Cobbett, *Parliamentary History*, XXXVI, 686–97.

4. Grenville spitefully reminded Cornwallis of this exchange at the start of the next parliamentary session, 23 November 1802: ibid., 934.
5. *The Times*, 2 July 1802.
6. Cornwallis to Ross, 30 June 1802: Ross/III, 491.
7. Cornwallis to Ross, 2 July 1802: NAM/1997/04/115/4.
8. Cornwallis to Ross, 7 July 1802: ibid.
9. Cornwallis to Marsden, 19 July 1802: Lecky, *Eighteenth Century Ireland*, V, 470–1.
10. Cornwallis to Ross, 2 September 1802: Ross/III, 493.
11. Ibid., 492–3.
12. Cornwallis to Ross, 27 October 1802: Ross/III, 494–5.
13. Cornwallis to Ross, 12 November 1802: ibid., 495.
14. Cornwallis to Ross, 18 November 1802: ibid., 496.
15. Cornwallis to Ross, 12 November 1802: ibid., 495–6.
16. Cornwallis to Ross, 18 November 1802: ibid., 496.
17. Cornwallis to Ross, 14 November 1802: NAM/1997/04/115/4; Cornwallis to Ross, 18 November 1802: Ross/III, 496. Addington eventually agreed that Brome should have a reversionary tellership of the Exchequer when a vacancy occurred: Cornwallis to Ross, 13 February 1803: ibid., 498.
18. Cornwallis to Ross, 10 December 1802: NAM/1997/04/115/4.
19. Cornwallis to Ross, 19 December 1802: Ross/III, 496–7.
20. Cornwallis to Ross, 13 February 1803: ibid., 498.
21. Cornwallis-West, *Admiral Cornwallis*, 388–9.
22. *The Times*, 23 June 1803.
23. Fedorak, *Henry Addington*, 161–5.
24. *Morning Chronicle*, 29 July 1803.
25. Cornwallis to Ross, 1 August 1803: Ross/III, 498–9.
26. Cornwallis to Ross, 19 August 1803: ibid., 500–1.
27. Cornwallis to Ross, 1 August 1803: NAM/1997/04/115/4.
28. Cornwallis to York, 6 September 1803: Ross/III, 502.
29. Cornwallis to Grisdale, 26 September 1803: ibid., 503–4.
30. Cornwallis to Ross, 1 November 1803: ibid., 505–6.
31. Cornwallis to Ross, 6 September 1803: ibid., 502.
32. Cornwallis to York, 6 September 1803: ibid., 502.
33. York to Cornwallis, 8 September 1803: ibid., 503.
34. Cornwallis to Grisdale, 26 September 1803: ibid., 503–4.
35. Cornwallis to Ross, 5 October 1803: ibid., 504–5.
36. Cornwallis to Ross, 1 November 1803: ibid., 505–6.
37. Cornwallis to Ross, 18 December 1803: ibid., 508–9; Glover, *Peninsular Preparation*, 232–7.
38. Cornwallis to Ross, 13 February 1804: ibid., 511–12.
39. Cornwallis to William Cornwallis, 7 June 1804: HMC, *Report on Various Collections*, VI, 403–4.
40. Cornwallis to William Cornwallis, 12 August 1804: ibid., 405.
41. Cornwallis to Ross, 6 August 1804: Ross/III, 515.
42. Cornwallis to Ross, 16 August 1804: NAM/1997/04/115/4.
43. Cornwallis to Ross, 11 September 1804: Ross/III, 518.
44. Cornwallis to Grisdale, 6 October 1804: ibid., 518–19.
45. Cornwallis to Ross, 18 November 1804: NAM/1997/04/115/4.
46. Cornwallis to Grisdale, 6 October 1804, Ross/III, 518–19.
47. Cornwallis to Ross, 14 October 1804: ibid., 519.
48. Cornwallis to Ross, 24 October 1804: ibid., 521.
49. Cornwallis to Ross, 25 November 1804: NAM/1997/04/115/4.
50. Cornwallis to Ross, 6 December 1804: Ross/III, 522–3.
51. Ibid.
52. Cornwallis to Ross, 7 December 1804: Ross/III, 523–4.
53. Cornwallis to Ross, 12 December 1804: NAM/1997/04/115/4.

54. Cornwallis to Ross, 9 January 1805: Ross/III, 527.
55. Cornwallis to Ross, 4 January 1805: ibid., 524–5.
56. Grant to Cornwallis, 4 January 1805: IOR/H/379.
57. *The Times*, 7 January 1805.
58. Cornwallis to Kennaway, 13 January 1805: Ross/III, 527.
59. *The Times*, 21 March 1805.
60. Cornwallis to William Cornwallis, 25 March 1805: HMC, *Report on Various Collections*, VI, 409.
61. Plowden to Cornwallis, 6 April 1805: PRONI, Castlereagh Papers, D/3030/2026.
62. Cornwallis to Plowden, 7 April 1805: ibid. The publication of the history was advertised in the *Morning Chronicle*, 7 May 1805. Thomas Bartlett, *The Fall and Rise of the Irish Nation: The Catholic Question, 1690–1830* (Dublin, 1992), 260–1, absolves Cornwallis and Castlereagh of sharp practice in their dealings with the Catholics.
63. Last will and testament, 5 April 1805: PRO/30/11/278.
64. *Morning Chronicle*, 6 April 1805.
65. Ibid., 16 April 1805.
66. Cornwallis to Brome, 6 May 1805: Ross/III, 532.
67. Gore to William Cornwallis, 23 January 1806: HMC, *Report on Various Collections*, IV, 417.
68. Nightingall to Ross, 15 January 1806: Ross/III, 560.
69. *The Times*, 9 January 1806.
70. Cornwallis to Brome, 23 July 1805: Ross/III, 532–3.
71. Spencer (ed.), *Hickey Memoirs*, IV, 318–19.
72. Ibid., 320–1.
73. Narrative of Lord Cornwallis's administration, 1805: PRO/30/11/210. The author of this document was probably George Robinson.
74. Cornwallis to Lake, 30 July 1805: Ross/III, 533.
75. Cornwallis to the Directors, 1 August 1805: ibid., 535.
76. Cornwallis to Ross, 4 August 1805: ibid., 536.
77. Ibid.
78. Gore to William Cornwallis, 23 January 1806: HMC, *Report on Various Collections*, VI, 417.
79. Nightingall to Brome, 15 January 1806: Ross/III, 560.
80. Cornwallis to Court of Directors, 9 August 1805: ibid., 537–9.
81. Cornwallis to Castlereagh, 9 August 1805: ibid., 540.
82. Cornwallis to Secret Committee, 28 August 1805: ibid., 543–5.
83. Cornwallis to Lake, 1 September 1805: ibid., 546–7.
84. Cornwallis to Malcolm, 14 August 1805: ibid., 541–2.
85. Cornwallis to Lake, 30 August 1805: ibid., 545–6.
86. Cornwallis to Lake, 23 September 1805: ibid., 555–7.
87. Robinson to Castlereagh, 25 September 1805: ibid., 557.
88. Robinson to Ross, 26 September 1805: ibid., 558–9.
89. Nightingall to Brome, 15 January 1806: ibid., 560–1.
90. Gore to William Cornwallis, 23 January 1806: HMC, *Report on Various Collections*, IV, 417.
91. Nightingall to Brome, 16 March 1806: Ross/III, 561.
92. *Calcutta Gazette*, 12 October 1805, reprinted in *Morning Chronicle*, 31 January 1806.
93. T.C. Hansard, *The Parliamentary Debates from the Year 1803*, first series, 41 vols (London, 1812–20), VI, 120–2.
94. Ibid., 122–8.
95. *The Times*, 31 January 1806.
96. Motion of Charles Grant and George Smith, 6 February 1806: PRO/30/11/58.
97. Court of the East India Company, 12 February 1806: ibid.
98. *The Times*, 13 February 1806.
99. Sophia Crichton-Stuart, marchioness of Bute (ed.), *The Private Journal of the Marquess of Hastings*, 2 vols (London, 1858), I, 118.

100. There is a sketch of the mausoleum, dated 2 January 1819, in the Cornwallis papers: PRO/30/11/58.

101. George Otto Trevelyan, *The American Revolution*, 3 vols (London, 1899–1907).

102. Lecky, *History of Ireland*, V, 331.

103. C.A. Bayly and Katherine Prior, 'Cornwallis, Charles, first Marquess Cornwallis (1738–1805), governor-general of India and lord lieutenant of Ireland', *Oxford Dictionary of National Biography*, XIII (2004).

104. Prakash (ed.), *Lord Cornwallis*.

Bibliography

PRIMARY MANUSCRIPTS

India Office Records, British Library, London

Commissions, Instructions, Military Papers – IOR/H
Committee Reports, Memorandum and Correspondence – IOR/D
Minutes of the East India Company – IOR/B
Minutes, Letter Books of the Board of Control – IOR/F
Political and Secret Department – IOR/L/PS
Proceedings of Bengal Government – IOR/P/B

Kent Record Office, Maidstone

Amherst Papers – U/1350
Mann–Cornwallis Papers – U/24
Pratt Additional Mss – U/1968
Pratt Mss (Camden Papers) – U/840
Sackville (Amiens) Papers – U/269

National Archives, Kew

Amherst Papers – WO/34
Chatham Papers – PRO/30/8
Cornwallis Papers – PRO/30/11
Dorchester Papers – PRO/30/55
Foreign Office Papers – FO/27
Home Office Papers – HO/100
Inspection Returns – WO/27
Military Headquarters Papers, North America – WO/36
Ordnance Board Papers – WO/46
Secretary at War Out-letters – WO/4

National Army Museum, London

Cornwallis Ross Correspondence – 1997/04/115

BIBLIOGRAPHY

National Library of Ireland, Dublin

Genealogical Office – Mss 96
Littlehales Letter Book – Mss 42,451
Lord Lieutenants' Correspondence – Mss 886–7

National Library of Scotland, Edinburgh

Melville Papers – Mss 3385–88

National Records of Scotland (formerly Scottish Record Office), Edinburgh

Letter Book of Thomas Graham – GD/29/2148
Melville Papers – GD/51

New-York Historical Society

William Cornwallis Letter Book

Public Record Office of Northern Ireland

Castlereagh Papers – D/3030
Portland Transcripts – T/2905

William L. Clements Library

Cornwallis Orderly Book
Germain Papers
Henry Clinton Papers

NEWSPAPERS

London Evening Post, 1763–85
Morning Chronicle, 1760–1800
The Times, 1785–1806

PRIMARY PRINTED SOURCES

Abbatt, William (ed.). *Major André's Journal: Operations of the British Army under Lieutenant-Generals Sir William Howe and Sir Henry Clinton, June 1777 to November 1778* (Tarrytown, 1930).
Abbott, William W., et al. (eds). *The Papers of George Washington: Revolutionary War Series*, 28 vols (Charlottesville, 1985–ongoing).
Almon, John (ed.). *The Parliamentary Register or History of the Proceedings and Debates of the House of Commons, First Series: 1774–1780*, 17 vols (London, 1775–80); *Second Series: 1780–1796*, 45 vols (London, 1784–96); *Third Series: 1797–1802*, 12 vols (London, 1797–1802).
Aspinall, Arthur (ed.). *The Later Correspondence of George III*, 5 vols (Cambridge, 1962–68).
— *Correspondence of George, Prince of Wales, 1770–1812*, 8 vols (London, 1963–70).
Baring, Mrs Henry (ed.). *The Diary of the Right Honourable William Windham, 1784–1810* (London, 1866).
Buckingham and Chandos, Richard Temple-Nugent-Brydges-Chandos-Grenville, duke of (ed.). *Memoirs of the Courts and Cabinets of George III*, 4 vols (London, 1853–55).
Bulger, William T. (ed.), 'Sir Henry Clinton's "Journal of the Siege of Charleston"', *South Carolina Historical Magazine* 66 (July 1965), 147–74; 149.
Cannon, Garland (ed.). *The Letters of Sir William Jones*, 2 vols (Oxford, 1970).
Cannon, John (ed.). *The Letters of Junius* (Oxford, 1978).
Cobbett, William. *The Parliamentary History of England from the Earliest Period to the Year 1803*, 36 vols (London, 1806–20).

Corbett, Julian (ed.). *Private Papers of George, Second Earl Spencer, First Lord of the Admiralty, 1794–1801*, 4 vols (London, 1913–24).

Cornwallis, Charles, first Marquess Cornwallis, *An Answer to that Part of the Narrative of Lieutenant-General Sir Henry Clinton, KB, which Relates to the Conduct of Lieutenant-General Earl Cornwallis . . .* (London, 1783).

Davies, K.G. (ed.). *Documents of the American Revolution, 1770–1783*, 21 vols (Dublin, 1972–81).

Diron, Alexander. *A Narrative of the Campaign in India which Terminated the War with Tippoo Sultan in 1792* (London, 1794).

Fitzpatrick, John C. (ed.). *The Writings of George Washington from the Original Manuscript Sources, 1745–1799*, 39 vols (Washington, DC, 1931–44).

Fortescue, Sir John (ed.). *The Correspondence of George the Third, from 1760 to December 1783*, 6 vols (London 1927–28).

Gilbert, John Thomas (ed.). *Documents Relating to Ireland, 1794–1804* (Dublin, 1893).

Gruber, Ira D. (ed.). *John Peebles' American War: The Diary of a Scottish Grenadier, 1776–1782* (London, 1998).

Historical Manuscripts Commission. *Report on the Manuscripts of Mrs Stopford-Sackville, of Drayton House, Northamptonshire*, 2 vols (London, 1904–10).

—— *Report on Manuscripts in Various Collections, Volume 6: The Manuscripts of Cornwallis Wykeham-Martin Esq.* (London, 1909).

—— *Report on the Manuscripts of the Late Reginald Rawdon Hastings, Esq., of the Manor House, Ashby de la Zouche*, 4 vols (London, 1928–47).

Howe, William. *The Narrative of Lieutenant-General William Howe, in a Committee of the House of Commons on the 29 April 1779 Relative to His Conduct during His Late Command of His Majesty's Troops in North America* (London, 1780).

Jackson, Donald and Dorothy Twohig (eds.), *The Diaries of George Washington*, 6 vols (Charlottesville, 1976–79).

Lamb, Roger. *An Original and Authentic Journal of Occurrences during the Late American War: From Its Commencement to the Year 1783* (Dublin, 1809).

—— *Memoir of His own life* (Dublin, 1811).

Londonderry, Charles Vane, marquess of (ed.). *Memoirs and Correspondence of Viscount Castlereagh, Second Marquess of Londonderry*, 12 vols (London, 1848–53).

Lords. *Journal of the House of Lords*, vols 30–7 (London, 1767–1830).

Malmesbury, James Howard Harris, earl of (ed.). *Diaries and Correspondence of James Harris, First Earl of Malmesbury*, 4 vols (London 1844).

Maurice, F.J. (ed.). *The Diary of Sir John Moore*, 2 vols (London, 1904).

McKenzie, Frederick. *The Diary of Frederick McKenzie, Giving a Daily Narrative of His Military Service as an Officer of the Regiment of Royal Welch Fusiliers during the Years 1775–1781 in Massachusetts, Rhode Island and New York*, 2 vols (Cambridge, MA, 1930).

McKenzie, Roderick. *Strictures on Lt Col. Tarleton's 'History of the Campaigns of 1780 and 1781 in the Southern Provinces of North America'* (London, 1787).

Muenchhausen, Friedrich Ernst von. *At General Howe's Side, 1776–1778: The Diary of General William Howe's Aide-de-Camp, Captain Friedrich von Muenchhausen*, trans. Ernst Kipping (Monmouth Beach, 1974).

National Archives of India (ed.). *Fort William–India House Correspondence, 1748–1800*, 21 vols (Delhi, 1949–85).

Pellew, George (ed.). *Life and Correspondence of the Right Hon. Henry Addington, First Viscount Sidmouth*, 3 vols (London, 1847).

Rogers Jr, George C. (ed.). 'Letters of Charles O'Hara to the Duke of Grafton', *South Carolina Historical Magazine* 65 (July 1964), 158–80.

Ross, Charles (ed.). *Correspondence of Charles, First Marquis Cornwallis*, 3 vols (London, 1858).

Saberton, Ian (ed.). *The Cornwallis Papers: The Campaigns of 1780 and 1781 in the Southern Theatre of the American Revolutionary War*, 6 vols (Uckfield, 2010).

Showman, Richard K., et al. (eds). *The Papers of General Nathanael Greene*, 13 vols (Chapel Hill, 1976–2005).

Simcoe, John Graves. *A Journal of the Queen's Rangers* (Philadelphia, 1844).

Smith, William James (ed.). The Grenville Papers, 4 vols (London, 1852–53).

Spencer, Alfred (ed.). *Memoirs of William Hickey*, 4 vols (London, 1913–25).

Tarleton, Banastre. *A History of the Campaigns of 1780 and 1781, in the Southern Provinces of North America* (London, 1787).

Teignmouth, John Shore, Baron. *Memoir of the Life and Correspondence of John, Lord Teignmouth*, 2 vols (London, 1843).

Thacher, James. *A Military Journal during the American Revolutionary War from 1775–1783* (Boston, 1827).

Tustin, Joseph P. (ed.). *Diary of the American War: A Hessian Journal: Captain Johann Ewald, Field Jaeger Corps* (New Haven, 1979).

Verney, Harry (ed.). *The Journals and Correspondence of General Sir Harry Calvert* (London, 1853).

Wickham Jr, William (ed.). *The Correspondence of the Rt Hon. William Wickham*, 2 vols (London, 1870).

Willcox, William B. (ed.). *The American Rebellion: Sir Henry Clinton's Narrative of His Campaigns, 1775–1782, with an Appendix of Original Documents* (New Haven, 1954).

SECONDARY PRINTED SOURCES

Alavi, Seema. *The Sepoys and the Company: Tradition and Transition in Northern India, 1770–1830* (New Delhi, 1995).

Alden, John. *Stephen Sayre: American Revolutionary Adventurer* (Baton Rouge, 1983).

Aspinall, Arthur. *Cornwallis in Bengal: The Administrative and Judicial Reforms of Lord Cornwallis, 1786–1793* (Manchester, 1931).

Babits, Lawrence E. *Devil of a Whipping: The Battle of Cowpens* (Chapel Hill, 1998).

Babits, Lawrence E. and Joshua B. Howard. *Long, Obstinate and Bloody: The Battle of Guilford Court House* (Chapel Hill, 2009).

Bartlett, Thomas. *The Fall and Rise of the Irish Nation: The Catholic Question, 1690–1830* (Dublin, 1992).

Bartlett, Thomas and David Dickson (eds). *The 1798 Rebellion: A Bicentennial Perspective* (Dublin, 2003).

Bartlett, Thomas and Keith Jeffery (eds). *A Military History of Ireland* (Cambridge, 1996).

Bass, Robert D. *The Green Dragoon: The Lives of Banastre Tarleton and Mary Robinson* (Orangeburg, SC, 1973).

— *Swamp Fox: The Life and Campaigns of General Francis Marion* (Orangeburg, SC, 1974).

Bates, Crispin. *Subalterns and Raj: South Asia since 1600* (Abingdon, 2007).

Baugh, Daniel. *The Global Seven Years War, 1754–1763* (Harlow, 2011).

Bayly, C.A. *Rulers, Townsmen and Bazaars: North Indian Society in the Age of British Expansion, 1770–1870* (Cambridge, 1983).

— *Indian Society and the Making of the British Empire (The New Cambridge History of India)* (Cambridge, 1988).

— *Imperial Meridian: The British Empire and the World, 1780–1830* (Harlow, 1989).

Beatson, Robert. *A Political Index to the Histories of Great Britain and Ireland*, 2 vols (London, 2nd edn, 1788).

Bernstein, Jeremy. *Dawning of the Raj: The Life and Trials of Warren Hastings* (Chicago, 2000).

Bew, John. *Castlereagh: Enlightenment, War and Tyranny* (London, 2011).

Bilias, George (ed.). *George Washington's Generals and Opponents: Their Exploits and Leadership* (New York, 1994).

Blackstock, Alan. *Loyalism in Ireland, 1798* (Martlesham, 2007).

Bolton, G.C. *The Passing of the Irish Act of Union: A Study in Parliamentary Politics* (Oxford, 1966).

Borick, Carl P. *A Gallant Defense: The Siege of Charleston, 1780* (Columbia, 2003).

Bowen, H.V. *The Business of Empire: The East India Company and Imperial Britain, 1756–1830* (Cambridge, 2006).

Bowler, R. Arthur. 'Sir Henry Clinton and Army Profiteering: A Neglected Aspect of the Clinton–Cornwallis Controversy', *William and Mary Quarterly* 31 (January 1974), 111–22.

— *Logistics and the Failure of the British Army in America, 1775–1783* (Princeton, 1975).

Breen, Kenneth. 'Graves and Hood at the Chesapeake', *Mariner's Mirror* 66 (February 1980), 53–65.

Breen, Timothy. *American Insurgents, American Patriots: The Revolution of the People* (New York, 2010).

Brereton, J.M. and A.C.S. Savory. *The History of the Duke of Wellington's Regiment (West Riding), 1702–1992* (Halifax, 1993).

Broers, Michael. *Napoleon, Volume 1: Soldier of Destiny, 1769–1805* (London, 2014).

Brooke, John. *King George III* (London, 1972).

Brown, Gerald S. *The American Secretary: The Colonial Policy of Lord George Germain, 1775–1778* (Ann Arbor, 1963).

Brumwell, Stephen. *Turncoat: Benedict Arnold and the Crisis of American Liberty* (New Haven, 2018).

Buchanan, John. *The Road to Guilford Court House: The American Revolution in the Carolinas* (New York, 1997).

— *The Road to Valley Forge: How Washington Built the Army that Won the Revolution* (New York, 2004).

Burne, A.H. *The Noble Duke of York: The Military Life of Frederick Duke of York and Albany* (London, 1949).

Callahan, Raymond. *The East India Company and Army Reform, 1783–1798* (Cambridge, MA, 1972).

Carpenter, Stanley D.M. *Southern Gambit: Cornwallis and the British March to Yorktown* (Norman, 2018).

Cashin, Edward J. *The King's Ranger: Thomas Brown and the American Revolution on the Southern Frontier* (Athens, Georgia, 1989).

Chhabra, G.S. *Advanced Study in the History of Modern India, Volume 1: 1707–1813* (New Delhi, 2011).

Connolly, S.J. *Divided Kingdom: Ireland 1630–1800* (Oxford, 2008).

Conway, Stephen. 'British Army Officers and the American War for Independence', *William and Mary Quarterly* 41 (April 1984), 265–76.

— '"The Great Mischief Complain'd of"': Reflections on the Misconduct of British Soldiers in the Revolutionary War', *William and Mary Quarterly* 47 (July 1990) 370–90.

— *The War of American Independence, 1775–1783* (London, 1995).

— *The British Isles and the War of American Independence* (Oxford, 2003)

Dalrymple, William. *The Anarchy: The Relentless Rise of the East India Company* (London, 2019).

Datta, Rajat. *Society, Economy and the Market: Commercialization in Rural Bengal, c. 1760–1800* (New Delhi, 2000).

Davis, Burke. *The Cowpens Guilford Court House Campaign* (Philadelphia, 2002).

Davis, Robert P. *Where a Man Can Go: Major General William Philips, British Royal Artillery, 1731–81* (Westport, CT, 1999).

Debrett, John. *The Peerage of the United Kingdom of Great Britain and Ireland* (London, 1820).

Duffy, Michael. *Soldiers, Sugar and Seapower: The British Expeditions to the West Indies and the War against Revolutionary France* (Oxford, 1987).

Dull, Jonathan. *The French Navy and American Independence: A Study of Arms and Diplomacy, 1774–1787* (Princeton, 1975).

Duncan, F. *History of the Royal Regiment of Artillery*, 2 vols (London, 1879).

Ehrman, John. *The Younger Pitt*, 3 vols (London, 1969–96).

Elliott, Marianne. *Wolfe Tone: Prophet of Irish Independence* (New Haven, 1989).

Embree, Ainslie Thomas. *Charles Grant and British Rule in India* (London, 1962).

Englund, Steven. *Napoleon: A Political Life* (New York, 2004).

Fedorak, Charles John. *Henry Addington, Prime Minister, 1801–1804: Peace, War and Parliamentary Politics* (Akron, 2002).

Ferling, John. *Almost a Miracle: The American Victory in the War of Independence* (New York, 2007).

Fisch, Jorg. *Cheap Lives and Dear Limbs: The British Transformation of the Bengal Criminal Law, 1769–1817* (Wiesbaden, 1983).

Fischer, David Hackett. *Washington's Crossing* (New York, 2004).

Fischer-Tiné, Harald and Michael Mann. *Colonialism as Civilizing Mission: Cultural Ideology in British India* (Wimbledon, 2004).

Fitzgibbon, Elliot. *The Earl of Clare: Mainspring of the Union* (London, 1960).

Flexner, James T. *George Washington in the American Revolution* (Boston, 1967).

Forbes, A. *A History of the Army Ordnance Services*, 3 vols (London, 1929).

Forrest, Denys. *Tiger of Mysore: The Life and Death of Tipu Sultan* (London, 1970).

Fortescue, John. *A History of the British Army*, 13 vols (London, 1899–1930).

Freeman, Douglas Southall. *George Washington: A Biography*, 7 vols (New York, 1948–57).

Geoghegan, Patrick M. *The Irish Act of Union: A Study in High Politics, 1798–1801* (Dublin, 1999).

Gibney, John (ed.). *The United Irishmen, Rebellion and the Act of Union, 1791–1803* (Barnsley, 2018).

Glover, Richard. *Peninsular Preparation: The Reform of the British Army, 1795–1809* (Cambridge, 1988).

Golway, Terry. *Washington's General: Nathaniel Greene and the Triumph of the American Revolution* (New York, 2005).

Grainger, John D. *The Amiens Truce: Britain and Bonaparte, 1801–1803* (Woodbridge, 2004).

— *The Battle of Yorktown, 1781: A Reassessment* (Woodbridge, 2005).

Greene, Jerome A. *The Guns of Independence: The Siege of Yorktown* (New York, 2009).

Gregory, Desmond. *Malta, Britain and the European Powers, 1793–1815* (Madison, NJ, 1996).

Gruber, Ira D. 'The American Revolution as a Conspiracy: The British View', *William and Mary Quarterly* 26 (July 1969), 360–72.

— *The Howe Brothers and the American Revolution* (New York, 1972).

— *Books and the British Army in the Age of the American Revolution* (Chapel Hill, 2010).

Guha, Ranajit. *A Rule of Property for Bengal: An Essay on the Idea of Permanent Settlement* (Durham, NC, 3rd edn, 1996).

Hardy, Peter. *The Muslims of British India* (Cambridge, 1972).

Harlow, V.T. *The Founding of the Second British Empire, 1763–1793*, 2 vols (London, 1964).

Harris, Robin. *Talleyrand: Betrayer and Saviour of France* (London, 2007).

Hawes, Christopher J. *Poor Relations: The Making of an Eurasian Community in British India, 1773–1833* (Richmond, 1996).

Higginbotham, Don. *Daniel Morgan: Revolutionary Rifleman* (Chapel Hill, 1961).

— *George Washington Reconsidered* (Charlottesville, 2001).

Higgins, W. Robert (ed.). *The Revolutionary War in the South: Power, Conflict and Leadership: Essays in Honor of John Richard Alden* (Durham, NC, 1979).

Hogg, O.F.G. *The Royal Arsenal: Its Background, Origin and Subsequent History*, 2 vols (London, 1963).

Hoock, Holger. *Scars of Independence: America's Violent Birth* (New York, 2017).

Islam, Sirajul. *The Permanent Settlement in Bengal: A Study of Its Operation, 1790–1819* (Dakha, 1979).

Johnson, Donald F. 'The Failure of Restored British Rule in Revolutionary Charleston, South Carolina', *Journal of Imperial and Commonwealth History*, 42 (2014), 22–40.

Jupp, Peter. *Lord Grenville, 1759–1834* (Oxford, 1985).

Kagan, Frederick W. *The End of the Old Order: Napoleon and Europe, 1801–1805* (Philadelphia, 2006).

Kavanaugh, Ann C. *John FitzGibbon, Earl of Clare: Protestant Reaction and English Authority in Late Eighteenth-Century Ireland* (Dublin, 1997).

Keay, John. *The Honourable Company: A History of the English East India Company* (London, 1991).

Keogh, Dáire and Kevin Whelan (eds). *Acts of Union: The Causes, Contexts and Consequences of the Act of Union* (Dublin, 2001).

Ketcham, Richard. *Victory at Yorktown: The Campaign that Won the Revolution* (New York, 2004).

Kite, Elizabeth. *Brigadier-General Louis Lebegue Duportail: Commandant of Engineers in the Continental Army, 1777–1783* (Philadelphia, 1933).

Kranish, Michael. *Flight from Monticello: Thomas Jefferson at War* (New York, 2010).

Kumar, Dharma and Meghnad Desai (eds). *The Cambridge Economic History of India, Volume 2: c. 1757–c. 1970,* (Cambridge, 1983).

Lambert, Robert Stansbury. *South Carolina Loyalists in the American Revolution* (Columbia, 1987).

Lecky, William Edward Hartpole. *A History of Ireland in the Eighteenth Century*, 5 vols (London, 1913).

Lengel, Edward G. *General George Washington: A Military Life* (New York, 2005).

Long, J.C. *Lord Jeffery Amherst: A Soldier of the King* (New York, 1933).

Maas, John R. 'The Greatest Terror: Cornwallis Brings His Campaign to Goochland, June 1781', *Goochland County Historical Society Magazine* 41 (2009), 12–27.

Mackenzie, Roderick. *Strictures on Lt Col. Tarleton's 'History of the Campaigns of 1780 and 1781 in the Southern Provinces of North America'* (London, 1787).

Mackesy, Piers. *The War for America, 1775–1783* (Cambridge, MA, 1964).

— *War without Victory: The Downfall of Pitt, 1799–1802* (Oxford, 1984).

Macleod, Emma Vincent. *A War of Ideas: British Attitudes to the Wars against Revolutionary France, 1792–1802* (Abingdon, 2020).

Majeed, Javed. *Ungoverned Imaginings: James Mill's 'The History of British India' and Orientalism* (Oxford, 1992).

Majumbar, N. *Justice and Police in Bengal, 1765–1793: A Study of the Nizamat in Decline* (Calcutta, 1960).

Marshall, P.J. *Bengal: The British Bridgehead: Eastern India, 1740–1828 (The New Cambridge History of India)* (Cambridge, 1988).

— *The Making and Unmaking of British Fortunes in Eighteenth Century India* (Oxford, 2005).

— *The Making and Unmaking of Empires: Britain, India and America, c. 1750–1783* (Oxford, 2005).

— *Problems of Empire: Britain and India, 1757–1813* (Abingdon, 2019).

Marshall, P.J. (ed.). *The Oxford History of the British Empire, Volume 2: The Eighteenth Century* (Oxford, 2001).

— *The Eighteenth Century in Indian History: Evolution or Revolution?* (Oxford, 2003).

McCowan, George. *The British Occupation of Charleston, 1780–1782* (Columbia, 1972).

McDowell, R.B. *Ireland in the Age of Imperialism and Revolution, 1760–1801* (Oxford, 1979).

McGuire, T.J. *The Philadelphia Campaign*, 2 vols (Mechanicsburg, 2006–7).

McIntyre, James R. *Johann Ewald: Jaeger Commander* (Louisville, 2020).

McLane, John R. *Land and Local Kingship in Eighteenth Century Bengal* (Cambridge, 1997).

McNally, V.J. *Reform, Revolution and Reaction: Archbishop John Thomas Troy and the Catholic Church in Ireland, 1787–1817* (Dublin, 1995).

Metcalf, Barbara D. and Thomas R. Metcalf. *A Concise History of Modern India* (Cambridge, 3rd edn, 2012).

Middlekauf, Robert. *The Glorious Cause: The American Revolution, 1763–1789* (Oxford, 1982).

Middleton, Richard. *The Bells of Victory: The Pitt-Newcastle Ministry and the Conduct of the Seven Years' War, 1757–1762* (Cambridge, 1985).

— *The War of American Independence, 1775–1783* (Harlow, 2012).

— 'The Clinton–Cornwallis Controversy and Responsibility for the British Surrender at Yorktown', *History* 98 (July 2013), 370–89.

— 'Naval Resources and the British Defeat at Yorktown, 1781', *Mariner's Mirror* 100 (February 2014), 29–43

Mill, James. *The History of British India*, abridged and with an introduction by William Thomas (Chicago, 1975).

Misra, B.B. *The Central Administration of the East India Company, 1773–1834* (Manchester, 1959).

Moon, Penderel. *The British Conquest and Dominion of India* (London, 1989).

Mukherjee, S.N. *Sir William Jones: A Study of Eighteenth Century British Attitudes to India* (Cambridge, 1968).

Murray, Alexander (ed.). *Sir William Jones, 1746–1794: A Commemoration* (Oxford, 1998).

Namier, Lewis and John Brooke, *The House of Commons, 1754–1790*, 3 vols (London, 1964).

Nelson, Paul David. *General Horatio Gates: A Biography* (Baton Rouge, 1976).

— *Anthony Wayne: Soldier of the Early Republic* (Bloomington, 1985).

— *General James Grant: Scottish Soldier and Royal Governor of East Florida* (Gainesville, 1993).

— *Francis Rawdon-Hastings, Marquess of Hastings: Soldier, Peer of the Realm, Governor-General of India* (Madison, NJ, 2005).

Norton, Mary Beth. *The British Americans: The Loyalist Exiles in England, 1774–1789* (London, 1974).

O'Donnell, James H. *The Southern Indians in the American Revolution* (Knoxville, 1973).

O'Shaughnessy, Andrew J. *The Men Who Lost America: British Command during the Revolutionary War and the Preservation of the Empire* (New Haven, 2013).

Pakenham, Thomas. *The Year of Liberty: The Story of the Great Irish Rebellion of 1798* (London, 1997).

Pancake, John S. *This Destructive War: The British Campaign in the Carolinas, 1780–1782* (Tuscaloosa, 1985).

Patterson, Benton Rain. *Washington and Cornwallis: The Battle for America, 1775–1783* (Lanham, 2004).

Philips, C.H. *The East India Company, 1784–1834* (Manchester, 1961).

Porter, Whitworth. *A History of the Corps of Royal Engineers*, 2 vols (London, 1889).

Potts, Louis W. *Arthur Lee: A Virtuous Revolutionary* (Baton Rouge, 1981).

Prakash, Om (ed.). *Lord Cornwallis: Administrative Reforms and British Policy (Encyclopaedic History of Indian Freedom Movement Series)* (New Delhi, 2002).

Ray, Aniruddha. *Tipu Sultan and His Age: A Collection of Seminar Papers* (Calcutta, 2002).

Reitan, Earl A. *Politics. Finance, and the People: Economical Reform in England in the Age of the American Revolution, 1770–1792* (Basingstoke, 2007).

Rodger, N.A.M. *The Command of the Ocean: A Naval History of Britain, 1649–1815* (New York, 2004).

Roy, Kaushik. *War and Society in Colonial India* (Oxford, 2010).

— *War, Culture and Society in Early Modern South Asia, 1740–1849* (Abingdon, 2013).

Roy, Tirthankar. *The East India Company: The World's Most Powerful Corporation* (New Delhi, 2012).

Royster, Charles. *Light Horse Harry Lee and the Legacy of the American Revolution* (New York, 1981).

Schecter, Barnet. *Battle for New York: The City at the Heart of the American Revolution* (New York, 2002).

Scotti, Anthony J. *Brutal Virtue: The Myth and Reality of Banastre Tarleton* (Bowie, MD, 2002).

Simms, Brendan. *Three Victories and a Defeat: The Rise and Fall of the First British Empire* (London, 2007).

Sinha, Narendra Krishna. *The Economic History of Bengal from Plassey to the Permanent Settlement*, 2 vols (Calcutta, 1956–62).

— *The Permanent Settlement in Bengal: A Study of Its Operation, 1790–1815* (Dakha, 1979).

Smith, David. *'Whispers across the Atlantick': General William Howe and the American Revolution* (London, 2017).

Smyth, Jim. *Revolution, Counter-Revolution and Union: Ireland in the 1790s* (Cambridge, 2000).

Spring, Matthew H. *With Zeal and with Bayonets Only: The British Army on Campaign in North America, 1775–1783* (Norman, 2008).

Stedman, Charles. *The History of the Origin, Progress, and Termination of the American War*, 2 vols (London, 1794).

Stokes, Eric. *The English Utilitarians and India* (Oxford, 1959).

Stryker, William S. *The Battles of Trenton and Princeton* (Boston, 1898).

Sutherland, L.S. *The East India Company in Eighteenth-Century Politics* (Oxford, 1952).

Syrett, David. *The Royal Navy in American Waters, 1775–1783* (Aldershot, 1989).

— *Admiral Lord Howe: A Biography* (Annapolis, MD, 2006).

Taaffe, Stephen R. *The Philadelphia Campaign, 1777–1778* (Lawrence, 2003).

Tharoor, Shashi. *An Era of Darkness: The British Empire in India* (New Delhi, 2016).

Thomas, Peter D.G. *Lord North* (London, 1976).

Travers, Robert. *Ideology and Empire in Eighteenth Century India: The British in Bengal* (Cambridge, 2007).

Whitridge, Arnold. *Rochambeau: America's Neglected Founding Father* (New York, 1965).

Wickwire, Franklin and Mary Wickwire. *Cornwallis and the War of Independence* (London, 1971).

— *Cornwallis: The Imperial Years* (Chapel Hill, 1980).

Wilkinson, David. ' "How Did They Pass the Union?": Secret Service Expenditure in Ireland, 1799–1804', *History* 82 (April 1997), 223–51.

Willcox, William B. *Portrait of a General: Sir Henry Clinton in the War of Independence* (New York, 1964).

Wilson, David K. *The Southern Strategy: Britain's Conquest of South Carolina and Georgia, 1775–1780* (Columbia, 2005).

Wood, W.J. *Battles of the Revolutionary War, 1775–1781* (New York, 1995).

Zastoupil, Lynn and Martin Moir (eds). *The Great Indian Education Debate: Documents Relating to the Orientalist–Anglicist Controversy, 1781–1843* (Richmond, England, 1999).

Index

Locators for maps are entered in *italics*.
Relationships in brackets are to Charles Earl Cornwallis.
Unattributed actions refer to Charles Earl Cornwallis.